DISEASED CINEMA

For My Only Begotten Son
– Robert

For Lucy and Ben
– Merle

For Zoe and All the Other Pro-Democracy Protesters in Israel, 2023
– Lee

DISEASED CINEMA

Plagues, Pandemics and Zombies in American Movies

Robert Alpert, Merle Eisenberg and Lee Mordechai

EDINBURGH
University Press

Edinburgh University Press is one of the leading university presses in the UK. We publish academic books and journals in our selected subject areas across the humanities and social sciences, combining cutting-edge scholarship with high editorial and production values to produce academic works of lasting importance. For more information visit our website: edinburghuniversitypress.com

© Robert Alpert, Merle Eisenberg and Lee Mordechai, 2024

Grateful acknowledgement is made to the sources listed in the List of Illustrations for permission to reproduce material previously published elsewhere. Every effort has been made to trace the copyright holders, but if any have been inadvertently overlooked, the publisher will be pleased to make the necessary arrangements at the first opportunity.

Edinburgh University Press Ltd
The Tun – Holyrood Road
12(2f) Jackson's Entry
Edinburgh EH8 8PJ

Typeset in 10/12.5 Adobe Sabon by
IDSUK (DataConnection) Ltd

A CIP record for this book is available from the British Library

ISBN 978 1 3995 2165 9 (hardback)
ISBN 978 1 3995 2166 6 (paperback)
ISBN 978 1 3995 2167 3 (webready PDF)
ISBN 978 1 3995 2168 0 (epub)

The right of Robert Alpert, Merle Eisenberg and Lee Mordechai to be identified as the authors of this work has been asserted in accordance with the Copyright, Designs and Patents Act 1988, and the Copyright and Related Rights Regulations 2003 (SI No. 2498).

CONTENTS

Figures	viii
Preface	x

Introduction   1
  Disease Movies Past and Present   3
  Early Disease Movies from the Advent of Film to the Early 1990s   6
  The Rise of Viral Disease Movies and a Nostalgia for the Past   10
  Post-Apocalyptic Worlds and Posthumanity   12
  Future Pandemics in Movies   15

1. Early Disease Movies: American Norms and Containment   24
  Introduction   24
  The Origins of Disease Movies: From Silent Films to World War II   26
  The Heroic Public Servant and the American Dream: *Panic in the Streets* (1950)   30
  An Alternative Vision: *The Seventh Seal* (1957)   36
  Revealing the Rot in American Values: *Night of the Living Dead* (1968)   37
  A Critique of Values and a Global Pandemic: *Shivers* (1975) and *Virus* (1980)   41
  Conclusion   45

2. **Disease Movies in Transition: Globalization and Imagined Containment**   53
   Introduction   53
   The Disease Is Contained: *Outbreak* (1995)   56
   Prescient Transitions: *12 Monkeys* (1995) and *28 Days Later* (2002)   63
   Fast Zombies and Fragmentation: *Dawn of the Dead* (2004)   67
   Dark Disease Movies and a Pandemic Sequel: *28 Weeks Later* (2007)   73
   Conclusion   76

3. **Post-Apocalyptic Disease Movies: Pandemics and Posthumanity**   84
   Introduction   84
   Spiritual Faith in the Twenty-First Century: *Children of Men* (2006) and *Black Death* (2010)   86
   Individual Choice in a Fractured Society: *Contagion* (2011)   90
   Patriarchal Zombie Pandemics: *Zombieland* (2009) and *World War Z* (2013)   96
   Hope for a New Society: *Rise of the Planet of the Apes* (2011) and Its Sequels   100
   Conclusion   105

4. **Remaking Humanity:** *The Body Snatchers*   110
   Introduction   110
   The Infection of Small-Town America: *Invasion of the Body Snatchers* (1956)   113
   The Spread to Urban America: *Invasion of the Body Snatchers* (1978)   116
   An Aggressive Expansion across America: *Body Snatchers* (1993)   119
   The Attractive Threat: *The Invasion* (2007)   123
   The Happy, Bio-Engineered Transformation: *Little Joe* (2019)   127
   Conclusion   132

5. **Popularizing the Pandemic: The *Resident Evil* Franchise**   139
   Introduction   139
   Nostalgia for an Imagined Containment: *Resident Evil* (2002)   142
   Transitions and New Paradigms: *Apocalypse* (2004), *Extinction* (2007), *Afterlife* (2010) and *Retribution* (2012)   146
   The New Apotheosis: *The Final Chapter* (2016)   152
   Conclusion   155

6. **Movie Myths: The COVID-19 Pandemic**   161
   Introduction   161
   Consuming Movie Pandemics during COVID   163
   The Blurring of COVID and the Movie Pandemic Landscape   164
   The Wrong Lessons of Movie Stories   170

The Stories Missing in Movies	174
Conclusion	178

Conclusion — **192**

The Historical Arc of Disease Movies	192
Depicting an End of Times Landscape	196
The COVID Story	198
Movie Myths and Stories for the Future	200

Bibliography	206
Index	237

FIGURES

Figure I.1:	*Outbreak* (1995)	2
Figure I.2:	*Nosferatu* (1922)	8
Figure I.3:	The September 11, 2001 attacks on the World Trade Center	11
Figure 1.1:	*Dr. Ehrlich's Magic Bullet* (1940)	29
Figure 1.2:	*Panic in the Streets* (1950)	33
Figure 1.3:	*Night of the Living Dead* (1968)	39
Figure 2.1:	*Outbreak* (1995)	60
Figure 2.2:	*28 Days Later* (2002)	65
Figure 2.3:	*Dawn of the Dead* (2004)	69
Figure 3.1:	*Children of Men* (2006)	88
Figure 3.2:	*Contagion* (2011)	95
Figure 3.3:	*Rise of the Planet of the Apes* (2011)	103
Figure 4.1:	*Invasion of the Body Snatchers* (1956)	114
Figure 4.2:	*The Invasion* (2007)	124
Figure 4.3:	*Little Joe* (2019)	128
Figure 5.1:	*Resident Evil* (2002)	145
Figure 5.2:	*Resident Evil: Retribution* (2012)	151
Figure 5.3:	*Resident Evil: The Final Chapter* (2016)	155
Figure 6.1:	The real-life lessons of *Contagion*	165
Figure 6.2:	*World War Z* (2013)	166

Figure 6.3:	*12 Monkeys* (1995)	166
Figure C.1:	The warrior Achilles of the *Iliad*	193
Figure C.2:	*Black Death* (2010)	201
Figure C.3:	*The Seventh Seal* (1957)	202

PREFACE

Books require many behind-the-scenes actors, and all books have an origin story involving the authors themselves. This book is no exception. It began as a series of conversations between the authors in the spring of 2019 with the simple idea of co-writing an article about diseases in movies. We soon realized that the story we wanted to tell was much larger and could only be told through a book length study. The onset of COVID-19 in early 2020 forced us to reconsider our work yet again, leading us to incorporate the global pandemic within our narrative as well as reevaluate our reading of movies based on real time events. As with any book in which ongoing events shape how we think, the narrative must continue to change as the current pandemic, its perception and its memory develop over the coming years.

This book was a wholly collaborative effort, written (and re-written) by all three of us. Like all collaborations, it gave rise to both amazing moments of discovery and moments of sharp disagreement. We hope that this book demonstrates the power of those discoveries and disagreements to shape a critical literary work that surpasses what any of us could have written alone. Humanities research will benefit from more multi-authored collaborations in which multiple authors combine their perspectives to create a story that transcends each, and from which each might learn and develop still more stories to tell in the future.

This book could only be built upon the continued work of scholars, critics and journalists in the fields of movies, media, history and entertainment, to name but a few, over the past century. Engaging with their collective, often conflicting work has been a fascinating experience for us. We admittedly have only barely touched upon their extensive, widely varied viewpoints. This book could not have been written without the insights from the many guests, including Robert, who have appeared on Merle and Lee's podcast, *Infectious Historians*. Discussions with guests have both deepened our knowledge of the histories of disease, temporally and globally, and drawn our attention to a vast literature of newly developed ideas and theories. Their work is cited throughout this book, and we are deeply grateful to them for their time and fascinating discussions.

We also thank those who read parts or all of the manuscript. Thanks to the late Bob Stanley of Hunter College in NYC who early on read parts of the manuscript and graciously offered advice on how to engage readers. He is sorely missed. We would also like to thank Michelle Smirnova, who helped us mold this project at an early stage, along with Joel Suarez, Andrew Edwards and Emily Kern who provided advice, feedback and key ideas. Friends, colleagues and family members have read parts of this book or offered us helpful feedback on various ideas as well. We would like to thank Dana Alpert, Shane Alpert, Brendan Duke, Emily Forman, A. J. Herrmann, Pamela Klasova, Christian Mauder, Gal Mordechai and Ben Riemersma. Thanks as well to Meg Leja and Alex Chase-Levenson for answering our questions about the book process that saved us a lot of time.

We would also like to thank the anonymous reviewers who read earlier versions of this book. Their comments have done much to push us to improve the manuscript. Any failure to address their comments adequately is ours entirely.

Our deep appreciation goes to our mentors and teachers. Robert thanks my film school teachers, Andrew Sarris, Samson Raphaelson and Michael Stern, who years ago inspired my passion for the art of film, as well as *Jump Cut* co-founder and editor Julia Lesage, who patiently vetted my writings and encouraged my exploration of politics in art. Merle and Lee would like to thank Helmut Reimitz, John Haldon, William Chester Jordan, Timothy Newfield, Brent Shaw and Jack Tannous for encouraging us to ask interesting questions and pursue our intellectual interests wherever they might take us, including far beyond our training in medieval and Byzantine history.

Each of us has benefited enormously from the many insights of our students and audiences in the academic field. Robert thanks my many classes of students at Fordham University, especially those who have participated in my computer science course on movie robots and computers. Merle would like to thank my students in my history of disease course at Oklahoma State University as well as various audiences who heard parts of the book at Oklahoma State University, Princeton University, the University of Zurich, the University of Southern California, the University of Lincoln, Valencia College and the College of Staten Island. Finally, Lee thanks the students taking my course on epidemics in film in the history department at The Hebrew University of Jerusalem whose comments and coursework encouraged my continued writing of this book.

This book was made possible through the support of universities and research institutions. First, financial support was provided by the College of Arts and Sciences, Oklahoma State University. Thanks also to Princeton University, SESYNC (funded by NSF DBI 1639145), Penn State University and the Hebrew University of Jerusalem. Thanks to Michael Cook and the other members of *The Balzan Seminar on the Formation, Maintenance, and Failure of States in the Muslim World before 1800*.

At Edinburgh University Press we would like to thank our editor Gillian Leslie, who oversaw this project from the beginning, insisted upon its careful vetting and offered insightful perspectives on the improvement of our manuscript. Sam Johnson, our senior assistant editor, who patiently guided us through the lengthy publication process and Stuart Dalziel, the graphic designer, who showed us how to attract ordinary readers to a seemingly academic work. We also thank Kate Mertes for indexing the book.

Finally, we are grateful for the support of our families. Working on this book for over four years, especially during COVID, took its toll on them, too.

Robert thanks, in particular, his daughter Dana, whose weekly Sunday movie going with him as a child first enabled him to see movies through fresh eyes; his daughter Shane, who has enthusiastically encouraged his movie writing and teaching; and Marcia, his wife, who has embarked with him on this long, wonderful journey through film school, repertories, 42nd Street grindhouses, multiplexes, DVDs and streaming.

Merle would like to thank his children, Lucy and Ben, who have been part of this project from almost the beginning and who have loved to crash neverending Skype and Zoom calls with Dawah and Uncle Lee. He would also like to thank his wife, Alissa, who has put up with watching movies she is not a huge fan of and for taking the time out of her own busy work schedule to listen to his various takes on them.

Lee would like to thank, in particular, his dog Apollo, his daughter Zoe and his partner, Vered, for putting up with the continued work on this project, which took him away from longer walks, more playtime, and overall support at home. Vered was also willing to watch too many horror films with him, despite her early reservations, and hopefully Zoe might do so, too (in several years).

Despite the increasingly unsettled world over the past several years and our collective unknown futures, we hope this book will be of value (and enjoyment) to readers within and outside academia and that it will contribute to the ongoing conversations at the nexus of infectious diseases, movies, entertainment and capitalism. Thank you, our reader, for your time and attention. We hope that you take pleasure in our book, and we look forward to continuing the conversation with you.

INTRODUCTION

The theatrical release poster for *Outbreak* (1995) prominently depicts images of its leading actors, Dustin Hoffman, Rene Russo and Morgan Freeman, focusing their gaze outward next to a small, screaming monkey. The poster, like the film's title, implies a terrifying disease on the loose. Its plot follows heroic doctors successfully containing the deadly outbreak, which the monkey introduces from the jungles of Zaire (today, the Democratic Republic of Congo) to a small town in California. *Outbreak* was America's first blockbuster viral thriller, grossing $190 million on a $50 million budget.[1] It introduced a narrative depicting the public panic and fear resulting from a lethal disease outbreak in an ordinary, American town. The movie capitalized on the success of Richard Preston's 1992 nonfiction article in *The New Yorker*, "Crisis in the Hot Zone," and his 1994 expanded version of that article, the popular thriller book *The Hot Zone*, both of which focused on the Ebola virus. The similarities between the book and the movie were obvious to movie audiences, and fiction and reality blurred when newspaper headlines referred to both, stimulating further interest in the threat of disease.[2]

American audiences did not have to wait long for the next event. In May 1995, only a couple of months after *Outbreak*'s release, the media widely reported on an outbreak of Ebola in Kikwit, Zaire. At the time, *The Hot Zone* was still selling briskly (and would rise again to become number one on *The New York Times*' best-seller list), and *Outbreak* was still playing in theaters. As one commentator later summed it up, "The Kikwit epidemic received epidemic coverage."[3] The line between fiction and reality further blurred in

Figure I.1 *Outbreak* (1995): The American military dispatches its medical professionals in hazmat suits to identify and contain the disease in its colonial outpost.

real-time as media reports mixed information from both. Coverage of Kikwit used images and information from fictional and nonfictional accounts, such as *The Hot Zone*, *Outbreak* and *The Coming Plague*, a 1994 book which also focused on infectious diseases.[4] Preston went so far as to predict the inevitable collapse of civilization with hyperbolic op-eds about the future failure of medicine. He argued that "even with all of the advances of the past 100 years in medical technology, the world may be closer to the Middle Ages than policy makers realize."[5] The media, too, exaggerated the threat. Ebola was "the ultimate horror," a "doomsday disease," the "apocalypse bug" and a "biological Satan." CNN's special "The Apocalypse Bug" even opened by suggesting that microscopic killers might lead to the End Times, which humans were powerless to stop. Similar TV portrayals appeared in other countries.[6]

This excessive attention to and depiction of infectious diseases that began in the mid-1990s has remained central to American consciousness ever since. Most inflammatory accounts did not mention, however, that while outbreaks could be horrific, they were far from apocalyptic, or that even a dangerous virus like Ebola is neither particularly infectious nor necessarily deadly when treated with medical care. Ebola has resulted in tens of thousands of recorded deaths in Africa, but endemic diseases, such as malaria, are far deadlier with annual death tolls in the hundreds of thousands – and yet have played far less of a role in American thought. Infectious disease epidemics can be terrifying, but their death toll and their impact are not necessarily correlated with their role in the public imagination.

Disease Movies Past and Present

This book examines films about disease as a way to understand contemporary American culture. Within the broad category of disease films, we include movies that feature realistic diseases, diseases with extraterrestrial origins and zombie infections, all of which share common characteristics. Beginning in the early twentieth century, diseases in movies have represented an increasingly important way of reflecting American life. This book investigates the changes in these movies over time, rather than assume a consistent, identical disease narrative. It argues that certain themes have appeared, disappeared and reappeared in different forms over the course of the last century as films have explored disease through changing cultural paradigms.

This book demonstrates first how movies have transitioned through three broad time periods: the advent of film through the early 1990s, the mid-1990s through the mid-2000s and the late 2000s and afterward. Across these three periods, disease movies have shifted from featuring a contained outbreak to an imagined containment of a known disease and finally to a globalized, uncontainable pandemic of an unknown origin. As the projected impact of disease has grown exponentially, movies have adopted a narrative in which the focus has shifted from trying to identify the source of a disease and potentially stopping its spread to a dystopian, post-pandemic world in which humans simply try to survive. Nobody and nothing are safe anymore.

This change over time in the narrative of disease movies drives the book's second theme: the impact of disease on American society has changed from identifying social problems with potential solutions to highlighting America's failure to fulfill its basic duty of maintaining a viable social contract for the vast majority of its population. American society has offered ever less social cohesion and defense against the growing spread and encroachment of disease. Disease movies from the early and mid-twentieth century often identified the source of the disease as foreign-originating, told stories of how disease could be conquered, and occasionally critiqued aspects of American society that had caused disruption of social norms. The myth of individual heroism offered a means to fight against and contain disease, even as that myth became increasingly inadequate and unbelievable by the late twentieth century. This focus on problems within American society then largely disappeared from disease movies.[7] By the early twenty-first century such films begin to reflect a new myth in which reason and order give way to chaos and destruction. Increasingly pandemics wipe out much of the global population without regard to race, age, gender, ethnicity or class, even as biological and social features shape the differing impacts of diseases and pandemics in the real world. Recent disease movies are obsessed with projecting future outbreaks, encourage a sense of dread and fear of mass death, and, in the aftermath of a global apocalypse, focus on the creation of a new society and often the evolution of a new species.

As its third theme, this book argues that developments in capitalism drive these two changes. Capitalism as an economic system is driven by the needs of private owners of production and the investors of capital in production. Both supply goods and services to consumers in the marketplace to generate profits for further investment. In this book, though, capitalism is a shorthand for not only this economic system but also the intellectual and cultural ideas supporting it. Importantly, this idea of capitalism has changed over time as well. The beginning of cinema paralleled the continued development of industrial capitalism, and disease films, particularly from the 1930s onward, advocated for the state-managed capitalism underpinning the New Deal order.[8] Movies through the 1970s continued to advocate for scientific progress and the strengthening of American society. While these films might at times critique state-managed capitalism, whether its failure to enable narrowly defined Americans – white, Christian men – to achieve their material aspirations, or its failure to expand upon that definition to include others – women and persons of color – they accepted such failures in return for a belief in the American Dream of steady wage growth, a house and a loving family.

Beginning in the 1970s, the New Deal order began to collapse as a result of both economic stagnation and a conservative reaction against the inclusion of new groups into American society. This new form of capitalism, which is often described as neoliberalism and promotes freedom of choice, witnessed the expansion of low wage, service jobs – often employing women and workers of color – along with the rise of the financial sector and rapidly increasing wage inequality.[9] This new form of capitalism, which has metastasized through the expansion of the American empire, has led, among other things, to environmental destruction by multi-national corporations and the accelerated emergence and spread of new diseases.[10] Local social constraints have disappeared in its wake.

In the following decades, this global capitalism has continued to privilege individual success, transforming America from a job-based economy to one based on assets. Success (and survival) now requires the individual accumulation of assets as salaries largely stagnate. While the rich amass ever greater wealth, the majority must rely on individual debt, since the state no longer invests in the public good, such as education and healthcare. Individuals hope to transform themselves ("human capital") and their possessions into marketable assets in a society without a common good, which encourages social fragmentation.[11] It is not surprising, therefore, that many are concerned only with helping themselves and their immediate families.[12] Global capitalism with its massive collection of standardized data happily assimilates those with different genders, races and ethnicities – to list but a few characteristics of identity – in return for their acceptance of the economic and intellectual paradigm of contemporary capitalism. Only individual choice – the "right" decision – can result in success while failure – the "wrong" decision – is separated from any broader social context or structural limitations.

No one is immune from the destructive power of global capitalism and the forces it has unleashed, even if disease movies occasionally look back nostalgically to an earlier era for solutions, or superficially critique capitalism while massively profiting from it. As capitalism has become more ubiquitous through its global trade and newly developed technologies, disease movies either flatten all individual differences or increasingly advocate for a complete destruction of the present world to give humanity a fresh start and transform the species into some form of "posthumanity." The posthuman in the context of global capitalism represents an endorsement of the conformity of the human species through advanced technology in which differences disappear in an effort to further cultural assimilation, predictive surveillance and growth of capital even as the posthuman is presented as an evolutionary advancement of the species.[13] At the same time, today's disease films recognize that the end of the mid-century social contract requires a radical reappraisal: the collapse of civilization and the extinction of the species to meet the challenge of the contemporary disease of global capitalism itself. Under the guise of apocalyptic endings and posthumanism, Hollywood's disease stories advance an American, global capitalism that ignores real-world cultural intersections even if these films include a more diverse cast. The underlying ideology values seamlessness, efficiency and individual gain over individual differences, community identities and other forms of uniqueness.[14] In arguing for this transformation, these films paradoxically advocate for the global capitalism that they seemingly critique.

These three themes in disease movies are intertwined and reinforce one another even if a particular movie may differ in its focus on one or the other of them. This book, like others before it, is hardly neutral. For example, by naming myths, it empowers the ideas that drive our expectations or by labeling films as depicting containable outbreaks, we create a classification system that determines how we and others will view and act upon events in the real world. Likewise, the movies themselves are hardly neutral. These movies not only reflect contemporary events and ways of perceiving – and hence the popularity of movies at the time of their release – but also drive a broader discourse, including those of individuals, the media, governments, and academics, among others, in real-life outbreaks. In other words, the stories underlying these films become part of our lived reality.

This book demonstrates how these fictional cinematic stories have contributed to the disconnect between our expectations of a disease and the evidence of what it actually does. As the beginning of the COVID pandemic revealed, we now expect real diseases to massively disrupt societies like they do in movies, but these expectations remained unfulfilled – certainly not at the scale of societal collapse or the overt transformation of the human species.[15] Movie stories also leave out what does happen. Notably, marginalized people and communities are rarely centered in movies, except as a way for majoritarian communities to ostracize, police and condemn them as outside accepted social norms and disease carriers. When these groups do appear in films, their new or different experiences seldom challenge the movies' underlying capitalist perspective.[16] Moreover, films rarely acknowledge the more significant impact of infectious diseases on marginalized groups – long known in scholarship and more obviously evident during COVID – or focus on equitable solutions. The Hollywood ending to these movies similarly fails to depict the lingering effects of disease in the real world, where the "ending" of disease is almost always partial and selective and where for many there may be no clear ending whatsoever.

   Like all books, this book must be selective in what it covers, and while these choices are certainly subjective, they are illustrative of the key themes in disease movies. Since we offer a story to understand disease movies, we focus on movies that best demonstrate the group as a whole for a variety of reasons, including popularity (both at the time and in hindsight), contribution to "the nascent genre" of pandemic films, cultural importance, and, to a lesser extent, aesthetic significance.[17] Disease movies did not follow a single, inevitable path either, and outliers have always existed. These outliers could be at times prescient or at other times look back to an earlier era as a way to reach a more optimistic, if improbable, conclusion. This book also focuses on American movies. For better or for worse, American films have substantially and consistently influenced the global development of movies generally, and disease movies are no exception. Despite the important contributions of films such as *The Seventh Seal* (1957) or *28 Days Later* (2002), this book analyzes the core narrative of American disease films. Since our book examines these movies in the context of the historical development of American, global capitalism, our focus remains on the idea of the social contract that has shifted from one of cohesion to fragmentation of the body politic. While we discuss issues of identity, such as gender, age and race, the overarching story of the book reveals how global capitalism has consistently aimed to erode differences in identity to ensure the triumph of its economic system and ideology.

Early Disease Movies from the Advent of Film to the Early 1990s

Representations of mass human destruction are timeless. They date back to Near Eastern myths, such as those preserved in the Hebrew Bible with the flood that wiped out almost all of humanity and the ten plagues of Egypt during the Exodus story. Eighteenth and nineteenth century English-language novels, such as *A Journal of the Plague Year* (Daniel Defoe, 1722), *The Vampyre* (John Polidori, 1819), *The Last Man* (Mary Shelley, 1826), *The Strange Case of Dr. Jekyll and Mr. Hyde* (Robert Louis Stevenson, 1886) and *Dracula* (Bram Stoker, 1897), represent the beginnings of modern fictional interest in the horror of disease and epidemics. Movies, as a newly developed means of mass communication, continued that interest and depicted disease as early as the beginning of the twentieth century.[18]

Modern discussions of diseases and their depiction in film draw initially upon three connected foundations from the late nineteenth century: scientific breakthroughs connecting a pathogen and a disease ("germ theory"), major transformations in public and private hygiene and the globalization of diseases.[19] Thinkers around the turn of the twentieth century believed that only strong, advanced states could stop diseases, which originated in "backward" colonial regions. Raymond Crawfurd described this paradigm in literature and art a century ago, pointing out that suffering from a disease like plague was the price empires had to pay for the "enjoyment of [their] Oriental commerce," whether Venice in the past or Britain in his present.[20] Ironically and tragically, it was the supposedly scientific measures advanced states adopted to stop disease outbreaks in colonies that exacerbated the impact on people living in colonies, condemning them to further sickness and death. Nevertheless, this myth of difference between colonizers and the colonized remains embedded in how we think about disease today.[21]

As Chapter 1 discusses, films about disease from the first half of the twentieth century largely fell into two separate narratives. First, B-movie, low-budget horror films depicted disease outbreaks as the result of abnormal sexuality or other "asocial" behavior and highlighted the role of "the other" – whether blacks, Jews or Eastern Europeans – in introducing the disease often in the form of monsters. By showing the defeat of "the other," the movies restored the "natural" order by excluding those who threatened it. In depicting how those enslaved to these monsters, particularly through zombification, rebel against their enslavers, these movies also enacted stories about a class struggle in which labor rebels against its capitalist master. Both themes continued to reverberate in later disease movies, but in different forms as disease became a character rather than a lens to examine social issues.[22]

Among the most striking of these types of early movies is the silent German film *Nosferatu: A Symphony of Horror* (1922). Based upon Bram Stoker's 1897 novel *Dracula*, *Nosferatu* depicts how a rat-carrying disease infects a town.[23] Yet, the real source for the plague is a vampire known as Nosferatu, who is the Jewish other: an emaciated, pale foreigner with a prominently protruding nose, a bald head and claw-like fingers.[24] Zombie movies, too, depicted a creature of

DISEASED CINEMA

Figure I.2 *Nosferatu* (1922): The foreigner Nosferatu infects an ordinary, middle-class town through his rats.

horror, the dead brought back to life, that originated in individual, moral corruption during the 1930s and 1940s. They were set in a foreign environment, the Caribbean, and focused on voodoo creations.[25] The first, *White Zombie* (1932), attributes the making of these undead creatures to a voodoo master and emphasizes how abnormal sexuality, which transgresses social norms, results in zombification. *White Zombie* also reflected the horror of turning humans into mindless drones in order to supply the cheap labor of black slaves.[26]

The second disease narrative consisted of mainstream, historical dramas that examined the major advances in science and medicine during the mid-twentieth century. Although mainstream is an ambiguous concept that changes over time, it encompasses movies that clearly reflect the social norms of their era, regardless of commercial success or popularity.[27] In this case, as scientists developed vaccines and cures to diseases, it seemed that infectious diseases could be eradicated or at least contained. Wealthy countries had vanquished disease at home and had begun to eradicate it in their former colonies as well.[28] Attention to previous pandemics, such as the Influenza Pandemic of 1918–1920, waned because they were no longer central to how people thought about disease. Technological utopianism, the idea that science could and would solve all of humanity's problems, dominated.[29] Disease movies served to educate the public about contemporary scientific advances, such as the identification and cure of diseases, while also portraying those toiling in public health as heroes. Simultaneously, these movies also advocated for the role of American capitalism as the centerpiece of historical progress.

Jezebel (1938), a mainstream movie, illuminates the benefits of science and social progress in conquering disease. This antebellum story critiques Southern ignorance and racism in anticipation of the future benefits of Northern capitalism in combating obliviousness through commerce and science. Where the South foolishly shoots off canons to purify the air and unsuccessfully tries to quarantine those who contract yellow fever, the North improves public health by draining swamps. Mainstream movies also told stories about specific diseases and their cure, such as *The Story of Louis Pasteur* (1936). It advocated for the development of science, the compassionate practice of medicine and a valuing of the public good. The film depicts Pasteur, a chemist in 1860 Paris, speaking out against a medical profession that refuses to acknowledge its own ignorance in an effort to maintain its own privileged position. Although Emperor Napoleon III exiles him, the later installation of a new, democratic government results in the discovery anew of Pasteur in a remote French province, where he had been busy developing a vaccine immunizing sheep from the "black plague" of anthrax. On his return to Paris, he soon also develops a vaccine for rabies. Pasteur, a great man, contributes "to the welfare and progress of mankind," according to his own speech at the end of the film.

The narrative focus of disease movies slowly shifted from the mid-twentieth century onward. As René Girard argued and Susan Sontag made famous in the 1970s, illness from disease increasingly became a metaphor for broader social illnesses.[30] Filmmakers applied the metaphor to all types of societal problems from violence to race. As also discussed in Chapter 1, *Panic in the Streets* focuses on the foreign origin of a New Orleans outbreak, namely an unlawful immigrant, and disease serves to illuminate the benefits and difficulties of America's middle class. Films with science fiction overtones, such as *Invasion of the Body Snatchers* (1956 and 1978, discussed in Chapter 4) or *The Stuff* (1985), meanwhile depict disease as originating from outer space as a metaphor for the threat of social conformity within American society.

The most influential of the Cold War-era movies was George Romero's *Night of the Living Dead* (1968), which transformed the zombie genre, moving it from stories about the violation of norms to critiques of those norms.[31] Romero depicted the undead as an infectious disease, but shifted the backdrop from the exotic to the mundane America of rural Pennsylvania.[32] Although some disease movies, such as *Shivers* (1976) and *Rabid* (1977), end with the spread of the disease unchecked, there is nevertheless a logical progression in the spread of the disease, and the eventual infected are often presented sympathetically before succumbing. There is a sense of shock in how a mass of undifferentiated undead snatch and absorb Barbra in *Night of the Living Dead*, or in how the body of Rose, *Rabid*'s main character and the source of its sexually transmitted disease, is casually tossed onto a heap of garbage at the film's end. Disease reveals greater societal problems; it is not the problem itself.

The 1980s and subsequent decades witnessed a change in these ideas due to the increased presence of infectious disease in American consciousness. The AIDS epidemic of the 1980s overturned the widespread assumption that scientific and technological progress could contain and defeat disease.[33] As a result, some observers began framing diseases as world-changing events throughout history, describing AIDS, for example, as the Black Death of the twentieth century.[34] Although the AIDS epidemic was ubiquitous in the news and included high profile cases within the entertainment industry, Hollywood largely ignored it. AIDS's association with LGBTQ+ culture and sexuality also led to its suppression, stereotyping and further deaths, particularly in the conservative Reagan era.[35] Later AIDS films, such as *Longtime Companion* (1989) or *Philadelphia* (1993), aimed to teach audiences about the disease and LGBTQ+ culture more generally. The few other disease movies released in the 1980s such as *Parasite* (1982) or *I Was a Teenage Zombie* (1987), were B-movies that continued to showcase disease as a social metaphor.[36] While infectious diseases returned as objects of dread, they did not change the movie paradigm.

The Rise of Viral Disease Movies and a Nostalgia for the Past

Disease outbreaks became more common in movie narratives beginning in the mid-1990s. New diseases, which scientists formally classified as "emerging infectious diseases," gained attention as the developed world realized that the continued destruction of natural environments, together with global climate change, would lead to new pandemics.[37] At the same time, increased globalization at the end of the Cold War brought the world ever closer. The combination of both developments resulted in a terrifying realization that films soon visualized: a lethal disease could now spread around the world in a matter of days.

These environmental concerns had certainly been building for decades before their connection to disease. Rachel Carson's *Silent Spring* (1962) and the celebration of Earth Day beginning in 1970 reflected a growing public consciousness of the consequences of environmental destruction.[38] Disaster films, such as *The Poseidon Adventure* (1972) and *Towering Inferno* (1974), introduced American moviegoers to an increasingly threatening environment. They underscored the instability of human society while depicting the environment as physically unstable, turning, for example, an ocean liner upside down. With rare exceptions, however, until the 1990s, disaster films rarely featured disease outbreaks as a main plot device.

Globalization was hardly new either. Historically goods, people and ideas had moved across large regions of the world for millennia. Over the past century, however, globalization has intensified with commodities that flow across the world through long supply chains and ubiquitous commercial flights that have made long-distance travel cheaper and faster than ever before. These networks have also increasingly facilitated the movement of diseases, while the ease of global communications contributed to the global awareness of these diseases. 9/11, in particular, played a key role in the perception of globalization as a growing threat. While the United States historically engaged in imperialist actions ranging from the Philippines to Cuba before 9/11, it had long viewed its own continental boundaries as sacrosanct. The destruction of the World Trade Center in 2001 introduced the perceived threat of terrorism to daily life. The anthrax envelope attacks a few weeks later and threats of additional biological attacks heightened such fears. Like an infectious disease, this threat at home was foreign-originating and could quickly spread almost invisibly.[39]

As discussed in Chapter 2, the key movie in this cultural shift is *Outbreak*, whose success was predicated on increased interest in diseases, the environment and globalization alongside the contingent timing of the Kikwit events. Yet, even as disease movies of this period recognized the impact of environmental

Figure I.3 Following the September 11, 2001 attacks on the World Trade Center, global America's borders are no longer secure.

destruction and globalization, they did not dispense with the earlier, simplistic hero and villain narrative featuring an individual who could thwart or spread the disease. While movies still offered hope of a cure, fear of disease increasingly overwhelmed a belief in science. These films remained grounded in the present even if they viewed that present as increasingly unstable and looked nostalgically to the past.

Scholars from diverse fields have observed how central the mid-1990s were to American thinking about disease. As early as July 1995, Malcolm Gladwell noted the interplay of four elements – books, movies, real events and the media – that had pushed the United States into "the grip of paranoia about viruses and diseases." Gladwell attributed the change primarily to Preston's work.[40] A few years later, Sheldon Ungar offered a sociological analysis of the same shift. By analyzing coverage of the Ebola outbreak, he identified the key framework as a "hot crisis" followed by containment. He focused on how a newly mutated disease emerged, infected humans and then was, in turn, contained. The key stakeholders in this framework included, what he called, the "Hollywood factor" that turned an outbreak into a standard story, such as *Outbreak*.[41] Others have argued that all of the different types of media demonstrate how these ideas are commonly accepted across American society.[42]

Scholarship has also examined the formation of disease stories. The historian of medicine Charles Rosenberg famously described epidemics as playing out in a series of acts in a specific order, like a play (or one might add a movie). These acts have helped structure how each new outbreak can be easily accommodated within our culture.[43] That these acts reflected cinematic stories thereafter was hardly surprising. The literary scholar Priscilla Wald wrote about the centrality of this new key disease story, which she named the "outbreak narrative." This narrative, according to Wald, is a powerful idea that "in its scientific, journalistic, and fictional incarnations – follows a formulaic plot that begins with the identification of an emerging infection, includes discussion of the global networks through which it travels, and chronicles the epidemiological work that ends with its containment."[44] Wald traced the longer history of American thinking about disease but identified various elements – contagious others, problems of public health, humanity's inevitable destruction and the collapse of scientific authority – as leading almost inevitably toward the outbreak narrative. The perception of disease outbreaks had become a self-fulfilling myth.

Post-Apocalyptic Worlds and Posthumanity

In Chapter 3, the book turns to the most recent developments in disease movies. Beginning in the late 2000s, disease films have shifted from outbreaks in single locations to pandemics that sweep across the globe when containment fails as a result of the disappearance of social norms. Even before COVID, the unending list of emerging disease threats that received extensive media coverage, such as SARS or MERS, continually reminded society of the ever-present threat of a global pandemic. Although these diseases had minor impacts on a global scale, Americans have come to expect rapidly-spreading, future pandemics that will end in large-scale catastrophes.[45] Partially through movies, the fear of outbreaks became so prevalent that it resulted in repeated, apocalyptic projections in which science and medicine fail to contain a pandemic. Christos Lynteris has labeled this focus on the next pandemic and the end of the world the "pandemic imaginary." Global capitalism has now become equated with human nature itself, making it impossible for human choices to prevent the inevitable end of humanity or even imagine alternative outcomes.[46]

The 2011 film *Contagion* reflects this most recent cinematic turn. It centers on a pandemic that affects everyone from Hong Kong to a small Midwestern town, killing tens of millions and leading to severe disruptions. The vaccine, which the film heralds as a solution, is merely a temporary fix against inevitable future diseases. Upon its release, scientists praised *Contagion* for its realism. That scientists have increasingly been called upon to comment on disease films (and even participated in their production) demonstrates how disease narratives have become integral to contemporary culture.[47]

By the second decade of the twenty-first century, pandemics in which the human species failed to ensure its own survival have become the norm on screen. Yet, there is also an incongruity about these pandemic movies. Despite the horrific impacts of the worst past pandemics, such as the Influenza of 1918–1920 or the Black Death, they did not result in the collapse of society, let alone the End Times. Perhaps given this reality, pandemic movies have increasingly taken the form of zombie movies.[48] The twenty-first century explosion in zombie books, films and TV shows is massive, and, while these movies serve as a way to explore such issues as race, gender and ethnicity, they also offer a parallel narrative in which the human species is transformed.[49] That zombie movies may accommodate both the horror genre, including the dread of bodily decay and death, and science fiction, including futuristic, unimaginable, apocalyptic End Times, confirms their suitability in addressing these twin obsessions of the early twenty-first century. Even the CDC has acknowledged the aptness of zombies to contemporary discussions by using them in a viral media campaign to increase awareness of infectious disease.[50]

Zombie films from the 2010s, such as *World War Z* (2013) or *Train to Busan* (2016), have extended fears of a global disease into a dystopian future in which humanity is nearly annihilated. These new apocalyptic zombie movies have even spawned a series of parodies, such as *Zombieland* (2009), and romantic comedies, such as *Warm Bodies* (2013), which explore and normalize the aftermath of the world's end. These movies increasingly highlighted the failure of present-day institutions and argued that humans through technology must transform themselves into some form of posthumanity. The *Planet of the Apes* trilogy (2011–2017), discussed in Chapter 3, both examines humanity's failure to maintain a viable social contract and depicts ape society as its successor. These long-term changes are also exemplified by the five versions of *The Body Snatchers* movies over almost 70 years. These movies, as discussed in Chapter 4, maintain the same overarching plot (and even similar characters until the fifth movie), while changing from stories of containment in a small American town in the 1950s to the twenty-first century's inevitable, global spread. They also shift from embracing individual identity as necessary to a lively "free" society to a growing advocacy for uniformity as the solution for a disintegrating social contract. They have shifted, in fact, from a critique of managed capitalism to embracing global capitalism.

Scholars have noticed these changes. Building on Wald's "outbreak narrative," Neil Gerlach and Sheryl Hamilton identified this 2010s shift as creating a "pandemic narrative," identifying globalization (rendering national borders moot), the failure of core human ideals and the centrality of apocalyptic ideas as the key themes. The result, in their telling, is a "pandemic culture" that permeates society.[51] At the same time, Ungar revisited his earlier analysis to demonstrate the internet-based standardization of news reports, drawing more attention to global events instead of local news. The globalization of communication has thereby facilitated a single, cultural consensus.[52] Dahlia Schweitzer has also followed this trend to argue that since the mid-1990s the government, journalists and Hollywood have encouraged the production of disease movies and that the capitalist profit motive drives this production. Succinctly put: "Hollywood reads the zeitgeist in order to translate it into box office profits."[53] The industry feeds upon the public's seemingly insatiable desire for such stories while also reinforcing the same desire in a straightforward cycle that follows other genres, such as horror-slasher films.

The six films in the *Resident Evil* franchise, discussed in Chapter 5, best exemplify Schweitzer's view. Released between 2002 and 2016, these movies were an enormous financial success, making over a billion dollars, notwithstanding their critical drubbing. Although the filmmakers' aim was to maximize profit, the *Resident Evil* movies also reflected the changes disease movies underwent from the late 1990s to the 2010s. The same fictional disease in the first and second movies is containable but results in the near annihilation of humankind in the third movie. By the last two movies, *Resident Evil* argues for a posthuman transformation. While Schweitzer's approach helps explain why such movies were produced from a monetary perspective, the *Resident Evil* movies demonstrate that the cultural transformation in America is part of a larger, ideological change.

INTRODUCTION

FUTURE PANDEMICS IN MOVIES

The contemporary interpretation of past diseases is often ahistorical, depicting diseases as an unchanging biological event, while ignoring their historical context. Scholars have drawn a straight line from Daniel Defoe's *Journal of a Plague Year* to the present, with stops along the way for Mary Shelley and George Romero.[54] Pre-1995 disease films and even those before the late 2000s are lumped together, since they belong to the same genre, notwithstanding the stark differences in these films and the periods in which they were produced. Yet, today the notion of a disease as containable to a single location or the possibility of quickly conquering disease through modern science – the standard before the mid-1990s – is unimaginable.[55] Equally unimaginable is the earlier notion of disease as a metaphor for strengthening the social fabric. Fictional twenty-first century diseases are a means for tearing down and reconstructing society anew. Social bonds, which had nearly always guaranteed the survival of the film's protagonists until the late twentieth century, no longer suffice. If horror and science fiction differ in their concerns, with the former focused on the emotional, the body and a moral order, while the latter focuses on the cognitive, a sense of wonder and the social, recent disease movies increasingly partake of and merge the two.[56] Reason and logic are no longer adequate. While paying tribute to science, movies express a sense of dread and fear, which contemporary institutions, particularly global capitalism, cannot allay.

George Romero's first and penultimate zombie movies are a useful snapshot to highlight the extent of this change. Romero, in effect, remade *Night of the Living Dead* forty years later in *Diary of the Dead* (2007). Both movies focus on the night when the dead were reanimated. Where, however, the former critiqued a culture in which mid-century norms, such as family and gender, constrain its characters, the latter depicts the stultifying effects of family and ends with the literal entombment through wealth of the surviving humans. *Diary of the Dead*, a "found footage" film, also self-consciously focuses upon human communication as destroying the species. As the movie's protagonist Debra explains, "The more voices there are, the more spin there is. The truth becomes that much harder to find." If in 1968 America glimpsed but failed to achieve a revolutionary vision of humanity, by 2007 America had dissolved in a cacophony of images and sounds amidst a battle royale of distinct tribes.[57]

To reveal these changes, this book traces the development of disease movies in chronological detail in the first three chapters, which are roughly grouped into mid-twentieth century films, 1990s to early 2000s films and the late 2000s films to the present. Each chapter focuses on two movies, one about a supposedly realistic disease and one about a speculatively imagined disease, with fictional creatures, whether zombies or enhanced apes, as illustrative examples of the period. Each chapter also offers short takes on other films that offered alternative viewpoints. Chapter 4, which discusses the remakes of *The Body Snatchers*, highlights these changes through the differing critique and shifting perceptions of what it means to be human. As Chapter 5 on *Resident Evil* demonstrates, this shift occurs regardless of artistic merit or box office success.

The COVID-19 pandemic that began in 2020 has codified these trends. Mario Slugan has suggested that COVID has retrospectively catalyzed these previously disparate films into a new genre: "pandemic movies."[58] In an important recent book, Qijun Han and Daniel Curtis likewise discuss in the context of COVID how these films have historically examined pressing social issues, including the need for communal cohesion, trust towards authorities and state institutions, and the depiction of the poor and other marginalized groups.[59] Both the breadth and scope of Han and Curtis' analysis – movies from across the globe for over a century – indicate that many of the key features of these movies are not new in film (or real life), even if the focus of specific films and real life discussions may change. What these writers demonstrate unequivocally is that the increase in the number and popularity of these films in the last few decades has shaped audience expectations of what a pandemic should do, and how society should react to it.

We began writing this book a year before COVID and continued drafting it during the pandemic to include an analysis of the impact of movies during the pandemic. Chapter 6 examines the conflicts between expectations and reality. It traces how people used their existing disease frameworks and re-watched disease movies to better understand what might happen, or was happening, during COVID. As movies guided audiences in reaching assumptions about how this pandemic would result in apocalyptic doom, those same movies also enabled audiences to overlook many of COVID's effects, such as its varied impact on different social groups. The COVID pandemic did not end human civilization, but it did make clear those structural effects of race and gender (among others) that disease films from the 1990s onward had ignored. COVID has featured few obvious moments of heroism, and significant, at times horrific, human suffering has occurred unseen for many.[60] Disease movies' apocalyptic visions were not only unrealistic and false but more importantly propagated stories that allowed Americans to overlook real problems. The glaring inadequacies of American capitalism were laid bare to both Americans and the world.[61]

Although contemporary ideas about disease are well-established across many fields, this book does not examine other formats of popular culture, such as video and board games or TV series, which have played a key role in driving both the interest in disease and the changes to their discourse.[62] Millions around the world play games, such as the video game *Resident Evil*, the online game *Plague Inc.*, and the board game *Pandemic*. Similarly, TV shows, especially *The Walking Dead* and its spin offs, have created their own fields with significant specialized literature.⁶³ These other formats have different structures, and their portrayal of infectious diseases follows their norms. All of these different formats, however, have reinforced the development of the current view of pandemics as ubiquitous, totalizing and ahistorical.

Contemporary movies about disease are not the only films that project the assumed collapse of society. Disease movies are nearly indistinguishable from the apocalyptic depictions in such genres as the end-of-the-world dramas (caused by natural disasters), superhero franchises (such as *The Avengers*' fight against Thanos, who instantly kills half of all living things in the universe) and artificial intelligence stories (in which AI increasingly replaces the human species). Each of these genres reflects differing concerns, but they share a common view of the approach of the end of life as we know it and depict a future Judgment Day, the aptly named subtitle for *Terminator 2* (1991), an apocalyptic film about artificial intelligence that has taken over in the future.⁶⁴

Disease movies today posit that humanity must accept as inevitable a global apocalypse in which the species must transform to avoid extinction. The contemporary cultural obsession with a post-apocalyptic world is, in the end, reflective of a growing inability of Americans to control, or for that matter understand, their environment in a post-industrial, information society. It is also reflective of an inability to solve the enormous and growing structural inequalities both in America and globally. Americans find that capitalist culture fails to satisfy long-term, individual needs, let alone achieve a sense of salvation. Disease movies affirm the seemingly inevitable triumph of capitalism at the expense of Americans themselves.

Notes

1. Retrospectively, *Outbreak* was the first movie in the formation of a "pandemic genre." See Mario Slugan, "Pandemic (Movies): A Pragmatic Analysis of a Nascent Genre," *Quarterly Review of Film and Video* 39, no. 4 (2021): 890–918. For box office numbers, "Outbreak (1995) – Financial Information," *The Numbers*, https://www.the-numbers.com/movie/Outbreak.
2. Richard Preston, "Crisis in the Hot Zone: Lessons from an Outbreak of Ebola," *The New Yorker*, October 18, 1992, https://www.newyorker.com/magazine/1992/10/26/crisis-in-the-hot-zone; the book, Richard Preston, *The Hot Zone* (New York: Random House, 1994). For a discussion of the early popularity: Bernard Weinraub, "Two Films, One Subject. Uh-Oh. In Hollywood, the Race Is On." *The New York Times*, June 23, 1994, https://www.nytimes.com/1994/06/23/movies/two-films-one-subject-uh-oh-in-hollywood-the-race-is-on.html. Also, Laurie Garrett, "Plague Warriors," *Vanity Fair*, August 1, 1995, https://www.vanityfair.com/news/1995/08/ebola-africa-outbreak. Preston was not pleased at this comparison critiquing the movie as "Curious George gets the Andromeda Strain." See Valerie Kuklenski, "Germ Warfare," *People*, March 20, 1995, https://www.upi.com/Archives/1995/03/20/People/8649795675600/.

3. Susan D. Moeller, *Compassion Fatigue: How the Media Sell Disease, Famine, War and Death* (London: Routledge, 1999), 86.
4. For one of the first academic analyses of this outbreak, see Sheldon Ungar, "Hot Crises and Media Reassurance: A Comparison of Emerging Diseases and Ebola Zaire," *British Journal of Sociology* 49, no. 1 (1998): 36–56; see also Laurie Garrett, *The Coming Plague: Newly Emerging Diseases in a World out of Balance* (New York: Farrar, Straus and Giroux, 1994).
5. Richard Preston, "The Vaccine Debacle," *The New York Times*, October 2, 1994, https://www.nytimes.com/1994/10/02/opinion/the-vaccine-debacle.html.
6. For these quotes, see Moeller, *Compassion Fatigue*, 89–90. For a news clip from Canada, *CBC News*, "Killer virus Ebola breaks out in 1995," https://www.youtube.com/watch?v=v2e7TeCR--w.
7. On public health officials as heroes in mid-twentieth century narratives, see Qijun Han and Daniel R. Curtis, *Infectious Inequalities: Epidemics, Trust, and Social Vulnerabilities in Cinema* (New York: Routledge, 2022), 71. See also Christos Lynteris, "The Epidemiologist as Culture Hero: Visualizing Humanity in the Age of 'the Next Pandemic,'" *Visual Anthropology* 29, no. 1 (2016): 36–53.
8. Steve Fraser and Gary Gerstle, eds., *The Rise and Fall of the New Deal Order, 1930–1980* (Princeton: Princeton University Press, 1989).
9. Wendy Brown, *Undoing the Demos: Neoliberalism's Stealth Revolution* (New York: Zone Books, 2017); for differences in wages based on gender and race, see Nancy Fraser, "Contradictions of Capital and Care," *New Left Review* 100 (2016): 99–117.
10. Global capitalism is closely associated with globalization, which is the growing connectivity and interdependence of economies, cultures and populations around the globe. A brief discussion of the topic is: Jürgen Osterhammel, *Globalization: A Short History* (Princeton: Princeton University Press, 2005).
11. Lisa Adkins, Martijn Konings, and Melinda Cooper, *The Asset Economy: Property Ownership and the New Logic of Inequality* (Medford: Polity Press, 2020).
12. On the link between families and this form of capitalism, see Melinda Cooper, *Family Values: Between Neoliberalism and the New Social Conservatism* (New York: Zone Books, 2017).
13. "Posthuman" has been described in a variety of ways. For examples, see Michael Hauskeller, Thomas D. Philbeck, and Curtis D. Carbonell, "Posthumanism in Film and Television," in *The Palgrave Handbook of Posthumanism in Film and Television*, eds. Michael Hauskeller, Thomas D. Philbeck, and Curtis D. Carbonell (New York: Palgrave Macmillan, 2015), 1–7; Rosi Braidotti, *The Posthuman* (Cambridge: Polity Press, 2013), 37–50; and, N. Katherine Hayles, *How We Became Posthuman: Virtual Bodies in Cybernetics, Literature, and Informatics* (Chicago: University of Chicago Press, 1999), 2–3. Some writers have advocated for a posthuman world resulting from the developing technology as ridding humanity of its oppressive cultural identities, such as gender and race. See Donna Haraway, "A Manifesto for Cyborgs: Science, Technology, and Socialist Feminism in the 1980s," *Socialist Review* 80 (1985): 65–108. Others, such as Shoshana Zuboff, have been more critical of the newly developing technologies and Zuboff coined the term "surveillance capitalism" to describe a new form of capitalism in the age of the

massive data collection. See *The Age of Surveillance Capitalism: The Fight for a Human Future at the New Frontier of Power* (New York: PublicAffairs, 2019).
14. For another view, see Han and Curtis, *Infectious Inequalities*, 85–106.
15. For a historical example of the disconnect between myth and reality, see Merle Eisenberg and Lee Mordechai, "The Justinianic Plague and Global Pandemics: The Making of the Plague Concept," *The American Historical Review* 125, no. 5 (2020): 1632–67.
16. See Kirsten Ostherr, *Cinematic Prophylaxis: Globalization and Contagion in the Discourse of World Health* (Durham: Duke University Press, 2005). Also, Han and Curtis, *Infectious Inequalities*.
17. For pandemic films as a genre: Slugan, "Pandemic (Movies): A Pragmatic Analysis of a Nascent Genre."
18. For collections of these films: Han and Curtis, *Infectious Inequalities*, 138–153; Walter Dehority, "Infectious Disease Outbreaks, Pandemics, and Hollywood – Hope and Fear Across a Century of Cinema," *JAMA* 323, no. 19 (2020): 1878–80. Also see Slugan, "Pandemic (Movies)."
19. On these developments, see George Rosen, *A History of Public Health*, expanded edition (Baltimore: Johns Hopkins University Press, 1993); for cultural change, Nancy Tomes, *The Gospel of Germs: Men, Women, and the Microbe in American Life* (Cambridge: Harvard University Press, 1998); on germ theory, Nancy J. Tomes and John Harley Warner, "Introduction to Special Issue on Rethinking the Reception of the Germ Theory of Disease: Comparative Perspectives," *Journal of the History of Medicine and Allied Sciences* 52, no. 1 (1997): 7–16.
20. Raymond Crawfurd, *Plague and Pestilence in Literature and Art* (Oxford: Clarendon Press, 1914), 161. This idea dates back to at least Thucydides' discussion of the Plague of Athens in 430 BC.
21. On this idea, see Ungar, "Hot Crises and Media Reassurance: A Comparison of Emerging Diseases and Ebola Zaire;" on zombies and this idea, Kyle Bishop, "The Sub-Subaltern Monster: Imperialist Hegemony and the Cinematic Voodoo Zombie," *The Journal of American Culture* 31, no. 2 (2008): 141–52. For a historical example of this process, Michael G. Vann, *The Great Hanoi Rat Hunt: Empire, Disease, and Modernity in French Colonial Vietnam* (New York: Oxford University Press, 2019).
22. For other cinematic themes, see Qijun Han and Daniel R. Curtis, "Suspicious Minds: Cinematic Depiction of Distrust during Epidemic Disease Outbreaks," *Medical Humanities* 47, no. 2 (2020): 248–256; Qijun Han and Daniel R. Curtis, "Epidemics, Public Health Workers, and 'Heroism' in Cinematic Perspective," *Visual Studies* 36, no. 4–5 (2021): 450–462.
23. On rats, Hans Zinsser, *Rats, Lice and History* (Boston: Little, Brown, 1935); on vermin and their cultural impact, Lisa T. Sarasohn, *Getting under Our Skin: The Cultural and Social History of Vermin* (Baltimore: Johns Hopkins University Press, 2021).
24. See Robin Wood, "The Dark Mirror: Murnau's Nosferatu," in *Robin Wood on the Horror Film: Collected Essays and Reviews*, ed. Barry Keith Grant (Detroit: Wayne State University Press, 2018), 119–32; Kevin Jackson, *Nosferatu: Eine Symphonie des Grauens* (London: Palgrave Macmillan, 2013).

25. Zombies have a longer history before film: Sarah Juliet Lauro, *The Transatlantic Zombie: Slavery, Rebellion, and Living Death* (New Brunswick: Rutgers University Press, 2015). There is a vast literature on zombies, see Peter Dendle, *The Zombie Movie Encyclopedia* (Jefferson: McFarland, 2010); Peter Dendle, *The Zombie Movie Encyclopedia, Volume 2: 2000–2010* (Jefferson: McFarland, 2012); also the essays in Deborah Christie and Sarah Juliet Lauro, eds., *Better off Dead: The Evolution of the Zombie as Post-Human* (New York: Fordham University Press, 2011); along with Kyle W. Bishop, *How Zombies Conquered Popular Culture: The Multifarious Walking Dead in the 21st Century* (Jefferson: McFarland, 2015); Todd K. Platts, "From White Zombies to Night Zombies and Beyond: The Evolution of the Zombie in Western Popular Culture," in *The Supernatural Revamped: From Timeworn Legends to Twenty-First-Century Chic*, eds. Barbara Brodman and James E. Doan (Madison: Fairleigh Dickinson University Press, 2016), 219–35.
26. Lauro, *The Transatlantic Zombie*.
27. During the 1930s horror movies produced by B-studios, such as Universal Studios, might be considered less mainstream than the movies of A-studios, such as MGM. In later decades this distinction begins to break down as the wider the theatrical release (and the greater the projected profits), the more the movie might be viewed as "mainstream" while the distinction between studios disappeared. The increasing presence of online streaming further blurs the definition of "mainstream." This breakdown in "mainstream" echoes the fragmentation of social norms in the disease movies.
28. Thomas Zimmer, *Welt ohne Krankheit Geschichte der internationalen Gesundheitspolitik 1940–1970* (Göttingen: Wallstein Verlag, 2017).
29. For this point, see Alfred W. Crosby, *America's Forgotten Pandemic: The Influenza of 1918*, 2nd edition, (New York: Cambridge University Press, 2003), xi; compared against the original edition, whose name reveals its focus on World War I: Alfred W. Crosby, *Epidemic and Peace, 1918* (Westport: Greenwood Press, 1976); and see the essays in Guy Beiner, ed. *Pandemic Re-Awakenings: The Forgotten and Unforgotten "Spanish" Flu of 1918–1919* (Oxford: Oxford University Press, 2021). On disease at this time, see William McNeill, *Plagues and Peoples* (Garden City: Anchor Books, 1976).
30. René Girard, "The Plague in Literature and Myth," *Texas Studies in Literature and Language* 15, no. 5 (1974): 833–50; Susan Sontag, *Illness as Metaphor* (New York: Farrar, Straus and Giroux, 1978); and David Steel, "Plague Writing: From Boccaccio to Camus," *Journal of European Studies* 11, no. 2 (1981): 88–110.
31. Dendle, *The Zombie Movie Encyclopedia, Volume 2: 2000–2010*; and Andrew Schopp and Matthew B. Hill, "Attack of the Livid Dead: Recalibrating Terror in the Post-9/11 Zombie Film," in *The War on Terror and American Popular Culture: September 11 and Beyond*, eds. Andrew Schopp and Matthew B. Hill (Madison: Fairleigh Dickinson University Press, 2009), 239–58.
32. It was also the first of a series of films about the undead that Romero would use to critique American culture: Robert Alpert, "George Romero's Zombie Movies: The Fragmentation of America," *Senses of Cinema*, no. 98 (2021), https://www.sensesofcinema.com/2021/feature-articles/george-romeros-zombie-movies-the-fragmentation-of-america/.

33. Elizabeth Fee and Daniel M. Fox, eds., *AIDS: The Making of a Chronic Disease* (Berkeley: University of California Press, 1992); and for the early period, see Richard A. McKay, *Patient Zero and the Making of the AIDS Epidemic* (Chicago: University of Chicago Press, 2017).
34. For this idea, see Ernest B. Gilman, *Plague Writing in Early Modern England* (Chicago: University of Chicago Press, 2009), 5; for an early reflection, Charles E. Rosenberg, "What Is an Epidemic? AIDS in Historical Perspective," *Daedalus* 118, no. 2 (1989): 1–17. For a twenty-first century perspective: Zachary Crockett and Javier Zarracina, "How the Zombie Represents America's Deepest Fears," *Vox*, October 31, 2016, https://www.vox.com/policy-and-politics/2016/10/31/13440402/zombie-political-history.
35. Monica Pearl, "AIDS and New Queer Cinema," in *New Queer Cinema: A Critical Reader*, ed. Michele Aaron (New Brunswick: Rutgers University Press, 2004), 23–36; for broader changes, see Allan M. Brandt, "How AIDS Invented Global Health," *New England Journal of Medicine* 368, no. 23 (2013): 2149–52; and a COVID perspective, E. Berryhill McCarty and Lance Wahlert, "Lessons on Surviving a Pandemic From 35 Years of AIDS Cinema," *AMA Journal of Ethics* 23, no. 5 (2021): 423–27.
36. For changes to production: Todd K. Platts, "A Comparative Analysis of the Factors Driving Film Cycles: Italian and American Zombie Film Production, 1978–82," *Journal of Italian Cinema & Media Studies* 5, no. 2 (2017): 191–210.
37. Garrett, *The Coming Plague*; for a reflection, see Joshua Lederberg, "Infectious History," *Science* 288, no. 5464 (2000): 287–93.
38. Rachel Carson, *Silent Spring* (New York: Fawcett Crest, 1962); for a look back at DDT and *Silent Spring*, see Elena Conis, *How to Sell a Poison: The Rise, Fall, and Toxic Return of DDT* (New York: Bold Type Books, 2022). On the early event that led to Earth Day, Kate Wheeling and Max Ufberg, "'The Ocean Is Boiling': The Complete Oral History of the 1969 Santa Barbara Oil Spill," *Pacific Standard*, April 18, 2017, https://psmag.com/news/the-ocean-is-boiling-the-complete-oral-history-of-the-1969-santa-barbara-oil-spill.
39. On disease and security, Alethia H. Cook, "Securitization of Disease in the United States: Globalization, Public Policy, and Pandemics," *Risk, Hazards & Crisis in Public Policy* 1, no. 1 (2010): 11–31; and Mika Aaltola, "Contagious Insecurity: War, SARS and Global Air Mobility," *Contemporary Politics* 18, no. 1 (2012): 53–70; see also Anjuli Fatima Raza Kolb, *Epidemic Empire: Colonialism, Contagion, and Terror 1817–2020* (Chicago: University of Chicago Press, 2021).
40. Malcolm Gladwell, "The Plague Year," *New Republic*, July 17, 1995, https://newrepublic.com/article/62521/the-plague-year.
41. Ungar, "Hot Crises and Media Reassurance: A Comparison of Emerging Diseases and Ebola Zaire."
42. Peter Washer has suggested that these ideas "emerge spontaneously." Peter Washer, "Representations of SARS in the British Newspapers," *Social Science & Medicine* 59, no. 12 (2004): 2561–71; for further discussion, see Peter Washer, *Emerging Infectious Diseases and Society* (New York: Palgrave Macmillan, 2010); on media and science, Brigitte Nerlich and Christopher Halliday, "Avian Flu: The Creation of Expectations in the Interplay between Science and the Media," *Sociology of Health & Illness* 29, no. 1 (2007): 46–65.

43. Rosenberg, "What Is an Epidemic? AIDS in Historical Perspective"; and for a look back during COVID: Charles Rosenberg, "What Is and Was an Epidemic," *Bulletin of the History of Medicine* 94, no. 4 (2020): 755–57.
44. Priscilla Wald, *Contagious: Cultures, Carriers, and the Outbreak Narrative* (Durham, NC: Duke University Press, 2008), 2.
45. But for problems with these expectations: Carlo Caduff, *The Pandemic Perhaps: Dramatic Events in a Public Culture of Danger* (Oakland: University of California Press, 2015).
46. Christos Lynteris, *Human Extinction and the Pandemic Imaginary* (New York: Routledge, 2020), 5–13.
47. Neil A. Gerlach and Sheryl N. Hamilton, "Trafficking in the Zombie: The CDC Zombie Apocalypse Campaign, Diseaseability and Pandemic Culture," *Refractory: A Journal of Entertainment Media* 23 (2014), https://refractory-journal.com/cdc-zombie-apocalypse-gerlach-hamilton/; Neil A. Gerlach, "From Outbreak to Pandemic Narrative: Reading Newspaper Coverage of the 2014 Ebola Epidemic," *Canadian Journal of Communication* 41, no. 4 (2016); and for epidemiologists as key figures, Lynteris, *Human Extinction and the Pandemic Imaginary*, 99–103.
48. For the new zombie movies: Schopp and Hill, "Attack of the Livid Dead"; and Dendle, *The Zombie Movie Encyclopedia, Volume 2: 2000–2010*; also, Dahlia Schweitzer, *Going Viral: Zombies, Viruses, and the End of the World* (New Brunswick: Rutgers University Press, 2018).
49. See Stephanie Boluk and Wylie Lenz, "Introduction: Generation Z, the Age of Apocalypse," in *Generation Zombie: Essays on the Living Dead in Modern Culture*, eds. Stephanie Boluk and Wylie Lenz (Jefferson: McFarland, 2011), 1–17; and also Dave Beisecker, "Afterword: Bye-Gone Days: Reflections on Romero, Kirkman and What We Become," in *"We're All Infected": Essays on AMC's The Walking Dead and the Fate of the Human*, ed. Dawn Keetley (Jefferson: McFarland, 2014), 201–14. For a recent view, Megen de Bruin-Molé, "Killable Hordes, Chronic Others and 'Mindful' Consumers: Rehabilitating the Zombie in Twenty-First-Century Popular Culture," in *Embodying Contagion: The Viropolitics of Horror and Desire in Contemporary Discourse*, eds. Sandra Becker et al. (Cardiff: University of Wales Press, 2021), 159–78.
50. Melissa Nasiruddin et al., "Zombies – A Pop Culture Resource for Public Health Awareness," *Emerging Infectious Diseases* 19, no. 5 (2013): 809–13; for a negative view of the CDC's campaign, Dahlia Schweitzer, "Pushing Contagion: How Government Agencies Shape Portrayals of Disease," *Journal of Popular Culture* 50, no. 3 (2017): 445–65; and Sara Polak, "Preparedness 101: 'Zombie Pandemic' and the Ebola Scare How the CDC's Use of Zombie Pop Culture Helped Fan a Nationalist Outbreak Narrative," in *Embodying Contagion: The Viropolitics of Horror and Desire in Contemporary Discourse*, eds. Sandra Becker et al. (Cardiff: University of Wales Press, 2021), 41–59.
51. Gerlach and Hamilton, "Trafficking in the Zombie."
52. Gerlach, "From Outbreak to Pandemic Narrative." Internet-based media was, of course, not alone in this process, see Neil A. Gerlach, "Visualizing Ebola: Hazmat Suite Imagery, the Press, and the Production of Biosecurity," *Canadian Journal of Communication* 44, no. 2 (2019): 191–210; Sheryl N. Hamilton, "Mediating Disease

Cultures," *Canadian Journal of Communication* 44, no. 2 (2019): 151–56; and Scott Mitchell and Sheryl N Hamilton, "Playing at Apocalypse: Reading Plague Inc. in Pandemic Culture," *Convergence* 24, no. 6 (2018): 587–606.
53. Schweitzer, *Going Viral*, 22.
54. For examples that use literature across time: Elana Gomel, "The Plague of Utopias: Pestilence and the Apocalyptic Body," *Twentieth Century Literature* 46, no. 4 (2000): 405–33; Jennifer Cooke, *Legacies of Plague in Literature, Theory and Film* (New York: Palgrave Macmillan, 2009); Stephanie Boluk and Wylie Lenz, "Infection, Media, and Capitalism: From Early Modern Plagues to Postmodern Zombies," *Journal for Early Modern Cultural Studies* 10, no. 2 (2010): 126–47; and Douglas Kellner, "Social Apocalypse in Contemporary Hollywood Film," in *The Routledge Companion to Cinema and Politics*, eds. Yannis Tzioumakis and Claire Molloy (London: Routledge, 2016), 13–28.
55. For historical narratives and few alternatives, see Mary E. Fissell et al., "Introduction: Reimagining Epidemics," *Bulletin of the History of Medicine* 94, no. 4 (2020): 543–61.
56. Barry Keith Grant, "Sensuous Elaboration: Reason and the Visible in the Science-Fiction Film," in *Alien Zone II: The Spaces of Science-Fiction Cinema*, ed. Annette Kuhn (New York: Verso, 1999), 16–30.
57. For further discussion, Robert Alpert, "George Romero's Night of the Living Dead and Diary of the Dead: Recording History," *CineAction* 95 (2015).
58. Slugan, "Pandemic (Movies)."
59. Han and Curtis, *Infectious Inequalities*.
60. Han and Curtis. "Epidemics, Public Health Workers, and 'Heroism' in Cinematic Perspective," express hope that a new paradigm will emerge. Also, Han and Curtis, *Infectious Inequalities*, 80–1 and 136.
61. See presciently: Lynteris, *Human Extinction*, 78.
62. For an example of change over time in another genre, see Christopher B. Menadue, "Pandemics, Epidemics, Viruses, Plagues, and Disease: Comparative Frequency Analysis of a Cultural Pathology Reflected in Science Fiction Magazines from 1926 to 2015," *Social Sciences & Humanities Open* 2, no. 1 (2020): 100048.
63. As just one example, see Dawn Keetley, ed. *"We're All Infected."*
64. As Sarah Connor, the mother of humanity's future heroic leader against the machines repeats, "The future's not set. There's no fate but what we make for ourselves." It is questionable whether the film, a classical Hollywood construction, endorses that view. For TV and the End Times, see Michael G. Cornelius and Sherry Ginn, eds. *Apocalypse TV: Essays on Society and Self at the End of the World* (Jefferson: McFarland, 2020).

CHAPTER 1

EARLY DISEASE MOVIES: AMERICAN NORMS AND CONTAINMENT

Introduction

Films featuring diseases date back to the earliest days of motion pictures. These films coincided with the development of germ theory and the ensuing bacteriological revolution that for the first time allowed humans to identify the cause of disease, which in turn facilitated the development of vaccines. Cures, however, were often not immediately available.[1] The earliest disease films from the first half of the twentieth century reflected this limitation. Humans could identify the source of disease, but treatment remained medically elusive. The solution for disease on screen remained as it had been for centuries: quarantine and containment of marginalized groups blamed for the spread of disease. Limiting the spread of the disease was necessary to ensure the survival of "civilized," in essence, culturally acceptable people who adhered to existing norms.[2] The perceived threat of disease would eventually begin to shift after World War II when cures for disease became more widespread through the use of antibiotics and more vaccines. During the first half of the twentieth century, American disease movies nevertheless also remained consistently optimistic, whether through successful quarantine or faith in social and spiritual progress in addressing disease. Outsiders remained the source of disease, so these stories also continued to affirm the myths surrounding American norms.

This chapter investigates key mid-century disease movies that sustained majoritarian ideals typically through the identification of norms and the punishment of those who transgressed them, resulting in a temporary failure of containment that was resolved by the ending of these films. While these early films sometimes depicted individuals who violated norms or critiqued society as problematic, they remained committed to shared values and offered a vision of a better world, even if it was not always immediately obtainable or available to everyone.[3] These films are optimistic in the ability to maintain or improve upon American norms. Any pessimism results from frustration at the difficulty in achieving these norms and their associated values at a time when the biological effects of disease were considered less important than the consequences associated with the social disruption caused by disease.[4] While capitalism underlies the socio-economic structure of these films, it remains in the background and is rarely critiqued.

This chapter also offers a baseline to understand the historical transformations that have occurred over the last three decades of disease films that feature in the next two chapters. It opens with a discussion of pre-World War II films. These films consisted of either horror movies about vampires and zombies, which focus upon the foreign origin of disease, or more mainstream movies, which depict real-life diseases, such as yellow fever, cholera and syphilis, so as to affirm existing values. It then examines some of the dominant norms and social critiques of American society through two illustrative movies, *Panic in the Streets* (1950) and *Night of the Living Dead* (1968). *Panic in the Streets* identified the source of the infection as foreign as well as criticizes the unfairness of the social contract in its denial of the idealized comforts of the middle-class American Dream to white, male patriots. Yet, it also continues to advocate for the moral and professional efforts of the "average" American couple as well as reaffirms a narrative in which society conquers disease. *Night of the Living Dead* was central to the change beginning in the late 1960s when films about disease shifted from a focus on containment of undesirables to an expression of discomfort with the social norms of contemporary American society. It revised the zombie genre and highlighted the problems of family, gender and race during the height of America's war in Vietnam and the Civil Rights era. It suggested that resolving these issues was impossible during that era but envisioned a future of an America less savage and more equitable and just.

This overarching trend of disease movies is interspersed with brief discussions of a few influential non-American movies that offered alternatives. *The Seventh Seal* (1957) has a perspective based on the personal ideas of its Swedish director, Ingmar Bergman. It pictured the horrific impact of the fourteenth century Black Death pandemic and advocated that individuals seek personal redemption through spiritual transcendence, despite the vices of the society in which they live. Its alternative view demonstrates how a non-American film focused its critique on these different values before the era of globalized capitalism of the late twentieth century. *Shivers* (1975), a Canadian production, offered a reactionary perspective to the dangers of the recent sexual revolution coming from America. Even this reactionary perspective, though, remained centered on curing social problems and restoring "traditional" values, such as those *Panic* endorsed and *Night* had critiqued. Finally, the Japanese disaster film *Virus/Day of Resurrection* (1980) told of a pandemic that could not be contained, viewing its effects through a Cold War lens. While *Virus* was optimistic in suggesting that international cooperation and the creation of a new society that included citizens of all nations might result in a more inclusive, post-pandemic society, its apocalyptic ending featuring the near annihilation of the human species suggested the difficulties faced in achieving these new possibilites. An outlier at the time, its themes would resurface two decades later.

The Origins of Disease Movies: From Silent Films to World War II

Disease horror movies during the first half of the twentieth century from both Europe and the United States shared a common view of the source of disease: outsiders to the proper, "civilized" members of society. While the plague in the German *Nosferatu: A Symphony of Horror* (1922) seems to originate with rats, the disease source is plainly an Eastern European, Semitic creature who spreads his infection through sexually deviant behavior. Nosferatu, whose name likely means disease-carrier, hides under the name Orlok and has resided alone for centuries in a towering Transylvanian castle in the Carpathian Mountains.[5] His appearance draws on anti-Semitic tropes while another stereotypical Jew assists him. Nosferatu's lust for a married, Christian woman eventually defeats him, since he continues to suck her blood while she is lying upon her bed when a cock crows to announce the dawn. Proper moral behavior and a woman's sexual purity, and to a lesser extent medical knowledge, defeat the disease represented by the evil Nosferatu. The American produced *Dracula* (1931) also underscores the sexual, syphilitic nature of the vampire's infection and hence the social deviance of the foreigner. The Hungarian-born Bela Lugosi portrayed this Transylvanian vampire, and the film's anti-Semitism is even starker, reflected in the Star of David Dracula wears. The vampire threatens the moral order of London society through his sexual seductions that spread the disease across the city. Only the polymath Professor Van Helsing resists his hypnotic, magical powers and defeats him through appropriate items, including wolfsbane and a wooden stake. As in *Nosferatu* and other films of the period, society and its sexual norms must be protected against insidious outsiders, who can be identified and contained.

Early zombie movies similarly focus on the violation of social norms, using disease as a metaphor for the need to contain supposedly non-normative behavior and defeat the foreign-originating source of the zombies. In *White Zombie* (1932), a foreign voodoo master in Haiti transforms a married, white woman into a zombie in order to satisfy the sexual lust of a wealthy plantation owner, and in *I Walked with a Zombie* (1943), a married woman is transformed into a zombie, because she has seduced her husband's half-brother. These movies on occasion also critiqued capitalism during an era when many saw Marxism as an alternative to capitalism or fascism.[6] For example, the voodoo master in *White Zombie*, Legendre (played again by Bela Lugosi), seeks to persuade the wealthy plantation owner of the benefits of using zombies by observing, "They work faithfully. They are not worried about long hours." These early critiques of capitalism focused on how people performed work – monotonously in factories – and how the behavior of a largely black population contradicted the norms of a supposedly respectable white society. These critiques of capitalism in B-movies disappeared, however, during World War II when they were replaced with stories supporting the war effort against fascism, another foreign-originating disease. In *King of the Zombies* (1941), foreign spies use zombified black natives to obtain classified information about Panama Canal fortifications, and in *Revenge of the Zombies* (1943) a white enslaver transforms the dead, both white and black, into zombies to create an undefeatable Nazi army.

The plots of these anti-Semitic and racist movies featured the successful containment of disease represented by those viewed as outsiders to the then dominant, American cultural values.[7] More mainstream American movies about disease also consistently developed and affirmed those cultural values, and disease served as a metaphor in such films for a belief in the public good, the inevitability of social progress and a faith in the spiritual rightness of American exceptionalism. While disease in these movies could play an incidental or central role in their narrative, these movies typically affirmed existing social values, expressed a continued faith in America's progress at solving problems and envisioned a hopeful future.[8] *The Painted Veil* (1934), for example, tells of a pampered Austrian woman who out of boredom marries a British research bacteriologist and then has an affair in Hong Kong with an equally bored and married British embassy attaché. When she is forced to travel with her husband inland to fight a raging cholera epidemic, she comes to admire how he has devoted himself to helping the ignorant Chinese peasants. She soon joins him in his humanitarian efforts, devoting herself, unbeknownst to her husband, to the local convent which cares for Chinese orphans, and rejects the attaché who wishes to renew their extramarital affair. Disease is the motivating plot device for a bored white woman to end her affair, love her husband and help the "exotic" other. *Pacific Liner* (1939) likewise features the exotic other and affirms American norms. Its "Asiatic cholera" originates in an Asian stowaway on a luxury passenger ship bound for America, and the movie critiques the wealthy, upper class passengers, who fail in their normative (if paternalistic) duty to protect society and instead continue to party. It simultaneously critiques as "uncivilized" the lower-class workers who are kept in line by quarantine only through the efforts of the chief engineer, a brutish officer appropriately nicknamed Crusher. The film ends happily when the ship arrives ahead of schedule in San Francisco as a result of Crusher's efforts, while the ship's doctor and nurse renew their romantic relationship. Quarantining along class lines enables the professional, educated middle class to contain the disease while continuing to flourish.

No film, however, better illustrates disease as a metaphoric affirmation of American values than the so-called woman's picture *Jezebel* (1938). It focuses on the antebellum belle Julie Marsden as both benefitting and suffering from a prejudicial and preindustrial society.[9] Julie challenges the gender norms of New Orleans in 1852 and serves as the key fulcrum to explore the place of disease and progress. At an important business meeting, which Julie unsuccessfully tries to interrupt, her fiancé Pres advocates for an investment in railroads, which he foresees as a threat to the Southern monopoly on commerce, while simultaneously another town resident, Dr. Livingstone, advocates for preventing another outbreak of yellow fever. Pres eventually breaks off his engagement with Julie due to her failure to conform to gender norms and travels North where he marries a Northern woman. A year later Pres returns and argues at Julie's homecoming party that in a civil war Northern commerce with its machines will prevail over the South's unskilled, slave labor and that to cure yellow fever the town must drain its swamps instead of mindlessly shooting off canons and placing the sick on an island for lepers. Julie, in turn, mocks Pres for prioritizing his bank and urges him to acknowledge that the South "isn't tame and easy like the North. It's quick and dangerous, but you trust it." The film ends with Julie accompanying Pres, who has caught yellow fever from a mosquito bite on Julie's plantation, to the lepers' island. The film uses disease to contrast the preindustrial, unscientific South with the capitalist and scientifically advanced North. In contrast to the ignorant South, Northern commerce, banks and industrialism will prevail over the disease by draining the Southern swamps. While the film labels Julie as a "Jezebel," a woman "who did evil in the sight of God" and outside the bounds of correct behavior, it depicts her as straddling these two worlds. Northern capitalism will one day cleanse Southern patriarchy of its Jezebels and revert to proper gender roles just as it would soon free black slaves in the Civil War.

Other mainstream movies depict diseases as their main plot element. They espouse the development of science through curiosity, a compassionate practice of medicine and the value of American beliefs, including the public good and spiritual faith. *Green Light* (1937), for example, highlights the advancement of American medical science through a combination of social progress and spiritual development. It depicts a young surgeon, Newell Paige, who resigns from an urban hospital and moves to a remote region of Montana, where spotted fever ticks have been killing off the local population for decades. He eventually finds a cure by serving as a human guinea pig for the vaccine he develops.

Paige's story serves to confirm the spiritual advice of a clergyman, Dean Harcourt, who asserts faith in the progress of humankind in which civilization is an inexorable march to eternity. Together, science and faith drive progress. Life is not a story about the survival of the fittest, as Paige's nurse argues. Instead, it consists of a search for a purpose in life by the inherently good, such as Paige, who are receptive to the "green light" enabling the progression of civilization. The film ends on both the establishment of the Rocky Mountain Laboratory of the US Public Health Service and a choir singing Amen in Dean Harcourt's church. Socially good works are spiritually progressive.

Dr. Ehrlich's Magic Bullet (1940) likewise reiterates the unity of the secular and the sacred. Released between the start of World War II and America's entry into the war and directed by the Jewish German immigrant Daniel Dieterle, who had previously directed *The Story of Louis Pasteur* (1936), the film affirms the American values of assimilation, individualism and capitalism as spiritually uplifting. The villains, such as Drs. Hartmann and Wolfert at the German hospital where Paul Ehrlich initially works, insist on knowing one's place, obeying rules and conforming. Ehrlich refuses, instead privately experimenting on the development of dyes to stain microbes and later persisting in research on the

Figure 1.1 *Dr. Ehrlich's Magic Bullet* (1940): A heavenly light illuminates the deceased Dr. Ehrlich, who successfully fought bodily diseases and diseases of the soul.

seemingly irrelevant (snake venom) and the socially disreputable (syphilis). If money plays a role as a "necessary evil," according to Ehrlich, the film argues that while it may encourage the small minded, it can also facilitate social good. A state budget committee strips Ehrlich's research facility of funding in the midst of his efforts to find a cure for syphilis, because Dr. Wolfert, who had earlier criticized Ehrlich for being Jewish, observes that Ehrlich employs Dr. Hata, an "Oriental." "What has race to do with science?!" Ehrlich asks enraged, but soon finds alternative funding through Franziska Speyer, the wealthy widow of a banker who wishes to use her money for the "greatest public good." Her investment enables Ehrlich not only to find a "magic bullet" but also mass produce it. Even when 38 people die from Ehrlich's not yet fully tested "magic bullet," these are "martyrs" for the "public good." Lying on his deathbed, Ehrlich tells those gathered around him that diseases of the body are inseparable from diseases of the soul. "There will be epidemics of greed, hate, ignorance," he predicts. "We must fight them in life as we fought syphilis in the laboratory." A heavenly light then illuminates the deceased figure of Ehrlich as his wife closes the door. Disease offers Ehrlich, a Jew, an opportunity to pursue his magnificent obsession, which coincides with American exceptionalism in its valuing of innovation, industry and religious faith.

The Heroic Public Servant and the American Dream: *Panic in the Streets* (1950)

By the mid-twentieth century, scientists had significantly tempered the effects of infectious disease in the United States through vaccines, antibiotics and eradication campaigns, which enabled movies to examine through stories about disease the ideals and disappointments of American social norms. Mid-century disease movies sought both to find meaning in middle class American life as well as reflect upon the problems members of the middle class experienced. Like their earlier counterparts, these movies also helped define cultural norms, articulated their failings, examined the effects of their transgressions, and proposed ways to defeat or at least buffer these failings and transgressions. American society had to be protected through state-managed capitalism, even if it meant that some individuals, including white, Christian men who should benefit from social norms, had to sacrifice some material happiness for the common good.

Elia Kazan's *Panic in the Streets* is the quintessential disease movie of 1950s, Cold War America. Representative of its time, the film received positive reviews and even an Academy Award for Best Story.[10] The movie reflects an expansive fear of "the other," exemplified not only by the unlawful immigrant who introduces disease to the American mainland but also by other infected foreigners as well as lower-class workers and gangsters. These outsiders, while supposedly seeking to achieve the American Dream, threaten the social containment of the disease, since they do not share American values. They instead seek to benefit from their own personal, economic gains at the expense of the common good and may also be equated with the Communists then supposedly threatening American capitalism.[11]

Kazan uses disease as a key plot element to examine American society from different perspectives. Stopping the disease outbreak, including by ostracizing and punishing outsiders, enables society to continue to function and keeps the American social contract inviolate. The movie exemplifies its idealization of society as white, male and middle-class through its protagonist Lieutenant Commander Clinton Reed (Richard Widmark), a doctor in the US Health Service. At the same time, the film critiques the middle-class life of the public servant as economically unfulfilling in comparison to work in the private sector. Despite Reed's education and public service, he fails to achieve the American Dream. Reed nonetheless continues to protect society and his community, since he maintains his belief in the rightness of the American social contract. While he may not achieve the materialistic heights he hopes for, or even recognition for what he has done, he is content with his role in defending the American way of life. The film's lesson is clear. Everyone should know and accept their place in American society.

The movie's plot is straightforward. Often working alone, Reed tries to contain an outbreak of pneumonic plague to prevent its spread beyond New Orleans. The movie identifies the plague's origin as a foreign cargo ship transporting illegal immigrants into the United States. An immigrant named Kochak has contracted the plague and transmits it to others in New Orleans, although gangsters soon kill and rob him.[12] Reed races around the city to identify Kochak and those with whom Kochak came into contact to prevent the outbreak from spiraling out of control. All the suspected or confirmed cases of plague involve foreigners and lower-class individuals: Kochak's cousin Poldi, Asian seamen, the wife of a Greek restaurant owner and the antagonist, the sadistic gangster Blackie (Jack Palance).

While a big budgeted movie, *Panic in the Streets* adopts a low budget style combining documentary and film noir. It has documentary-like, on location shooting and uses non-professional actors while filmed in starkly contrasting black and white photography.[13] The opening shots depict unknown, low-life characters gambling above a bar followed by the hunting and brutal killing of Kochak. The next morning's light reveals the immigrant's body washed ashore. The small talk of the morgue workers contrasts with Kochak's body lying on the coroner's table. He is just another dead foreigner in America. Even the bright morning daylight thereafter in Dr. Reed's middle-class home offers no respite, since Reed and his wife engage in a lengthy discussion about money and unpaid debts. Yet, the contrast between these sharply differing neighborhoods of New Orleans representative of the different parts of American society is stark, in turn reinforcing the dichotomy between those who uphold norms and those who through selfishness or their foreignness will seek to tear it down.

Panic in the Streets uses plague to illuminate early 1950s life in America, in particular, the tensions between communal cohesion and individualistic aspirations within the middle class. Throughout the film, Reed continually tries to enlist others from the public sector to help him find the plague's origin. While everyone acknowledges that the plague would overwhelm the United States if it escapes from New Orleans, other officials repeatedly frustrate his efforts, demonstrating how even those in charge do not necessarily understand how best to protect the country. The mayor does not want his job, while the police department and its individual officers go through the motions of interviewing hundreds of potentially diseased suspects but assume they will fail. The mayor's assistant is the most obvious contrast to Reed. He is self-centered and clueless, insisting that the "problem lies right here in our own community" and that the plague will not spread. Reed replies,

> Community? What community? Do you think you're living in the Middle Ages? . . . I could leave here today and I could be in Africa tomorrow. And whatever disease I had would go right with me . . . We're all in a community, the same one!

Reed's perception of who is included in American society offers a viewpoint of each person's place within that society as well as in the larger, surrounding world. If a global America includes unwanted, foreign elements, it also offers an ideal. Everyone working together may build a better world under America's benign leadership, reflecting the new post-war order manifested famously in the post-World War II rebuilding projects of the Marshall Plan. In this new world order, cure and containment are feasible but require hard, constant work – just like the work demanded by America's growing, cultural, economic and political hegemony in the Cold War.

Dr. Reed and Police Captain Warren (Paul Douglas) represent the film's ideal of heroic Americans who are willing to sacrifice their materialistic gains to build a better society. They symbolize the government professional class who now defend the world in the aftermath of World War II in the same way that American GI's put aside their personal lives and sacrificed during the war. Both are middle-class civil servants committed to their duties, regardless of financial remuneration. Warren, like the other police officers, is initially skeptical of Reed's motives, offering only pro forma assistance. Yet, Warren eventually accepts Reed's public role as a heroic American serving to protect American values, and Reed, in turn, acknowledges Warren's professionalism in upholding these American ideals. To prevent "panic in the streets," Warren puts his career and pension in jeopardy by arresting a reporter who decides that he

Figure 1.2 *Panic in the Streets* (1950): Working together, Dr. Reed and Captain Warren, two middle-class, American public servants, will contain the plague.

must publish the story about the plague, notwithstanding that its publication will lead to chaos and a failure of containment. Reed later notes that Warren, who is only a high school graduate, "prov[es] he's four times the man I'll ever be." Warren's change represents how a public servant can become an American hero. While the mayor later releases the reporter and gives Reed and Warren only four hours to find the source of the plague before the news story will be published, the two men are successful. They prevent the gangster Blackie and his sidekick Fitch (Zero Mostel) from leaving the city.[14] The self-centered mayor's assistant, in contrast, uses those same four hours to evacuate his kids to their grandmother's house upriver. He only cares about his family – a sentiment the film condemns.

The movie also highlights the limits of public institutions, notwithstanding Reed's success through sheer force of personality. In that respect, like many film noir movies, *Panic in the Streets* critiques American capitalism, which financially rewards those in the private sector and relegates its public servants to a second-tier status. Reed cannot support his family, which has placed a strain on his relationship with both his wife and his son. His wife Nancy's (Barbara Bel Geddes) household budget is insufficient to pay a longstanding $42 bill, which embarrasses her, and the couple regret they cannot afford a second child. Reed confesses to Nancy his failure as the family breadwinner, noting that he has only $38 in savings. Money problems extend also to their son Tommy, who has already spent his allowance and begs for another quarter to go to the movies. He laments how he wished they had a larger house and that he had a set of electric trains like Mr. Redfield, the painter who lives next door. The blue-collar Mr. Redfield with this larger house represents the success of private enterprise. His train set, which Tommy envies, is symbolic of American capitalism, since railroads during the late nineteenth century opened the American West and unified the country. Not surprisingly, Reed dreams of quitting his public service job and working for a private oil company laying a pipeline in Arabia or serving as a medical advisor for expeditions in Chile.

The film contrasts Reed's white, middle-class home with the seedier parts of New Orleans inhabited by lower class, foreign immigrants. The coroners repeatedly denigrate Kochak, who introduces the plague to America, as a foreigner and later describe his appearance as Eastern European, Armenian, Czech or some other type of "mixed blood." In contrast to the glamorous Hollywood physical appearances of Richard Widmark and Barbara Bel Geddes (Reed and Nancy), the underworld Kochak joins is inhabited by the "less Hollywood looking" Jack Palance and Zero Mostel, who play the unsavory-looking gangsters Blackie and Fitch. Blackie and his gang resemble animals as they hunt down and kill Kochak, and Fitch's wife later calls Blackie a "big ape." Blackie's nickname surely refers to his "darker," Eastern European background as well as is a racist characterization of non-Western Europeans or "proper" Americans. The film writes out black Americans, even though it was shot in the heavily black city of New Orleans using local extras. This reflects the open racism of the movie industry (and America) at the time but simultaneously reinforces how certain groups are invisible in the discussion of the American image.[15] The foreign origin of the disease also extends to the ship on which Kochak contracted the plague. It is named the *Nile Queen* and came from Algeria, and its crew is largely Asian and black. The disease will later spread to other foreign immigrants, such as a Greek couple who own the restaurant that Blackie and his gang frequent. These unkempt members of the lower class do not always accept their place in society, and their selfishness threatens the American social fabric.

The underworld character Blackie serves as a double to the middle class Reed, demonstrating what can go wrong in America if American ideals are not carefully managed. While Reed selflessly hunts to find the source of the disease, Blackie runs his own investigation for personal profit, mistaking the police dragnet to stop the plague as an indication that the infected Kochak must have smuggled something valuable into the United States. The danger posed by Blackie is underscored by the presence of the lower-class entertainment of pinball machines and jazz music in the ordinary coffee shops which

Reed frequents. Blackie represents what Reed could become, if he focused on personal profit rather than on the American ideal.

If the film argues for a moral, if precarious, vision of American middle-class life, it also offers a gendered vision of America in which women are relegated to a domestic setting. Yet, they, too, have a specific part to play in upholding American values by serving as the social conscience and moral guide to working men. A key, late-night discussion between an exhausted Reed and his wife underscores this perspective. While Nancy's face reveals horror upon hearing that plague is in New Orleans, her voice expresses confidence in her husband. "Well, at least they have you. You've been through it," she assures him. Reed, and people like him, will ensure that society survives and thrives. He acknowledges her trust in him and calls her "little miss sunshine," who always looks for and sees the better outcome. With romantic music playing on the soundtrack, Reed and Nancy speak of his dreams. Nancy insists that his public health position is the job he had always wanted and with the plague outbreak, he is now the most important man in the city. She also tells him that he is also no longer a kid and needs to grow up and let go of his childish fantasies of working for the private sector. She announces that she decided weeks ago that Tommy will not be an only child. Everything will be resolved, and they can have their two children, live in a house of their own and finally enjoy their version of the American Dream. Nancy voices how Reed represents the American ideal, which requires individual sacrifice for the common good, and she ensures that he continues to fulfill that public role to preserve a functioning society.

In contrast, Blackie as Reed's double does not "like a smart cracking dame" and does not heed the good advice of women. Instead, the gangster sidekick Fitch plays the woman's role in his relationship with Blackie. He packs Blackie's suitcase, cannot explain to Blackie why he did not stay single, and eventually tries to escape the city (and his marriage) with Blackie. Lower class women often transgress their gender roles leading to the further spread of disease. Rita, the wife of the owner of the Greek restaurant where Kochak met Blackie and his gang, persuades her husband not to identify Kochak to the authorities. They lie to Reed and Warren, resulting in Rita's death from plague and the quarantine of their entire lower-class neighborhood. Angie, Fitch's wife, is likewise inappropriately aggressive, not afraid of Blackie, and chastises her husband for letting Blackie run him around "like a dog on a leash."[16] Unlike Nancy, she does not know her "proper" place in a marriage. These women represent debased caricatures of Nancy, demonstrating the risks confronting American society if gender roles are transgressed.

In the film's happy ending, Dr. Reed and Captain Warren contain the plague, and Captain Warren then drops Dr. Reed off at his small home and returns to the everyday grind of being a cop. Reed, in turn, encounters his neighbor, Mr. Redfield, who again exhorts Reed to spend more time with his son, telling him that "your own son comes first." Redfield, like the mayor's assistant, represents prioritizing the personal over the public good. With romantic music on the soundtrack, Nancy runs to greet her husband and is now happily pregnant (even if realistically impossible), though she still cannot afford to pay the cleaner's bill. The heroic doctor has successfully saved the public, but his own life remains far from perfect. Reed's sacrifices are necessary so that American society may continue to function properly. His heroic performance is a counterpart to the dark undercurrent of the film noir world just beyond the neighborhood of his small home. *Panic in the Streets* uses plague to affirm and reinforce America's threatened values through the heroes serving in its public sector. Their cooperation in triumphing over the disease augurs well for the newly emerging American cultural, economic and political global order. *Panic in the Streets* is both a celebration of and a fantasy about American society, in which everyone knows and accepts their place in the social contract.

An Alternative Vision: *The Seventh Seal* (1957)

The 1950s witnessed other movies about infectious diseases, such as *The Killer that Stalked New York* (1950). It tells the story of how a smallpox epidemic spreads throughout New York City and a public service doctor successfully identifies the source of the disease and contains it. Its themes resonate with *Panic in the Streets*. The most celebrated movie, however, is the Swedish director Ingmar Bergman's *The Seventh Seal* (1957). While it, too, uses plague as a backdrop, it differs from the Hollywood-produced *Panic in the Streets* in that, as a low-budget, non-mainstream Swedish art film, it focuses on questions of a personal nature and reflects alternative ideas about how individuals should live within their society. It advocates for distinctly different values at a time when foreign film production had not yet become – as routinely would become the case in decades hence – largely assimilated within the American model. The movie follows the disillusioned knight Antonius Block and his squire Jöns returning from the Crusades to find plague ravaging Sweden.[17] When Death comes for Block, the knight challenges him to a chess match and uses his remaining time on Earth to try to find meaning in his life which has otherwise seemed purposeless. As he confesses to Death, he seeks knowledge, not faith, and wants God to speak to him to acquire that knowledge. *The Seventh Seal* is, like Block's search, an allegory about Bergman's view of humankind's place on Earth. The film echoes American mainstream movies of the 1930s in its focus on the role of spiritual faith, but aims at finding personal redemption rather than depict an effort at achieving material progress, let alone furthering a mythical, American society.

The movie examines the questions raised in Reed's banter with Nancy in *Panic in the Streets* about the individual's place in a seemingly uncaring universe. If Reed sacrificed his prosperity for the greater good of society and accepted his role within seemingly uncaring institutions, *The Seventh Seal* critiques these uncaring institutions, particularly the church, for stifling individual enlightenment. The church has offered good deeds, such as the Crusades, to glorify God. The Crusades, however, caused thousands of deaths in faraway lands, created social chaos at home, led to Block's abandonment of his family, and has resulted in his inability to hear God. Underscoring his disillusionment, the knight discovers that the cleric who had encouraged him to go on Crusade has left the church. That same cleric also attempts to rape a peasant woman and later nearly kills the helpless actor Jof to please a crowd of drunken peasants. Other church followers whom the film criticizes include a procession of self-flagellants and a small group of soldiers who burn a religious heretic at the stake.[18] Returning to his castle at the film's end, Block finds his wife alone and, alluding to Christ's "last supper," eats one last meal with her and his followers. Death then enters the vast hall to claim them all, leading them the next morning in a Dance of Death.[19]

The Seventh Seal rejects Block's search for meaning just as it rejects the church's claim that it creates a cohesive society through deeds and rituals. In contrast to other films from the mid-century, Bergman's film offers the possibility of redemption by envisioning the personal development of each individual within a small community. Salvation, it posits, is possible through personal faith and revelatory artistic visions. In his travels, Block meets Jof, an artist who experiences visions, such as his early vision of the Virgin Mary and a young, playful Christ child. In the film's most celebrated scene, which underscores the centrality of personal faith, Jof and his family offer the knight secular communion in the form of a picnic of milk and wild strawberries. Block declares, "I shall remember our words and shall bear this memory between my hands as carefully as a bowl of fresh milk and this will be a sign and a great content."[20] By observing the simple, happy existence of Jof and his family, Block understands the possibility of an earthly heaven and transcendence beyond material existence. Shortly afterwards, he distracts Death, allowing Jof and his family to escape a night storm and survive. Death symbolically "passes over" them. The film offers a belief in Jof (a stand in for Bergman) who has a faith in and accepts the unknown. In contrast to the plague of *Panic in the Streets*, which serves as a social critique, the plague in *The Seventh Seal* serves as a metaphor for reminding its audience of the possibility of grace in artistic visions.[21] The film offers hope in human empathy, which, in turn, assures a better and more cohesive society for everyone.

Revealing the Rot in American Values: *Night of the Living Dead* (1968)

Bergman's vision of individual grace as the key to a better world in the face of disease remains an outlier to this day. There were other outliers, such as *The Last Man on Earth* (1964), an American movie adaptation of Richard

Matheson's novel *I Am Legend* (1954). A global plague has turned humans into vampires, except for a small group. The members of that group hold the infection at bay by repeatedly injecting themselves with a vaccine but also eventually kill the only surviving human, extinguishing any hope for a better future. More representative of the films of this period was George Romero's *Night of the Living Dead* (1968). Inspired by Matheson's novel and using disease in the paradigmatic way – as a critique of society – *Night of the Living Dead* is far more critical of the cultural cohesion for which *Panic in the Streets* had advocated but continues to maintain a belief that America can cure itself. Independently directed by then novice filmmaker George Romero, the film popularized the myth of the undead, "ghouls" (as Romero first called them) or "zombies" (as they became popularly known). As Romero acknowledged, the movie "was never really about them. They were just the problem driving the characters – it could have been anything, like a Hitchcock MacGuffin."[22] If earlier zombie films featured a local story that took place in the Caribbean and presented zombies as individually controlled creatures, *Night of the Living Dead* featured zombies as a faceless horde of uncontrollable creatures attempting to take over the American East Coast in a widespread epidemic, even if the film's story takes place almost entirely in an isolated rural house. Extraordinarily successful as a low budget, black and white horror movie, *Night of the Living Dead* enabled (as well as compelled) Romero to develop a career in zombie movies in which he would continue to explore cultural criticism.[23]

Night of the Living Dead uses three key lenses – family, gender and race – to critique the social contract that *Panic in the Streets* had supported. In *Night of the Living Dead*, these three pillars must be modified to create an improved, more inclusive society that offers a place and potential success for everyone. It does not, however, advocate tearing down the social fabric itself.[24] Nor does the movie focus explicitly on capitalism or even mention it. The film follows a small group of strangers from different backgrounds in an isolated Pennsylvania farmhouse to keep out the growing numbers of undead during a single night. The disease in *Night of the Living Dead* is never identified, and a TV broadcaster simply announces that the source of the reawakened dead, who eat the flesh of the living, is likely a space satellite or a Venus space probe that became contaminated from radiation and blew up in the Earth's atmosphere. Its outer space origin evokes the Cold War and alludes to the 1960s space race between the United States and the Soviet Union.[25] While all the main characters die, American society seemingly contains the disease at the film's end and restores the pre-epidemic "normality," though that "normality" attests to America's failure to include those who differ.

As many have observed, the film is unrelenting in its criticism of the nuclear family, emphasizing the repression that underlies many horror movies about family.[26] Drawing inspiration from *Psycho* (1960), in which Norman Bates' mother turns him into a psychotic killer, *Night of the Living Dead* depicts family as a source of horror.[27] In the famous opening scene, a brother and sister, Johnny and Barbra (Judith O'Dea), visit their father's gravesite. Johnny contemplates reburying their father closer to their home for convenience, complaining that "mother wants to remember so we trot two hundred miles into the country and she stays at home." While at the cemetery, an undead man attacks the siblings and kills Johnny. As a result, Barbra becomes emotionally unhinged. When she later recovers from her catatonic state and attempts to rescue another farmhouse survivor, her brother Johnny, now undead, pulls her into the undead crowd, who devour her.[28] Two young lovers, Tom (Keith Wayne) and Judy (Judith Ridley), are also undone by their attachment to one another. Tom heroically ventures outside to fill a car with gasoline, but Judy refuses to let him go out alone. When her jacket is inadvertently caught in the car door, the car catches fire, they burn together, and the dead eat their charred remains. The familial attachment of Harry (Karl Hardman) and Helen Cooper (Marilyn Eastman), a middle-aged married couple, likewise leads to their demise. They tend in the fruit cellar to their ill daughter Karen, who has been bitten. When she is reanimated as one of the undead, she devours her father and then kills her mother. Family, the cornerstone of American life, fails in its most basic function – to protect its members – implying how family will in turn lead to the undoing of broader society.

The film is equally critical of mid-twentieth century gender roles, which define characters and limit their ability to protect the nascent community in

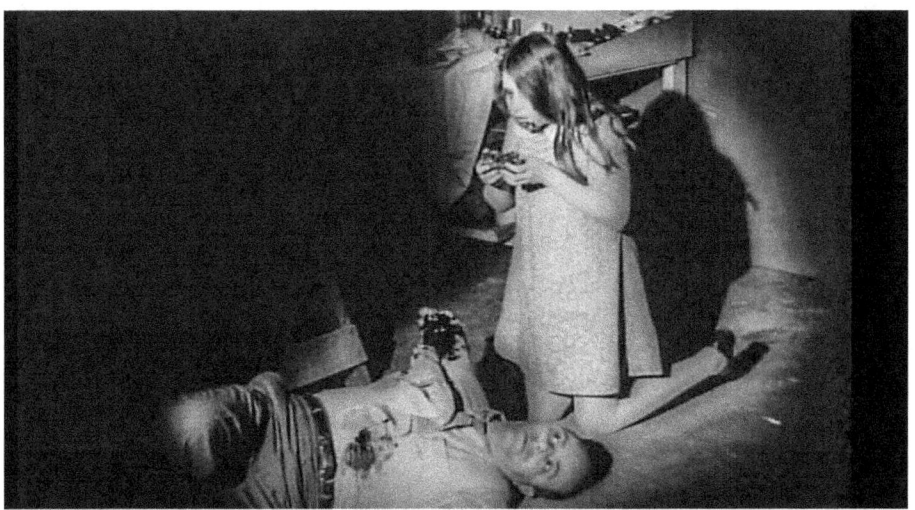

Figure 1.3 *Night of the Living Dead* (1968): Family devours its own.

the farmhouse. Barbra is depicted as the clichéd, hysterical woman, cowering in the corner of the farmhouse obsessively asking, "What's happening?" and later becomes silent. Judy is the clichéd, subservient woman, accommodating Tom, for example, when he condescendingly asks, "Where's that big smile for me?" when the situation begins to worsen. And Helen is the clichéd housewife. Her introduction to Barbra – "I'm Helen Cooper, Harry's wife" – reveals that her personal identity is wholly defined by her marital status. The men, such as Ben (Duane Jones) and Harry, in turn, exhibit stereotypical male territoriality. After arguing over who is in charge, Ben aggressively asserts, "Get the hell down in the cellar. You can be the boss down there, but I'm boss up here." By insisting that only the basement offers them safety, Harry similarly warns Ben and the others that he will lock them out once he goes downstairs. Only Helen observes, "That's important, isn't it?" To which Harry responds only with confusion as Helen clarifies, "To be right, everybody else to be wrong." Too wrapped up in this contest of male egos, Harry cannot even understand her comment, asking, "What do you mean by that?" Notwithstanding his ostensible advocacy of cooperation among them, Ben, too, cannot overcome his masculinity and insists that they barricade and defend themselves upstairs. Normative gender roles have reduced the capacity of this microcosm of society to resist the zombies, leading to their destruction.

While Ben, the only character in the makeshift farmhouse community who does not have a family, succeeds in surviving the undead onslaught, his heroic actions are undone by the film's third social critique: racism. He finds practical solutions to stop the undead, using tools to board up windows and doors, discovering a rifle with ammunition, improvising Molotov cocktails and locating a radio and later a TV to learn how to survive. Yet, because he is a black man in a rural area, the local white militia members identify him as one of the undead, shooting him in the head "by mistake" in an early morning rag-tag militia campaign to kill the undead. Evoking the contemporary American war in Vietnam (with helicopters overhead), the operation to kill the undead more closely resembles a white male hunting expedition than a state-organized effort to deal with a major threat. During the closing scenes, a sheriff and his deputies pursue the undead with dogs on leashes and use meat hooks to dispose of the bodies, including that of Ben, whose body is added to the burning pyre.[29] These scenes evoke the images of lynchings and other racist attacks on black Americans during the Civil Rights movement. Elements of America might come together to pacify the countryside, but they do so at the expense of the heroic black man who would otherwise have survived. Society is worse off by his death. The dominance of white men as the embodiment of the state represents an underlying problem with American society that upholds the shared values of only certain people, leading to the deaths of others.

In addition to these critiques of family, gender and race, the film also critiques the broader failure of the national government to address the crisis and meet its obligations. Reflecting the disillusionment with government during the 1960s war in Vietnam, the US military in *Night of the Living Dead* tries to cover up the source of the apparent origin of the disease and threatens civilian scientists for speculating to reporters (one of whom is played by Romero) about its possible origin. The White House conference on the crisis is more concerned with assigning blame than finding a solution. The movie's criticism reflects the social and political turmoil in the United States during the late 1960s, including the assassinations of Martin Luther King and Robert Kennedy, the continued, horrific war in Vietnam, race riots in major US cities and a police riot at the Democratic National Convention in Chicago. The movie criticizes the national government's failure to recognize, let alone cure, the disease infecting America through its exclusion of America's disparate racial and gender groups. The state fails not only its individual citizens but also fails to perform its basic public health mission.

Night of the Living Dead exposes, through its disease narrative about the undead, the seemingly intractable problems of American society. The film depicts the suffocation of family, the stereotyping of gender and the structural oppression of racism. If no immediate cure is offered, it maintains a sense of the urgent changes necessary to improve the social contract in the context of rotting social structures. Even this darkest of visions, however, allows for some optimism about America's future. If 1950s movies, including *Panic in the Streets*, critiqued the inadequacies of the American Dream, they affirmed American middle-class norms. *Night of the Living Dead* reflects a still darker image with its fears for a future in which American society literally eats itself alive. But it, too, remains committed to the ideals of an American vision in which change remains possible. The empty farmhouse remains standing at the film's end, offering refuge to its next family.

A CRITIQUE OF VALUES AND A GLOBAL PANDEMIC:
SHIVERS (1975) AND *VIRUS* (1980)

The years following *Night of the Living Dead* witnessed the release of additional movies about disease outbreaks. These movies used disease to critique society but differed in their perception of what its flaws were. Moreover, society could not always contain the pathogen. For example, *The Omega Man* (1971), the second remake of Matheson's novel *I Am Legend*, anticipates later apocalyptic narratives, focusing on a biological war between the Soviet Union and China that has caused a global pandemic and has killed nearly everyone. The exceptions are the few hundred nocturnal mutants who seek to destroy any remaining technology. In contrast to the earlier remake, *The Last Man on Earth*, it has a somewhat happier ending in which the protagonist, a scientist and the sole immunized human, sacrifices himself to produce a serum for a vaccine from his own blood. Yet, only a handful of youthful mutants are willing to take the serum, while the rest flee into the wilderness. Romero's *The Crazies* (1973) blames the American military for the creation of a bioweapon that renders irrational its victims and is more pessimistic about the possibility of successfully containing the disease. When a scientist finds a possible cure, the military mistakenly quarantines him, and an infected mob later crushes him underfoot.

The Andromeda Strain (1971) also blames the American military, in this case for an extraterrestrial microbe organism that the military has sought to weaponize. The film, however, is more optimistic. At first glance, it appears to endorse the scientific explanations and highly advanced technology focused on the threat posed by this unknown microbe. Nonetheless, the movie demonstrates that science and technology alone fail. While Dr. Jeremy Stone serves as team leader of the experts, Dr. Mark Hall, an ordinary but iconoclastic surgeon, is the film's hero. While reprimanded by the authorities for flirting with a female recorded voice, he best fulfills the "odd man hypothesis" as an unmarried and dispassionate man who ranks highest on the "index of effectiveness." Dr. Hall discovers the vulnerability of the microbe and disarms the self-destruct nuclear device that might have destroyed the facility as well as spread the Andromeda Strain. Where Dr. Stone wants to destroy the small, rural town of Piedmont, the US president insists on waiting 48 hours, which avoids the globalization of the microbe. Dr. Ruth Leavitt, the only woman on the team, pointedly notes that science is not pure, critiques the military for its attempt to weaponize the microbe, and recognizes why the young are dropping out of society. Significantly, an old man and a baby, the only survivors of Piedmont, all "good, decent, normal folks," provide Dr. Hall with the solution for destroying the microbe. While criticizing science, the military and irrational prejudice and fear, *The Andromeda Strain* is optimistic about America's future by placing its faith in a broad spectrum of Americans, such as those of the town of Piedmont, Drs. Hall and Leavitt and the President.

David Cronenberg's *Shivers* (1975) offered a more reactionary, pessimistic perspective about society.[30] Produced in Canada, it critiques institutions and the contemporary social contract in response to Romero's *Night of the Living Dead* released only several years earlier. The film unfolds in an idyllic, middle class apartment complex just outside of Montreal and tells how a mad scientist, Dr. Emil Hobbes, whose name alludes to Thomas Hobbes, develops a parasite that combines elements of a venereal disease and an aphrodisiac, turning the world into "one beautiful, mindless orgy."[31] As a result of Dr. Hobbes' affair with a young woman, to whom he introduces the parasite and who, in turn, has affairs with other men, the parasite quickly spreads throughout the complex and infects all of its residents, including the hero Dr. Roger St. Luc.

Shivers depicts the middle class as already corrupt and valueless, offers no cure for the virus that "came from within" and critiques out-of-control, sexual norms and the ongoing sexual revolution.[32] Viewing humans as inherently evil, that is, Hobbesian, it advocates for the return to pre-1960s values, similar to *Panic in the Streets*, but this time in reaction to a 1960s world in which liberal values had run amok.[33] Only conservative, shared values, represented by heteronormative families, can ensure a cohesive society.

Shivers' opening underscores the corruption of human values by repeatedly cross-cutting between seemingly ordinary residents, showing how the parasite has already begun to spread. While occasionally humorous, such as when one resident vomits a penis-shaped slug several stories down onto the umbrella of an elderly woman walking with her friend, the film's horror resides in how easily the parasite becomes part of daily life. The viral slug attacks a resident doing her laundry in the basement, an infected mother and daughter spread it by attacking a security guard, and an infected father tries to spread it by offering the sexual services of his daughter. While Dr. St. Luc is a rational scientist who tries to understand the outbreak, Nurse Forsythe, who works in his office, displays evidence of sexual corruption even before her infection. As Dr. St. Luc learns of Dr. Hobbes' creation of an aphrodisiac parasite, she strips naked for St Luc in their office and then seductively invites him to her apartment for dinner. The contemporary disease has already undermined societal values, the film posits, and the parasite merely accelerates the process.

Shivers inverts numerous clichéd scenes from a variety of genres to highlight its reactionary social critique. For example, Dr. St. Luc and Nurse Forsythe evoke the protagonists from *Invasion of the Body Snatchers* (1956). Where, however, the male protagonist of *Invasion of the Body Snatchers* escapes, St. Luc instead succumbs to the mass of infected residents. The movie's ending likewise reverses the Biblical myth of rebirth. Evoking Noah's Ark and its repopulation of a new world, the infected exit the basement garage of the apartment complex in cars, two by two, in order to spread the disease across the country.[34] Where the TV broadcaster in *Night of the Living Dead* identified shelters to hide in, the radio announcer in *Shivers* misleads the public, repeating the Montreal police's characterization of reports about the apartment complex as "irresponsible and hysterical." The parasite disease symbolizes the contemporary corruption of humanity with its savage nature. *Shivers* expresses disgust with the sexual revolution of the 1960s counterculture that has accelerated the spread of this disease to the middle class. It rejects the progressive, social narrative of *Night of the Living Dead*, and wants society to return to conservative values as a way to ensure societal cohesion in the future.[35]

If *Shivers* looked backward in reaction to cultural changes, the Japanese film *Virus'* release (1980) coincided with contemporary fears about environmental destruction and with Hollywood's production of disaster movies, a popular, big-budget genre that depicted catastrophic events with happy endings. *Virus* follows this disaster movie format – an unexpected disaster leads to a worldwide pandemic and an attempt for survival against the odds – but has a pessimistic ending.[36] Directed by Kinji Fukasaku, *Virus*' depiction of a global pandemic was an outlier in its time, depicting the uncontained spread of a disease as a critique of both Cold War superpowers. It was an enormously budgeted Japanese movie that included internationally well-known actors.[37] Resources from countries allied with the United States, such as Canada and Chile, were used in making the film, which expresses allies' concerns about the implications of American power and supports international cooperation to create a better, global society.[38]

The film is divided into three acts: the failure of the contemporary world system, the creation of a new society after the apocalypse and a failed attempt by this new society to prevent its own annihilation. The first act focuses on the pandemic of the "Italian Flu," which is a creation of the American military and is accidentally released into the atmosphere. Within months, the virus kills over 99.9% of the world's population. After creating the virus, the US military not only jails an American professor who threatens to reveal this biological weapon, but also lies to the US president, claiming that the Soviet Union created the virus. Once the president finds out the truth, he, too, insists that American scientists maintain a "lid of complete secrecy" over the virus' origin.[39] An East German scientist sums up the movie's view of American power – "Any student of history can tell you that a rational mind is not always a prerequisite for a position of power." In light of diplomatic and military fiascoes, such as the Vietnam War, the film argues, America has used its global power incorrectly and must change its ways.

The second act focuses on the survivors in international research bases in Antarctica, since the virus is dormant in cold temperatures. The movie advocates for global cooperation as an antidote to the virus and, more broadly, a potential nuclear war that would destroy the real world. The American president during his last broadcast beseeches all the survivors in Antarctica with the obvious message of the movie: "This time, try to work it out together, please." The 11 nations with bases in Antarctica – 855 men and 8 women – unexpectedly succeed in creating a new, cooperative government which they name the Federal Council of Antarctica. Although the representatives to the Council occasionally squabble, the Council represents a collaborative effort to ensure a scientifically rational society. At the behest of one of the surviving women, it adopts, for example, a rotation system that designates the scheduled mating of men and women, ignoring any instinctive desires or personal feelings to assure a future for humankind. In response to a critique of this system, one of the men simply states, "Unless we can [cooperate], there is no future." A child is soon born and heralded as "the dawn of a new day," and at a Christmas party a year later all the women are holding babies. A French scientist even develops a vaccine for the disease.

Despite this optimism, the movie ends grimly. In the final act, a team of two (with the Japanese Dr. Yoshizumi as the hero) travels to Washington, D.C., in an effort to disarm a doomsday American nuclear system that will be triggered by an earthquake off Washington (and will, in turn, set off a similar Soviet, automated system), destroying Antarctica.[40] The duo arrives moments too late in Washington, and nuclear destruction follows, evoking both the atomic bombs the United States dropped on Japan at the end of World War II and the satiric ending of *Dr. Strangelove* (1964) with its "doomsday weapon." The ensuing, automated nuclear weapon attacks destroy Antarctica. While a skeletal male crew and all 8 women (and their children) reach safety in an ice breaker, four years later the few survivors are holed up in a small hut in southern Chile. Many, including children, have died and are buried in a nearby cemetery. While Yoshizumi eventually rejoins these survivors after walking south across the desolate Americas, the "happy ending" in which the romantic couple reunites is bleak. As he collapses into his Norwegian lover Marit's arms, Yoshizumi repeats his colleague's earlier last words – "Life is wonderful," an allusion to the cynically titled *It's a Wonderful Life* (1946). While maintaining faith in international cooperation, *Virus* is an unapologetic warning about how easily the global political order, human relationships and the rational mind may be defeated by irrationality and an obsessive desire for power, leading to humanity's demise. *Virus* anticipates the movies that decades later will feature pandemics that result in the annihilation of the species but attributes it to the Cold War-era political order rather than capitalism.

Conclusion

With the exception of a number of B-movies, often humorous body horrors, such as *Bloodsuckers from Outer Space* (1984) and *Night of the Creeps* (1986), disease movies largely disappeared from the screens for about a decade, while conservative changes came to dominate political thinking in the United States. *Virus'* release coincided with the election of Ronald Reagan as president of the United States and his advocacy of a free market economy. Individual freedom would increasingly trump social equality, and this shift in cultural ideology would soon spread around the globe. Alongside this change would be the fracturing of American society into different and increasingly siloed groups on the left and the right.[41] This process would lead to the disappearance of common values, which had formerly been at the center of disease movies critiques.

Some disease movies of the decade did react against or were explicit critiques of the ideological shift in culture. Romero's *Day of the Dead* (1985) humorously critiques the military-industrial complex and offers its dissenting characters, who are a mix of races, genders and nationalities, a paradisiacal island in which to start over. Humans must create a new type of society in the context of the failure of American capitalism to promote human-focused values. Critiques of consumer capitalism took center stage in other disease movies as a reflection of the growing dominance of corporations in daily life. Larry Cohen's *The Stuff* (1985) depicts an addictive white, yogurt-like material that bubbles out of the ground and then takes over the human brain, mutating people into zombie-like creatures. Companies market and distribute this product nation-wide for profit. Likewise, John Carpenter directed a curious, non-disease take on the *Invasion of the Body Snatchers*, *They Live* (1988). Wearing a special pair of sunglasses, a drifter named Nada discovers that wealthy people, the media and advertisers are aliens who exercise control over the population through subliminal messages on billboards or broadcast over a special frequency, urging the population to obey, sleep, buy, consume, don't think and conform.[42] American capitalism had become recognizable as a problem, and these films insist upon identifying and critiquing it, lest it become more pervasive in American, and increasingly global, culture.

Aside from these exceptions, science fiction movies filled the gap disease movies left open during the 1980s and early 1990s. Movies such as *Blade Runner* (1982), *Terminator* (1984) and *Total Recall* (1990) questioned humanity's future while avoiding disease themes. Technological developments, such as the introduction of personal computers and digital communications, increased this particular genre's popularity. These movies tended to substitute a critical examination of science and reason for the horror of disease movies. They underscored the growing distrust of science to further human progress and advance the evolution of the human species. A few movies, such as the *Alien* franchise – *Alien* (1979), *Aliens* (1985) and *Alien 3* (1992) – creatively combined horror and science fiction, reflecting the view that both mind and body were under attack in this new ideological environment, and criticized the corporate model for its dehumanization of its workers. But these movies were few and far between. With their focus on the heroic individual, movies like *Star Wars* with its space opera optimism, *Superman* with its American "can do" attitude and *Star Trek* with its depiction of the conquest of space, proliferated.[43] This shift is best exemplified when Reagan explicitly referred to *Back to the Future* (1984) in his 1986 State of the Union, offering a succinct slogan for this new ideology: "Where we're going, we don't need roads."[44] Global neoliberalism was ascendant.[45]

Early disease movies, ranging from vampire and zombie movies to mainstream movies, such as *Jezebel*, *Panic in the Streets* and *Virus*, to low budget movies, such as *The Killer that Stalked New York*, *Night of the Living Dead* and *Shivers*, had offered shared values and proposed that cure and containment remained possible (if not always depicting a happy ending). As an alternative to American stories and values, *The Seventh Seal* depicted a deadly pandemic but envisioned the possibility of personal redemption against a backdrop of its devastation. The disease movies that would re-emerge after the 1980s would initially retain the optimism of shared values, despite the seeming incoherence of that message in an increasingly fractured and individualistic country, but by the 2000s would turn far darker than their science fiction predecessors. These later disease movies would become stories about pandemics that would devastate the human species with its lack of moral purpose or reason for survival. Social despair at the growing fragmentation of cultural values would eventually overwhelm the search to find a cure and that darker despair would soon eclipse the social critique of early disease movies.

Notes

1. For cultural changes related to germ theory, see Tomes, *The Gospel of Germs: Men, Women, and the Microbe in American Life*. For the link between visual media, specifically photography, and disease, Christos Lynteris, *Visual Plague: The Emergence of Epidemic Photography* (Cambridge: MIT Press, 2022).
2. Girard put it succinctly: "The medical plague has become a metaphor for the social plague." René Girard, "The Plague in Literature and Myth," 835; for further discussion, see Ostherr, *Cinematic Prophylaxis*.
3. For discussion of this period at the time: Girard, "The Plague in Literature and Myth;" Sontag, *Illness as Metaphor*; and Steel, "Plague Writing: From Boccaccio to Camus."
4. For a representative example of the period's scientific consensus: L. Fabian Hirst, *The Conquest of Plague* (Oxford: Clarendon Press, 1953); for a discussion, see Wald, *Contagious*, 158–61.
5. One of the etymologies proposed for the name is a combination of the Greek *nosos* (disease) and *phoros* (bearing).
6. Tyler Malone, "The Zombies of Karl Marx: Horror in Capitalism's Wake," *Literary Hub*, October 31, 2018, https://lithub.com/the-zombies-of-karl-marx-horror-in-capitalisms-wake/.
7. For an overview of zombies, see Kyle W. Bishop, *How Zombies Conquered Popular Culture*; and the essays in Sarah Juliet Lauro, ed. *Zombie Theory: A Reader* (Minneapolis: University of Minnesota Press, 2017). For this early period in more detail, see Roger Luckhurst, *Zombies: A Cultural History* (London: Reaktion Books, 2015), 75–84.
8. Han and Curtis, *Infectious Inequalities*, 27–43.
9. Bette Davis played Julie Marsden, for which Davis won the Academy Award for Best Actress. Jeanine Basinger has discussed how the movie is a "woman's picture." "Commentary by Jeanine Basinger," *Jezebel* directed by William Wyler (1938; Burbank: Warner Home Video, 2000), DVD. *Jezebel* is also a variation on the story of the movie *Gone with The Wind*, which was released one year later.
10. Kazan had already directed the controversial, if celebrated, *Gentlemen's Agreement* (1947), a story about anti-Semitism, and would later direct several social critique movies, such as *A Streetcar Named Desire* (1951), *Viva Zapata!* (1952), *On the Waterfront* (1954), *East of Eden* (1955) and *A Face in the Crowd* (1957). On his filmmaking, see Elia Kazan, *Elia Kazan: A Life* (New York: Knopf, 1988).

11. For literature on "the other" and alterity, see Bernhard Leistle, ed. *Anthropology and Alterity: Responding to the Other* (New York: Routledge, Taylor & Francis Group, 2017). Only two years after the film's release, Kazan gave testimony before the House Committee on Un-American Activities (HUAC), identifying individuals in Hollywood who had been members of the Communist Party. At times *Panic in the Streets* foreshadows Kazan's HUAC testimony, such as when merchant marine seamen refuse to identify an illegal immigrant. It is hard not to equate the Eastern European source of the disease with Kazan's own anti-Communism. See Brian Neve, *Elia Kazan: The Cinema of an American Outsider* (London: Bloomsbury Academic, 2009), 1–32. For a retrospective, Alexandra Minna Stern and Howard Markel, "The Public Health Service and Film Noir: A Look Back at Elia Kazan's Panic in the Streets (1950)," *Public Health Reports* 118, no. 3 (2003): 178–83. On HUAC, see Brian Neve, "Elia Kazan's First Testimony to the House Committee on Un-American Activities, Executive Session, 14 January 1952," *Historical Journal of Film, Radio and Television* 25, no. 2 (2005): 251–72.
12. The story is not epidemiologically factual, since pneumonic plague does not require rats to spread, although Reed and others attempt to find rats. For types of plague: CDC, "Symptoms | Plague | CDC," Centers for Disease Control and Prevention, https://www.cdc.gov/plague/symptoms/index.html; these differences were known, see Robert Pollitzer, *Plague* (Geneva: World Health Organization, 1954). There was plague in New Orleans at the time, see Vernon B. Link, *A History of Plague in the United States of America* (Washington, DC: US Government Printing Office, 1955), 43–56.
13. Other examples of this style of film include *Side Street* (1950) and *99 River Street* (1953). On film noir, see Paul Schrader, "Notes on Film Noir," *Film Comment* 8, no. 1 (1972): 8–13. For its importance, see Adrian Danks, "Panic in the Streets," *Senses of Cinema* 2, January 2000, http://sensesofcinema.com/2000/feature-articles/panic/.
14. As they contain the disease, a rat "guard" symbolically prevents Blackie from boarding an outgoing vessel, connecting Blackie to the stereotypical carrier of the plague.
15. Rebecca Kaplan, "A Silent, Savage Menace: Reassessing 'Panic in the Streets,'" *Science History Institute – Distillations: Using Stories from Science's Past to Understand Our World,* June 30, 2020, https://www.sciencehistory.org/distillations/a-silent-savage-menace-reassessing-panic-in-the-streets.
16. Blackie is seen coming down a staircase and is hunched over like a "big ape" only moments after Angie has described him in those terms.
17. While Bergman, like Kazan, began his career in the theater, Bergman had already become internationally known for intimate dramas like *Sawdust and Tinsel* (1953) and *Smiles of a Summer Night* (1955). He would later direct movies known for their focus on personal, not political, concerns, such as identity (*Persona*, 1966), the difficulties of marriage (*Scenes from a Marriage*, 1973) and Bergman's childhood (*Fanny and Alexander*, 1983). On Bergman, see Peter Cowie, *Ingmar Bergman: A Critical Biography* (New York: Limelight Editions, 1992). For a brief discussion of the film see Girard, "The Plague in Literature and Myth," 847.
18. For a survey of the Black Death: Ole Jørgen Benedictow, *The Black Death, 1346–1353: The Complete History* (Rochester: Boydell Press, 2004); but for a different

take on its impact, see Samuel K. Cohn, "The Black Death: End of a Paradigm," *American Historical Review* 107, no. 3 (2002): 703–38.

19. On the Dance of Death, see Seeta Chaganti, *Strange Footing: Poetic Form and Dance in the Late Middle Ages* (Chicago: University of Chicago Press, 2018), 99–143.

20. Translation from *The Seventh Seal*, directed by Ingmar Bergman (1957: New York, The Criterion Collection, 1998), DVD. Bergman offers a similar scene of momentary happiness at the end of *Cries and Whispers* (1972) and described in a 2001 interview how he developed that entire movie from his envisioning one image of a room in red. "Introduction by Ingmar Bergman," *Cries and Whispers*, directed by Ingmar Bergman (1972; Stockholm, Sweden, The Criterion Collection, 2015), DVD.

21. It is clearly set in Sontag's metaphor world. See Sontag, *Illness as Metaphor*.

22. Steve Biodrowski, "Interview: George Romero Documents the Dead," *Cinefantastique*, February 15, 2008, https://web.archive.org/web/20160404150058/http://cinefantastiqueonline.com/2008/02/interview-george-romero-documents-the-dead-part-1/. A MacGuffin as used by director Alfred Hitchcock is a "pretext" or "gimmick" that is integral to the plot, but in fact, "of no importance whatever." Francois Truffaut, with the collaboration of Helen G. Scott, *Hitchcock* (New York: Simon & Schuster, 1967), 98.

23. For discussions of Romero and his career, see Paul R. Gagne, *The Zombies That Ate Pittsburgh: The Films of George A. Romero* (New York: Dodd, Mead, 1987); Tony Williams, *The Cinema of George A. Romero: Knight of the Living Dead*, 2nd edition (London: Wallflower Press, 2015). For a discussion of his zombie movies, see Robert Alpert, "George Romero's Zombie Movies: The Fragmentation of America."

24. This is partially the view of: R. H. W. Dillard, "Night of the Living Dead: It's Not Just Like a Wind That's Passing Through," in *American Horrors: Essays on the Modern American Horror Film*, ed. Gregory Albert Waller (Urbana, IL: University of Illinois Press, 1987), 14–29.

25. For the movie as focused on environmental concerns, see Carter Soles, "'And No Birds Sing': Discourses of Environmental Apocalypse in *The Birds* and *Night of the Living Dead*," *ISLE: Interdisciplinary Studies in Literature and Environment* 21, no. 3 (2014): 526–37. Romero was ambivalent about the Cold War connections saying, "The radiation scenario that people feel is an explanation in *Night of the Living Dead* was actually one out of three that were advanced in the original cut of the film, but the other ones got cut out and people have adopted that radiation thing as the reason why the dead are coming back. I really didn't mean that to be." Tony Williams, *George A. Romero: Interviews* (Jackson: University Press of Mississippi, 2011), 48.

26. See Robin Wood, *Robin Wood on the Horror Film: Collected Essays and Reviews*, ed. Barry Keith Grant (Detroit: Wayne State University Press, 2018), 57–62; and Robin Wood, *Hollywood from Vietnam to Reagan . . . and Beyond*, expanded and revised edition (New York: Columbia University Press, 2003), 85–119. For a discussion of horror movies and the role of the repressed, see also pp. 63–84.

27. On the connection between the movies, see Kim Paffenroth, *Gospel of the Living Dead: George Romero's Visions of Hell on Earth* (Waco: Baylor University Press,

2006), 36; and for Romero's reflections, see Williams, *George A. Romero*, 97. Also, Alpert, "George Romero's Night of the Living Dead and Diary of the Dead."

28. On Romero and gender, see Barry Keith Grant, "Taking Back the Night of the Living Dead: George Romero, Feminism, and the Horror Film," in *The Dread of Difference: Gender and the Horror Film*, 2nd edition, ed. Barry Keith Grant (Austin: University of Texas Press, 2015), 228–40.

29. Romero claimed that the race of actor Duane Jones, who played Ben, was irrelevant to his casting, "When John Russo and I collaborated on the final screenplay, the character was white. And we consciously, deliberately didn't change the script when Duane agreed to play the role. He was simply the best actor from among our friends. And then, we finished the film, we were actually driving it to New York to see if anyone would want to distribute it, and that night, on the car radio, we heard that King had been assassinated. And all of a sudden, the film took on the feel of a racial statement. That was not intended at all. The same things happened to that character when he was white. The posse shot him, because they thought he was a zombie." Tim Robey, "George A. Romero: Why I Don't like The Walking Dead," *Telegraph*, November 8, 2013, https://www.telegraph.co.uk//culture/film/10436738/George-A-Romero-Why-I-dont-like-The-Walking-Dead.html. Nevertheless, the scene in which the unexpected glare of headlights dramatizes the sudden appearance of a black man in the context of a lone, hysterical white woman is stark, and while Romero claimed Martin Luther King Jr.'s murder in April 1968 did not affect the film, viewers undoubtedly made the connection, since the film was released in October 1968.

30. Cronenberg would become famous for movies that focused on "body horror." Later movies included *Rabid* (1977), *The Brood* (1979), *Scanners* (1981), *Videodrome* (1983), *The Fly* (1986) and *eXistenZ* (1999). See Luke Aspell, *Shivers* (Leighton Buzzard, UK: Auteur, 2019); and for a discussion of the middle-class critique, see Thomas Caldwell, "Shivers," *Senses of Cinema* 19 (2002), http://sensesofcinema.com/2002/cteq/shivers/; and see the essays in Piers Handling, ed. *The Shape of Rage: The Films of David Cronenberg* (Toronto: New York Zoetrope, 1983); and William Beard, *The Artist as Monster: The Cinema of David Cronenberg* (Buffalo: University of Toronto Press, 2001). For a different view, see Robin Wood, "Cronenberg: A Dissenting View," in *The Shape of Rage: The Films of David Cronenberg*, ed. Piers Handling (Toronto: New York Zoetrope, 1983), 115–35. His movies, though, showcase a change in their focus over time, see Lianne McLarty, "'Beyond the Veil of Flesh': Cronenberg and the Disembodiment of Horror," in *The Dread of Difference: Gender and the Horror Film*, ed. Barry Keith Grant (Austin: University of Texas Press, 1996), 259–80.

31. This reflects Hobbes's famous idea that life in the state of nature was nasty, brutish and short, and humans, if unchecked, would do anything they wanted (such as Dr. Hobbes's experiments). For his key works, Thomas Hobbes, *Three-Text Edition of Thomas Hobbes's Political Theory: The Elements of Law, De Cive, and Leviathan*, ed. Deborah Baumgold (Cambridge: Cambridge University Press, 2017).

32. "They Came From Within" was the film's Canadian subtitle and the title of the film as initially distributed in the US. See Holly Luhning, "Cronenberg's: Contagion and Community," in *Body Horror and Shapeshifting*, eds. Jessica Folio and Holly Luhning (Leiden: Brill, 2014), 33–40.

33. For further discussion: Robin Wood, "An Introduction to the American Horror Film," in *American Nightmare: Essays on the Horror Film*, ed. Andrew Britton (Toronto: Festival of Festivals, 1979), 7–28; but for a different reading of gender, David Sanjek, "Dr. Hobbes's Parasites: Victims, Victimization, and Gender in David Cronenberg's 'Shivers,'" *Cinema Journal* 36, no. 1 (1996): 55–74; and Allan MacInnis, "Sex, Science, and the 'Female Monstrous': Wood Contra Cronenberg, Revisited," *CineAction* 88 (2012): 34–43.
34. Genesis 8:19.
35. Cronenberg's next film, *Rabid* (1977), continued his endorsement of those values.
36. Mainstream movies in the genre included *Airport* (1970), *The Poseidon Adventure* (1972), *The Towering Inferno* (1974), *Earthquake* (1974), *The Swarm* (1978) and *Meteor* (1979). For the genre: Stephen Keane, *Disaster Movies: The Cinema of Catastrophe*, 2nd edition (New York: Wallflower Press, 2006); and Nik Havert, *The Golden Age of Disaster Cinema: A Guide to the Films, 1950–1979* (Jefferson: McFarland & Company, 2019). Two versions of *Virus* were released, but the long version of 155 minutes represents the director's preferred version, which was released at the 1980 Cannes Film Festival as a "work in progress." The film was released in a shortened American video version (108 minutes). An even shorter version (93 minutes) was shown on television in the US. On this history, see Stuart Galbraith IV, *The Toho Studios Story: A History and Complete Filmography* (Lanham: Scarecrow Press, 2008), 323; and for a discussion of Fukasaku's films Olivier Hadouchi, *Kinji Fukasaku: un cinéaste critique dans le chaos du XXème siècle* (Paris: Harmattan, 2009). The movie is not discussed frequently, but see Tony Williams, "Doomsday, Past, Present and Future: Kinji Fukasaku's Virus," *Asian Cinema* 19 (2008): 215–31.
37. These include: Chuck Connors, Glenn Ford, Olivia Hussey, George Kennedy, Edward James Olmos and Robert Vaughn. Fukasaku had previously co-directed the ensemble, large-budgeted *Tora! Tora! Tora!* (1970) about the Japanese attack on Pearl Harbor. *Virus* was the most expensive ($16 million) film made in Japan at the time.
38. Japan preferred to maintain economic relations with the Soviet Union while receiving American military support. Michael Schaller, "Japan and the Cold War, 1960–1991," in *The Cambridge History of the Cold War: Volume 3: Endings*, eds. Melvyn P. Leffler and Odd Arne Westad (Cambridge: Cambridge University Press, 2010), 156–80.
39. The Soviet Union appears briefly, but only as a counterbalance to American power, China is absent, and East Germany, the only Soviet bloc country depicted, is represented by a well-intentioned scientist. He seeks to find an antidote for the virus, but instead triggers the outbreak as a result of shady dealings with disguised Americans and the East German military.
40. *Virus*'s pessimism is apparent in its many suicides. Yoshizumi's pregnant fiancée, a nurse overwhelmed by the virus in a Tokyo hospital, chooses to take her own life, after giving sleeping pills to the son of her friend. Likewise, one of Yoshizumi's colleagues in Antarctica, a five-year-old boy who is alone but cannot hear Yoshizumi and his colleagues over the radio, and the entire staff of the Norwegian station all choose to take their own lives.

41. Fredric Jameson in 1984 articulated the basis for neoliberalism as the separation of reality (the signified) from simulation (the signifier) and the increased substitution and acceptance of the latter in place of the former. Fredric Jameson, *Postmodernism, or, The Cultural Logic of Late Capitalism* (Durham: Duke University Press, 1991). For an overview, see Daniel T. Rodgers, *Age of Fracture* (Cambridge: Belknap Press, 2012).
42. For this neoliberal process of changes, see Arjun Appadurai, "Disjuncture and Difference in the Global Cultural Economy," *Theory, Culture & Society* 7, no. 2–3, (1990): 295–310; and David Harvey, *A Brief History of Neoliberalism* (New York: Oxford University Press, 2005); for a broader view, see Anthony Giddens, *The Consequences of Modernity* (Stanford: Stanford University Press, 1990).
43. The original *Star Wars* franchise includes: *Star Wars: A New Hope* (1977), *The Empire Strikes Back* (1980) and *Return of the Jedi* (1983). The *Superman* franchise initially includes *Superman* (1978), *Superman II* (1980), *Superman III* (1983) and *Superman IV: The Quest for Peace* (1987). The *Star Trek* franchise had films based upon the original TV series – *Star Trek: The Motion Picture* (1979), *Star Trek II: The Wrath of Khan* (1982), *Star Trek III: The Search for Spock* (1984), *Star Trek IV: The Voyage Home* (1986), *Star Trek V: The Final Frontier* (1989) and *Star Trek VI: The Undiscovered Country* (1991) – as well as many later entries based on the Next Generation TV sequel series and movie reboots.
44 "1986 State of the Union Address," C-SPAN.org, February 4, 1986, https://www.c-span.org/video/?125975-1/1986-state-union-address.
45. For example, see Robert Kuttner, "Free Markets, Besieged Citizens," *New York Review of Books,* July 21, 2022, https://www.nybooks.com/articles/2022/07/21/free-markets-besieged-citizens-gerstle-kuttner/.

CHAPTER 2

DISEASE MOVIES IN TRANSITION: GLOBALIZATION AND IMAGINED CONTAINMENT

Introduction

The appearance of new, unknown diseases from the 1980s onward led to public concern and even at times panic. The mid-twentieth century's high hopes of creating a "world without disease" collided in the 1980s with a somber reality in the form of the AIDS epidemic. AIDS not only revealed the continued presence of infectious diseases but also highlighted science's inability to find a cure.[1] The cultural prejudices associated with AIDS and LGBTQ + culture also, however, resulted in a paradox: despite AIDS' real-world effects, movies largely ignored it for years.[2]

These developments in the field of public health occurred alongside an increasingly globalized, capitalist and connected world. Changes to communications and commerce reconfigured networks in furtherance of efficiency and maximizing profit. This greater connectivity, however, also helped accelerate a resurgent fear of infectious diseases that could easily spread along these networks as well as fostered the movement of both refugees and ideologies. The 9/11 attacks, in particular, marked a watershed moment in American society by increasing the feelings of insecurity and uncertainty as reflected in the growing concerns about terrorism as well as more specific bioterrorism attacks. While continuing to exercise an outsized influence upon the world through a Pax Americana that secured economic benefits for American elites, America no longer seemed a fortress shielded from the political and military turmoil of other countries.

The simmering possibility of novel pathogens during the late 1980s led many scientists to raise awareness of these using a new term: emerging infectious diseases. Key among these figures was Joshua Lederberg, a Nobel laureate and biologist who had been warning the public about diseases for decades. His views began to gain traction by the end of the 1980s, first among peers and then among the public. In his crusade, Lederberg met Richard Preston, a journalist interested in disease stories. Lederberg told Preston about an outbreak of a deadly, Ebola-like virus in a monkey quarantine facility in Reston, a suburb of Washington, DC. The virus had mutated and become airborne, resulting in all the monkeys dying by infection or euthanization. Preston's write-up of the incident in *The New Yorker*, "Crisis in the Hot Zone," in late 1992, included alarming language that discussed the possibility that a third of the world's population might die from a hypothetical AIDS mutation that became airborne.[3]

The article was extraordinarily popular, and Preston received "at least 30 calls" from producers who wanted to buy the rights just 24 hours after the article's publication.[4] He would go on to expand the article into a book, *The Hot Zone*, which was released in 1994 and became a best-seller.[5] Preston also sold his movie rights to 20th Century Fox for a $100,000 option against $450,000 to be paid if the movie was, in fact, made.[6] Fox's planned big-budget ($55 million) movie, however, got bogged down in early production and was eventually cancelled. In the meantime, Warner Brothers developed its own big-budget ($50 million) disease movie based on Preston's outline but changed the details to avoid copyright issues and make the plot more dramatic.[7] The resulting movie, *Outbreak* (1995), opened with an alarmist quote from Lederberg himself: "The single biggest threat to man's continued dominance on the planet is the virus." Although the movie received mixed reviews, it was a commercial success, reaching number one at the box office.[8] Coincidentally, as *Outbreak* was playing in theaters, an Ebola outbreak that emerged in Kikwit, Zaire, received significant attention in TV news stories. As discussed in this book's Introduction, the line between reality and fiction soon blurred, foreshadowing the COVID-19 pandemic a quarter century later. Public fascination with infectious disease had entered popular perception. There was no turning back.

Infectious diseases returned to movie screens in the 1990s and their fictional depictions changed as a reflection and reification of these real-life ideas. Movies began to emphasize the globalized nature of disease, and containment became ever more difficult. As the risk of outbreaks grew, solutions to global infections seemed increasingly distant. The growth of global communications and the simultaneous splintering of local communities in the face of international trade and competition had triggered and accelerated the disappearance of common values as the new asset economy began to take hold.[9] Public institutions no longer had the ability, or more darkly no longer wanted, to put in place adequate preventative measures to protect people. Individuals were now on their own. Movies also began exploring the seemingly obvious next step: humanity's possible extinction and life in a post-apocalyptic world. Despite these changes, however, the movies of this period often stopped short of suggesting the complete breakdown of society, even as norms had weakened or disappeared, but instead featured heroic attempts to prevent the outbreak and, more often than not, individuals succeeded in containing (or escaping) the disease. Films maintained a nostalgia for the idea of a cohesive society working together and containing the disease through heroic action even as they recognized that society itself might not be worth protecting.

This chapter examines two key films from this period to illuminate both these changing stories about diseases on screen and the continuing fragmentation of the American social contract. It begins by discussing *Outbreak* (1995) that reflected the newly emerging disease moment. Its themes – globalization, the fraying of the social fabric and the role of the military – blended together nostalgic ideas about how to contain disease with contemporary fears of infectious diseases. *Outbreak* is the paradigmatic example of the mid-1990s idea of disease, but its conclusion – in which the white male American hero saves the day, stops a disease originating in a colonial location from spreading in the homeland, and reunites with his ex-wife – envisions a happy ending reflective of the 1950s and *Panic in the Streets* than the globalized world of the 1990s. It is a movie fighting against its contemporary reality: romantic altruism incongruously contains a deadly, almost instantaneous outbreak.

The chapter then offers a brief interlude through a discussion of *12 Monkeys* (1995) and *28 Days Later* (2002). Released the same year as *Outbreak*, *12 Monkeys* focused upon a post-apocalyptic pandemic world where a time traveler attempts to stop an outbreak in pre-pandemic times. Its plot, too, tells the story of a global outbreak and efforts at its containment. Yet, *12 Monkeys* reached the opposite conclusion from *Outbreak*: the pandemic spreads, kills billions and romantic sacrifice cannot stop it. It reflects a different, in retrospect prescient, idea of what a disease might do in a globalized world, but which in the mid-1990s was not yet the norm. The British *28 Days Later* also depicted a catastrophic epidemic, albeit limited to the United Kingdom. It helped lead the global resurgence in zombie movies which would become far more common beginning in the early 2000s as an alternative way to explore a disease outbreak. In addition, *28 Days Later* harnessed the perception of a rapidly changing, global landscape and the idea of the extraordinarily fast spread of a virus to the depiction of zombies that now sprint at "viral" speed rather than shamble. While the original ending depicted the death of the male protagonist, audiences viewed it as too dark and hence the filmmakers reshot the ending so that the protagonists survived the epidemic.[10]

Dawn of the Dead (2004), a remake of George Romero's decades earlier critically and commercially successful zombie movie, accelerated and successfully commercialized this lethal combination of a super-fast spreading disease and a post-outbreak setting, reinforcing the development of a new type of zombie movie. It serves in that respect as a key transitional movie. It highlighted the fragmentation of America and increasingly individualistic behavior that was leading to its social disintegration. Unlike the original, however, it masked these pessimistic reflections through the viscerally pleasurable action genre in which masses of undead repeatedly and ferociously attack humans. If *Dawn of the Dead* initially ends with heroic individuals sacrificing themselves so that a handful of survivors might escape to an isolated island, the producers were no longer constrained to offer a happy ending. The zombies seem to overwhelm these last few survivors in the found footage of the end credits. The end of humanity appeared inevitable, with nothing left of society to save.

The chapter ends on a brief look at other movies of this era and focuses, in particular, on the British sequel *28 Weeks Later* (2007). While released only a few years after the original, it no longer offers the nostalgic view of its predecessor or relegates humanity's demise to the end credits. The spread of the viral disease and the triumph of the zombies instead are the logical conclusion to a narrative in which all institutions have failed.

The Disease Is Contained: *Outbreak* (1995)

Directed by Wolfgang Petersen, who had previously directed war and action movies, such as *Das Boot* (1981) and *In the Line of Fire* (1993), *Outbreak* turned the disease movie into an action-thriller.[11] The movie's plot follows the spread of the fictional, deadly Motaba disease, a hemorrhagic fever uncannily similar to Ebola.[12] It opens with an outbreak of Motaba in central Africa in 1967, where two US military doctors collect samples and then order the firebombing of a field hospital with hundreds of patients. The Motaba virus re-emerges in present-day Zaire, 28 years later, and soon arrives in the United States as the result of animal trafficking of an infected monkey. The virus then mutates and spreads as an airborne disease in the small, California town of Cedar Creek. The protagonists, Colonel Dr. Sam Daniels (Dustin Hoffman), who leads a team of military doctors, and his ex-wife Dr. Roberta "Robby" Keough (Rene Russo), who had recently left his team to join the Centers for Disease Control (CDC), a civilian public health organization, race to find a cure and save the town. Two senior US Army medical officers, Donald "Donnie" McClintock (Donald Sutherland) and William "Billy" Ford (Morgan Freeman), are the antagonists who had ordered the 1967 bombing and now advocate bombing Cedar Creek to hide their development of Motaba as a biological weapon.

Outbreak updates the plot of *Panic in the Streets*, adjusting it to the fit the "golden age" of American triumph after the Cold War following the fall of the

Soviet Union and the continued global expansion of the American empire. In revisiting the 1950s film, *Outbreak* argues for conservative, nostalgic solutions to the problems of the mid-1990s at a time when such answers no longer made sense in a globalized world of emerging, infectious diseases.[13] Both films focus on white collar professionals, featuring a military doctor as the central character who fights a deadly disease that has slipped through US Customs. Both doctors encounter institutional resistance: the police and city government in the earlier movie and the American military and federal government in *Outbreak*. Despite these obstacles, both doctors contain the disease because of their own efforts, breaking rules and sacrificing for the greater good. Some plot details and scenes are almost identical. Both doctors, for example, investigate failures at US Customs and identify the disease's source as a foreign ship with an Asian crew. Both films are also marital dramas in which a couple must reconcile career demands with the family's needs – strained finances represented by a son who admires a wealthier neighbor in the first film and a broken marriage represented by fights over the custody of two dogs in the second.

The differences between the films highlight the historical changes that have occurred between the release of *Panic in the Streets* in 1950 and the release of *Outbreak* 45 years later. While *Panic in the Streets* takes place in the city of New Orleans, *Outbreak* adopts a global perspective even if the action in its second half takes place in an idyllic, small town. If *Panic in the Streets* takes for granted the military status of its public service hero, *Outbreak*'s post-Cold War narrative highlights the divide between civilians and the military and is far more critical of the latter. Unlike *Panic in the Streets*, *Outbreak* features black actors, but casts them in subordinate military roles, such as Billy and Major Salt (Cuba Gooding Jr.) reporting to Donnie and Sam, respectively, or as largely anonymous Africans through a colonial lens. The role of the heroic doctor's romantic partner has also changed from a housewife in *Panic in the Streets* to an independent, career-oriented ex-wife in *Outbreak*. It is, however, the film's reaffirmation of the social values of *Panic in the Streets* and its advocacy of the message that love and heroism can conquer a disease that seems most at odds with the changed world of the 1990s. By the time of *Outbreak*'s release, cultural idealization of individual choice and the need for personal success had gone mainstream, endorsing individuals fighting on their own to grab what they can from American society, and was cinematically symbolized, if satirized, by Gordon Gekko's celebrated mantra in *Wall Street* (1987) that "greed is good." *Outbreak*'s depiction of heroic individuals successfully containing the fictional Motaba disease simply ignores the disappearance of the common good as a cultural touchstone.

The filmmakers of *Outbreak* sought to make a scientifically accurate movie or at least promoted it as such. They marketed the film using the medical credentials of one of the screenwriters, Dr. Lawrence Dworet, who claimed,

"I got so into this story that, as a physician, I terrified myself."[14] Dworet and other screenwriters talked to disease experts and stressed how they "are fanatics about realism."[15] They deliberately modeled Motaba after Ebola with the depiction of Ebola-like heavy bleeding from "everywhere on the body." The marketing material for the film included Dworet's claims that there is no cure for these viruses and that "one drop of blood of the Motaba virus has the power to kill one billion people," which would make it a thousand times deadlier than the Influenza Pandemic of 1918–1920.[16] The cast also joined in promoting the film's medical realism. Having met with virologists, Russo described her experience in these meetings as "very scary."[17] Patrick Dempsey, who played Jimbo, the smuggler of the infected monkey, pointed out during the premiere:

> With everything that's going on today, it's, it's very scary. There's been a lot in the news about this actual thing [an outbreak] happening, I mean it's been changed slightly for the film, but this could happen at any time . . . It happens a lot faster. It can take like very few, not even a day, and I think the more we start messing with the environment and our planet, the more trouble we're gonna have.[18]

Contrary, however, to what the creators and actors suggested, the film's science appeared dubious to many reviewers at the time of its release. It may have been a more realistic portrayal of a disease than earlier films, but this was a low bar.[19]

The film's realism is instilled through an emphasis on gore. *Outbreak* uses the realism introduced in films like *Jaws* (1975), in which the film shocks its audience into an acceptance of its supposed realism through a variety of techniques, such as fast cutting, special effects and shot perspective. *Outbreak* includes horrific images of the disease's effects to achieve its supposed realism.[20] In this sense, it attempts to cajole and compel audiences that this could happen rather than persuade and enlighten them about causes and possible solutions. It shows the Motaba virus graphically by initially offering viewers a blurry image of the bloodied face of the victim reflected through the mask of a doctor in a hazmat suit. Only later does the camera zoom out to show the virus's full carnage with blood, pus and gore strewn about. The verbal descriptions are no less extreme. On one occasion Robby phones Sam to tell him about an autopsy she conducted. "Christ, Sam, I opened this guy up, looked like a bomb went off inside. His pancreas, liver . . . all the organs were liquefied."[21]

Outbreak's plot highlights how diseases arrive in America in a globalized world, but that portrayal, like the earlier *Panic in the Streets*, is stereotypical and xenophobic. The movie has a colonial, racist view of Africa, which is portrayed as a backward, superstitious region that threatens "civilized" society. The virus lurks in the water of a village well, but the ignorant villagers fail to recognize that well as the source of the infection. The local witch doctor is unable to cure the virus and blames instead nearby road construction for it. He claims that the "gods were awoken from their sleep . . . This [virus] is a punishment."[22] African professionals cannot help the village. While the local medical doctor's knowledge of medical science allows him to pinpoint the well as the source of the disease, the heroic American military doctor, Sam, must be dispatched from the United States with a team of virologists to take control. Only modern American science can cure the problems that globalization (ironically through the building of the roads which the witch doctor identified) has created. Power and knowledge are situated in the imperial center, which dispatches its legates to solve problems in the colonies, which are unable to follow proper modern health practices.

The fictional, small town of Cedar Creek (population: 2,618) stands in contrast to the African village. Like *Panic in the Streets*' New Orleans, the town is almost entirely white, which highlights the nostalgic feeling of what America "should" look like. The effect of the disease on this supposedly typical, all-American town is made clear by its military invasion and occupation. A two-minute, dialog-less scene shows the military takeover of Cedar Creek – a convoy of heavily armed military vehicles and choppers arriving at night while shocked residents watch in awe from their windows. After more troops are deployed to patrol and quarantine the town, a reporter observes, "It's like a war zone here."

The movie personalizes the disease's effect on this small town in a variety of ways to demonstrate how anyone, anywhere in America could contract a horrific disease. Several scenes are set within the town's small hospital, highlighting the chaos the disease has caused among the town's residents, while another scene occurs in the local cinema, which is the super spreader event in which a carrier of Motaba infects many in the audience.[23] While town residents remain anonymous, *Outbreak* personalizes their experiences by lengthy scenes that do not advance the plot or feature the named characters in the movie. In one scene, the mother of a Cedar Creek family realizes she is sick, leaves her husband and young daughters and voluntarily enters military quarantine. We later watch her die, and the military transports her corpse to a body bag filled barn, which the military then burns to the ground. If these families of this fictional, small town of Cedar Creek are intended to evoke audience sympathy and demonstrate that individuals and their personal lives matter, they also simultaneously demonstrate that in the globalized world of the 1990s individuals are at the mercy of an estranged military and distant American elites. Individual deaths are simply collateral damage. While the film personalizes the outbreak in this small town, it simultaneously shows how individuals, families and local communities no longer matter when disease threatens.

Protecting an anonymous, global community – the far-flung reaches of the American empire – is what drives the film's military to occupy and nearly annihilate Cedar Creek. In a key scene, which would be repeated in subsequent disease movies, Donnie presents a model of the potential spread of Motaba at a White House briefing. According to his dramatic projections, the virus will spread throughout the continental United States in 48 hours. Donnie's solution is straightforward: drop an incendiary bomb on the town of Cedar Creek and wipe out its inhabitants to protect the nation and the world. "The containment procedure must be viewed objectively ... Be compassionate, but be compassionate globally," he tells the assembled group. The camera repeatedly returns its focus to Donnie, who emotionlessly watches the debate which he has initiated unfold around him.[24] The military's suggested action to contain the disease is to annihilate the town's population, rendering their lives inconsequential. Small-town America, the supposed core of American identity, must be sacrificed and cleansed to save the rest of the world.

Paradoxically, *Outbreak* maintains a naïve hope in civilian institutions to check the worst intentions of the American military in advocating for the cold calculations of globalization. While the movie critiques the military in a way that would appear "unpatriotic" after 9/11, it reenacts the myth of the classic

Figure 2.1 *Outbreak* (1995): General Donnie McClintock (center) listens while the White House Chief of Staff approves dropping an incendiary bomb on the small town of Cedar Creek to protect the American nation and its empire.

American Western, believing the good guys will stop the bad guys.[25] National security and military action are invoked to justify almost any decision both in 1967 and in the movie's present. In 1967, the military needs to contain the outbreak and wants to weaponize the virus, which it deems sufficient to justify the bombing of a field hospital filled with sick, American mercenaries. In the film's present, the White House readily endorses the military perspective with no dissenting voice. Following Donnie's presentation, the White House Chief of Staff quotes the Fifth Amendment to the US Constitution. "No person shall be deprived of life, liberty or property without due process."[26] He underscores the gravity of the decision by throwing photos of infected citizens on the table in front of everyone, emotionally asserting that "these are not statistics, ladies and gentlemen, they're flesh and blood!" Yet, he asks no questions of Donnie and falls in line with the proposed military solution, asking only that those in the room provide unwavering support in the form of political loyalty in telling the American people that there were no other options. While the outbreak should require more justification to firebomb American citizens, Donnie's brief presentation at the White House suffices. The film recognizes that a militaristic order that is willing to sacrifice everyone and anyone in the pursuit of global empire is here to stay, even as it naively struggles against such an order and eventually offers a classic, Hollywood happy ending.[27]

The movie's two romantic protagonists, Sam and Robby, reflect this clash between the military and civilian realms and between cold calculations and human emotions. Sam works for the military in Maryland at the Medical Research Institute of Infectious Diseases, while his ex-wife Robby, who had formerly worked under him, found that military life made their marriage impossible and now works for the CDC. *Outbreak* has updated her role from Nancy as a housewife in *Panic in the Streets* to a career-driven woman with professional independence, but this has helped destroy their marriage, since Robby was unwilling to take a backseat to Sam's career ambitions. The conflict in their relationship is underscored when Sam pressures Robby to care for their two dogs, because he must fly to Zaire to investigate the Motaba outbreak. He then fails to return at the time he had promised her just as he had failed at so much else in their marriage. Sam's commitment to the military is in conflict with his relationship with Robby. His romantic feelings cannot be reconciled with the obligations of his military service.

Sam's transformation from military to civilian perspective, with his eventual reconciliation with Robby, defines his character arc in which individual, civilian needs take priority over collective, military obligations. Sam's change is reflected by his two parallel interactions with Billy, his direct commander. When Sam first sees the military giving the residents of Cedar Creek an antiserum, he asks Billy how the military developed it so quickly. Billy cryptically replies, "We have to work together, Sam." But Sam is skeptical. "Are we? . . .

Are we working together, sir?" he asks but accepts the reply. Later, Sam again confronts Billy after Robby and one of his subordinates have become infected.[28] This time Sam is insistent, observing that had the antiserum been administered earlier, the virus might not have mutated. Billy replies by claiming that they are both to blame, since "'we' includes you, Sam, unless you resigned from the army." He emphasizes that they are soldiers first. "We have done all we can as doctors and we have to go on as soldiers." This time, however, Sam refuses to accept Billy's explanation and mutinies. He steals a military helicopter to search for the disease host (the smuggled monkey) to develop an antiserum. Sam even later persuades Billy through an emotional appeal to reject his military outlook, melodramatically arguing that bombing Cedar Creek will result in killing "a big piece of the American soul." Having effectively resigned from the military, Sam can save the town of Cedar Creek and his marriage.

In equating Sam's confrontation with the military as the means by which he reunites with his ex-wife, *Outbreak* is also a romantic comedy. Released during the revival of romantic comedies in the early 1990s, it features constant banter between the recently divorced couple. At times their fight against the military and their effort to find a cure for the virus seem merely background noise to a domestic dispute.[29] Russo (Robby) even stated at the movie's premiere, "Dustin [Sam] kept us hysterical most of the time . . . I had such a good time. I laughed. It felt like a comedy."[30] The romance at the heart of the movie is symbolically reflected in the movie theater's super spreader event when the screwball comedy *What's Up Doc?*, a movie released in 1972, is just coincidentally playing decades later in this small town. Alluding to Sam and Robby, that movie had starred Barbra Streisand and Ryan O'Neal as a seemingly mismatched couple.[31]

The containment of the Motaba virus succeeds alongside Sam and Robby's romantic reconciliation and their affirmation of civilian, domestic values, including their love for one another and a renewal of their marriage. There is surely no gesture more romantic (if incredibly cheesy) than when Sam, fearing that he will lose Robby to the virus, pulls off his mask and cries, "Please don't leave me!" She caresses his face, and he soon returns to inject her with the newly developed antiserum. The film's last scene in which Robby and Sam are reconciled underscores the equating of the virus with their marriage. After Robby observes that her contracting the Motaba virus was a "pretty unique experience," Sam replies, "Sort of like living with me. Would you go through it again?" To which she replies, "Maybe now that I have the antibodies," suggesting that she is now immune to their earlier marital problems. The movie ends on that positive note. The white, heterosexual, professional couple reasserts their love, the virus is cured and American society will be restored.

Outbreak is a paradoxical movie. After a long hiatus of infectious disease movies, it offered a frightening vision of a world in which globalization and the American empire could result in an infection spreading to the small towns of America. At the same time, the movie maintained a nostalgic perspective which imaginatively projects a happy, fictional ending. The heroic husband in a romantic couple successfully averts the excesses of American globalization, demonstrates the desirability (but absence) of a competent, civilian government, and ultimately prevents the destruction of America, upholding the US Constitution. While the film recognized the new paradigm of militarism and globalization, it continued to cling to older notions of American idealism in which individuals working together could still act to save society as well as avert the extinction of humanity by containing the disease. It is, in this sense, a conservative film, because it recognizes that the historical values of America have irrevocably changed, but it does not critique that process of change. Instead, it naively assumes heroes working within the framework of the American empire will continue to protect the nation, so long as modern medical science and altruism remain in charge.

PRESCIENT TRANSITIONS: *12 MONKEYS* (1995) AND *28 DAYS LATER* (2002)

Outbreak was the most visible Hollywood manifestation of a disease movie during the mid-1990s. Other contemporary films, however, depicted disease and its potential impact as far more catastrophic. Released only months after *Outbreak*, Terry Gilliam, an American-born British film director (who had been a member of the celebrated Monty Python comedy troupe), directed *12 Monkeys*. Anticipating future movies, it depicted a failure to contain a global virus and the resulting apocalyptic ending for humanity, using disease to critique society, including consumer capitalism. Likewise, *28 Days Later*, a British production, depicted a post-apocalyptic world in which a biotech experiment goes awry, resulting in raging zombies that quickly overwhelm the United Kingdom. If *Outbreak* was a cautionary tale for the present, both *12 Monkeys* and *28 Days Later* imagined how a virus would inevitably overwhelm the human species in the near future.

Projecting an ominous near-future, *12 Monkeys* was ahead of its time. The film narrates how in 1996 (a year after the movie's release, highlighting the urgency of the matter) a deadly virus wiped out 99.9 percent of humanity, forcing the survivors to take refuge underground. The movie opens in a future 2035, when James Cole, a prisoner incarcerated for an unknown crime but known for his "disregard of authority," is offered a bargain. Cole will be freed if he agrees to travel back in time to 1996 to discover the virus' origin so scientists in 2035 can find a cure. Cole accepts the offer and struggles throughout the film to identify the origin of the disease in two years: 1990 and 1996.

Where *Outbreak* updated *Panic in the Streets* for a post-Cold War world, *12 Monkeys* updated the experimental short film *La Jetée* (1962), an exercise in radical filmmaking that consisted of a series of still photos with a voiceover. In contrast to *Outbreak*, *12 Monkeys* points to capitalism, particularly consumerism, as the cause of the pandemic by its exploitation of the environment.

Outbreak accepts the globalized world as necessary, if problematic, but *12 Monkeys* directly criticizes the adverse effects of globalization.[32] It portrays humanity in the 1990s as destructive of the natural environment and offers a discouraging prognosis about the species' future. Several characters openly suggest that perhaps humanity should be wiped out as punishment for its excesses. Although Cole, who has traveled from the future into the pre-pandemic past, knows about the pandemic and convinces others to believe him, he cannot prevent it from happening or even escape it himself. The immediate cause of the pandemic is a lone wolf eco-terrorist who deliberately releases a bio-engineered virus developed in his own lab. If one person could save thousands in the small town of Cedar Creek in *Outbreak,* one person likewise can annihilate almost the entire world's population in *12 Monkeys*, highlighting the dark side to the power of the individual in a globally interconnected environment. As a result, *12 Monkeys* is a pessimistic film in its depiction of the human species' inevitable self-extinction.

The film is, however, the more dramatically logical outcome for the mid-1990s. Rather than imagining containment, *12 Monkeys* serves as a warning for its contemporary world with its increasing anxiety towards emerging, infectious diseases. Yet, the film failed to change the American disease film paradigm, since American movie myths had yet to confront the new realities of a global empire. America was still enjoying its unprecedented hegemony, capitalism had not yet been perceived to have hollowed out American social norms, and ideas about disease, despite the warnings of Lederberg and others, had not yet concluded that containment was impossible. While outbreaks occurred, Americans still believed that infectious diseases largely originated and could be contained within the global South. That, in turn, only further reinforced colonialist, racist ideas about the global North as separate, privileged and protected. Americans continued to believe in the 1990s that Sam could save them, rather than believe that Cole's attempts at averting an apocalyptic future were doomed to fail.[33] While *12 Monkeys* was commercially successful, its depiction of a dystopian future had not yet become the norm.

American beliefs began shifting by the early 2000s. The 9/11 terrorist attack on America's financial center shattered the notion of American privilege and exceptionalism. America's global empire exposed the country to the newly recognized fear that borders and containment might no longer suffice. *Outbreak*'s individual heroism increasingly appeared anachronistic. Zombie movies had usefully critiqued the very fabric of what had become America's empire – consumerism and capitalism – in the 1960s and 1970s but had then largely disappeared from mainstream screens for over a decade from the mid-1980s. Now newly revived and adapted to the newly emerging fears, these reimagined zombie movies became the perfect vehicle to explore the potential effects of a global pandemic. Popularized by enormously successful video game franchises that had originated in Japan, such as *Resident Evil* (1996) and *The House of the Dead* (1996), these initially consisted of a series of low-budget zombie films.³⁴ The mainstream resurgence of zombie movies dates, however, to the 2002 release of the low-budgeted, British-produced *28 Days Later* and the larger-budgeted, American-produced movie *Resident Evil*.³⁵ The movie *28 Days Later*, in particular, rejected George Romero's format, in which zombies were hulking corpses of undead reanimated and whose bite after hours or days could "turn" the living into zombies. It depicted instead "the infected" as technically still living people, not undead, who displayed insatiable rage, sprinted at full speed and infected victims in seconds.³⁶ These changes made zombies more visceral and their threat more immediate.

Figure 2.2 *28 Days Later* (2002): Jim wanders alone through the streets of London, pausing before the Houses of Parliament and Big Ben.

The narrative of *28 Days Later* evoked contemporary events and in particular 9/11.³⁷ The "missing persons" flyers in early scenes in London recall similar flyers in New York City after 9/11, and London's empty streets echo the images of a post-9/11 New York City under threat of terrorists.³⁸ These allusions conveyed how disease reflected the inability of humans to resolve their conflicts and the failure of institutions to contain, let alone cure, the deadly pandemic symbolic of those conflicts. The opening scene in *28 Days Later* shows video clips of human violence from around the world and the release by an animal rights group of a chimpanzee forced to watch those videos and upon whom scientists have experimented. Afterwards, the monkey bites the female activist who releases it from its cage, evoking the myth of Pandora's box, and the experimental disease spreads to humans throughout London almost instantly.[39]

The film depicts the failure of both individual efforts and institutions to defeat the virus. It focuses on Jim, a working-class bicycle courier, who was hurt in a traffic accident and wakes up from his coma at a hospital 28 days later (hence the film's title) to find that the rage-inducing disease has turned nearly everyone into infected.[40] Mark and Selena, the two survivors whom Jim finds while roaming the streets of London, are only looking out for him or herself. The film depicts the new reality in a graphic scene in which Selena unhesitatingly slaughters Mark with a machete when she suspects that an infected has bitten him before unapologetically telling Jim that she would readily kill him, too, if necessary.[41] Traditional institutions also fail. When Jim asks Selena and Mark, "What about the government, what are they doing?" Selena's answer – "there's no government" – is incomprehensible to Jim. Mark must further explain, "There's no government, no police, no army, no TV, no radio, no electricity." Similarly, as Jim wanders through London he seeks refuge in a church where he encounters for the first time the infected: a priest and infected parishioners.[42] The church, too, fails to offer refuge or relief.

If the movie portrays biological families as unable to survive in this new world – Jim's parents take their own lives, and Mark's father becomes infected after Mark's other family members are trampled underfoot by a massive crowd – it proposes the close-knit, surrogate family as an alternative. Soon after Mark's death, Frank, a cab driver who lives in a high-rise London building with his daughter Hannah, rescues Jim and Selena from the infected. He soon shares with them a military radio broadcast, calling for survivors to head for a roadblock near Manchester. The subsequent road trip by these four survivors in Frank's cab to that roadblock results in the creation of a new family. Working together, they succeed in fixing a flat tire, evade the infected, happily shop for groceries and camp in the picturesque English countryside. Frank even teaches Jim about the finer points of Scotch, and the unexpected image of four horses running freely across the countryside symbolizes the sense of momentary grace associated with their newly formed family.[43]

Yet, such families are hardly guarantors of change to outmoded social traditions. The small group of soldiers whom the four encounter at the military blockade represents a corrupted surrogate family. After brutally killing an infected Frank in front of the others, the officer in charge, Major Henry West, fails to replace Frank as Jim's father, reveals that he and his men intend to turn Selena and Hannah into sex slaves and orders the execution of the resistant Jim. This group also chains outside with a collar one of its own, an infected black soldier, as a substitute for the group's mistreated dog, and another of them, an apron-wearing male soldier, is a substitute mother who serves rotten eggs to the group, claiming that he thought "the salt might cover the taste."[44]

Moreover, the idealized family of Jim, Selena and Hannah in the end perpetuates only patriarchal gender relations. While Jim increasingly demonstrates his heroism, Selena and Hannah become increasingly passive.[45] Selena begins the movie as a strong individualist but is quickly domesticated in her new surrogate family. When the soldiers plan to rape both women, Selena offers Hannah pills so that she does not care. In the film's final scene her transformation is complete. She is busy sewing at home, a domestic female role, and Jim approvingly comments that she "looked alright" in the red dress that the soldiers had forced her to wear.

Yet, the film's theatrically released ending also underscores that the public was still not ready to accept the dark ending toward which the film had pointed. During the protagonists' escape from the mansion overwhelmed by the infected, Major West shoots Jim before the infected snatch him as well. The filmmakers' proposed original ending showed Selena and Hannah unable to save the wounded Jim, and Jim's death in a hospital both echoed the opening in which Jim awakens alone in a hospital as well as served as a punishment for his collaboration and identification with the infected. Too dark for audiences, the revised theatrical ending shows the surrogate family of Jim, Selena and Hannah driving off in Frank's cab and finding refuge in a secluded, countryside home.[46] The movie ends 28 days later. Jim has recovered, and the family's giant "HELLO" cloth banner attracts the attention of a jet flying overhead. Yet, even this released version ending is ambiguous.[47] When seen from high above, the HELLO cloth banner appears briefly without the letter "O." The new post-apocalyptic world is "HELL."

Fast Zombies and Fragmentation: *Dawn of the Dead* (2004)

Dawn of the Dead (2004), an all-American remake of a George Romero zombie movie, confirmed the arrival of the reimagined zombie as a viral disease movie. While George Romero had transformed the zombie movie in his low budget, black and white *Night of the Living Dead* (1968), his second movie, the much higher budgeted *Dawn of the Dead* (1978), in color, was his most commercially and critically successful. Romero's *Dawn of the Dead* ignored the disease's source and opened with scenes of social chaos and zombies already overwhelming America. The movie focuses on a makeshift community of two SWAT team members and two TV staffers who create a place of safety for themselves in a large, suburban mall. Romero's movie critiques consumer capitalism in late 1970s America. The mall serves as a "temple to consumerism" and attracts both the living and the dead.[48] Comically satirizing and critiquing American consumerism, the film depicts how the characters' fantasies of material comfort, the pleasures of violence and even romance spiral out of control over a few months before the undead eventually overrun the mall. The black SWAT team member Peter (Ken Foree) describes what motivates these undead to surround the mall: memories of their consumer capitalist life. "They're after the place," he remarks. "They don't know why. They just remember." He also articulates that there is no difference between the living and the dead, observing, "They're us. That's all." Romero intended that the undead seem familiar and that each have an individual story, just like each surviving human, which he emphasized by dressing each zombie with a distinctive wardrobe including a nun and a softball player.[49] Peter quotes his grandfather, a priest in Trinidad, in order to explain what has happened. "When there's no more room in hell, the dead will walk the Earth." While Peter and the pregnant TV staffer Fran (Gaylen Ross) escape by flying off at dawn in a helicopter, the ending remains ambiguous, since the duo has little fuel left, even as Fran's pregnancy offers some hope of a new beginning.

Dawn of the Dead was remade in 2004.[50] Zack Snyder, who would go on to direct a series of graphic novel and comic book movies, such as *300* (2007), *Man of Steel* (2013) and *Justice League* (2017), directed the remake as his feature debut. James Gunn, who would have a directorial career in odd horror movies, such as *Slither* (2006), as well as comic book movies, such as *Guardians of the Galaxy* (2014, 2017, 2023) and *The Suicide Squad* (2021), wrote the screenplay. The remake follows Romero's original in its setting: a group of humans barricading themselves within a suburban mall and holding off a horde of surrounding zombies. Yet, the remake reimagines this story, shifting from a critique of consumer capitalism to an action movie that revels in its graphic violence. In the remake, the suburban mall is just a stage on which these characters perform. The zombies likewise serve more to create dramatic tension rather than seriously threaten the protagonists. As such, they kill fewer human characters than the humans themselves.[51]

The shift in the remake's focus is evident in how its narrative is also no longer an intimate drama about a handful of survivors but instead has an expansive cast, resulting in little character development. The movie initially focuses on five individuals, Ana (Sarah Polley), a nurse in a local Milwaukee hospital where an early victim appears, black police sergeant Kenneth Hall (Ving Rhames), TV salesperson Michael (Jake Weber), the black criminal Andre (Mekhi Phifer) and Andre's white, pregnant, Russian wife Luda (Inna Korobkina). It quickly expands to include three security guards at the mall, CJ (Michael Kelly), Bart and Terry, and thereafter adds a motley group of eight additional survivors who escape into the mall from a nearly overwhelmed truck. Once these characters are inside, the movie follows a series of barely connected subplots, such as the effort to restart the mall's emergency generator, which serve only as an impetus for violent action. Most characters are, in fact, barely developed, stereotypical and disposable, and we hardly learn some of their names. They evoke the reality TV show contestants whom Ana and her husband watch in a pre-credits scene and whose names are similarly unknown.

DISEASE MOVIES IN TRANSITION

The remake offers instead the pleasures of CGI. Like a video game, the film features numerous zombie headshots and the firing of substantial ammunition in its depiction of humans shooting these endless numbers of fast-moving zombies. It is entirely fitting that the survivors at one point literally play a game in which the barricaded gun store owner Andy shoots zombies who resemble real-world celebrities, such as Jay Leno, Burt Reynolds and Rosie O'Donnell. Where the zombies in the original movie were slow moving undead dressed in their prior life attire, only these lookalike celebrity zombies are distinguishable from the mass of zombies who tirelessly race after and rage at humans like the zombies of *28 Days Later*. If some of the violence is amusing, most of it is graphic and meant to shock and awe. In an early scene in Ana's suburban home, a young child, as though possessed, hurls herself against the locked bedroom door behind which Ana desperately administers a rag to her bitten husband's neck. Later, the few survivors trying to escape from the mall in reinforced buses blow up massive numbers of zombies only to find that the horde almost immediately recovers and renews its attack. In contrast to the original, there is no fake, red-colored liquid on the drooling faces of these undead, but instead realistic-looking human blood is splattered across the white bathroom floor and walls of Ana's home.

The film conveys pleasure in the utter devastation of the neatly laid out patterns of typical American suburban sprawl. The ordered housing in the evening's light offers a stark contrast to the chaotic violence the next morning. The audience shares Ana's perspective as she looks upon her secure world rapidly

Figure 2.3 *Dawn of the Dead* (2004): Zombies swarm like a hive mind and nearly overwhelm the fortified vehicles of the few human survivors.

collapsing around her, unable to make sense of what is happening. A long shot view of the Greater Milwaukee area as Ana drives off to escape makes plain the spreading zombie apocalypse. After she then crashes her car and falls unconscious, the introductory credits roll and show a series of gratuitous, barely discernable long shots and close ups of the spreading zombie outbreak, beginning with a grainy image of an undifferentiated mass of Muslims praying at a mosque, civil unrest, which devolves into chaos, ineffective political and military action, and zombies swarming and devouring humans, including in front of the White House and in an identifiably Muslim country. In a movie that features no other Muslim-related content, the clear Muslim framing in the opening credits underscores the film's evocation – and exploitation – of fears aroused in America about 9/11, while simultaneously enabling its audience to enjoy the visual pleasures of cultural collapse.[52]

Moreover, the remake adopts a distanced, sardonic attitude, featuring a tone of knowingness, hipness and condescension. This is best reflected in the constant cynicism expressed by the successful businessman Steve (Ty Burrell), beginning with his observation about infighting between survivors. "It's nice to see that you've all bonded through this disaster," he sarcastically remarks at one point. Where others may momentarily engage in romance, such as Ana and Michael, Steve instead has casual, voyeuristic sex with Monica, a survivor about whom almost nothing is known. Openly self-centered and uncaring of others, he allows the zombies to enter the mall by leaving his post at a locked door and later abandons the other survivors of his armored vehicle during their escape, though he soon succumbs to a zombie bite. In an example of the film's black humor, Ana then shoots the infected Steve as she had mockingly earlier promised to do. That same black humor extends to the narrative itself. Steve's offhanded suggestion – that the remaining survivors "drop by the marina" in which he has anchored his luxury boat and "take it for a pleasure cruise" – leads to Ana's incredible reply that that is a good idea. "There's islands out on those lakes," she explains with strained logic. "There's not many people on them." This absurd, farcical plan – which the characters themselves acknowledge is farfetched, almost breaking the movie's fourth wall – frames the remaining narrative. The movie is self-aware and in on the joke but also contemptuous of its audience in challenging it to enjoy the absurdity of its narrative.

The *Dawn of the Dead* remake is both more pessimistic and nihilistic than the original, with a dystopian view of the world. No longer are zombies, for example, equated with the living in their attraction to the mall's consumer goods. They are instead reanimated without purpose or aim other than to spread the infection. A televangelist (played by Ken Foree, who had played the SWAT team member Peter in the original) defines the moral lesson of the zombies when he reformulates the original film's definition of hell. "Hell is overflowing. And Satan is sending his dead to us," he lectures his audience. "Why?

Because you have sex out of wedlock. You kill unborn children. You have man-on-man relations. Same-sex marriage. How do you think your god will judge you? . . . When there is no more room in hell, the dead will walk the earth." In expressing this absolutist view of morality, the televangelist reflects the religious right of the early 2000s. Yet, if the movie mocks his viewpoint, it also critiques a secular view of morality, which Kenneth articulates. According to Kenneth, hell is a form of punishment in which cause and effect explain the moral order of the universe. "You saw hell yesterday. Now you're scared of going to hell for all the bad things you've done," he sarcastically admonishes the petty criminal Andre. "I'll tell you what. Go in the stall, say five Hail Marys, wipe your ass, and you and God can call it even." Religious rituals, too, offer no comfort. When the few remaining survivors collect their dead and request Glen, a church organist, to "say something" about these dead, he flatly refuses. "I don't believe in God," he admits. "I don't see how anyone could."

With religious and secular institutions no longer as options, the movie identifies human nature as the cause of the disintegration of American life but identifies individual choice as its possible savior. The movie mocks, for example, the lower-class security guard CJ for selfishly refusing, at least initially, to allow other survivors to enter the mall. "This is our place and you can't stay here," he tells them, asserting his instinct for survival. "I'll kill each and every one of you to stay alive." If he grudgingly allows them into the mall, he insists that he is "going to give everybody a job" and then locks them up at night to prevent them from "stealing shit." Later reading a woman's magazine on how to develop a marital relationship, he suddenly develops self-awareness and is transformed from a frightened, bullying and dim-witted security guard to a heroic character who sacrifices himself for the others. More caricature than character, CJ represents the film's view in which individual choice will rescue humanity, especially the uneducated lower class. American capitalism, too, praises those few who succeed for their hard work, condemns the vast majority who succumb to their human nature, and, in the end, disposes of even those who supposedly succeed, like CJ.

This same focus on individual choice motivates the other characters as well, although this makes clear the limitations inherent in individual choice. The protagonist, the middle-class nurse Ana, is the most altruistic voice in the group, convincing the others to rise up against and disarm the obstinate mall security guards and accept unexpected newcomers. Yet, even Ana's altruism is qualified by her earlier refusal to open her car to a neighbor who pleads for help during the initial outbreak. The otherwise rational Kenneth articulates this message. Speaking over the newly dead in place of Glen, he acknowledges the compelling instinct for survival when he recalls his former days as a marine and current life as a police officer. "Been to a lot of funerals. Folded the flag and given it to a lot of wives and fathers and kids. I told them how sorry I was. But that's not what I was really feeling. In the back of my mind, I was always saying, 'Better them than me.'" If the upper-middle-class Steve serves as an antagonist, he is simply more candid about his own selfish interests. While some characters may exhibit Hollywood-like, heroic gestures, no common purpose unites this group other than the momentarily collective, animal instinct for survival.

Moreover, *Dawn of the Dead* depicts the failure of the patriarchal family to offer refuge from the enveloping social chaos. Michael, for example, acknowledges that he has divorced three times.[53] Nicole has already lost her entire family and receives little sympathy when the others execute her infected father. Kenneth repeatedly voices his plan to reunite with his brother in Fort Pastor but never acts on his intent given its apparent futility. And Andre is disturbingly obsessed with creating a family, hiding pregnant Luda's infection from the others, delivering the birth of a zombie baby in the film's most troubling scene, and then shooting Norma (who has shot the zombified Luda and retaliates by shooting Andre). These families are hardly the bedrock of a new society in this chaotic world.

Dawn of the Dead has gender, racial and queer diversity, but such diversity is circumscribed by the capitalist paradigm. The main character, Ana, is a woman of pragmatic resourcefulness and leadership. Glen is the rare (for 2004) LGBTQ+ character, who discloses his sexuality to the narrow minded CJ and Bart, and horrifies, in particular, the misogynistic Bart.[54] Norma is an older truck driver who is skilled in the use of guns. Two of the initial five survivors are black and Andre and Luda are an interracial couple.[55] Yet, this diversity offers only a cosmetic change: a diversity in casting but without that diversity affecting the film's perspective on individualistic behavior. For example, Ana as a woman offers little alternative to the individualistic, masculine-gendered approach of this new zombie world. Moreover, her critique of "the boys" shooting celebrity-lookalike zombies ("you guys had really rough childhoods") is delivered emotionlessly and superficially. In offering a diverse cast, the movie offers equality to everyone, regardless of identity, but the film's focus remains on the corruption of human nature and a sentimental belief in individual heroism. That, of course, results in the ineffectiveness of those seeking refuge in the mall to escape the ferociously assimilating zombies. By attributing the disease to human nature and insisting upon heroics, the film offers no alternative and instead endorses capitalism in which each person is alone and out for him or herself.[56]

If the movie is about redemption, according to its screenwriter, then that redemption is consistent with Hollywood's movie mythology of individual heroism. Gunn explained that the movie sought to remove characters' identities, whether social or professional, so that they might "become who they really are . . . and some of the people are redeemed and end up becoming good people and some of them are not redeemed and they end up, you know, not redeemed."[57] Michael is the quintessential example. He transforms himself from a TV salesperson at Best Buy, who had failed at all his careers, to Davy Crockett (Steve's term), an American frontier hero. Realizing at the end of the movie that he's been bitten and is infected, he assures Ana that "it's gonna' be alright." While she replies that "it won't," he continues to insist that it will. When a bloodied Kenneth, too, asks whether he's sure he wants to do this, Michael assures him that he is just going to stay awhile on the dock and "enjoy the sunrise." The movie then cross-cuts between Michael standing tall and alone on the dock and a shot of Ana alone in the boat next to an American flag as the boat in longshot heads into the sun. Michael puts a handgun to his head, the film cuts to Ana and the screen goes black as a single shot is heard. If everyone is out for him or herself, then helping others represents merely another individual choice rather than a collective or public good.

The film's ending underscores the transition from containment to apocalypse. If the audience-driven, revised ending of *28 Days Later* depicts the three survivors of the zombie attack being rescued by an overhead aircraft through their strategic placement of the sign "HELLO" *Dawn of the Dead* repeats that image – but earlier in the film with a rooftop sign, "Help Alive Inside." These survivors, however, are not rescued by the helicopter flying overhead. Moreover, while the movie could have ended with Michael's heroic sacrifice, it ends instead with camcorder found footage that unexpectedly appears during the end credits.[58] That footage initially shows Steve partying with an unknown woman, but it soon devolves into footage of the four survivors, Ana, Kenneth, Nicole and Terry, exhausting their food and gas supplies, landing on an unknown island and then encountering a swarm of zombies who ferociously rush at them. Individual heroism comes to naught.

Like Romero's *Night of the Living Dead*, the remake of *Dawn of the Dead* seemingly mocks American rednecks and patriotism. After watching a media interview of a sheriff on how to get rid of zombies ("shoot 'em in the head, then you gotta burn them"), the lower class CJ enthusiastically exclaims to Bart and Terry, "What did I tell you boys? America always sorts its shit out!" Yet, *Dawn of the Dead* is hardly a paean to such patriotism, since the military fails to contain the zombie apocalypse. At the same time, individual heroism also fails to create or even envision a new world. *Dawn of the Dead* teeters in its double ending between both reassuring and cautioning its audience as to the species' future. The movie emphasizes the pleasures of kinetic visuals, creates a chaotic if occasionally incoherent narrative, but thoroughly entertains.[59]

DARK DISEASE MOVIES AND A PANDEMIC SEQUEL: *28 WEEKS LATER* (2007)

Disease movies proliferated in the new millennium and increasingly expressed, if with occasional hesitancy, pessimism in acknowledging the changed American landscape. *Cabin Fever* (2002), released the same year as *28 Days Later*, tells of five college students on spring vacation in a remote cabin where there are already signs of infection with a disease of an unknown origin. That disease quickly spreads to the group when the students brutally set fire to an infected, local hermit whose dead body then infects the local reservoir. Recalling Romero's *Night of the Living Dead*, the local police shoot and burn the one survivor in a bonfire along with nearly all of the other students. The infection, however, spreads to the town through children selling lemonade and beyond the town in a truck transporting bottled spring water.

Romero, too, continued to direct zombie movies critiquing American culture. *Land of the Dead* (2005) focused on the inequality divide in America between the wealthy, white male minority and the vast numbers of an impoverished population. While a small group of friends successfully escape in an armored vehicle for Canada after zombies overrun the fortified city within which the humans had barricaded themselves, a farewell shot of colorful firecrackers exploding in the sky announces the triumph of the zombies who have become self-aware. Big Daddy, a black zombie, successfully leads other zombies in a workers' revolt against their human masters. Reanimated zombies, according to the film, increasingly represent an attractive alternative to the contemporary capitalist culture of an urban environment comprised of a small group of elites and a mass of submissive human workers.

Meanwhile *I Am Legend* (2007), the third adaptation of Richard Matheson's novel, underscored the oftentimes reactionary retreat in the face of the changed landscape. A celebrated, arrogant scientist, who has apparently found a "miracle cure" for cancer by reprogramming an existing disease "designed by nature," causes a viral outbreak that has infected and transformed nearly the entire world's population into frenzied, emaciated creatures who attack in packs as a hive.[60] Black US Army virologist, Robert Neville, seeks to find a cure for the infection for which only he and 1 percent of the population are immune and insists that he remain alone in New York City, "ground zero," to try to develop that cure. While Neville eventually develops a cure from his own blood, he only succeeds when he acknowledges God and God's plan. While the film advocates for an end to racism and hate, closing with Bob Marley's celebrated words "light up the darkness," the film's last images depict a sanctuary in the walled community of Bethel, Vermont, an iconic New England community of magnificent fall foliage and church bells playing conspicuously in the background. Here the only solution to the inevitable spread of viral infection is a retreat behind high walls and a nostalgic reimagining of America's long-gone past.

The continuing shift to an increasingly dark perception of infectious diseases is best illustrated by *28 Weeks Later*. The success of *28 Days Later* led its British producers to conceive of a "28" trilogy. The second film in that trilogy, *28 Weeks Later*, was released five years later in 2007, though the third film has yet to materialize. The sequel unfolds in London 28 weeks after the onset of infection and follows a British family during the NATO-led reconstruction and repopulation of London. The father, Don, had abandoned his wife, Alice, to the infected who had attacked their hideout during the initial outbreak. Surviving that attack, Don secures a contracting job and brings into this newly secured, reconstructed London safe zone his children, who had been abroad during the initial outbreak. The children soon discover that their mother is alive as an asymptomatic carrier of the virus but delirious. When she infects Don, a series of events results in an outbreak in the secure zone, which the military is unable to contain. Two American soldiers, a sniper and a medical officer, help Don's two children escape from the zone, sacrificing themselves to do so. The children, at least one of whom shares Alice's asymptomatic carrier gene, eventually evacuate to the European mainland, where they spread the infection. Containment has failed, and the zombie apocalypse will inevitably spread worldwide.

The sequel *28 Weeks Later* continues to explore the themes of *28 Days Later* but is far darker in its view of humanity's future. It, too, focuses on the failure of society and its institutions, especially the military. If the small military unit under Major West's command in *28 Days Later* failed, the expeditionary force in *28 Weeks Later* can neither stop the spread of the rage infection nor safeguard the citizens under its protection. Moreover, the family in both its nuclear and surrogate forms, the latter of which had been a source of hope in the original, becomes the source for the infection.[61] Don abandons his wife, and she, in turn, infects him when she accepts his plea for forgiveness and kisses him. The sniper and the medical officer sacrifice themselves for their two surrogate children, but the results are catastrophic, leading to a global apocalypse. If *28 Days Later* balanced uncertainly on the cusp of a new disease paradigm, then *28 Weeks Later* knowingly embraces it.

Moreover, *28 Weeks Later* explicitly alludes to contemporary political events and hence is far more confident in its view that efforts to prevent the end of the world – or at least the world as we know it today – are futile.[62] Using the virus as an allegory for contemporary events, the movie critiques the US-led Iraq War (2003–2011) and the subsequently failed reconstruction, which had led only to greater chaos internationally and further acrimony domestically.[63] London is equated with Baghdad, the center of American military operations in Iraq. Both cities feature a heavily militarized safe zone, and both experience a quick, early success followed by a bloody and ultimately unsuccessful effort to control the occupied territory.[64] Global politics in the years between the first and the second movies, including the American military adventures in the Middle East, reinforced the growing belief in a terminal, incurable societal failure.[65] The happy ending of *28 Days Later* which preview audiences insisted upon contrasts with the ending in *28 Weeks Later* in which a happy ending is no longer possible. The sequel foresees the inevitability of humanity's extinction from the global forces accelerating changes inconsistent with human needs.

Conclusion

The disease movies released during the 1990s and 2000s reflect a growing unease with global developments in which events around the world appeared ever closer and more connected, but also increasingly beyond individual, human control. *Outbreak* was released on the precipice of the change from an analog to a wholly digital world which threatened mid-century hierarchies and common values. The turn of the twenty-first century witnessed an acceleration in technological connections as personal computers became ubiquitous, while the internet spread throughout the developed world and into much of the developing world, resulting in easier communication, greater access to varied content, and the increasing speed of commerce. At the same time, the 24-hour news cycle came to dominate not only television but also news websites, with near-immediate, worldwide coverage of events ranging from the Iraq War to the 2004 Indian Ocean tsunami.

The events of 9/11 played a key role, shattering America's perceived inviolability. It also revealed how American political and commercial interests coincided. Trade transformed from local to global supply chains in far off countries in which cheap labor and materials magnified the "know how" of American capitalism. If the decades following the Great Depression and World War II offered the possibility of collective action and Pax Americana had offered a safety net to those who fit the definition of Americans, the newly emerging global order emphasized corporate profits and individual material benefits. These changes greatly accelerated the increasing disintegration of local communities across the United States, particularly small towns. It paradoxically resulted in a growing social fragmentation even as the global network supposedly drew everyone within the western culture of capitalism closer and made them more similar to one another. Movies continued to nostalgically grasp at mid-century norms, including hierarchies and institutions, even as they receded from reality.

If many of the changes to disease films described in this chapter broke new ground, these movies also sit uneasily between the past and future. *Dawn of the Dead* may have helped usher into the mainstream a new type of infected, but its inclusion only in the end credits, camcorder found-footage scenes suggests that studios believed (whether correctly or not) that audiences had yet to fully transition to a new paradigm in disease movies. From a vantage point two decades later, the change in themes is apparent. If *Outbreak* had refused to acknowledge that the world, or at least our view of it, had changed, *Dawn of the Dead*, while hesitant in its choice, tentatively recorded that change. Within the next few years movie diseases would fully embrace it. Heroic action soon became openly nostalgic, often depicting reactionary reenactments of outmoded narratives and taking place in a post-pandemic world in which social institutions were plainly incapable of coping with the realities of a pandemic. The proliferation of zombie movies during the next decades would mirror this new reality in which the source of the infection is often unknown or irrelevant.

The zombie-infested, post-apocalyptic world had, however, arrived. Measured by twenty-first century standards, *Outbreak* is slow, almost boring, since the virus took days to spread within a single quarantined town and did not spill over to other populations. By contrast, in *Dawn of the Dead,* the American Midwest is quickly overrun and annihilated in what seems to be a few days at most, despite the American military's brief attempts at containment measures. The change in the effects of infectious disease in movies was not yet complete. What should replace these failed systems and how should humans survive in this new apocalyptic landscape remained open questions that would only be answered in the next decade.

NOTES

1. On this again: Zimmer, *Welt ohne Krankheit: Geschichte der internationalen Gesundheitspolitik 1940–1970*; and for the changes over the twentieth century, see J. N. Hays, *The Burdens of Disease: Epidemics and Human Response in Western History*, revised edition (New Brunswick: Rutgers University Press, 2009), esp. 243–282; and Peter Washer, *Emerging Infectious Diseases and Society*.
2. There was, for example, a several year delay between the book *And the Band Played On* in 1987 and its making into a television drama in 1993. For the book, see Randy Shilts, *And the Band Played On: Politics, People, and the AIDS Epidemic* (New York: St. Martin's Press, 1987). The few other early movies addressing AIDS include *Longtime Companion* (1989) and *Philadelphia* (1993).
3. Richard Preston, "Crisis in the Hot Zone: Lessons from an Outbreak of Ebola."
4. Bernard Weinraub, "Wrestling a Virus to the Screen," *The New York Times*, March 19, 1995, https://www.nytimes.com/1995/03/19/movies/film-wrestling-a-virus-to-the-screen.html. But see Weinraub, "Two Films, One Subject. Uh-Oh. In Hollywood, the Race Is On."
5. Richard Preston, *The Hot Zone.*
6. Weinraub, "Wrestling a Virus to the Screen."
7. Weinraub, "Two Films, One Subject. Uh-Oh. In Hollywood, the Race Is On."
8. For the film's mixed critical success, see "Outbreak," *Rotten Tomatoes*, https://www.rottentomatoes.com/m/outbreak. For the film's commercial success see: "Outbreak (1995)", *Box Office Mojo*, https://www.boxofficemojo.com/title/tt0114069/. The book's introduction has further bibliography.
9. For a discussion of one of the ways in which this changed environment has affected individuals, see Sherry Turkle, *Alone Together: Why We Expect More from Technology and Less from Each Other* (New York: Basic Books, 2011).
10. Commentary by Danny Boyle and Alex Garland, "Alternative Theatrical Ending," *28 Days Later*, directed by Danny Boyle (2002; London, 20th Century Fox Home Entertainment, 2003), DVD. Boyle and Garland were surprised by the audience reaction, since they viewed the effort in the hospital to revive Jim as focusing on the

strengths of Selena and Hannah and confirming their likely survival in this post-apocalyptic world.
11. The movie's production was tortuous, although the details are disputed. Since Warner did not own the rights to *The Hot Zone*, producer Arnold Kopelson hired a longtime friend, Lawrence Dworet, and a co-writer, Robert Roy Pool, to draft the script. The resulting script was unsatisfactory, with Dustin Hoffman, the leading star, also complaining early on about the script and Kopelson bringing in several screenwriters and introducing still more revisions to the script. See Weinraub, "Wrestling a Virus to the Screen."
12. Like Ebola, the Motaba virus is named after a river in Africa.
13. Ironically, the working title of *Panic in the Streets* was *Outbreak*. See "Panic in the Streets," *AFI Catalog of Feature Films: The First 100 years 1893–1993*, https://catalog.afi.com/Film/26448-PANIC-IN-THE-STREETS. For further discussion of *Outbreak*, Wald, *Contagious*, 37–67; and Dahlia Schweitzer, *Going Viral*, 38ff.
14. Judy Brennan "Just What the Doctor Ordered." *Los Angeles Times*, January 15, 1995, https://www.latimes.com/archives/la-xpm-1995-01-15-ca-20291-story.html.
15. EW Staff, "Inside 'Outbreak' Fever," *Entertainment Weekly*, April 21, 1995, https://ew.com/article/1995/04/21/inside-outbreak-fever/; and for further discussion Brent Lang, "'Outbreak' Writers on How the Movie's Deadly Illness Compares to the Coronavirus Pandemic," *Variety*, April 15, 2020, https://variety.com/2020/film/news/outbreak-writers-25-year-anniversary-coronavirus-covid-19-1234580608/.
16. Brennan "Just What the Doctor Ordered."
17. E! News, "'Outbreak' Sounds Like Coronavirus 25 Years Later: Rewind | E! News," https://www.youtube.com/watch?v=ga1yTAsXksk.
18. E! News, "'Outbreak' Sounds Like Coronavirus 25 Years Later: Rewind | E! News."
19. Duane Byrge, "'Outbreak': THR's 1995 Review," *The Hollywood Reporter*, March 10, 2020, originally published March 8, 1995, https://www.hollywoodreporter.com/news/general-news/outbreak-review-movie-1995-1281560/ called it "plausible." Janet Maslin, "The Hero Is Hoffman, The Villain a Virus," *The New York Times*, March 10, 1995, https://www.nytimes.com/1995/03/10/movies/film-review-the-hero-is-hoffman-the-villain-a-virus.html called it overheated, unrealistic and shallow. As late as 2003, scientists still cited it as one of the more realistic movies: Georgios Pappas et al., "Infectious Diseases in Cinema: Virus Hunters and Killer Microbes," *Clinical Infectious Diseases* 37, no. 7 (2003): 939–42.
20. Maslin, "The Hero Is Hoffman, The Villain a Virus."
21. Robby's words heavily allude to *The Hot Zone*'s description of the effects of Ebola on "Charles Monet," see Preston, *The Hot Zone*, 17–24. For further discussion of *Outbreak*, Ostherr, *Cinematic Prophylaxis: Globalization and Contagion in the Discourse of World Health*, 175–191.
22. Ironically, the building of roads does contribute to the transmission of diseases from its animal reservoir to new human hosts, and the later movie *Contagion* (2011) would vindicate the witch doctor's belief, since environmental destruction leads to a "spill over" event from animals to humans in that film. See David W. Redding et al., "Impacts of Environmental and Socio-Economic Factors on Emergence and Epidemic Potential of Ebola in Africa," *Nature Communications* 10, no. 4531 (2019);

and David Quammen, *Spillover: Animal Infections and the next Human Pandemic* (New York: W.W. Norton & Co., 2012).
23. Warner Brothers, an American corporation with a global reach, also used a similar approach to choose their filming site, the city of Ferndale (population: 1,450), which was recovering from a devastating earthquake in 1992. The damage convinced the town's residents to accept Warner Brothers' offer to film by pledging to pump $5 million into the local economy. The movie disrupted local life. One resident described the situation as "Helicopters. Tanks in the streets. It was like Budapest." While some felt under siege, other residents profited. A fruit merchant acknowledged "I made tons of money." Rob Haeseler, "Hollywood Invades Humboldt County / Ferndale Profits from 'Outbreak' Cash Infusion," *SFGATE*, April 17, 1995, https://www.sfgate.com/entertainment/article/Hollywood-Invades-Humboldt-County-Ferndale-3036529.php.
24. At the end of *Resident Evil: Apocalypse,* a nuclear bomb is dropped on Raccoon City to eliminate the T-virus, although this fails. See Chapter 5 for further discussion.
25. The US Department of Defense refused to collaborate with the production of the movie given its negative depiction of the military. Bernard Weinraub, "Wrestling a Virus to the Screen."
26. US Constitution, amendment V, provides, in relevant part: "No person shall be ... deprived of life, liberty, or property, without due process of law ..." Likewise, amendment XIV provides, in relevant part: "[N]or shall any state deprive any person of life, liberty, or property, without due process of law; nor deny to any person within its jurisdiction the equal protection of the laws."
27. Donnie's justification – "We are at war, Billy. Everybody is at war." – anticipates the unending American wars of the twenty-first century.
28. The infection of public health officials is a common theme. See Han and Curtis, *Infectious Inequalities,* 72–73.
29. Romantic comedies enjoyed a renaissance during the 1990s with the release of such films as *When Harry Met Sally* (1989), *Pretty Woman* (1990), *Sleepless in Seattle* (1993), *Groundhog Day* (1994) and *Four Weddings and a Funeral* (1994).
30. E! News, "'Outbreak' Sounds Like Coronavirus 25 Years Later: Rewind | E! News."
31. Screwball comedies, a subgenre of romantic comedies, became popular during the 1930s. *What's Up Doc?* was intended by its director, Peter Bogdanovich, to pay homage to the classic Howard Hawks screwball comedy *Bringing Up Baby* (1938). Gregg Kilday, "Peter Bogdanovich on Barbra Streisand: 'Funny, Cute and Kind of a Wiseass,'" *The Hollywood Reporter*, April 19, 2013, https://www.hollywoodreporter.com/news/peter-bogdanovich-barbra-streisand-funny-434860. In reality, residents of Ferndale had to drive sixteen miles to watch *Outbreak*. Haeseler, "Hollywood Invades Humboldt County."
32. Jeffrey Goines (Brad Pitt, an inmate in the asylum) observes that "We're consumers ... Buy a lot of stuff, you're a good citizen. But if you don't buy a lot of stuff, if you don't, what are you then, I ask you? What? Mentally ill." Dr. Peters (the terrorist) offers the link to ecocide, "Proliferation of atomic devices, uncontrolled breeding habits, pollution of land, sea and air, the rape of the environment. In this context, isn't it obvious that Chicken Little represents the same vision and that homosapiens' motto, 'Let's go shopping,' is the cry of the true lunatic?"

33. Ungar, "Hot Crises and Media Reassurance: A Comparison of Emerging Diseases and Ebola Zaire," compared with Sheldon Ungar, "Global Bird Flu Communication: Hot Crisis and Media Reassurance," *Science Communication* 29, no. 4 (2008): 472–97.
34. For example: a few dozen films in the 1980s and the early 1990s featured zombies, but they were neither popular nor influential. See Kyle W. Bishop, *How Zombies Conquered Popular Culture*. *Bio Zombie* (1998), *Wild Zero* (1999), *Junk* (2000) and *Versus* (2000) were among the later examples of low-budget zombie films. This later interest in zombies also spawned spin-offs into other media, such as the educational video game *The Typing of the Dead* (1999), where players were required to type words to kill zombies. Squakenet, "The Typing of the Dead Gameplay (PC Game, 2000)," February 12, 2015, https://www.youtube.com/watch?v=Zs3M6oDcPlU.
35. Non-American films often anticipate many ideas only later introduced in American films. See Robert Alpert, "AI at the Movies and the Second Coming," *Senses of Cinema* 88, October 2018, https://www.sensesofcinema.com/2018/feature-articles/ai-at-the-movies-and-the-second-coming/. Shot with a small budget and then lesser-known actors in the main roles, *28 Days Later* was initially released in the UK in November 2002. It was only later distributed more widely after a showing at the Sundance Film Festival and, even then, had a limited release in American theaters from June 2003. The scheduled showing of *28 Days Later* at the Sundance Film Festival seemed intended to underscore the film's dark story. The showing began at midnight and then finished at around 2 am – following which audience members rushed madly for the last buses of the night to their scattered lodgings, itself reminiscent of the film's sprinting zombies. Recollection of author R. A.
36. Although fast zombies, or at least running zombies had appeared in earlier films, such as *Life Force* (1985) and *Return of the Living Dead* (1985), these movies did not change the genre. For a take on fast zombies: Michael Newbury, "Fast Zombie/Slow Zombie: Food Writing, Horror Movies, and Agribusiness Apocalypse," *American Literary History* 24, no. 1 (2012): 87–114; also: Peter Dendle, "Zombie Movies and the 'Millennial Generation,'" in *Better off Dead: The Evolution of the Zombie as Post-Human*, ed. Deborah Christie and Sarah Juliet Lauro (New York: Fordham University Press, 2011), 175–86. Reviewers did not consider *28 Days Later* a pandemic movie when it first came out, although its director Danny Boyle mentioned in 2003 that he and others working on the movie had read Preston's 1994 book *The Hot Zone*. Slugan, "Pandemic (Movies)," 897, 906.
37. For a discussion of the movie in the context of 9/11, Anna Froula, "Prolepsis and the 'War on Terror': Zombie Pathology and the Culture of Fear in 28 Days Later . . .," in *Reframing 9/11: Film, Popular Culture and the "War on Terror,"* eds. Jeff Berkenstein, Anna Froula and Karen Randell (New York: Continuum 2010), 195–208.
38. They were actually based on a disaster in China. Schweitzer, *Going Viral*, 23. For similar comparisons in the movie, see: the scene in the church where Jim sees piles of corpses is based on the Rwandan genocide; the scene in the diner where Jim notices a dead mother clutching her dead baby parallels a photo from Saddam Hussein's gassing of Iraq's Kurdish populations; and the scene where Jim is led to his execution referenced a photo from Bosnia. See Kim Newman. "The Diseased

World," *Filmmaker Magazine*, Summer 2003, https://www.filmmakermagazine.com/archives/issues/summer2003/features/diseased_world.html.
39. A graphic novel published in 2007 to bridge the gap between *28 Days Later* and its sequel, *28 Weeks Later*, clarified that the Rage virus was designed to follow Ebola. See Steve Niles, *28 Days Later: The Aftermath* (New York: Dey Street Books, 2007). Of course, neither the representation of the disease nor these themes were wholly original with *28 Days Later*, since they had featured in earlier films. The writer of *28 Days Later*, Alex Garland, admitted this, remarking, "You could say, 'Look, he's [Garland] ripped that off Day of the Triffids, and that off of Dawn of the Dead,' and I accept that and say, 'Sure I did,'" Newman, "The Diseased World." For women as spreaders of disease, Han and Curtis, *Infectious Inequalities*, 85–106 (with a brief discussion of *28 Days Later* on p. 93).
40. The film's director, Danny Boyle, does not consider *28 Days Later* a zombie movie. Richard Newby, "How '28 Days Later' Changed the Horror Genre," *The Hollywood Reporter*, June 29, 2018, https://www.hollywoodreporter.com/heat-vision/have-get-a-quiet-place-killed-zombie-genre-1121491. On the UK-US connections, Lindsey Decker, "Transatlantic Genre Hybridity in Danny Boyle's *28 Days Later*," *Horror Studies* 7, no. 1 (2016): 95–110.
41. For a broader picture of this process in zombie media, Kathryn A. Cady and Thomas Oates, "Family Splatters: Rescuing Heteronormativity from the Zombie Apocalypse," *Women's Studies in Communication* 39, no. 3 (2016): 308–25. For a discussion of Selena, Barbara Korte, "Envisioning a Black Tomorrow? Black Mother Figures and the Issue of Representation in *28 Days Later* (2003) and *Children of Men* (2006)," in *Multi-Ethnic Britain 2000+*, eds. Lars Eckstein et al. (Leiden: Brill, 2008), 315–25; also: G. Christopher Williams, "Birthing an Undead Family: Reification of the Mother's Role in the Gothic Landscape of 28 Days Later," *Gothic Studies* 9, no. 2 (2007): 33–44.
42. See the discussion in Karl Martin, "The Failure of a Pseudo-Christian Community in a Nation-State in Crisis: *28 Days Later*," *Journal of Religion & Film* 18, no. 2 (2014), Article 6.
43. For other views on this family process, Sarah Trimble, "(White) Rage: Affect, Neoliberalism, and the Family in *28 Days Later* and *28 Weeks Later*," *Review of Education, Pedagogy, and Cultural Studies* 32, no. 3 (2010): 295–322; Karl Martin, "The Failure of a Pseudo-Christian Community;" and Nick Muntean and Matthew Thomas Payne, "Attack of the Livid Dead: Recalibrating Terror in the Post-9/11 Zombie Film," in *The War on Terror and American Popular Culture: September 11 and Beyond*, eds. Andrew Schopp and Matthew B. Hill (Madison, NJ: Fairleigh Dickinson University Press, 2009), 239–58.
44. Trimble, "(White) Rage: Affect, Neoliberalism, and the Family in *28 Days Later* and *28 Weeks Later*," 305. Korte, "Envisioning a Black Tomorrow?" 319, sees the black soldier as just like the white soldiers.
45. For a more positive view of female agency, especially Selena, Korte "Envisioning a Black Tomorrow?"
46. Commentary by Danny Boyle and Alex Garland, "Alternative Theatrical Ending."
47. While the entire movie was shot on digital video, the ending was shot on 35 mm film, providing "superior sharpness, much finer grain and wider range of contrast,"

offering the visual equivalent to waking up from a nightmare. See Steve Biodrowski, "Retro Review: 15th Anniversary Screening of 28 Days Later w/John Murphy," *Hollywood Gothique*, December 2, 2017, http://new.hollywoodgothique.com/retro-review-15th-anniversary-screening-28-days-later-w-john-murphy/. And, in more detail on these aspects of the film, Rüdiger Heinze and Jochen Petzold, "No More Room in Hell: Utopian Moments in the Dystopia of 28 Days Later," *Zeitschrift für Anglistik und Amerikanistik 55*, no. 1 (2007): 53–68.
48. Toronto International Film Festival, "George A. Romero Interview" (Toronto, November 2, 2012), https://www.youtube.com/watch?v=uCpJKakWVRc.
49. Toronto International Film Festival, "George A. Romero Interview."
50. The later released director's cut DVD version discussed in this section is about nine minutes longer than the theatrically released version. Most of the additions consist of more gore. Some, however, expand upon characters and in the case of one character, the security guard CJ, the director's cut softens his character to justify his eventual self-sacrifice. See "Dawn of the Dead (Comparison: Theatrical Version and Director's Cut)", *Movie-Censorship.com*, https://www.movie-censorship.com/report.php?ID=1988.
51. Humans killed by humans: Michael (suicide), Andre (shot by Norma), Luda (shot by Norma), their baby (shot by Ana), Norma (shot by Andre), Glen (bus accident), Monica (chainsawed by Glen), Frank (killed by Michael before turning) and Tucker (shot by CJ). Humans killed by zombies: Bart, Andy (killed by zombies that follow Nicole's dog), Steve (bitten by a zombie and transformed off-screen) and CJ (fighting zombies).
52. Notably, the Muslim-themed introductory footage was not part of the original script. James Gunn and Michael Tolkin, "Dawn of the Dead (Screenplay)", April 24, 2003, http://www.horrorlair.com/movies/scripts/dawnofthedead_2004.pdf.
53. He also says his best job was being a dad but never expands on that.
54. While Bart exhibits sexual bravado and is demeaning in his treatment of Ana, ironically he and CJ are undressing and literally going to bed together. See Kevin J. Wetmore Jr., *Back from the Dead: Remakes of the Romero Zombie Films as Markers of Their Times* (Jefferson: McFarland, 2011), 150–1.
55. The race of several characters changed from script to movie. Andre's character was originally named Randall and there is no indication that he was black. Ana's character changed from Latina to ostensibly white between the scripts of April and August 2003. Compare James Gunn and Michael Tolkin, "Dawn of the Dead (Screenplay)" from April with: James Gunn, Michael Tolkin and Scott Frank, "Dawn of the Dead (Screenplay)," August 19, 2003, https://www.scriptslug.com/assets/scripts/dawn-of-the-dead-2004.pdf.
56. Lynteris, *Human Extinction*, 5.
57. The full quote is: "I think that in the end, Dawn of the Dead is about redemption because it's about a bunch of people who have lived certain lives, who have maybe not been the best people, and suddenly they have everything that they've used to define themselves: Their careers, their churches, their jobs, their families are stripped away. They're gone. They start at nothing and they have to become who they really are in the face of all that and some of the people are redeemed and end up becoming good people and some of them are not redeemed and they end

up, you know, not redeemed. And that's what kind of drove me throughout the story, was it was a story about redemption. Jeff Otto, "An Interview with Writer James Gunn," *IGN*, March 26, 2004 (updated May 21, 2012), https://www.ign.com/articles/2004/03/26/an-interview-with-writer-james-gunn?page=1.

58. The end credits scenes were not scripted and do not appear in the screenplays of April or August 2003, see James Gunn and Michael Tolkin, "*Dawn of the Dead* (Screenplay)"; James Gunn, Michael Tolkin, and Scott Frank, "*Dawn of the Dead* (Screenplay)."

59. Unsurprisingly, George Romero reacted poorly to the remake. According to Romero "It was a good action film . . . but it sort of lost its reason for being. It was more of a video game. I'm not terrified of things running at me; it's like Space Invaders. There was nothing going on underneath." Ben Walter, "Simon Pegg Interviews George A. Romero," *The Tomb, Time Out Movie Blog*, September 8, 2005, https://web.archive.org/web/20070217113705/http://www.timeout.com:80/film/news/631.html.

60. *I Am Legend* links contemporary capitalism as the source of the virus. Prior to the TV station's interview with the scientist who claims to have cured cancer and presumably makes millions as a result of her research, it broadcasts a lengthy news report on the free agent signings of ballplayers and the upcoming World Series. The link is clear. Like those signing baseball contracts, biotechnology companies and their celebrated scientists reap enormous financial rewards at the public expense.

61. See Brian Michael Goss, "Unmasking the Monster(s) in *28 Weeks Later*," *Film International* 15, no. 2 (2017): 99–113. The Trojan horse theme, a minor plot point in the original, is repeated five times in the sequel. They are: (1) the survivors at the beginning of the movie bring the child into their hideout; (2) Don brings his children to London; (3) the children and Alice are brought back to the safe zone; (4) Don visits Alice in her quarantine; and (5) the children are evacuated to Europe at the end of the movie.

62. For a discussion of imperialism in the original movie, see Froula, "Prolepsis and the 'War on Terror.'"

63. For films of the Bush presidency, see Douglas Kellner, *Cinema Wars: Hollywood Film and Politics in the Bush-Cheney Era* (Malden: Wiley-Blackwell, 2010); and for a brief discussion of the reasons behind these films, Richard Beck, "Talking Point: Inanimate Fact and Iraq War Experience," *Film Quarterly* 62, no. 1 (2008): 8–9.

64. A partial list of other parallels: the US as a foreign occupier, Don as a corrupt contractor, Alice as a torture victim recalling the brutal treatment of Iraqis at Abu Ghraib prison and rooftop snipers.

65. *28 Weeks Later* failed to attract the same attention as *28 Days Later*, particularly in the US. While both films had similar international sales ($39.6 million for *Days* vs. $36.4 million for *Weeks*), American audiences did not watch *Weeks* in theaters as often (*Days* $45 million vs. *Weeks* $28.6 million). "28 Days Later," *Box Office Mojo*, https://www.boxofficemojo.com/title/tt0289043/ vs. "28 Weeks Later," *Box Office Mojo*, https://www.boxofficemojo.com/title/tt0463854/. Other mid-2000s films that depicted the war in the Middle East moved away from a critical stance towards it, presenting either a glorification of war, as in *The Kingdom* (2007) and *300* (2006), or a mixed understanding, as in *Jarhead* (2005) and *The Hurt Locker* (2008).

CHAPTER 3

POST-APOCALYPTIC DISEASE MOVIES: PANDEMICS AND POSTHUMANITY

INTRODUCTION

In 2007 alone, studio-released disease movies included *The Invasion*, *Rec*, *28 Weeks Later*, *I Am Legend* and *Resident Evil: Extinction*, all of which focused on the possibility of humanity's extinction. While they may have differed in their approach, including the specific pathogen and its impact, almost all had post-apocalyptic stories, and many depicted the undead or zombies as threatening humanity and forcing the few uninfected humans to create new social strategies to survive.[1] If non-American movies offered similar stories, their disease narratives occasionally reflected local, social critiques on the effects of the absorption by the American, global empire of their values. The Canadian-produced *Pontypool* (2008) portrayed the English language itself as infectious, forcing characters to use French to communicate safely. *Blood Quantum* (2019), also Canadian, featured indigenous people as immune to a disease that turns their white, colonialist neighbors into zombies. The Korean-produced *Train to Busan* (2016) depicted an indiscriminate infection that turns masses of people into zombies, while critiquing capitalism that has permeated Korean society. As the release of disease movies accelerated, comedies appeared to mock the genre, including *Zombieland* (2009) and its sequel *Zombieland: Double Tap* (2019) or the Japanese, independently produced *One Cut of the Dead* (2017) and its French remake, *Final Cut* (2022), along with the idiosyncratic *The Dead Don't Die* (2019).[2]

These movies share certain broad characteristics even if they differ in their details. Where the disease movies of the 1990s and early 2000s still focused upon efforts to contain and find cures for diseases, the new wave of films accepts catastrophic disease as a given and instead focuses upon reactions to these pandemics. The globalized pandemic in the real world represents a ubiquitous, constant threat, and attempts to discover why these pandemics happen or to mitigate them largely disappear.[3] Movies became more pessimistic about American society. Each individual faces the threat of disease alone as the state and its institutions fail in efforts to contain or cure the pathogen. Social norms and cohesion during these moments of crisis were rarely remarked upon, since no one on screen believed in them anymore. If a film did not end apocalyptically, then only individuals acting heroically, against all odds and outside stifling incompetent government bureaucracies prevented the End Times. More often, however, an increasingly common solution to a pandemic was, like the biblical flood, the annihilation of all existing institutions, communities and societies and the reinvention of the species through technology into some form of posthumanity. *Resident Evil: The Final Chapter* (2016) explicitly perceives the pandemic itself as offering a means to such a solution. Yet, the depiction of the posthuman species in these movies simply replicates and reinforces American global capitalism of the early twenty-first century, including the privileged role of its elite. These apocalyptic-focused disease films endorsed and furthered the values of a world in which supposed equality masked the sharp divide between owners and workers of the American model gone global. Movies have become so intertwined with that model that their producers cannot imagine, even in the context of a cinematic fantasy, a future that might differ in its perspective.

This chapter surveys this shift in movies through an exploration of two movies released the same year, *Contagion* (2011) and *The Rise of the Planet of the Apes* (2011). Both movies were successful commercially and depict an infectious disease that spirals out of control. *Contagion* is a drama that aims to depict realistically how a deadly pandemic could overwhelm global institutions and cause the collapse of American society, focusing on how a few individuals successfully negotiate these unprecedented challenges. Scientists praised it as an accurate depiction of a twenty-first century pandemic, and it would receive massive attention again with the outbreak of COVID in early 2020. Notably, the eventual defeat of the pandemic – through a rapidly developed vaccine – seems both fortuitous and only temporary. *The Rise of the Planet of the Apes*, a science fiction action movie, has a darker message.[4] A biotech company develops a potential cure for Alzheimer's, but the drug's use on apes unexpectedly enhances their intelligence. The inadvertent release of the drug then results in a deadly pandemic that kills most of the world's human population. Two sequels, *Dawn of the Planet of the Apes* (2014) and *War for the Planet of the Apes* (2017), expanded upon this depiction of the future extinction of the human species as well as the apes' search for their promised land and their development of a new society. Both movies reveal the continued decay of the social fabric of contemporary America and the pervasive failure of its institutions. But both movies also embrace American capitalist ideals, even as they expose its failings. The apes' new world, as depicted in the two sequels, reimagines American capitalism for apes.

This chapter also briefly touches upon several additional movies. It opens with a discussion of two films that portray future and past pandemics, respectively, *Children of Men* (2006) and *Black Death* (2010). *Children of Men* is a grim film which maintains some hope, and *Black Death* is a dark, mainstream film that sharply contrasts with the decades earlier *Seventh Seal*. Both films comment from a religious perspective on the assumed failure of state institutions and the collapse of society. This chapter also discusses two zombie films, the action movie *World War Z* and the satirical comedy *Zombieland*. Both depict a global, zombie pandemic of unknown origin and nostalgically advocate for the return of the patriarchal hero even as they acknowledge that this myth of the macho male offers at best a temporary solution in early twenty-first century America.

Spiritual Faith in the Twenty-First Century: *Children of Men* (2006) and *Black Death* (2010)

It is hardly surprising that disease movies might return their focus to religion and faith as a counter to the material secularism of an enveloping, global capitalism. *Children of Men* and *Black Death*, as non-American movies, raised questions about science and reason in the context of non-curable, non-containable diseases and searched for a religious or spiritual faith which might offer humanity an alternative to contemporary capitalism. If secular capitalism had led humanity astray, then the sacred might offer a new path. The path to faith consisted not of organized religion but instead a search for individual faith, portrayed as a way to potential salvation. *Children of Men* envisioned a future in which a global infertility pandemic has brought the human species to imminent, future extinction. Science might make life in the present better for the wealthy, but it fails to address the real threat humanity is facing. *Black Death* looks to the medieval past of the Black Death as the historical moment in which science in the form of new technology worsened human civilization. If *Children of Men* is the more optimistic of the two in positing that faith offers a path to salvation, both movies conclude that social institutions have failed and view with skepticism the ability of humans to cure these diseases on their own.

Like the earlier outlier *12 Monkeys*, *Children of Men* focuses on the near extinction of the human species. Set in 2027, the film tells of an unexplained, worldwide pandemic of human infertility. The protagonist Theo (derived from the word "god" in Greek) is a flawed, disillusioned character who gradually becomes more active in trying to improve the world, even as the film exposes post-pandemic society's spiritual and social decay. Recruited by his ex-wife,

Theo shields the miraculously pregnant refugee, Kee, against the state and its dissidents and delivers her to a mysterious ship manned by scientists trying to cure the pandemic. Theo transforms during the film from a bureaucratic drone to a Christ-like figure offering salvation to the world. The film's dark setting is relieved only by fleeting interactions between unrelated, often dissimilar individuals, such as Jasper, Theo's best friend and a disillusioned, former political activist turned drug dealer, and Miriam, the spiritual yet uneducated midwife accompanying Kee.

Children of Men critiques secular capitalism and offers through individual acts, not social institutions, a path to humanity's renewal and rebirth. It depicts the failure of the democratic social contract and its replacement with an authoritarian police state that coerces its subjects in all aspects of life and in which science assists the state in controlling its subjects rather than curing the disease. Military force and propaganda control and pacify the population, including an increasing number of refugees trying to escape the even more chaotic world outside the United Kingdom. Local residents are urged to report these refugees, and sheltering them is a serious crime. The military routinely transports refugees in caged vehicles before torturing and killing them, and the "refugee detention camp" through which Theo briefly passes is a *de facto* concentration camp.[5] The state has dispensed with all pretense of buy-in from civil society and exists to exert power to maintain the current elite.

Science, which had featured as a solution in films from the mid-twentieth century and even through the 1990s, offers no hope. To the contrary, a newspaper article suggests that a supposed drug to cure the pandemic had instead killed those who took it, and yet another article alludes to the death of "Test Tube Daisy," a failed scientific solution to infertility. To control its population in this dystopian future, the state harnesses science for its own corporate ends by marketing drugs such as Niagra (a male erectile dysfunction pill) and Bliss (an anti-depressant). Ads for another drug, Quietus, a freely distributed suicide drug, are promoted everywhere with the slogan "You Decide When." If this slogan fails to persuade sufficient numbers of people to end their lives, then the state offers three additional incentives: "Up to £2,000 to your next of kin," "Painless transition [death] guaranteed," and "Illegals [refugees] welcome." While the state offers suicide for the masses, it encourages the wealthy in the meantime to enjoy themselves through abundant consumerism, organ transplants, plastic surgery and cytogenesis. Each individual is alone, and the wealthier simply benefit more in this authoritarian, capitalistic sinking Titanic.

Agnostic spiritual faith offers the only hope. New religious groups, such as the Renouncers, who flog themselves, or the Repenters, who kneel for a month at a time, as well as other religious groups that declare that "Infertility is Gods! [sic] punishment!" are presented as hollow solutions.[6] The film views instead reborn spiritual faith, not symbolic rituals, as the source for

Figure 3.1 *Children of Men* (2006): Theo sacrifices himself so that Kee and her miraculously born baby, whom she holds in her arms, might live.

redemption, and the film's title, *Children of Men*, underscores that view.[7] Only individual actions, including martyrdom combined with faith, offer hope for salvation. Thus, several characters sacrifice themselves to protect Kee and her baby. Jasper stalls a terrorist group and is then tortured and killed for doing so. The midwife Miriam feigns mania to draw attention away from Kee and is then taken off a bus and presumably tortured.[8] The movie's plot follows Theo's own journey as one of self-sacrifice, an unexceptional act that offers hope for the future. Kee's pregnancy, which is never explained, represents a divine miracle, and Theo's sacrificial death at the end of the film reflects a belief in redemption. Kee's new baby offers the human species the possibility of renewal, which is underscored by the laughter of children playing as the credits roll. That Kee is poor, uneducated and black highlights how humanity's salvation lies among the multi-cultural, destitute classes, not the white elite. The film offers a romantic, alternative path for humanity, but its message of inclusion and diversity to build a better future was an outlier not followed by other wide-release films.

Most films rejected even minimal optimism. *Black Death*, a 2010 British-German production, is typical. It depicts the quintessential historical outbreak in 1348 CE, the second plague pandemic (popularly known as the Black Death). The film tells of a knight, Ulric, sent by his bishop to capture a necromancer, Langiva, whose village has not suffered from the plague. It also focuses on Osmond, a young monk whom Ulric enlists as a local guide and who is conflicted as a result of violating his monastic vows of celibacy through a relationship with a young woman, Averill. The film ends with Ulric deliberately infecting the village and the death of most villagers and soldiers. Ulric's only surviving soldier, Wolfstan, drags off the village elder to present him as the necromancer. Osmund, after mistakenly killing Averill and barely surviving his adventure, embarks on a lifelong crusade to kill Langiva who has escaped. Institutionalized religious faith is depicted as inextricably intertwined with human social institutions and its inevitable failure.

Society from the film's perspective is incapable of offering solace. Where *Children of Men* had offered hope of redemption through faith and self-sacrifice, *Black Death* critiques the failure of religious and secular beliefs, decries human actions as the cause of earthly suffering, and views human nature as self-destructive. The social contract, whatever its institutional embodiment, is doomed to failure. Tellingly, *Black Death* evokes the narrative of and repeats scenes from *The Seventh Seal* (1957) but reverses their meaning. Both films feature a knight on a journey with a group of followers, depict the church as claiming that the plague is God's punishment for human sin, and include numerous comparable scenes, such as a procession of flagellants.[9] *Black Death*, however, rejects the idea of redemption and revels in body counts, gore and emotional conflict. In contrast to a similar scene in *The Seventh Seal* in which the knight offers herbs to lessen the suffering of the woman whom soldiers intend to burn at the stake, Ulric kills a woman whom he intervenes to save from the villagers and assures the others in his group that the villagers would have killed her later anyway. The film is an endless series of horrors. When Ulric is about to be quartered by the villagers, he reveals his plague infection and then revels in his power to infect them, too, as a manifestation of God's wrath. The monk Osmund is eventually transformed into an inquisitor who tortures and burns countless women whom he sees as the village necromancer Langiva. The film likewise critiques Langiva. While she observes that the church has engaged in "thirteen centuries of control and intimidation" and substitutes secular love for the church's advocacy of divine love, she merely replaces the church's theocratic order with her own. Her village followers, who initially appear as an idyllic community, torture and kill Ulric and his soldiers, no different from what the soldiers want to do. Humans require miracles, magic and myths to make sense of their world, Langiva tells Osmund, and she maintains her hold over the village by exploiting that need. All human institutions, the film argues, deceive and result in the torment and death of their followers.

Wolfstan represents the film's moral center with his message of moderation to ensure at least some modicum of human survival amid the wreckage of the world. His viewpoint is reflected in his final voiceover as he surveys alone the carnage of both villagers and soldiers: "There is nothing beautiful or uplifting in returning people to God. There is no place in heaven for those who kill. The pestilence claimed no higher purpose." While the most level-headed observer in the movie, he perceives only the darkest of futures for humankind. He recounts early in the film how the English first used longbows in battle, a technological advancement, to defeat a larger French army, littering the field with the dead. That day, in Wolfstan's telling, marked the end of chivalry and by extension civilized society and its norms. King Edward ordered his army to slaughter any surviving French so that "god's greatest army descended into savagery," thereby inviting death, in the form of the plague, among them. Wolfstan's tale demonstrates how even his own moderation is at odds with human purposes. *Black Death* offers no hope of social cohesion other than that which is based on false miracles, magic and myths. There is no transcendence, whether religious, as in *Children of Men*, or secular, as in *The Seventh Seal*. Civilized society has failed to offer salvation, and a global pandemic represents the logical result of any such society unable to offer an alternative path.

Individual Choice in a Fractured Society: Contagion (2011)

No movie better underscores the changes to disease movies than Steven Soderbergh's *Contagion* (2011), a supposedly realistic depiction of a global pandemic. Soderbergh, who had directed independent features, such as *Sex, Lies, and Videotape* (1989) and *The Girlfriend Experience* (2009), as well as commercial projects, such as *Erin Brockovich* (2000) and the three *Ocean* movies (2001, 2004, 2007), is known for his liberal critiques of capitalism. *Contagion* is a return to the big-budgeted, realistic disaster movie with an ensemble of famous actors, like *Virus* from thirty years earlier. Its global pandemic kills tens of millions in a few weeks, and while it does not end as pessimistically as *Virus*, with the virtual extinction of humankind, its defeat of the virus is temporary. Scientists develop a vaccine to counteract the MEV-1 virus, but the film foresees similar pandemics in the near future. *Contagion* in the meantime depicts society's rapid disintegration from the MEV-1 virus, forcing individuals to act on their own, including taking steps to protect their families. Although institutions, international organizations and governments do not disappear, *Contagion* argues that fortuitous, individual, heroic action – in contrast to bureaucratic paralysis – results in the finding of a vaccine. Individual choice and chance, not social norms and values, reduce the impact of the disease. While global capitalism facilitates the successful development, production and distribution of a vaccine, the film's final scene blames this same capitalism for the pandemic through its exploitation and destruction of the environment. Humanity may have avoided one Judgment Day through individual heroism, a few conscientious institutional actors and good luck, but the film's ending makes clear that judgment has merely been postponed. *Contagion*'s endorsement of heroic individualism as the solution to the pandemic underscores that, notwithstanding its explicit critique of a capitalist culture, the movie can only offer a capitalist solution of individual heroics in the face of collective, structural failures.

In contrast to most disease movies that identified the source of the disease early in the movie, *Contagion* does so only in its final scene, as part of the film's reveal that the outbreak was the result of a random series of events. *Contagion*'s influenza-like disease, MEV-1, originates in southeast Asia where it infects what the film identifies as "patient zero," Beth Emhoff (Gwyneth Paltrow), who is on a business trip for a global company identified only as AIMM Alderson.[10] While gambling, eating and drinking at a Hong Kong casino, she becomes infected (by shaking the hand of a chef who had handled an infected pig) and then soon begins infecting others. Both the nature of Beth's work and the scenes of her mingling with other international travelers at the casino and elsewhere highlight the pervasiveness of global capitalism and its role as the underlying cause of the pandemic. After flying back home to the United States, she has an affair during a Chicago layover with a former lover, whom she infects, and then arrives home to her husband and family in Minneapolis, where she infects her son. The disease quickly spreads to other countries, including mainland China, Japan and England, as a result of people whom Beth had met at the casino or at the airport.

The film then depicts the frantic efforts to find the origin of the disease and develop a vaccine through several, loosely connected plotlines that often demonstrate an obsessive concern for scientific "accuracy" and "realism."[11] It focuses, in particular, on three American families as a way not only to highlight the individual effects of the disease but also to reveal the increasing social disintegration resulting from the pandemic. These families represent how Americans experience daily, pandemic life against a disrupted and collapsing social fabric. If *Contagion* reveals the flaws of all three families, it ultimately endorses the importance of familial bonds as the only ones that endure amidst a growing social disintegration.

The first family consists of Beth and Mitch Emhoff (Matt Damon), both of whom have a child from a former marriage but who have created a new family that includes all four members. The pandemic serves as a source of punishment for Beth's social transgressions at the beginning of the film – drinking and gambling at a Hong Kong casino as well as an extra-marital affair. She dies, followed by her son, as a biblical punishment for her sins.[12] The innocent Mitch is immune to the disease. After expressing shocked disbelief at the sudden, unexplained deaths of Beth and her son, he spends most of the film trying to protect his natural, teenage daughter, Jory, from the virus and the growing chaos, including looting and violence. Not surprisingly, the pandemic strains the father-daughter relationship. Mitch must separate Jory physically from her boyfriend both to protect her from the virus and to maintain her chastity as a counterweight to Beth's adultery. If Beth's adultery is punished by death, including the death of her lover, Mitch's protection of Jory's virginity, which conforms to conservative social norms, ensures her survival.[13] Underscoring this binary morality, the film's happiest moment is when Jory celebrates the development of a vaccine by dancing at home with her boyfriend at a makeshift, romantic prom that Mitch has arranged. The individual choice to sin or not determines whether this family's members die or live.

The second family consists of Dr. Ellis Cheever (Laurence Fishburne) of the CDC and his fiancé, later wife, Aubrey. Cheever uses his position at the CDC to favor his family, a violation of his ethical duty and contrary to CDC policy, by warning Aubrey to leave Chicago just prior to a military quarantine imposed on the city. Yet, the movie portrays Cheever sympathetically. He appears in a number of scenes as hard-working and friendly. Moreover, audience empathy with his actions is underscored when those actions are publicized in a national broadcast by the corrupt blogger Alan Krumwiede (Jude Law) and the head of Homeland Security informs Cheever that he will become the scapegoat for the government's inadequate response to the pandemic. Cheever represents the government bureaucracy's failure to solve the crisis and is then blamed by his politically appointed superiors for that failure. Yet, despite his supposed professional humiliation, Cheever claims that he would repeat his favoritism and, in fact, he later abruptly marries Aubrey so that she might receive an early vaccine due to her new marital status. Cheever's attitude is normalized as reflected in his admission when he administers the vaccine to Aubrey, "Like you said, baby. Just taking care of everybody that's in my lifeboat."[14]

The audience in the meantime continues to identify with Cheever, since the movie advocates for protecting one's family as the key goal in an uncaring, institutional world. This, of course, contrasts with early movies, such as *Panic in the Streets*. Dr. Reed, that movie's hero, shares information about the disease with his wife Nancy, but neither of them considers leaving New Orleans, whereas the mayor's assistant, whom the movie condemns, rushes to send his family to safety outside of the city. These earlier norms of the social contract have given way to a fragmentation in which individuals and their families are ranked according to an implicit social ladder of class and wealth. Individualism by good elites, such as Cheever, is no longer a problematic social characteristic, except by superiors shirking their responsibility, since everyone is expected to indulge in this practice. Social fragmentation prioritizes the individual clawing for the personal safety and comfort of "my lifeboat."

The movie simultaneously depicts how individuals who respect the social contract by seeking to protect society and advance the interests of the common good are easily tossed aside. Self-sacrifice for this common good is not rewarded. Cheever sends the family-less Dr. Erin Mears (Kate Winslet), a mid-level CDC official, to Minnesota to investigate the initial outbreak. She identifies Beth Emhoff as the source of the disease and sets up triage facilities in a stadium for the growing numbers of sick and dying, but soon contracts the virus. The saintly Mears takes care to track and warn those with whom she had come into contact and later as she lies dying offers her blanket to the sick man lying next to her. The state for which she works, however, abandons her. Cheever is unable to evacuate her, since the plane that might have flown her home is commandeered by a local politician looking out for themself. Mears dies from the disease, her heroic, altruistic efforts are quickly forgotten, she is buried in an unmarked, mass grave, and she is mourned only momentarily by a recent acquaintance. She is the 2011 version of Dr. Reed or Sam Daniels, but this time her altruism leads to her own death.

The film's third family consists of Dr. Ally Hextall (Jennifer Ehle), a CDC scientist who reports to Cheever, and her father who is a physician treating infected patients. Hextall acts outside the CDC chain of command to develop a vaccine. She initially works with an academic researcher who grows the virus in his lab against CDC protocols and soon injects herself with an experimental vaccine that she has developed. Hextall then visits her father who has been hospitalized from the virus as a result of devoting himself to his patients. When he protests that she cannot risk exposing herself to the virus, she reminds him that he is sick because he took the same risk when he continued treating his patients after everyone else had gone home. When her father then observes that she may win the Nobel Prize for her actions, she replies by kissing him on the forehead. Her motivation is familial. She is a dutiful daughter following in the footsteps of her role model father. If Hextall's actions are reckless, the film judges her testing of the vaccine on herself as morally correct.[15] Her individual choice has succeeded where the state failed, and she is the model of correct behavior.

The film also acknowledges, however, that faceless institutions can undermine the success of individuals and their families. The subplot about a Chinese official, Sun Feng (Chin Han), who resorts to kidnapping World Health Organization (WHO) scientist Dr. Leonora Orantes (Marion Cotillard) during her investigations of MEV-1's origins in Hong Kong, exemplifies this stark, unpleasant reality. Feng's extreme behavior is motivated by his hope at saving the survivors of his village. Like the American Cheever, the Chinese Feng transgresses institutional norms to save those closest to him, insisting that he will release Orantes when his village has received the vaccine that is in short supply. Individual need justifies inappropriate behavior. Orantes over the course of her kidnapping, however, finds herself identifying with this community, especially the young children whom she teaches, and Feng's motives, once sinister, increasingly appear similar to Cheever's. Feng eventually releases Orantes in response to the delivery of vaccines by the Chinese government and a WHO official's assurance that the vaccine "is effective. I promise." Yet, the same official soon reveals to Orantes that the vaccines are only placebos to discourage future kidnappings. When Orantes rushes back to inform the villagers of this deception, the film leaves no doubt that it favors this local community over institutional behavior and that communities, too, must act on their own if they are to survive. Everyone is on their own.

The blogger Krumwiede represents the film's conflicted view of the tension between individual action and social norms. Krumwiede is the obvious antagonist of the film, and his choices contrast with the altruistic behavior of others. Personal profit, not protecting family, motivates him. Thus, while he correctly identifies an early outbreak of MEV-1 in China, he uses his newfound fame to benefit financially. As his popularity surges, he falsely claims that forsythia, a homeopathic cure, is effective against MEV-1, even staging an online demonstration of his own supposed recovery after using forsythia. Millions then believe in forsythia as a cure and unruly mobs overwhelm pharmacies with their demands for this miraculous cure.[16] Yet, Krumwiede also darkly mirrors those whom the film admires insofar as he, too, adopts a go it alone attitude. He justifies his behavior by observing that he is not the first person to profit off a disaster but is simply gaming the capitalist system, pointing to the pharmaceutical industry (which surely profits off the development of the vaccine, albeit off screen) as a model for his behavior. Moreover, he is never punished for his selfish behavior. When he is at last arrested, his followers quickly put up the necessary bail for his release. Whereas Beth Emhoff dies, Cheever must appear before a Congressional committee, and Mears is buried in an unmarked grave, Krumwiede persists in his conspiratorial career.

Contagion's pessimism stems, in part, from its insistence upon its own realism, and MEV-1 reveals in this context the growing fragmentation of the American social contract as a result of the increasing importance placed upon individual behavior at the expense of the common good. While science can offer explanations about the disease's R0 factor, mortality and case fatality rates, it does not possess answers to the questions raised by the values of a twenty-first century world. It also can offer no comforting values of its own. When Mitch Emhoff learns of his wife's sudden death, for example, the hospital doctors are unable to provide him with any details or causal explanation other than vague medical jargon and an admonition to seek counseling. America quickly devolves into social chaos between Thanksgiving and Christmas, with the looting of supermarkets for food and supplies, the setting of fires in urban downtown areas and shootings in suburban homes. When the police can no longer respond, Mitch Emhoff breaks into a neighbor's abandoned home and arms himself with a weapon, which he will later brandish against his daughter's boyfriend. As basic government functions are increasingly disrupted, American society seems to turn Hobbesian, and each family is responsible for its own survival. Where earlier, big-budget disaster movies had often depicted its movie stars as rising to the challenge of the unexpected, *Contagion* shows an interconnected world in which the efforts of the individual often fail to overcome larger social constraints. For an audience expecting movie stars to play leading, heroic roles, the surprising early deaths of Gwyneth Paltrow and Kate Winslet reflect a cultural fatalism about the future direction of humankind.

Echoing *Contagion*'s appeal to a global audience, unrestrained multinational corporations cause the pandemic's Frankenstein-like creation and rapid spread worldwide. In the movie's ending, the audience learns that Beth Emhoff had travelled to Hong Kong for the groundbreaking ceremony of a new factory by her international employer. The ensuing environmental destruction dislodged a bat, which then dropped its food next to a pig on an industrial farm. The pig ate the now-contaminated food and is soon slaughtered and prepared as a meal by a chef with whom Beth shakes hands. As a result of this highly unusual series of interconnected events, the virus spreads to humans and quickly becomes global. The film's last image is of Beth and the chef posing together with the caption "Day 1." As the movie comes full circle to explain the origin of the pandemic, it underscores the inevitability of a future pandemic as non-fiction writers from the mid-1990s had suggested.[17]

Where, however, the pandemic in *Outbreak* resulted from capitalist expansion but was quickly contained, *Contagion* posits that future, random events will continue to lead to subsequent pandemics. As Hextall observes in describing the origin of MEV-1, "Somewhere in the world the wrong pig met up with the wrong bat." There is a randomness, too, to the spread of this disease. Beth contracts the disease after shaking hands with the chef. She then infects an anonymous, Ukrainian model who graciously returned the phone Beth had left behind. A Hong Kong waiter likewise contracts the disease, because he

Figure 3.2 *Contagion* (2011): Beth Emhoff and the Hong Kong chef pose together on Day 1.

has cleared away Beth's glass from the table. A local Minneapolis official later observes, if gratuitously, to Mears that Minneapolis is clearly unlucky, and within a matter of days, Mears' luck runs out. Even receiving the vaccine cure for the pandemic involves chance, since the government administers the vaccine by drawing balls at random from a container based on dates of birth. Although the human species survives the MEV-1 virus, *Contagion* says that we may not be so lucky next time. It depicts a global, capitalist culture in which science and its enlightened perspective are unable to contain the forces of nature, including the environment, over which the human species foolishly views itself as master. Society offers no safety against the inevitability of probabilities, and individuals are on their own in a dangerous world.

Patriarchal Zombie Pandemics: *Zombieland* (2009) and *World War Z* (2013)

Contagion's bleak story about a future pandemic is shown through a realistic lens. Zombie movies, too, such as *Zombieland* (2009), a comedy, and *World War Z* (2013), a superhero-like action movie, adopt this same, dark projection about the future, though unrestrained by the demands of realistic drama. Both movies assume that a virulent disease is inevitable and that the undead will overwhelm the living. If both are unconcerned about identifying the source of the deadly virus, they both project a future by looking backward to earlier, socially acceptable norms and values. Both movies re-affirm the authority of the white male. Their post-apocalyptic landscapes recreate an imagined past that will offer a more coherent future in a nostalgic context.

Zombieland (2009) dispenses with the pandemic's source and the search for a cure, but focuses instead on what comes next: reinventing the social order. *Zombieland*'s protagonist is a socially inept young man named "Columbus" who attempts to reach his parents' home in Columbus, Ohio, during a zombie apocalypse. When Columbus's car breaks down, he hitches a ride with a confident, older man named "Tallahassee," and the two, in turn, soon join two sisters, "Wichita" and "Little Rock." Following a series of misunderstandings and conflicts, Columbus and Tallahassee eventually rescue the sisters. Their final battle in an amusement park against hordes of zombies reaffirms the group's bonding together as well as fulfilling the men's individual desires: Columbus wins Wichita's affection and Tallahassee finds a Twinkie.

Zombieland parodies traditional zombie movies and relies upon deadpan humor to underscore its message. Columbus is introduced as the nerdy college student, a social misfit, who has spent all his time playing video games and only succeeds in even talking to his attractive hallway classmate when she is on the verge of becoming a zombie. He repeatedly discusses his newly developed survival rules, which comically pop up on the screen, as well comments on his "zombie kill of the week" award. Deaths, too, are depicted humorously, such as the unexpected death of Bill Murray, played by Bill Murray (and whom Columbus mistakes for a zombie when Murray demonstrates to Tallahassee how he has survived by passing as a zombie), the gratuitous killing of zombies throughout the film, and the slaughter of patrons of stripper zombies.

Yet, notwithstanding its deadpan sense of humor, *Zombieland* sentimentally offers the surrogate, patriarchal family as the favored response to this post-apocalyptic world. Tallahassee becomes the father to Columbus and Little Rock, while Columbus becomes the son that Tallahassee had lost. Columbus and Wichita are the adolescent couple from countless teen movies in which the naïve, socially inept man proves himself worthy of the more worldly, attractive woman. In the film's ending Columbus melodramatically overcomes his fear of zombie clowns and rescues Wichita, the woman of his dreams, who then kisses and discloses her real name to Columbus.[18] In contrast to Jim in *28 Days Later*, who returns to his parents' home and mourns their loss, Columbus cares little about his pre-apocalyptic, biological family. A rumor that Columbus, Ohio, may have been overrun is enough for him to abandon any effort at trying to reach his parents. As he remarks in a voiceover, "I'm not sure what's more tragic, that my family is gone, or the realization that I never really had much of a family to begin with." The apocalypse has freed Columbus from his social obligations and enabled him to find both family and true love. The film advocates for this newly transformed world, which it identifies as the "United States of Zombieland."

The values of this new social order are stereotypically juvenile, patriarchal and consumerist. Columbus summarizes the film's lesson in his new rule, 32: Enjoy the little things. These "little things" consist of material goods and adolescent antics, such as Tallahassee's search for Twinkies, driving expensive cars, shooting automatic weapons, engaging in mass killings of zombies, visiting a theme park, and squatting in Bill Murray's mansion while watching his films in a private screening room. Moreover, as Columbus comments, the best thing about the zombie apocalypse is that there are "no Facebook status updates."[19] Without exhibiting any self-awareness, *Zombieland* maintains that the surrogate family enables the adolescent male to enjoy the shared joys of fleeting but superficial antics. The world may end for reasons unknown but that is of little or no concern to Columbus, who wins the heart of the woman he desires. He gets to enjoy all the "little things" in life.

World War Z likewise adopts a standard solution for addressing a zombie apocalypse whose origin also remains unknown.[20] Although the search for the disease's origin drives the plot like in *Contagion*, *World War Z* appeals to the heroism of the white male savior to create a post-pandemic society. The film focuses on Gerry Lane, a former United Nations investigator who finds himself in the midst of a pandemic that turns humans into fast moving zombies in a matter of seconds.[21] These zombies swarm like insects and act like a hive mind trying to infect and transform all of humanity into an undifferentiated mass.[22] These zombies represent a direct threat to American individualism. Gerry and his family eventually find safety in an offshore fleet, and Gerry is tasked with accompanying a scientist along with an elite group of soldiers to investigate the outbreak's source. When the scientist accidentally kills himself, Gerry continues the investigation by traveling first to Israel and then Wales. He eventually finds a temporary solution by injecting himself with a deadly pathogen, which camouflages him from the zombies. The authorities then develop a vaccine, while Gerry is reunited with his family. *World War Z* is the story of the heroic American's triumph and the restoration of patriarchal hierarchies.

Like other movies in this chapter, *World War Z* focuses on family in the twenty-first century. It validates, however, Gerry as the patriarch of the nuclear family. The movie opens in the Lanes' suburban home in which Gerry, after ending his war zone forays, has become a stay-at-home dad who makes pancake breakfasts for his working wife Karin and their two daughters. Gender roles are reversed. Gerry's family will provide him during the course of the film not only with a motive for survival but also a means to demonstrate his masculinity and restore gender norms. When the family first encounters a zombie outbreak, for example, Gerry resumes his role as protector, asserts dominance over his family, and directs their escape while his wife fades into the background. Only men can be in charge. When Gerry later leaves his family on the offshore vessel, he instructs the young Tommy, his newly adopted Latino son, to "take care of the ladies." In contrast, his wife repeatedly places Gerry in danger, such as when her phone call arouses the zombies at the moment that he is trying to pass by silently. The film's portrayal of women's role is regressive even compared to Nancy Reed from the 1950s *Panic in the Streets*. If Nancy provided moral support and served as a social conscience to her husband, Karin is meek and incompetent. Gerry's family serves only to legitimize and encourage his actions as the prototypical male hero.[23]

Institutions and individuals other than Gerry consistently fail. The Israeli soldier who helps Gerry escape from the hordes of zombies who overrun the country is named only by her military rank, Segen (Hebrew for lieutenant), and Gerry later remedies her transgression of gender norms as a female action hero by chopping off her arm when she is bitten in a symbolic castration. The film critiques, too, science and its intellectuals, who are helpless to solve the pandemic. The genius Harvard professor joins Gerry's special mission, unexpectedly trips and fatally shoots himself upon landing at the Korean DMZ.[24] When zombies overrun a section of the WHO facility in Wales, the surviving scientists seal themselves off and do nothing. The state is equally ineffective. The American government is barely present. Moreover, local police officers utterly fail to contain the first outbreak in Philadelphia and soon afterwards stop even trying as, for example, when a police officer ignores the attack on

Gerry's wife. It falls to Gerry to protect her by quickly disposing of her attacker. The only states that successfully address the pandemic are either wholly coercive, such as North Korea (which removes the teeth of its twenty-three million citizens) or imaginative, such as Israel (which follows a "10th man" protocol later undercut by Palestinian crowds).[25]

In elevating the male warrior as reflective of a world in which each person must act alone to survive, *World War Z* offers a vision of twenty-first century American capitalism in which human value is measured solely as a function of the outcomes achieved. The United Nations, while framing its actions as serving the common good, threatens to remove Gerry's family from its offshore vessel unless he agrees to help discover the virus' origin. Surveying the mass of people onboard the ship, a United Nations representative articulates to Gerry that "everyone here serves a purpose." Idle members of society, categorized as such through unstated reasons by unknown authorities, will be removed. Human value corresponds to social utility. Gerry, the macho patriarch, is at the apex of those who serve a purpose, but even he must constantly demonstrate his value. When the United Nations loses communication with Gerry and mistakenly believes him dead, the ship's commanding officer promptly removes Gerry's family members from the ship and transports them to a less secure location on land.

The movie's message is pessimistic, beginning with the opening scenes in which contemporary America fails to contain the zombie apocalypse. The streets of Philadelphia are quickly overrun with chaotic violence, and a long-shot view discloses an urban devastation as a military voiceover observes that "containment failed." America must transform itself by returning to mid-century values. While Gerry fails at finding the origin of the virus, he succeeds in discovering on his own a vaccine that temporarily camouflages humans from the zombies. His solution is neither intellectual nor scientific. It is instead a male gendering of instinct in the face of randomness. His immediate reward, and his happiest moment, is the brief pleasure of loudly opening and then drinking a can of Pepsi from a bright blue soda machine as zombies part before him like the Red Sea before Moses. That Gerry's victory is celebrated by the most glaring corporate product placement in the movie highlights the corresponding conquest by an American, global brand. Gendering the disease and reinforcing the need for patriarchal control, the Harvard scientist had earlier confided to Gerry, "Mother Nature is a serial killer. No one's better or more creative . . . And she loves disguising her weaknesses as strengths. She's a bitch." It is up to the aggressive American male to tame and reestablish his control over this random, violent force through an equally violent, individual heroism. The alternative is human extinction. Ironically reflective of the sequel that was never made, the movie ends on Gerry's observation, "Our war has just begun."

Hope for a New Society: *Rise of the Planet of the Apes* (2011) and Its Sequels

Zombie pandemics in both *Zombieland* and *World War Z* advocated for a return to a patriarchal order and implicitly looked back to and argued for an industrial capitalism in which the few governed the many in a gendered hierarchy. *Rise of the Planet of the Apes* (2011) is set in the contemporary world of informational capitalism. American tech companies collect vast amounts of public and private information and use this information to convey a sense of material abundance by seemingly personalizing all human transactions while, in fact, exercising control through the offering of such choices and furthering their bottom line. [26] *Rise of the Planet of the Ape* envisions in this context a posthuman world with the creation of a newly enhanced, dominant species – intelligent apes that inherit the Earth from a corrupt humanity and offer the promise of a more just society. *Rise of the Planet of the Apes* was the first movie in a trilogy that included *Dawn of the Planet of the Apes* (2014) and *War for the Planet of the Apes* (2017), and it rebooted and sharply departed from the iconography of the original *Planet of the Apes* (1968–1973) movie franchise. Underlying the trilogy, however, is a pessimism about the transformation of the species and the evolutionary benefit of this posthuman society.

The original *Planet of the Apes* had depicted the rise of the apes as a result of humanity's self-destructiveness through an apocalyptic nuclear war. Its focus on nuclear war as opposed to the new trilogy's focus on disease reflects each period's assumptions about the causes of the End Times. But the original movies had also portrayed the apes as an inferior version of humans. The apes in the original are intolerant and fearful of those who differ from them and enforce a rigid caste system in which the orangutans govern, the gorillas serve as brutal workers and warriors, and the chimpanzees are ineffectual intellectuals. The American astronaut, George Taylor (Charlton Heston), who returned from a voyage in deep space to crash on an unknown planet, exemplified the superiority of humans over apes through his uprightness and intelligence. With few exceptions, only the humans, whom the apes mistreat and lock in cages like animals in a zoo, are sympathetic. In the 1960s, humanity had not deserved to become jailed and enslaved.

In contrast, the apes in *Rise of the Planet of the Apes*, who are biologically enhanced, surpass humans in intelligence and elicit sympathy in their creation of a functioning, equitable community. The film portrays the apes as an evolutionary necessity for progress against a backdrop of humanity's penchant for self-destruction. The inhuman, corporate environment that reflects the capitalist human drive for individual profit, material goods and status has replaced the social contract that had previously fostered human connections. Science, which served as the solution in earlier disease movies, is now thoroughly corrupted in the human drive for maximizing profit, leading to the near-extinction of humanity. In short, humans no longer deserve to be saved. If *Children of Men* or *Contagion* had offered hope, albeit in different ways, *Rise of the Planet of the Apes* and its sequels are devoid of any optimism about the future of humanity.

Rise of the Planet of the Apes focuses initially on Dr. Will Rodman (James Franco), who has developed the drug ALZ-112 for a pharmaceutical company to cure Alzheimer's. Rodman steals the drug from his company's lab and administers it at home to his father, Charles (John Lithgow), who suffers from Alzheimer's. The film then focuses on Caesar (Andy Serkis), the baby son of the lab ape ("Bright Eyes") to whom Rodman had experimentally administered the drug. Rodman decides to raise Caesar who has inherited the effects of ALZ-112 and soon exhibits human-like intelligence at a rate surpassing that of a human child. They live peacefully for several years, but when Caesar defends Charles from an attack by a neighbor, local animal control services place him in an ape "rescue" facility. After the facility's caretakers torture him and Rodman is unable to have him released from the facility, Caesar comes to identify with the other members of his species. He soon becomes their leader, orchestrates their escape, and enhances their intelligence with the more advanced ALZ-113. The apes ultimately find shelter in the nearby redwood forest, and the end credits show how ALZ-113, with which a worker at Rodman's lab has accidently become infected and which is fatal to humans, quickly spreads around the globe as a pandemic.

Rise of the Planet of the Apes condemns the human species through its repeated reversals of the original *Planet of the Apes* as well as its allusions to classical mythology. In the original, for example, Taylor hid his intelligence by remaining mute until he unexpectedly shouted, "Take your stinking paws off me, you damn dirty ape!" Caesar likewise learns to hide his intelligence when an orangutan at the facility cautions him that humans do not like intelligent apes and then unexpectedly announces his intelligence by shouting "NO" in reply to a caretaker shouting "Take your stinking paw off me, you damn dirty ape!" Caesar plays a Moses-like figure, evoking the role for which Charlton Heston, who played Taylor, was best known (Moses in *The Ten Commandments*, 1956). He is raised among humans but then transforms to defeat the humans, leading his species to the promised land of the nearby redwood forest. Moreover, his name Caesar refers to Julius Caesar, the Roman leader who is associated with the overthrow of the Roman Republic and founded a new imperial order.[27] Rodman, in turn, through his development of the drugs ALZ-112 and ALZ-113, which enhances ape intelligence, plays the role of Prometheus, the titan who stole fire from the gods and brought intelligence to humanity. His relationship with Caesar also evokes the story of *Frankenstein; or The Modern Prometheus*, in which the doctor (Rodman) creates a "monster" (Caesar) that humanity wrongly shuns and with whom the audience sympathizes.[28]

Rise of the Planet of the Apes targets capitalism as the villain in contrast to the hope offered by Caesar's new world order. Central to *Rise of the Planet Apes'* story is an American pharmaceutical company. Its motivation for the development of ALZ-112 and ALZ-113 as a possible cure for Alzheimer's is profit-driven, and scientific curiosity or altruism plays no part. The corporate head of the Alzheimer's project, Steven Jacobs (David Oyelowo), seeks only to increase shareholder profit and materially benefit himself, and his villainy is symbolized by his obsessive purchase of yet another expensive car. As Jacobs pointedly comments to Rodman, they are running a business, not a "petting zoo," so that compassion for the apes plays no role. Thus, he instructs the euthanization of all the lab apes when it appears that the ALZ-112 experiment has failed by turning Bright Eyes ferociously aggressive.

Family life, too, offers no sanctuary, as it did in earlier movies. The pharmaceutical company, which cares nothing about individuals or families given its focus on maximizing financial returns, mistakes Bright Eyes' maternal, if aggressive, protectiveness of her baby for madness and kills her. Likewise, the police later mistake as unprovoked aggressiveness Caesar's protectiveness of his mentally disoriented "grandfather" Charles against the attack of a neighbor who is defending his prized, material possession, again a sports car. Family merely serves to underscore Rodman's hubris but is unable to divert his misplaced focus. In an idyllic family picnic scene, Rodman's romantic partner, a primatologist, accuses Rodman in his development of ALZ-112 of possessing the hubris of Prometheus and creating a Dr. Frankenstein "monster." It is wrong, she observes, to try to control that which is not meant to be controlled. Yet, nothing changes after that conversation.

In contrast to the venality of humans, Caesar chooses empathy over power and consensus over divisiveness, while insisting upon a community inclusive of dissenters. He creates a new social contract that includes apes of all species, and by analogy to all human races, genders and classes. Although the apes in the shelter initially behave according to a Darwinian perspective in which only the fittest survive, Caesar soon gains their trust and the authority to guide them, including his former rivals. The apes represent the next evolutionary step. Even though the humans torture and kill apes in captivity and later prepare to massacre them on the Golden Gate Bridge, Caesar refuses to sanction the killing of humans (with the exception of Jacobs, who has repeatedly sinned against the apes), and the apes return during the closing scene to the paradisiacal, redwood forests.[29] Caesar's evolution is complete when he tells Rodman in that forest, "Caesar is home." Climbing to the tops of these majestic trees, Caesar, the noble savage, sees before him the majesty of a new Eden. His view is Nietzschean.[30] With Caesar as their leader, a Spartacus to the enslaved, the apes have ostensibly cast off the corrupting effects of civilization, including the capitalist values of profit and materialism, for the greater freedom

Figure 3.3 *Rise of the Planet of the Apes* (2011): Climbing to the top of a majestic forest, Caesar, the noble savage, surveys before him San Francisco and the future.

offered by returning to nature. These apes, whose intelligence humans have enhanced, have become "more human than humans."[31] The post-apocalyptic world hinted at during the closing credits offers a new beginning for a posthuman species. That the global spread of this viral disease is easily missed in these credits only underscores the inevitability of human extinction, since that dispersion is less important than the venality of the humans that causes their extinction and the consequent rise of the apes.

The two sequels, *Dawn of the Planet of the Apes* and *War for the Planet of the Apes*, continue the story of humanity's extinction, but with a different director. Rupert Wyatt directed *Rise of the Planet of the Apes* while Matt Reeves directed the two sequels, which shift the focus to the inherent corruption of human and ape natures, even if the apes are triumphant.[32] They also simultaneously depict the transitoriness of the hope offered by this posthuman ape species in the evolutionary process. By the end of these sequels, the differences between apes and humans, whom the apes have replaced, have largely disappeared, and the trilogy has become merely a prequel to the original *Planet of the Apes* – but without the comforting presence of the patriarchal Charlton Heston. Evolution has failed to transcend the corruptive effects of contemporary capitalism. Tellingly, the critique of American capitalism in *Rise of the Planet of the Apes* disappears in its two sequels, shifting the focus to the inherent corruption of human and ape natures, even if the apes are triumphant. The ending to the trilogy recalls the ending of George Orwell's novel *Animal Farm* (1946). "Twelve voices were shouting in anger, and they were all alike. No question, now, what had happened to the faces of the pigs. The creatures outside looked from pig to man, and from man to pig, and from pig to man again; but already it was impossible to say which was which."[33]

Dawn of the Planet of the Apes opens by repeating the image of the global spread of the viral disease, which humans have named the "Simian flu," and the rapid, global turning out of the lights on human civilization. The sequel initially focuses on the efforts of a small group of human survivors, who are led by the engineer Malcom, to literally turn on the lights of a desperate San Francisco community. The movie soon devolves into a story about a battle between the warring factions of human survivors (led by Malcom) and apes (led by the ape Koba, after he overthrows Caesar). Although Caesar describes the apes as family and rejects human behavior, including the adoption of technology, the sequel underscores the similarity of the two species, including their corruption.

Caesar remains the ape leader, only because, as he acknowledges, the others fear him as the strongest. Yet, as he eventually concludes, "I always think ape better than human. I see now how much like them we are." If he acknowledges, too, that Malcom is a "good man" and nostalgically recalls Rodman as a "good man," Caesar rejects Koba, because he is "no ape" in the same way that humans rejected apes, because they are "animals."[34] By recategorizing Koba as a non-ape, Caesar can reconcile his killing of Koba with the ape commandment – or prime directive – that "apes not kill apes."[35] While apes may replace humans, nothing has changed by the end of the movie. Apes have become increasingly indistinguishable in their barbarism from humans.

The final episode of the trilogy, *War for the Planet of the Apes*, concludes the humans' self-destructive process and the rise of the apes as the dominant species. Yet, the movie qualifies that rise. The film depicts humans through Colonel McCullough (Woody Harrelson), the leader of a merciless remnant of the United States army that marches each morning to the beat of the American national anthem. It identifies humans with the madness of Colonel Kurtz of *Apocalypse Now* (1979). In contrast, Caesar, whom the colonel criticizes for displaying emotions and taking war personally, is again identified with Moses. Like the Egyptians in the Bible, Caesar's oppressors, too, are drowned in the film's concluding battle, though in an avalanche of snow, and like Moses, Caesar leads his apes across the desert and into a verdant valley, a promised land he cannot enter. Yet, as he also concludes, "I am like Koba." Caesar has adopted human technology, blindly pursued vengeance, and killed others in that pursuit. Human sins have infected ape society, and the film suggests that this new social order will over time reflect that of the humans whom they have replaced.

War for the Planet of the Apes highlights the inevitability of this outcome by underscoring the trilogy as a prequel to the original *Planet of the Apes* with the apes as a replacement species for humanity. Alluding to the original *Planet of the Apes*, *War for the Planet of the Apes* depicts how humans as a result of a mutation of the "Simian flu" are becoming mute and losing their intelligence, which, as Colonel McCullough notes, is what makes them human. Likewise, Nova, the name of a mute girl who joins the apes, not only anticipates the evolution of a "new" human species but also recalls the mute woman named Nova with whom Taylor became romantically involved in the original movie. If the colonel's "holy war" ends in human defeat, the film acknowledges the truth of his observation that "all of human history has led to this moment." Apes must replace humans. "That's the law of nature," the colonel observes, underscoring the inevitability of this evolution. In recalling the original movie, *War for the Planet of the Apes* reminds its audience, however, that the apes will eventually prove as corrupted as their human ancestors.

Rise of the Planet of the Apes and its two sequels represent a prequel to the fallen state of the decades earlier *Planet of the Apes*. In the original apes were the dominant species and the audience empathized with the enslaved, tortured humans. Produced in the 2010s, *Rise of the Planet of the Apes* critiques the global, corporate world of humans, including its technological advancements, focus on individualism and inability to create a functioning social order. It identifies with the apes. Its sequels, however, increasingly depict the flaws in ape society. The trilogy shifts from its depiction of the apes as noble savages in the context of a corrupt capitalism to members of an inherently flawed species that will inevitably evolve to tear apart its new world order. The increasing pessimism of the trilogy results from an increasingly reactionary view of the species. Where *Rise of the Planet of the Apes* offered a hopeful vision of a paradisiacal new world order, the ending of *War for the Planet of the Apes* deifies Caesar as a savior but underscores his powerlessness against the tide of history. There is no alternative to or escape from contemporary American capitalism, however corrosive its effects on all species.

Conclusion

Films about infectious disease have continued to proliferate, and their stories of human near extinction have become the norm. The titles alone of these movies convey the variety of sources for human extinction – *Blindness* (2008), *Carriers* (2009), *Antiviral* (2012), *Flu* (2013), *Plague* (2014), *Viral* (2016), *Pandemic* (2016) and *Mayhem* (2017). While these movies may vary in specifics, they increasingly share a sense of foreboding. In contrast to mid-twentieth century movies, the human species in its contemporary form is not worth preserving. In *Maggie* (2015), for example, even the aged 68-year-old action hero Arnold Schwarzenegger observes helplessly as his daughter slowly transforms into a zombie. The Korean military rescues the two survivors in *Train to Busan* (2016) and the two survivors in *#Alive* (2020), but these endings offer only a temporary respite from the zombie apocalypse. While a comedy such as *Warm Bodies* (2013) posits that romantic love might bridge the gap between the living and the dead, the self-aware comedy *The Dead Don't Die* is more typical. While it identifies the source of the zombie apocalypse as polar fracking, it also acknowledges the cultural sickness that has led to the inevitability of human extinction. By the movie's end, with the exception of "Hermit Bob," all the humans are either eaten or become zombies.

The growing distrust of science and reason corresponds to the recent difficulties in containing infectious diseases, such as Ebola, SARS and MERS, that have affected and threatened larger, mainstream populations. If the mid-twentieth century moment seemed to usher in the conquest of disease, re-emerging infectious diseases and the continued spread of older diseases have foreclosed this possibility. Recent disease movies reflect, too, a cultural acknowledgement that humanity remains conflicted by irrational fears and obsessions about what a disease might do, even as the COVID-19 pandemic demonstrated that American society is politically unwilling to commit its resources to stopping the spread of such diseases. Science and technology are no longer supposed panaceas, since both seem easily corrupted by corporate, capitalist interests. They are also increasingly in disfavor reflected in how horror often displaces science fiction in the narrative of disease movies. Contemporary disease movies depict the human inability to come to grips with this new reality in their stories about a post-apocalyptic world in which the human species is increasingly adrift and faces extinction.

Where decades ago disease movies were a metaphor for an attempt at revealing and curing the ills of society, recent movies depict a global pandemic whose source has become largely irrelevant and which cannot be contained or cured. Agreed upon norms have disappeared, and the myth of American capitalism with its supposed ideals of equal opportunity and individual freedom are transparently advantageous for only the select few. This fractured state of American society is all too obvious in these movies, and even the heroes of these movies largely lack the ability, or the will, to address these problems. Common values consist at best of sentimental, nostalgic evocations of predominantly masculine, heroic individuals and the venerated, often surrogate family. Enlightened reason has disappeared and been replaced by an unrelenting sense of fear of the unknown. The rise of a new species in this post-apocalyptic world represents the sought-for transformation of the human species in the context of such fear. Humans are reinvented in order to conform to the needs of a transformed, global community, which advances either the interests of American capitalism or a self-destructive populist revolt against those interests. The conclusion, however, is the same. Evolutionary development offers little or no hope in the face of a fearful transitoriness that mocks human ideals in progress or a faith in the transcendent. Human evolution represents merely change, not progress. In the end, like Caesar and his apes, humanity appears doomed to endlessly repeat and replicate the very structures that have caused its undoing.

Notes

1. This list is hardly exhaustive, since there has been an endless number of less commercial releases, such as, *Postal* (2007) and *Flight of the Living Dead* (2007), to name only two.
2. For the focus on the materialistic reason for explosion in the number of these films, see Dahlia Schweitzer, *Going Viral*. *Shaun of the Dead* (2004) was an early attempt to mock *28 Days Later* (2002), in particular, from a British perspective.
3. For a discussion of the paradigm shift: Neil Gerlach and Sheryl N. Hamilton, "Trafficking in the Zombie: The CDC Zombie Apocalypse Campaign, Disease-ability and Pandemic Culture"; and for the parallel in reality, Neil A. Gerlach, "From Outbreak to Pandemic Narrative: Reading Newspaper Coverage of the 2014 Ebola Epidemic," *Canadian Journal of Communication* 41, no. 4 (2016): 611–630.
4. While the movie falls within the genre of science fiction, several movie critics noted the events described in the documentary *Project Nim* (2011) as a possible influence on *The Rise of the Planet of the Apes*. See Manohla Dargis, "Looking Apocalypse in the Eye," *The New York Times*, August 4, 2011, https://www.nytimes.com/2011/08/05/movies/rise-of-the-planet-of-the-apes-stars-james-franco-review.html.
5. The song "Arbeit Macht Frei" ("work shall set you free") plays in the refugee camp, an obvious allusion to the German words on signs written above the entrances of Nazi death/concentration camps.
6. These are allusions to the responses to the Black Death, see Benedictow, *The Black Death, 1346–1353*.
7. The title is taken from Psalms 90:3 in the King James Version.
8. That she is tortured is suggested by the hooded person appearing nearby in a pose evocative of the infamous Abu Ghraib torture photo.
9. These are stock elements about the Middle Ages, including celebrated portrayals in Monty Python. On the Middle Ages and film, Paul B. Sturtevant, *The Middle Ages in Popular Imagination: Memory, Film and Medievalism* (London: I. B. Tauris, 2018); and on other myths, Winston Black, *The Middle Ages: Facts and Fictions* (Santa Barbara: ABC-Clio, 2019).
10. On the problem with origins of modern disease, see McKay, *Patient Zero*.
11. Movies have often identified the origin of their fictional diseases as originating from outer space, as in *Invasion of the Body Snatchers* (1956), *Night of the Living Dead* (1968) and *The Andromeda Strain* (1971). The military or the scientific community has also often featured as the source of the disease, as in *The Crazies* (1973) and *Rabid* (1977). Such concern for authenticity in identifying the origin of the disease also prophetically anticipates the search for the origin of COVID-19. See Christos Lynteris, "The Imperative Origins of COVID-19," *L'Homme*, no 234–235, no. 2 (2020): 21–32.
12. God normally visits the iniquity of the fathers, not the mothers, on their children (e.g., Exodus 20:5, 34:7). See Adia Benton, "Border Promiscuity, Illicit Intimacies, and Origin Stories: Or What Contagion's Bookends Tell Us About New Infectious Diseases and a Racialized Geography of Blame," *Somatosphere*, March 6, 2020, http://somatosphere.net/forumpost/border-promiscuity-racialized-blame/.

13. The classic work on the role of women in movies, including as virgin and whore, is Molly Haskell, *From Reverence to Rape: The Treatment of Women in the Movies*, 3rd edition (Chicago: University of Chicago Press, 2016).
14. At the same time, Cheever donates his own vaccine to the young son of the janitor in his office building after the janitor had earlier overheard Cheever's original warning to Aubrey to leave Chicago and had remarked to Cheever that he has family, too. The movie is ambiguous about whether Cheever donated his own vaccine to the janitor's son because of his conscience or because he is attempting to buy the janitor's silence in the face of the upcoming Congressional hearing.
15. For further discussion of health care workers as heroes: Lynteris, "The Epidemiologist as Culture Hero," esp. 40–41; and Lynteris, *Human Extinction*, 101–103; also Han and Curtis, "Suspicious Minds."
16. On fear and mistrust in the film, see Han and Curtis, *Infectious Inequalities*, 59–62.
17. Preston, "Crisis in the Hot Zone"; Stephen S. Morse, "Factors in the Emergence of Infectious Diseases," *Emerging Infectious Diseases* 1, no. 1 (1995): 7–15.
18. *Zombieland* parallels a long line of comedies in which the inept male is the film's focus and in which his loser status enables him not only to survive, but also to win the beautiful female. Examples include George McFly in *Back to the Future* (1984) and Gary Wallace and Wyatt Donnelly in *Weird Science* (1985). The final scene is also reminiscent of a quintessential fairy tale, in which the male hero rescues the female love-interest from a tower guarded by a monster (in this case a theme park tower ride guarded by a zombie clown) as a way to demonstrate his masculinity.
19. Jesse Eisenberg, who plays Columbus, would go on to portray Mark Zuckerberg one year later in *The Social Network* (2010). Ironically, in *The Social Network* the adolescent fantasy of true love will turn sour. He fails to win the girl and instead creates Facebook with all its problematic outcomes for society.
20. The film is loosely based on a profitable book of the same name and capitalized on the success of AMC's *The Walking Dead* (2010–2022) franchise that combined high-paced action with horror and adventure themes. For the book, Max Brooks, *World War Z: An Oral History of the Zombie War* (New York: Three Rivers Press, 2006).
21. Brad Pitt had previously starred not only as the mental patient Jeffrey Goines in *12 Monkeys* but also as traditional, swaggering male characters, such as Paul Maclean in *A River Runs Through It* (1992), Tyler Durden in *Fight Club* (1999) and Achilles in *Troy* (2004). Pitt often embodies the American ideal of male exceptionalism.
22. This change is similar to the transformation between the "bugs" in *Starship Troopers* the book and the movie, compare: Robert A. Heinlein, *Starship Troopers* (New York: G. P. Putnam's Sons, 1959) and *Starship Troopers* (1997); for the changes to zombies within the horror genre, Todd K. Platts, "The Unmade Undead: A Post-Mortem of the Post-9/11 Zombie Cycle," in *Shadow Cinema: The Historical and Production Contexts of Unmade Films*, eds. James Fenwick et al. (New York: Bloomsbury Academic, 2020), 251–66.
23. For example, Gerry sentimentally writes "tell my family I love them" when he believes that he will die from injecting himself with some unknown pathogen. For a different view of this character, Lynteris, *Human Extinction*, 105.

24. The poster that accompanied the film's release, which depicts Gerry as a Neanderthal emerging from a cave, conveys how only the primitive skills of the male brute ensure the continuation of that civilization, not intellect.
25. For further discussion of the movie, Haneen Shafeeq Ghabra and Marouf A. Hasian, "World War Z, The Zombie Apocalypse, and the Israeli State's Monstering of Palestinian 'Others,'" *Communication and Critical/Cultural Studies* 17, no. 2 (2020): 183–98. Also, Lynteris, "The Epidemiologist as Cultural Hero," 43–49.
26. On the personalizing of transactions and the collection of public and private data, see Zuboff, *The Age of Surveillance Capitalism*, 19. On the importance of inefficiency and randomness in human behavior, see Edward Tenner, *The Efficiency Paradox: What Big Data Can't Do* (New York: Knopf Doubleday Publishing Group, 2018).
27. While Julius Caesar was responsible for the immediate chain of events that de facto dissolved the Roman Republic, his nephew Octavian Caesar (also known as Augustus) founded the new imperial order.
28. Empathy for the creature created in the lab finds its origin in Mary Shelley's novel *Frankenstein*. Increasingly science fiction movies advocate for the artificially intelligent creation as not only worthy of empathy but also the wished-for next stage in the evolutionary development of the human species. See Robert Alpert, "AI at the Movies and the Second Coming". Also: Lynteris, *Human Extinction*, 78.
29. Critic Roger Ebert drew the connection between apes and zombies when he wrote in praise of the film's climactic battle on the Golden Gate Bridge: "There's a big climactic action scene that is more engaging than the countless similar scenes I've seen with zombies." Roger Ebert, "Pity they can't always remain babies," *RogerEbert.com*, August 3, 2011, https://www.rogerebert.com/reviews/rise-of-the-planet-of-the-apes-2011.
30. While viewing the evolutionary advancement of humans as surpassing apes, Friedrich Nietzsche articulated this same perspective: Friedrich Nietzsche, *The Portable Nietzsche*, ed. Walter Kaufman (New York: Viking Press, 1968), 124–26.
31. In *Blade Runner* (1982), Dr. Tyrell, a film version of Dr. Frankenstein, observed of his replicants, "Commerce is our goal here at Tyrell, 'More human than human' is our motto."
32. Wyatt had previously directed *The Escapist* (2008), which was not widely released, while, in contrast, Reeves is best known for his direction of *Cloverfield* (2008), *Let Me In* (2010) and *The Batman* (2022).
33. George Orwell, *Animal Farm* (New York: Harcourt, Brace and Company, 1946), 118.
34. Koba is a bonobo (a stereotypically more altruistic primate species compared to chimpanzees). He has been corrupted, however, by the suffering inflicted upon him in the corporate drug lab, killing Jacobs in *Rise of the Planet of the Apes*, and then seeking to kill Caesar and slaughter the remaining humans in *Dawn of the Planet of the Apes*.
35. The idea of recategorizing the enemy as enabling its killing originated in *Robocop* (1987). In the climactic scene of that science fiction film the CEO fires the Senior Vice President, enabling the android Robocop to overcome his programmed prime directive that had barred him from arresting, let alone killing, a corporate employee.

CHAPTER 4

REMAKING HUMANITY: *THE BODY SNATCHERS*

Introduction

As the previous three chapters have demonstrated, disease movies have transformed their plots, characters and messages over the last century. Movie remakes about diseases are, however, the most straightforward means for demonstrating these changes across different eras. Remakes play to contemporary audience tastes of a known theme and plot, offering more assured financial profits, as well as recast those themes and update cultural myths for the present. This permits a direct comparison of what has – or has not – changed over time. Although remakes have spanned nearly all genres, including westerns, gangster movies and dramas, they appear frequently in the horror and science fiction genres, particularly as these genres have increasingly appeared onscreen.[1]

This chapter follows the transformation of disease through the movies based on Jack Finney's novel *The Body Snatchers* (1955), which studios have periodically remade over the past seventy years.[2] This chapter traces the same transformation described in Chapters 1, 2 and 3, but reveals how cultural ideas about disease historically develop and change with a plot that remains constant. It examines how the changing concept of disease and its social meaning influence how movie remakes recast details from the origin and spread of the disease to larger issues, such as whether the disease can be contained. Even the most basic question – what is a disease? – changes across these movies: from an extraterrestrial, cancerous growth in the 1950s to a bio-engineered plant in the late 2010s.

The Body Snatchers remakes also reveal a transformation in American social cohesion and the role of capitalism. These movies evolve from a fear of conformity in the context of white, small-town America in which "father knows best" to increasingly broader and darker depictions that end with happy, zombie-like humans in a multinational, corporate world. At one level, these movies reflect the change in assumptions about the effects of disease and as such highlight how Americans understand disease. At a broader level, in the same way that movies about the undead have changed in ways reflective of their times, these remakes metaphorically reveal the underlying cultural change – from critiquing a rigidly hierarchical society that both lacks any diversity as well as demands conformity to the acceptance of a new social contract that replaces individual identity with a naïve contentment in a capitalist world of seeming material abundance. They are reflective of the historical change from state-managed capitalism to an asset and surveillance capitalism in which fear of similarity disappears amidst the growing acceptance and even yearning for that similarity as the solution to global problems.[3]

The first film adaptation, *Invasion of the Body Snatchers* (1956), came out just one year after the publication of Finney's novel.[4] Subsequent remakes have followed every few decades with increasing rapidity – *Invasion of the Body Snatchers* (1978), *Body Snatchers* (1993), *The Invasion* (2007) and *Little Joe* (2019) – confirming the continued relevance of this narrative.[5] Jack Finney's novel and all of *The Body Snatchers* movies feature a plot in which people's bodies and personalities are replaced without their knowledge and which is explained through an invasion of an extraterrestrial species. *Little Joe* is the exception that explains the transformation through the commercial development of a psychoactive plant, but that change is itself revealing of twenty-first century values. If in earlier versions aliens had come to infect and inhabit humans on Earth, in the last version humans have created the infection that has taken us over. The duplicated people are often colloquially referred to as "pods" or "pod people," referring to the plant-like pods that grow the human bodies being replicated. In the last version, the humans are identified, at times, as zombies.[6] While these movies evoke alien invasions or, in the case of the last, the threat of unregulated scientific research, they all conjure up the horror of disease through the fear of infection by an invasive species and feature the often futile effort by the protagonists to avoid infection by escaping those already infected.

As the remakes continued into the twenty-first century, the focus on American life gave way to a commentary on the need to resolve global questions, revealing an increasingly connected but fragmented world. While the earlier versions, particularly the 1956 movie, ignored cultural differences in order to examine middle-class conformity, later remakes have increasingly argued for overlooking cultural differences and embracing all people as similar and supposedly equal in a post-identity world. The trend in *The Body Snatchers* remakes is a movement from the feared loss of an implicitly white, middle-class identity, with no acknowledgment of other groups, to a view that other races, ethnicities, genders, ages and classes conflict with and undermine social cohesion and an efficient global capitalism. The later remakes, which are increasingly aimed at a global audience, argue that the solution is to subsume all identities into a featureless humanity with nothing to differentiate one person from the next, thereby erasing the features that make each person unique and human.[7] Pod people begin as a threat and, in the end, are a welcomed transformation.

The book *The Body Snatchers* is the baseline for the movies that followed. It describes an alien species that drifts from planet to planet, absorbing and killing the dominant species in each before moving on. The duplicate pod people lack emotion, cannot sexually reproduce, and possess a lifespan of only five years, forcing the alien species to continue their endless migration as a virus that repeatedly invades and destroys its hosts. This species arrives on Earth in a similar way, reaching the fictional, small town of Santa Mira, California outside of San Francisco. They use plantlike pods to duplicate and replace people while they sleep, absorbing the knowledge and memories of those whom they replace. Finney's novel focuses on Miles Bennell, a recently divorced town doctor, and his former high school sweetheart who has also recently divorced, Becky Driscoll. Although both encounter friends who claim that family members have lost their personality (have been replaced), Miles and Becky only accept the truth about the pods when their friends, the writer Jack Belicec and his wife Theodora, show them a pod in the Belicec home that is slowly duplicating Jack. While the source of the pods is outer space, Miles describes the threat as a real epidemic, using his medical expertise to compare it to a terrestrial pathogen.

The author Jack Finney has claimed that "the book isn't a cold war novel, or a metaphor for anything."[8] Yet, the novel is representative of a nostalgic paean to small-town America in the mid-twentieth century – a community of "ordinary," white Americans. Non-whites remain "others," such as the town's black shoeshine "boy" whose self-aware subservience to whites is compared to the pods' imitation of human emotion. The novel's villain is similarly an outlier: the biology Professor Bernard Budlong, an academic and intellectual who discovers the pods and later assists the aliens. In this vision of America, non-whites are aliens, and intellectuals have no place. The community of white Americans eventually succeeds in defeating and containing the alien infection. The aliens depart, because they see that ordinary Americans, including Miles, Becky, Jack and Theodora, will fight to retain their individualism. The book's vision of America is similar to *Panic in the Streets*, where heroic action stops the infection, leading to a return to the status quo that ignores everyone who does not fit this ideal image.

THE INFECTION OF SMALL-TOWN AMERICA: *INVASION OF THE BODY SNATCHERS* (1956)

The first movie, which Don Siegel directed and was released under the title *Invasion of the Body Snatchers*, is the closest to the original plot and retains many of the book's characters. It promotes the idea of individual freedom while expressing a fear of growing social conformity across the country.[9] The immediate analogy for contemporary audiences was "the red menace," with the pods symbolizing Communist infiltration of America.[10] Siegel observed that the political reference to totalitarianism was inevitable given the 1950s, Cold War symbols.[11] For example, when the only survivors flee from a crowd of townspeople, they hear a civil defense siren, alerting the entire town to pursue them. Later in their flight, they find shelter in a nearby cave, evoking a post-nuclear world in which civilization has been bombed back into the Stone Age.

Siegel denied the Cold War interpretation, however, and instead viewed the movie as a critique of the increasing conformity of Americans. "People are pods. Many of my associates are certainly pods," he observed. "They have no feelings. They exist, breath, sleep . . . [T]hat, by the way, is the world most of us live in. It's the same as people who welcome going into the army or prison." Uniformity, according to Siegel, characterizes how people increasingly act.[12] The film's character Wilma Lentz expresses that fear. She contrasts the physical resemblance of her now pod uncle with his utter lack of affect. "There's no emotion. None. Just the pretense of it. The words, the gesture, the tone of voice, everything else is the same, but not the feeling."

Siegel was not optimistic that there was any way to stop this change, since there is "a very strong case for being a pod," even if the end result is a "very dull world." Like Miles Bennell in the novel, Siegel compared the invasion in the film to a looming disease of his time, "like a cancer growth. The town, like a section of your body, is ill and it's going to spread."[13] His view largely conforms to the original book, which, in turn, echoes *Panic in the Streets*. What Siegel sought to save in America was a single-minded, male, white version of society, which was already bland, racist and misogynist. Yet, even this was too much, and his studio disagreed with his pessimistic ending in which the pods triumph. It required him to add a framing – a new opening, a happy ending and a voiceover to tie them together – in an effort to qualify Siegel's pessimism.

Despite this studio-imposed framing, the movie is largely a critique of the changes in American middle-class life. Miles Bennell (Kevin McCarthy), the film's protagonist, articulates Siegel's view. A doctor who serves as the town's general practitioner, he analogizes the invasion to a disease, commenting to Becky Driscoll (Dana Wynter), "Let's hope we don't catch it." He expresses

DISEASED CINEMA

Figure 4.1 *Invasion of the Body Snatchers* (1956): The small town of Santa Mira gathers on a Saturday morning to distribute alien pods to the surrounding towns.

Siegel's message throughout with such statements as "in my practice, I've seen how people have allowed their humanity to drain away. Only it happened slowly instead of all at once. They didn't seem to mind . . . All of us – a little bit – we harden our hearts, grow callous. Only when we have to fight to stay human do we realize how precious it is to us, how dear."[14] Miles's psychiatrist colleague who has become a pod person, Dr. Dan Kauffman (Larry Gates), explains the benefits of complete conformity in a lengthy discussion that will be repeated in some form in all of the remakes.[15]

> Dr. Kauffman: Miles, you and I are scientific men. You can understand the wonder of what's happening . . . Less than a month ago, Santa Mira was like any other town. People with nothing but problems. Then, out of the sky came a solution . . . Your new bodies are growing in there . . . Suddenly, while you're asleep, they'll absorb your minds, your memories and you're reborn into an untroubled world.
> Miles: Where everyone's the same?
> Dr. Kauffman: Exactly . . .
> Miles: I love Becky. Tomorrow, will I feel the same?
> Dr. Kauffman: There's no need for love.
> Miles: No emotion? Then you have no feelings, only the instinct to survive. You can't love or be loved! Am I right?
> Dr. Kauffman: You say it as if it were terrible. Believe me, it isn't. You've been in love before. It didn't last. It never does. Love. Desire. Ambition. Faith. Without them, life's so simple, believe me.

Becky and Miles resist such a bland world. "I want to love and be loved. I want your children," she melodramatically tells Miles in response to Kauffman's advocacy. "I don't want a world without love or grief or beauty. I'd rather die."

Yet, Becky symbolizes the seeming impossibility of stopping the spread of the disease of conformity. She and Miles flee town, but Miles briefly leaves her alone in the cave in which they have sought shelter when they hear the nearby sounds of a comforting, peaceful Brahms lullaby. "Miles, I've never heard anything so beautiful," Becky comments hopefully. "It means we're not the only ones left to know what love is." Miles is more skeptical. "Stay here," he replies, "and pray they're as human as they sound." Discovering that the music originates from a truck radio playing while pod people load pods onto trucks, he flees back to the cave disheartened. Upon his arrival, he discovers that Becky has been transformed into a pod person and acknowledges in a voiceover with a look of horror on his face that he had never known real fear until that moment.[16] Miles flees again and reaches a nearby highway in the hopes of alerting others outside the town to the threat of infection, while the townspeople stop chasing him secure in the belief that no one will believe him.

The movie critiques the contagion of social conformity, and hence the social contract writ large, in the context of a post-World War II America transformed through the growth of suburbs, national chain stores, interstate highways, nationwide broadcasting systems and rampant consumerism – the physical manifestations of state-managed capitalism.[17] This social conformity in the context of America's expansive, economic growth represents what we recognize today as a problematic vision of American identity. Santa Mira is an entirely white, middle-class town in which men commute to work each day while women tend to the home. While divorced, Miles is a respected figure within the community given his profession. Always immaculately dressed in a suit and tie, he, like Dan Kauffman, is a member of the medical profession. Even Jack Belicec, a mystery writer and the town intellectual (symbolized by his pipe-smoking), lives a secure, middle-class life with his wife, Teddy.

The portrayal of Becky underscores Siegel's male-centered view of America. She has only recently returned to Santa Mira and is divorced, but as a woman, her divorce places her in a precarious position with no defined role, and she must seek refuge in her parents' home. Her gender role is confirmed once Miles sexually desires her, since she soon acts the role of a dutiful wife. During a brief moment of calm, she serves Miles a breakfast of a two-minute egg, orange juice and coffee after sleeping at his home.[18] When he passionately kisses her later in the cave after she has become a pod, she stereotypically complains moments before as an exhausted housewife without sexual desire, "I'm so tired." Becky also becomes a stereotypical, hysterical woman. When Miles tells her to "show no interest or excitement" at one point so they can pass as pod people and escape from the town, she fails by crying out upon seeing a dog nearly run over. Indeed, she continues to fail, falling asleep when Miles briefly leaves her and subsequently betraying Miles after she has been transformed into a pod. If Becky had initially represented the American, white male's dream of marriage to his high school sweetheart, then Becky as a pod person represents the nightmare. She transforms from a helpless partner of the heroic male to become a femme fatale.[19] While Siegel sought to demonstrate his fear of conformity as represented by the pods, the movie – based on Siegel's understanding of what it means to be American – endorses an already bland white, middle-class town in which men control the narrative.[20]

Even within the confines of the supposedly average community of 1950s America, Siegel's *Invasion of the Body Snatchers* is unusually pessimistic about America's ability to cure the contagion of social conformity. Siegel had wanted the movie to end with Miles screaming on the highway to the drivers who ignore his pleas to stop the pods or call him a nutcase as he shouts, "You're next." In the studio-forced, tacked-on prologue, Miles recounts his story to a disbelieving psychiatrist at a Los Angeles hospital.[21] Only in the epilogue does the psychiatrist believe his ravings when in a highway accident a greyhound bus overturns a truck from Santa Mira, spilling pods onto the road.[22] Initiating an urgent, statewide quarantine, the psychiatrist alerts both the state law enforcement agencies and the Federal Bureau of Investigation. The imposition of this Hollywood ending does not undo, however, the pervasive disquiet and darkness that had already settled over the sunny town of Santa Mira. The movie's suggested solution of a top-down quarantine to Santa Mira's social conformity, which is mirrored in the national chains then spreading across America and promoted by a strong federal government, is ironically the federal government itself.[23] Siegel's film ends happily with the triumph of a national conformity that embraces the common characteristics of small-town America which Siegel idealizes – white, middle-class and male.

The Spread to Urban America: *Invasion of the Body Snatchers* (1978)

The period between the original version and its second adaptation witnessed twenty years of transformation, upheaval and strife in American life and culture. The version released in 1978, also titled *Invasion of the Body Snatchers*, reiterates many of the same concerns about social conformity but in a 1970s cultural context that took into account these reverberations in American society.[24] Directed by Philip Kaufman, the remake shifts the narrative from the small town of Santa Mira to the city of San Francisco, where the 1960s counterculture originated in the Haight-Ashbury neighborhood and a place Kaufman later described as "the city with the most advanced, progressive therapies, politics and so forth."[25] As Kaufman noted at the time, "The only way [the movie] could really be valid and relevant . . . would be if it played out in a city. You see, twenty years ago, the big cities were places that were secure, really. Small towns were in transition. Now big cities are falling apart, and there is paranoia in the streets. People are distrustful of other people. So we decided to run this theme through the streets of San Francisco."[26] The film reflects many of these contemporary issues of its time, such as pollution and environmental destruction as well as political conspiracies following the Nixon presidency and Watergate.[27]

Kaufman changes the pods from ungainly pea pods to beautiful, small, delicate flowers that grow to become pods. As Nancy Bellicec (Veronica Cartwright), the eventual sole survivor of the invasion, observes, the alien invaders are now "space flowers." They symbolize the flower power and flower children of the 1960s, and embody Kaufman's criticism of the ideals of the 1960s counterculture from his late 1970s vantage. The 1978 version critiques its contemporary cultural setting in which capitalism has absorbed the 1960s countercultural revolution. Moreover, this version sharply departs from both the book and the 1956 version, since while it critiques its society – similar to the 1956 version or even *Night of the Living Dead* – it simultaneously concludes with the pod takeover of San Francisco and, inevitably, the rest of America. This version recognizes the problems in America as the other disease movies from the late 1960s onward do but offers no solution or even hope that a favorable resolution is possible. Its conflicted approach also pairs well with *Virus*, which was released just two years later, and represents a vision of where disease movies could have gone but which they did not for decades, since diseases remained containable, not catastrophic.

The villain in this remake is the psychiatrist guru Dr. David Kibner, a close friend of the protagonist Matthew Bennell (Donald Sutherland). Kibner, a pod person, represents how people had mainstreamed the counterculture. Played by Leonard Nimoy, cast for his famous role as the coldly rational Dr. Spock in the *Star Trek* TV series, Kibner writes best-selling, self-help books.[28] He initially claims that "there's some kind of a hallucinatory flu going around. People seem to get over it in a day or two. All I can do is treat the symptoms." He soothingly persuades those who insist that their loved ones are no longer their loved ones that everything is ok through his guru techniques. He tries to assuage, in particular, the growing fears of Matthew and Matthew's work colleague, Elizabeth Driscoll (Brooke Adams), by insisting simply that "people are changing. They're becoming less human. It's happening all around us." When Kibner administers sedatives to Matthew and Elizabeth in a later scene as he tries to turn them into pod people, he comforts them with Dr. Kauffman's observation from the first version verbatim. "You'll be born again into an untroubled world."

Kibner symbolizes how easily humans can transform into emotionless Spocks in an untroubled world. His character represents the cultural assimilation of the countercultural revolution and reflects the 1970s "me decade" with its popular self-help books. Kibner ironically identifies ideas from the 1960s, such as the focus on individual, material pleasures and dropping out of society, as destroying the existing notions of morality and institutions that had formerly held society together. He advocates for a return to these "traditional" values. "People are stepping in and out of relationships too fast," he argues, "because they don't want the responsibility. That's why marriages are going to hell. The whole family unit is shot to hell." The author of a book entitled *The Universe Within You*, Kibner advocates finding cosmic meaning in personal feelings. As he later explains to Matthew, the aliens offer a straightforward reason for survival and the utility of conformity. "We came here from a dying world . . . We drift through the universe, from planet to planet, pushed on by the solar winds. We adapt and we survive. The function of life is survival." Nothing else matters in Kibner's world in which each person is both the center of the universe and indistinguishable from anyone else.

Kaufman's version is conflicted in its treatment of cultural identities. On the one hand, like the 1956 version, this 1978 version also depicts a white, middle-class setting, notwithstanding its urban San Francisco backdrop, and fails to challenge racial, ethnic and class norms that were increasingly no longer accepted. Its main characters, Matthew and Elizabeth, are "yuppies" before the term was coined, and San Francisco largely consists of picturesque, gentrified neighborhoods. It mentions neither the Civil Rights movement of the 1960s nor the feminist movement of the 1960s and 1970s when reflecting upon what has changed. There are no discussions of race as well. On the other hand, it is attuned to gender changes and advocates for the sensitive male, such as Matthew, criticizes the self-centered, sports-focused male, such as Elizabeth's boyfriend, and praises the financially savvy, perceptive female, such as Nancy Bellicec. It is a late 1970s movie that has absorbed some of the debates in American society over the previous decade and a half, but is silent about their meaning.

Moreover, in contrast to the 1956 movie, this version depicts its heroes, Elizabeth and Matthew, as middle-class civil servants who are easily ignored, and elevates a superficial network of literati symbolized by the capitalistically successful Kibner, in place of the talented intellectual, represented by the impoverished poet Jack Bellicec (Jeff Goldblum). The film notes differences in class but suggests that capitalist success, which permeates the movie's narrative, should be secondary to individual struggle for personal fulfilment. Jack Bellicec, who views Kibner's latest book as "post-industrial nonsense," articulates the film's lesson. "The rest of the world is trying to change people to fit the world. I'm trying to change the world to fit people," he dramatically asserts in describing his poetry, disregarding his own failure in even sustaining himself as an author. "Where's Homer? Where's Kazantzakis? Where's Jack London?" Jack acknowledges great intellectual authors, all of whom are also white men, hinting, however, at his own exaggerated self-perception. Ironically, Jack's question demonstrates how conformity is already required to thrive in his world based on his own list of great authors. If the aliens change the cultural imperative, they merely shift the focus from one of personal success to the survival of the species.

Philip Kaufman's remake is bleaker than Don Siegel's first version, reflecting the disillusionment and despair of the New Hollywood directors of the period.[29] Like Siegel, Kaufman, too, anguished over how "we must fight to preserve our humanity, because it is in danger of slipping away from us while we sleep."[30] The late 1970s represented "another 'pod' era, a lot like the 50s. In the 60s, there seemed to be a tolerance for diversity. Now, people are looking out for themselves again. We're going back to the conformist days . . ."[31] The 1978 version even features actors from the first version in cameo performances in which they are killed or taken over to drive this point home. Kevin McCarthy, who had played Miles Bennell in the 1956 version, screams in the streets of San Francisco at Matthew and Elizabeth, "You're next!" He is soon run over and lies dead on the street, surrounded by pod people. Don Siegel appears as a cab driver taking Matthew and Elizabeth to the airport. But he is a pod person and radios their whereabouts to other pod people to catch them. While Brahms' Lullaby had misled Miles to leave Becky in the original movie, Matthew is misled by the Christian hymn "Amazing Grace," which contains themes of forgiveness and redemption and whose playing conveys a far darker message. Finally, it changes the discovery of Elizabeth's replacement from a kiss to wake her up to Matthew watching as her desiccated body graphically collapses from within and her resurrection nearby as a naked pod person.

The ending is especially bleak. Where the first version had a studio-imposed prologue and epilogue that offered audiences a relatively happy ending, this remake ends with the triumph of the pod people. Rather than warn his fellow humans of the invasion, Matthew returns to work the next morning after Elizabeth's transformation to an office filled with his co-workers, including Elizabeth, who stare vacantly into the distance. At the end of the day, he marches with the other worker drones to exit the building. With "Amazing Grace" playing again in the background, he encounters Nancy Bellicec, who is still human and believes he is pretending to be a pod person just like she is. Only once she identifies herself does he reveal himself as an alien, point accusingly at Nancy, and emit a high-pitched, piercing scream ending the movie. The horror of the last scene demonstrates our inability, like Nancy Bellicec, to distinguish between Matthew, an average health worker, from Matthew, the pod person. Society has absorbed 1960s social critique, and that critique now disappears in the face of an American culture which "is trying to change people to fit."

An Aggressive Expansion across America: *Body Snatchers* (1993)

If the second version was set in a 1970s world, the next remake, *Body Snatchers* (1993), reflects the early 1990s. It was released shortly after the end of the Cold War, the emergence of the United States as the single remaining superpower and the American assertion of that power in the recently concluded Gulf War. The film focuses on the American military, rather than the medical profession or public health workers. Produced by Robert Solo, who had also produced the 1978 remake, and directed by the independent filmmaker Abel Ferrara, *Body Snatchers*, after opening at the Cannes Film Festival, it enjoyed a limited commercial release.[32] The film shifts the narrative to a different location: an American army base in the southern state of Alabama where a family is temporarily stationed.[33] The father, a chemist with a PhD who works for the Environmental Protection Agency, is assigned to investigate the environmental effects of chemical and biological weapons on the soldiers at the base and the surrounding countryside. The movie focuses, however, on Marti Malone (Gabrielle Anwar), the family's teenage daughter, and opens after the pod invasion has already begun at the base. Marti quickly falls in love with Tim (Billy Wirth), a helicopter pilot who has returned from the Middle East, tries unsuccessfully to save her half-brother Andy (Reilly Murphy) as well as her other family members, and eventually escapes with Tim to another army base.

If the first film critiqued middle-class conformity in a small town and the second film critiqued the counterculture in advancing conformity, then the third film accepts conformity as a given and focuses instead on the instrument implementing the sameness: the military. Anticipating 1995's *Outbreak*, the military, a pod society by its nature as an organization of assimilation, is the villain.[34] It is the tool for spreading the pods worldwide through American post-Cold War hegemony. The film critiques how individual identity and feelings create conflicts. The pods offer a way to erase these issues. Moreover, the film's depiction of the transformation is the most horrific yet. A hospital ward in one scene consists of humans and their pod duplicates lying next to one another. These human bodies, which are covered with transparent tendrils, become desiccated and then collapse one after another.

Body Snatchers replays several scenes from earlier versions, such as the confrontation between a pod person and a medical doctor, as well as visual effects from the 1978 version, such as the shrunken bodies and the duplicates' high-pitched scream. *Body Snatchers* is even more dystopian, presenting a universe that is cold and uncaring and in which the pod people are far more aggressive. It anticipates in this respect the transformation of zombies into the "fast zombies" of 2002's *28 Days Later* and 2004's *Dawn of the Dead*, and subsequent remakes will later adopt this same aggressiveness, such as, for example, *The Invasion*, where the infected spit their infection. Moreover, a sense of inevitability of the takeover pervades the 1993 version. It opens with Marti in the backseat of her family car with her half-brother Andy while recounting in a voiceover a dark present and a hostile future beyond human control.

Sometimes things happen that we don't understand. Maybe we shouldn't try to understand those things. My dad had been assigned to inspect the military southern sector of the EPA. My stepmother, my half-brother and I had to spend almost 2 months on the road with them. I can tell you it's not easy being stuck in a car with a 6-year-old and the woman who replaced your mom. But then again, nobody asked me what I wanted to do that summer. I guess things do happen for a reason, even if you don't like what that reason is.

Body Snatchers also breaks with the earlier movies in depicting many of its characters as already deeply flawed. Marti's stepmother, Carol Malone, for example, is distant and uncaring. Marti's new teenage friend, Jenn Platt (Christine Elise), who views Marti's dad as a "hippie" working at the EPA "saving the planet," brings Marti to her home where she introduces her unconscious, alcoholic mother. Jenn casually remarks that her father, the base commander, is an insomniac, because he fears that Jenn's mother will burn down their house due to her alcoholism. The family is already "shot to hell," and Marti will eventually kill the pod versions of both her father and her half-brother.

Where in the earlier movie versions humans sought to imitate and "pass" as the infected, the pod people now mimic humans, since they are self-aware and insidious, adding to the sense of despair. Marti's stepmother is already a replacement for Marti's biological mother, and her pod replacement later nearly seduces her husband into accepting becoming a pod person by acknowledging his anger, fear and pain.[35] When Tim points out to Marti that they can pass as pod people by displaying no emotion, as in the earlier remakes, the duplicate of Marti's father soon passes as a human to trap Marti and Andy, assuring both that he knows what he is doing and where he is going. A transformed Jenn later poses as a human, claims that she knows where Marti can find Andy, and then tricks Marti into revealing herself as human. Still later, Andy's duplicate, posing as human, nearly succeeds in destroying the helicopter in which Marti and Tim have fled. There is no longer a clear difference between the display of emotions by the humans and the simulation of emotions by the pods.

The film's bleakness is especially apparent in its replay of the standard scene about the clash between individuality and conformity in society. This time the scene takes place between the military base's understandably disturbed and paranoid human doctor, Major Collins (Forest Whitaker), and the base commander, General Platt, who has become a pod person. Like the equivalent scenes in the earlier films – between Miles and Dr. Kaufman and between Matthew and Kibner – General Platt explains to Major Collins the logic of the invaders. "When all things are conformed, there'll be no more disputes, no conflicts, no problems any longer." He describes how the aliens arrived after traveling "light years throughout the universe, always surviving, always growing stronger, because we've learned. It's the race that's important, not the individual." R. Lee Ermey, who plays Pratt, was celebrated for his role as the stone-cold marine drill instructor in *Full Metal Jacket* (1987), which underscores the equivalence of the soldiers with the pods. Collins' reply – "the individual is always important" – reveals how far the case for human individualism has fallen, since he stammers out, in a half-hearted manner, why humans, as individuals, should continue to exist. The crowd of pod people surrounding him respond more clearly: "Only unity guarantees survival . . . The human race left to its own devices is doomed. Accept it. It's a better way . . . It's a matter of survival." Collins has no answer and eventually uses his gun not against the pods but to blow his own brains out.

Forest Whitaker is notably the first prominent black actor in the series of remakes, and the film implicitly suggests, for the first time, that the pods may offer a solution to racism in America. An early scene highlights existing non-pod racism. When Marti uses a restroom at a local gas station in the American South prior to her family's arrival at the base, a black MP grabs her, threatens her with a knife and tells her, "They get you when you sleep." When Marti seeks help from the white owners of the station, they oblige by grabbing their guns and suggesting that they may lynch this black man for threatening a young white girl. While the human military pursues the American ideal of assimilation, it has no effect on the rest of America, which continues to physically threaten and kill those who are not white. Human society is deeply racist, while a pod takeover ironically offers the possibility of complete assimilation and an end to racism.

On the other hand, if Marti is the first female lead in the series of remakes, the film offers no change to gender norms, whether pre- or post-pod takeover. This same early scene at a rural gas station genders Marti through her sexualization in the eyes of the white owners who plainly view the black MP as sexually threatening her. Moreover, she remains an object of male gaze and desire throughout the film. After only briefly meeting Tim, she engages in a sexual relationship with him, even though she is much younger (and possibly underage). Later when Marti is almost taken over by the pod people, she is shown dozing off in a bath naked and covered by nothing but soap bubbles. Still later, her pod duplicate arises naked to seduce Tim into becoming a pod person in the same way that her stepmother nearly seduces her father.

The film's ending underscores the aliens' likely future triumph. The military, the protector of America's newfound global hegemony, intends to destroy the country from within by spreading pods everywhere. Tim and Marti from their military helicopter destroy the army trucks loaded with pods that fan out from the base. The ending, like that of *Outbreak*, is seemingly happy, since the protagonists appear to have stopped the alien takeover, but is also ambiguous and conflicted. Even Marti acknowledges both the inherent contradictions and the futility of their violent action that supposedly stops the pods. "They had destroyed everyone I loved. Our reaction was only human. Revenge, hate, remorse, despair, pity and most of all, fear. I remember feeling all those things as I watched the bombs explode." In contrast to the clarity of uniformity offered by the pod people, to be human is to experience the complex contradictions of human emotions, including a destructive desire for revenge through violence, which Marti suggests is the most human of reactions. The film ends with Marti's matter of fact statement that "they get you when you sleep but you can only stay awake so long." A deep, male voiceover then repeats the seductive chant of Marti's stepmother to her dad, "Where you gonna' go? Where you gonna' run? Where you gonna' hide? Nowhere, 'cause there's no one like you left." The film mourns the loss of individuality and darkly asserts that the alien infection will spread worldwide. If Siegel envisioned in the 1950s that his world was quickly changing to conform to those who welcomed entering the army or being imprisoned, *Body Snatchers* envisions a world in which conformity, spread by America's supposed defenders, the military, is already widespread across society.

The Attractive Threat: *The Invasion* (2007)

The Invasion was directed by Oliver Hirschbiegel and released in 2007, the first remake in a post-9/11 globalized world. It reverses the 1993 version in critiquing the American, civilian government, which is represented by a corrupt, disease-spreading CDC, and in featuring the American military as the source of the cure. While the earlier movies focus on an explicitly American setting, the 2007 version is aimed at an international audience with its Australian and British lead actors, Nicole Kidman and Daniel Craig, and it shifts the geographical focus to Washington, DC, so as to use a single location as a stand in for the international repercussions of the alien-originating, infectious disease. What happens in the capital of the United States spreads globally, which the movie shows through short news reports.[36] In threatening America, the alien-originating virus threatens the entire world. The 2007 version likewise advances the same development as other, then contemporary disease films – from imagined containment that contradicts global, structural changes to the spread of an uncontainable, viral pandemic – even if the movie ends with human triumph. It also suggests that human individualism has created the world's problems.

While reversing again gender roles from the original novel, the film returns to characters from the first two movies, with Kidman as the psychiatrist Carol Bennell and Craig as the medical doctor Ben Driscoll. The disease in this case originates in a fungus-like alien found on the crash site of an American space shuttle where it infects Dr. Tucker Kaufman (Jeremy Northam), Bennell's ex-husband and the director of the CDC. This alien disease infects people via an asymptomatic virus that takes control of the human brain during REM sleep, and Bennell spends the film trying to save her son Oliver, who is immune from takeover since he contracted a brain illness during early childhood. His immunity offers the possibility of developing a vaccine that can cure the disease. In contrast to the 1978 and 1993 remakes, the movie seemingly ends happily: Bennell protects her son, the military successfully develops a vaccine, the infected are cured (with no memory of what has happened), and the media announces an end to the global pandemic.

As with the earlier versions, the 2007 version reflects its historical context. For example, whereas pods were previously transported around in the trunks of cars to infect their human hosts or were placed near their human originals in basements and hospital wards, the aliens now spread by what had in the early 2000s emerged as a major fear of emerging infectious diseases such as SARS: person-to-person infection. A cough into the face of an uninfected human spreads the virus. *The Invasion* presents itself as a more realistic film for the 2000s. Only scientific progress and research that will eventually result in the development of a vaccine can contain the virus by also curing those already infected. Heroes matter, but science is king.

Yet, if the movie ends happily with the defeat of the alien virus, *The Invasion* is inconsistent in its views and sometimes advocates for the continued spread of the infectious disease. *The Invasion* seems to envision – and, at times, endorse – the triumph of the alien virus in its ability to resolve intractable world problems. In effect, it shows the outcome of what the pod people in the 1993 version had suggested – "no more disputes, no conflicts." In one scene, it

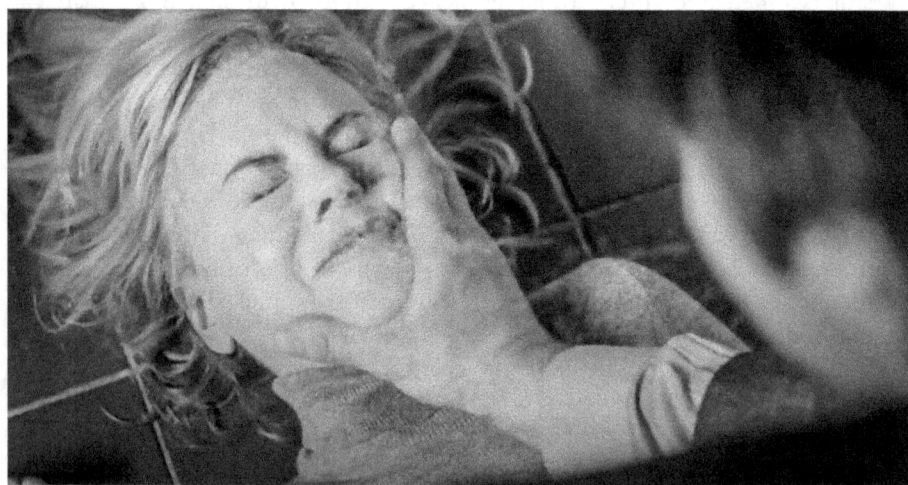

Figure 4.2 *The Invasion* (2007): Carrol Bennell's ex-husband infects her with an alien virus by forcibly holding her down and spitting saliva onto her face.

depicts the result of the global spread of the alien infection in news broadcasts: a global nuclear deal that includes North Korea, a peace treaty between India and Pakistan, China's release of political prisoners, a drop in suicide attacks against American soldiers in Kabul, a peace accord with Iran, universal health care in the United States, an end to the Darfur crisis and free AIDS vaccines around the world. Peace and prosperity have rapidly spread as a result of the virus so that what started in the capital of the United States quickly globalized.

Moreover, the film articulates the source of human conflict, which only the disease can cure: human nature. The key conversation occurs this time over an elegant dinner of caviar and champagne at the house of the Czech ambassador, which reflects the movie's global outlook and at which Bennell and Driscoll represent members of the global elite. During dinner, the Russian diplomat Yorish tells Bennell he is mystified by American belief in the ability to solve large, complex problems with a simple solution. Yorish asks Bennell, "Can you give me a pill to make me see the world the way you Americans see the world? Can a pill help me understand [the war in] Iraq, or [the crisis in] Darfur, or even [the horrific treatment of persons of color during the hurricane in] New Orleans?" Evoking Thomas Hobbes, he argues that civilization is a mere veneer and that violence is the human norm.

> All I am saying is that civilization crumbles whenever we need it most. In the right situation, we are all capable of the most terrible crimes. To imagine a world where this was not so, where every crisis did not result in new atrocities, where every newspaper is not full of war and violence. Well, this is to imagine a world where human beings cease to be human.

Bennell believes such solutions are possible as reflected in how she earlier prescribed pills for her patients, including one of whom claimed that her abusive husband was no longer her husband, because he was no longer abusive (and who had, in fact, been taken over).[37] In reply to Yorish, Bennell argues that humans "retain some basic animal instincts." She then continues,

> Our consciousness is changing. Five hundred years ago, postmodern feminists didn't exist, yet one sits right beside you today. And while that fact may not undo all of the terrible things that have been done in this world, at least it gives me reason to believe that one day things may be different.

Reflective of the film's reactionary narrative, Bennell seems only to pay lip service to the changed gender roles that feminism has produced. Her argument is delivered flatly, without a hint of emotion, as though required but disbelieved. Moreover, that Bennell has identified her patient as hysterical (because she accurately perceived her husband was no longer her husband) and prescribed a pill for her is the traditional, stereotypical reaction to a woman acting emotionally. Bennell does not believe her female patient could possibly know or understand what might be happening around her, and instead reduces her to a crazy woman. Bennell's empowerment as a feminist is solely focused on her success in her personal career. There is no attempt to change gender norms across the rest of society or substantively critique the male-centered capitalist world in which she partakes. Even Bennell's power is constricted and demonstrates that a woman's role remains that of a partner who supports and takes care of a man. When life returns to normal in the film's ending, Bennell is working in the kitchen while Driscoll drinks coffee and reads the newspaper. The scene returns to the gender norms of the original 1956 movie in which Becky Driscoll prepared breakfast and coffee for Miles Bennell. Human nature is a male-centered world.

The movie's pessimism about contemporary society focuses upon the inevitable failure of marriage and romantic love in this world, recalling Kibner's observation from the 1978 film that "the whole family unit is shot to hell." As Kaufman stalks Bennell in a closed room in one scene, he explains that the reason for the failure of their marriage was that he was placed third – after their son and her job. Even Bennell and Driscoll never enjoy a romantic moment. Their single kiss occurs only after both were drinking, and she explicitly identifies him as her "best friend." While Bennell's maternal love and search for her son is her most redeeming quality, every couple in the film is divorced, separated or in a broken marriage. An alternative is needed in the current world in which the nuclear family unit is loveless.[38]

The alien infection ironically offers the transformative pill that will permanently resolve Yorish's conundrum, and Kaufman, in fact, observes that Bennell should consider the virus as no different than the pills that she prescribes for her patients. Bennell is herself conflicted as a character and in her actions. That Kidman plays a psychiatrist, the role played by the leading pod person in two of the earlier films, suggests the ambiguity of her role. Moreover, in trying to persuade Bennell that the virus offers a world in which humans might live together in peace, Driscoll, who has become infected, reminds Bennell that she, too, had wondered while in Colorado "what it could be like if we could be more like those trees, completely connected with each other in harmony, as one."

The movie's "happy ending" is at best ambiguous, and the film instead seemingly at times endorses what the virus offers. As Driscoll, when a pod person, explains to Bennell, "there is no other" in the new world order so that fighting the aliens is "fighting for all the wrong things." Dr. Stephan Galeano (Jeffrey Wright), one of the scientists who has developed the vaccine at an army medical facility and the only prominent black actor in the cast, tells reporters that they have won, which headlines in newspapers confirm in reporting about renewed, worldwide violence. After all, he observes with a sigh and some disgust, "For better or worse we're human again." Dr. Galeano's delivery of this line underscores that human beings will continue to be divided and that no magic pill or vaccine will resolve racial, ethnic, class or gender differences. In contrast, the virus could have erased these differences, evidenced by a brief, early scene depicting the infected of many different backgrounds driving together in a car. If the military had spread the pod disease in the 1993 version, in a post-9/11 era the civilian government now spreads the disease through an inoculation program disguised as a flu vaccination and the military must intervene to stop it. A return to civilian control results in a world filled with conflict and discord. In a post-9/11 era, only the military can achieve global peace, but the only permanent source for such peace ironically originates with an alien virus.

The film concludes with the supposedly happy ending of a family breakfast scene in which Bennell sends her son Oliver to school (along with her newly adopted son Gene). Driscoll, who has become human again, ignores the family as befits a patriarchal father. His only contribution is to read headlines from *The Washington Post* about "83 more deaths in Baghdad" and then ask, "Is it ever going to end?" As the camera moves to a close-up of Bennell looking uncertain about her decision to help find a vaccine, Yorish's words about whether civilization is a veneer play in a voiceover, recalling the seductive, male voiceover that had ended the 1993 *Body Snatchers*. Bennell's doubts reflect the film's view that attempts to reconcile our differences by offering a place to those who have been excluded, will not save us from human nature and our state of fracture. An alien virus, which transforms human nature, is the seemingly preferred solution to the growing violence and fragmentation. Sameness is the implicit answer to the growing conflicts in an increasingly expansive American empire.

THE HAPPY, BIO-ENGINEERED TRANSFORMATION: *LITTLE JOE* (2019)

The most recent remake, *Little Joe* (2019), offers the most radical change in setting, plot and message. That the film's title does not refer to the "invasion" of the original book or of the prior remakes underscores the film's shift. Humanity's problem remains the same: individual identity results in cultural conflict and fragmentation. *Little Joe*'s narrative, however, depicts how humanity may successfully develop a solution by creating the viral agent of its own uniformity. The film's title identifies the infection, a genetically engineered plant, diminutively referred to as "Little Joe," and signals the film's welcoming of the resulting human transformation. It returns the movie to its roots as a localized story but acknowledges its global implications, since the plant and its infection will spread throughout the world. As with other contemporary disease films, the disease will overwhelm the world so as to create, through advanced technology, a better, "posthuman" society.

Little Joe had the only female director of the remakes, Jessica Hausner, an Austrian filmmaker who had directed non-commercial, art movies, such as *Lourdes* (2009) and *Amour Fou* (2014). It is also the only non-American remake. Independently co-produced by Austrian, German and British companies, the film shifts to the United Kingdom. The story takes place in London, where the protagonist, Alice Woodard (Emily Beecham), develops a new plant that emits the hormone oxytocin also known as the "mother hormone." Despite its non-American production, the movie reflects another step in the globalization of what had been an American, local narrative. The problems within American society have spread worldwide. Alice, a middle class, single mother, names the plant "Little Joe" after her adolescent son Joe (Kit Connor). She has genetically engineered Little Joe, a small plant with red tendrils, not to reproduce in order to control its commercialization. As a result, when its pollen is inhaled, it transforms people by causing them to experience happiness but also overriding their individuality and personal emotions. The evolved plant then encourages its own reproduction by urging humans to care for it and help spread its infection to other humans. Like the earlier remakes, *Little Joe*'s infection changes personalities, particularly those changes of the later remakes in which the infected became hostile and aggressive, not just unemotional workers. These changes begin in *Little Joe* with Bello, a dog that becomes hostile to its owner Bella, Chris (Ben Whitshaw), another co-worker who becomes sexually aggressive towards Alice, and then Joe, Alice's adolescent son who becomes rebellious towards his parents as well as sexually active.

Figure 4.3 *Little Joe* (2019): Alice Woodard and her assistant, Chris, tend to Alice's bio-engineered, neutered flowers whose scent transforms humans.

Hausner has advocated for a positive outlook of her film, since the plot ultimately vindicates Alice's need to accept Joe's maturity and suggests that Little Joe, in effect her other child, enables her and others to find joy.[39] As Karl, Alice's boss at her biotech firm, observes when Alice tells him that Little Joe is affecting people exposed to its pollen, "Who can prove the genuineness of feelings? Moreover, who cares?" Their biotech firm will make the world a "happier place." Contrary to those who viewed the movie's ending as apocalyptic, one interviewer commented to Hausner, "That's something I found interesting about the end of the movie. Maybe they've been brainwashed by this plant, but they're happy. And if they're happy, who are we to judge them?" Hausner agreed, replying, "And I'm so astonished, audiences or journalists ask me, 'Why is your film such a dark and dystopian look into the future?' I say, 'It's not! It's actually quite friendly.'"[40] *Little Joe* returns to the pessimism of the 1978 version, in which everyone is inevitably infected, but transforms this message by shifting the process of conformity from a pod grown from a delicate, reddish-pink alien flower that desiccates human bodies to a bioengineered flower with red tendrils that calms you into acceptance. Humans are not replaced, but transformed.

Little Joe's troubling message reflects the cultural context in which it was produced, advocating social conformity that emerges not from without, but from within, namely human, scientific engineering. If the infected Chris is admirable in finally declaring his feelings for Alice, he also invades the privacy of her home and twice forces himself upon her, including knocking her unconscious at the end of the film. When Alice insists that he leave her home, he fails to acknowledge any behavioral boundaries, choosing instead to declare, "I think I love you." While one of the film's few open expressions of positive feeling, Chris delivers the line in a flat, emotionless monotone. It reflects love in the post-Little Joe world, which is no different than the emotionlessness of pods. Hausner endorses the disconnect, observing, "My experience is that free choice is very limited even in a free world. We are very much manipulated in terms of how we should think and how we should behave."[41] The movie condones the plant's infection as a form of human evolution that might otherwise not have been possible, resulting in the disappearance of unnecessary privacy and a sense of happiness for everyone at Alice's biotech company and eventually throughout the world.

The movie specifically presents the virus as an attractive alternative to the intractable conflicts between generations. Throughout the film, Alice is concerned about her son's infection, but her resistance to accept the changes in him reflects her attempt to keep him in a state of permanent boyhood. As Alice's ex-husband comments, Joe is simply changing as a result of his adolescence. Moreover, after Joe later infects his girlfriend Selma, the two spend the remainder of the film together openly mocking Alice's unease with her son's developing independence. The virus offers an alternative to these seemingly incurable differences.

The movie endorses the infection as a societal good through a series of sessions between Alice and her psychiatrist. While Alice slowly seems to accept her need to allow Joe some measure of freedom, her own infection results in her consent to Joe's proposal that he live for a time with his father as reflective of his maturing into adulthood. Her calm acceptance is nothing short of miraculous. At the end of her last visit, Alice leaves her psychiatrist a Little Joe plant, and its bright red tendrils are identical to the bright red walls that cover the psychiatrist's office. Little Joe serves as a metaphor for a bioengineered solution to what would otherwise have taken Freudian analysis years to accomplish. Little Joe is the pill that Yorish had sought from Bennell in *The Invasion* to solve the inevitability of human conflict, including the unending violence and atrocities. *Little Joe* proposes that the solution to finding a balance between motherhood and a career is to become a pod.

Little Joe identifies with the infected as well as mocks uninfected humans. It endorses the lifestyle of the infected as equivalent and, in fact, superior to the uninfected humans, since it offers happiness to everyone, even if the film explicitly notes it turns people into zombies. Bella announces to those around her that she knows what is going on, and Alice confesses over lunch to Chris, who is now infected, her concern that the plant has mutated, resulting in a virus infecting the human brain. Chris rejects Bella's perception as originating from an emotionally unstable woman and scoffs at Alice's fears. "Right, stop looking at me as if I were a zombie," he says to Alice. Both women are held up to ridicule by their male colleagues for their paranoia, portrayed in the case of Bella as emotional imbalance or hysteria. Human emotions are reduced to madness that get in the way of a functioning society, whereas becoming an emotionless zombie is praised. In a particularly chilling scene at Alice's home, which evokes the confrontation scenes from the earlier remakes, the infected Joe confesses to his mother that he's infected but happy. He assures her that you do not notice the difference after infection, and Selma observes that the infected easily pass as uninfected. "It's like being dead," she adds. "You don't notice you're dead, do you?" After a few moments of stunned silence by Alice, Joe laughs with Selma, informing his mother that it was just a joke. Even Alice will later pick up on the joke when she confesses that Little Joe has mutated. When asked how she identifies the symptoms of the infected, Alice responds, "well, it's not like they become zombies." If people are happy, notwithstanding "imperceptible" changes and the loss of "genuine" feelings, then that is all that matters. Not surprisingly, Hausner has expressed her inability to distinguish in Siegel's 1956 movie the changed behavior of the pod people and was bored by the second half of the movie. She views *Little Joe* as "prolong[ing] the first half until the very end of the film" and resulting in a favorable transformation of society.[42]

Little Joe endorses a transformation in human consciousness, which it humorously identifies as becoming a zombie. In the traditional zombie narrative, turning into a zombie metaphorically represents the breaking of norms and usually entails a loss of consciousness. In *White Zombie* (1932) a foreign voodoo master uses a rose's smell to transform a woman into a zombie on her wedding day to satisfy the sexual desires of a supposed friend. In contrast, a red flower in *Little Joe* results in a supposedly positive outcome. While some early test subjects who have smelled the pollen exhibited imperceptible changes, these subjects are happy in the end, even if other family members are unhappy with these changes. The transformation represents a rational choice in a world in which truth, in this case whether it is good or bad to become a zombie, is elusive and how to judge that outcome is entirely subjective. Commercialized, global science offers humanity a utopia.

The closing scenes underscore the film's advocacy for this evolutionary transformation of the human species. Bella, despairing at the transformation of all of her co-workers, confesses to them in the company's lunch cafeteria that she had always "just pretended" – both in her inhaling of the pollen and in her relationship with the others, with the exception of her dog Bello. "You're all gone. You just don't know it," she tells them. "You are no longer your real selves." They, in turn, mock her. When Bella flees from the cafeteria, Karl and Chris chase her into a stairwell, and Alice soon finds her nearly dead at the bottom of the stairwell with Karl and Chris looking on. Karl's subsequent speech to the company workers about the accident (suicide? attempted murder?) assures them of the genuineness of his feelings – "I'm absolutely shaken," he states with a flat and emotionless voice. That does not prevent, however, the introduction of Little Joe at the upcoming flower fair, with further testing deemed unnecessary. Ironically, Alice's therapist, the role played in the earliest movies by the evil Drs. Kaufman and Kibner, echoes Bella's sentiment. Toward the end of the film, she counsels the now infected Alice, who is unusually calm, poised and with a smile on her face, "It would be a mistake to deny who you really are." The movie ends happily with the infected Alice smiling and saying goodnight to Little Joe. Little Joe, in turn, waves its red tendrils at Alice and says, as voiced by Hausner's own son, "Good night, mom."[43]

Alice has become the happy, contented worker for this new corporate state in which material satisfaction and personal happiness trump a belief in historical and social progress or in that which transcends human understanding. The film's immaculate compositions – from the vertiginous crane shot of unending rows of neatly aligned, distinctly colored plants in a corporate greenhouse to the long shot view at night through two townhouse widows of Alice and her son Joe playfully eating their takeout dinner at opposite ends of a dining room table against a backdrop of a lime green wall – underscore the inevitable logic of the film's viewpoint. In the film's contemporary world of material abundance, placidity and imagery have replaced the need for historical change and individual transcendence. Hausner's film advocates for the pod or simulated human over the real human.[44]

Conclusion

The Body Snatchers book and the movie remakes, with the possible exception of *The Invasion*, identify conformity as inevitable. Yet viewed over time, the films depict shifting attitudes towards this conformity – from absolute rejection to welcoming it. Siegel's *Invasion of the Body Snatchers* foresaw an inevitable conformity in small-town America but envisioned an alternate reality for the elite few, especially white males, for whom individual identity remained a possibility. Kaufman's remake twenty years later expanded that bleak vision to an even bigger stage, San Francisco, and depicted that conformity in the arrival of alien spores in the form of beautiful flowers. It attributed the invasion to the absorption of a counterculture which emphasized personal meaning and in which material comforts seduced America's white middle class. Ferrara's 1993 *Body Snatchers*, while envisioning the takeover of the pods from within the confines of a military base, envisioned a more aggressive and insidious infection in which the pods match, if not surpass, the film's humans but with none of their emotional infirmities. The mainstream *The Invasion* criticized American naivete in addressing the emerging infectious disease threat. It anticipated the attack upon the CDC as a deep state conspiratorial player during COVID. It also implicitly advocated for a global perspective in which American capitalism successfully resolved the conflicts of an increasingly expansive empire. From the perspective of historical American values, the most recent version of these remakes, the independently produced *Little Joe*, is the most radical and dystopian. Contemporary culture, it argues, requires neither broader perspectives nor the embrace of more groups into society that many have sought for the last half-century. It envisions an evolution of the species to a posthuman world in which capitalist technology transforms and smooths over any differences between individuals.

The remakes of Jack Finney's novel *The Body Snatchers* transition over the course of the past 70 years from the blissful ignorance of a segregated world in which the white, heterosexual male represents the norm to a post-cultural identity world in which everyone consciously chooses to be the same and in which capitalism enables and benefits from that sameness. These remakes also move from a local, American setting, such as Santa Mira and San Francisco, to a global network of communities in which culture is increasingly uniform, such as the elite residences of Washington, DC or the picturesque townhouses and the antiseptic, biotech lab in London. Finally, the source for the disease has changed from extraterrestrial, alien pods to person-to-person transmission of an alien virus to biochemically engineered plants. Even the protagonist no longer resists and fights against the spreading alien infection but now creates and brings her bioengineered flower with its infectious virus to her own home.

The conformity feared during the 1950s, which threatened humanity through its erasure of emotions, has been embraced by the contemporary need to adapt to a global, capitalist community in which differences are perceived as threatening human survival – or at least the capitalist structure – rather than enriching the species through those differences. Cultural identities on the screen disappear but with them the differences that distinguish each person from the next. Sameness, regardless of gender, race, ethnicity, class or age, becomes the norm, notwithstanding that fragmentation increasingly divides the world. If there are seemingly intractable political and social conflicts, then increasingly the solution, according to these remakes, is to transform people into pods or chemically altered beings, as a way to flatten humanity into an equality that erases all differences, including individuality and uniqueness. Recalling the enlightened naivete that had centuries ago declared that we live in the best of all possible worlds, these remakes increasingly assert an optimistic faith in solving the most intractable problems, including conflicts resulting from differences.[45]

In an era in which social hierarchies are depicted as limitations on human freedom and potential, these remakes also assert the relativism of moral values. In *Little Joe* the older, dissenting worker is characterized as unbalanced, and the adolescent becomes teacher to the parent. Moreover, a bioengineered plant offers a utopian, technological solution in which a reimagined counterculture enables the young to teach the old the limitless possibilities of the species that can be gained through science. This plant offers a personal happiness in which conflict ceases to exist. In a contemporary world in which historically transient cultural myths have replaced a belief in any coherent, transcendent ideals, these remakes now advocate for the technological development by a large pharmaceutical company of a virus that will globally transform humans into content, self-satisfied zombies.

Notes

1. The two *Robocop* movies (1987 and 2014) exemplify a science fiction remake. Where the original *Robocop* served as a social satire of Reaganism, the remake endorses American technology and a conservative political agenda. The two *3:10 to Yuma* movies (1957 and 2007) exemplify a Western remake, where the former focuses on family while the latter focuses on male bonding.
2. Finney's novel was originally published as a serial in 1954 in *Collier's* and differed in several respects from the novel *The Body Snatchers,* which was published a year later. The novel was, in turn, later republished in 1978 under the title *Invasion of the Body Snatchers* to take advantage of the second movie adaptation. See Kathleen Loock, "The Return of the Pod People: Remaking Cultural Anxieties in Invasion of the Body Snatchers," in *Film Remakes, Adaptations and Fan Productions: Remake | Remodel*, eds. Kathleen Loock and Constantine Verevis (London: Palgrave

Macmillan, 2012), 122–44, note 13; for summaries of the evolution of the *Body Snatchers* remakes, Neil Badmington, "Pod Almighty!; Or, Humanism, Posthumanism, and the Strange Case of *Invasion of the Body Snatchers*," *Textual Practice* 15, no. 1 (2001): 5–22, note 40. For further discussion about the book see Wald, *Contagious*, 188–99.

3. On these changes generally, Edward Tenner, *The Efficiency Paradox*; and Zuboff, *The Age of Surveillance Capitalism*. The *Body Snatchers* was not the first fictional work of the 1950s to envision an invasion in which aliens took control of humans. Robert Heinlein's 1951 *The Puppet Masters* is a story of slug-like aliens that attached themselves to and gained control over the nervous system of humans. It was adapted as a movie, *The Faculty*, in 1998. The movie's characters humorously discuss the similarities and differences between *The Body Snatchers* and *The Puppet Masters*. *The Faculty* is based on both.

4. There have been several book-length studies of Siegel's adaptation. For one example, Barry Keith Grant, *Invasion of the Body Snatchers* (London: Bloomsbury, 2010). For further bibliography see Murray Leeder, "Invasion of the Body Snatchers", *Oxford Bibliographies*, July 24, 2018, https://www.oxfordbibliographies.com/view/document/obo-9780199791286/obo-9780199791286-0297.xml.

5. This does not exhaust the remakes, adaptations and take-offs of the *Body Snatchers* movies. In 1977 the avant-garde Austrian movie *Invisible Adversaries* about an invasion of alien doubles was released, and in 2007 the low-budget *Invasion of the Pod People*, a "mockbuster," was released to take advantage of the release of *Invasion*. Several other movies, such as *The Thing* (1982), *Strange Invaders* (1983) and *Halloween III: Season of the Witch* (1983), share some themes. Since they are not a direct line of the remakes, they will not be discussed. For a further analysis of the similarities and differences in the plots, characters, and tone of the 1956, 1978, 1993 and 2007 movie adaptations, see Loock, "The Return of the Pod People."

6. The term "zombies" is not used in the earlier versions, although it is used often by commentators to discuss several of these films.

7. For a contrary view, Christian Knöppler, *The Monster Always Returns: American Horror Films and Their Remakes* (New York: Columbia University Press, 2017), 134, who concludes: "Yet, even though each film takes a dimmer view of humanity, the case for the pods only gets weaker as well."

8. Arthur LeGacy, "'The Invasion of the Body Snatchers': A Metaphor for the Fifties," *Literature/Film Quarterly* 6, no. 3 (1978): 285–92, here at 287.

9. Those involved in the production of the first movie adaptation of the novel were concerned that the title might be confused with Val Lewton's, *The Body Snatcher* (1945), which was then in re-release, but could think of no better title. See, Robert Cashill, "'There'll Be No More Tears': The Shifting Identities of Invasion of the Body Snatchers," *Cineaste Magazine* 44, no. 2 (2019): 3–7.

10. The alien absorption of human bodies with its analogy to Communist infiltration featured frequently in 1950s films, including: *Invaders from Mars* (1953), *It Came from Outer Space* (1953) and *I Married A Monster from Space* (1958).

11. Don Siegel spoke more of an existing allegorical subtext, but denied a strictly political point of view: "The political reference to Senator McCarthy and totalitarianism was inescapable but I tried not to emphasise it because I feel that motion pictures

are primarily to entertain and I did not want to preach." Alan Lovell, *Don Siegel: American Cinema* (London: British Film Institute, 1975), 54.
12. Stuart M. Kaminsky, "Don Siegel on the Pod Society (1976)," in *The Science Fiction Film Reader*, ed. Gregg Rickman (Milwaukee: Limelight Editions 2009), 136. See also Wald, *Contagious*, 199–204 for further discussion of the first movie.
13. Kaminsky, "Don Siegel on the Pod Society (1976)," 139. This predates Susan Sontag's ideas about illness and cancer. See Susan Sontag, *Illness as Metaphor*.
14. Daniel Mainwaring, the film's screenwriter "with left-wing associations," authored this famous and key line. See J. Hoberman, "Paranoia and the Pods," *Sight and Sound* 4, no. 5 (1994): 28–31.
15. This fear of conformity is reflected in much of the literature of the period, including David Riesman, *The Lonely Crowd; a Study of the Changing American Character* (New Haven: Yale University Press, 1950); and C. Wright Mills, *White Collar: the American Middle Classes* (New York: Oxford University Press, 1951). In the context of this critique of conformity, Dr. Kauffman represents the managerial technocrat who seeks to assuage corporate workers of the need to maximize efficiency and corporate profits.
16. Siegel described the scene in which Miles kisses Becky as: "[H]e knows she's a pod because she's a limp fish." Kaminsky, "Don Siegel on the Pod Society (1976)", 137. That "limp fish" reaction to Miles's kiss represents Becky's "lack of passion" for Miles "or, in Freudian terms, frigidity," according to Katrina Mann. "Moreover, it was not simply her lack of sexual response that was alarming but the patriarchal and paternal loss it signaled." Katrina Mann, "'You're Next!': Postwar Hegemony Besieged in 'Invasion of the Body Snatchers,'" *Cinema Journal* 44, no. 1 (2004): 49–68, here at 62.
17. There is a visually dark undercurrent to the small town of Santa Mira, which reflects Siegel's critique of invasive conformity. The film evokes a film noir atmosphere, such as the nighttime settings, odd camera angles, enclosed spaces, and the threatening mundane, daily objects, which is explicit in the posters on the wall of the Belicecs' dark poolroom that read "noir mirroir" and "femme fatale." See Paul Schrader, "Notes on Film Noir."
18. Several writers have found the early morning image of an ashtray of cigarettes at Miles's office symbolic of their having had sex. See Mann, "'You're Next!'," 61; and Grant, *Invasion of the Body Snatchers*, 91.
19. For a discussion of Becky's role as an independent woman who threatens Miles's masculinity, see Grant, *Invasion of the Body Snatchers*, 77–92. See also Nancy Steffen-Fluhr, "Women and the Inner Game of Don Siegel's 'Invasion of the Body Snatchers,'" *Science Fiction Studies* 11, no. 2 (1984), 139–153, who interprets the film as reflecting male fear and rejection of women. Conformity represents the male fear of changes in traditional gender roles and the pods' taking control during sleep alludes to the poetic association between the "little death" of orgasm and the "big death" of all living beings. Mann, "'You're Next!'," 62, sees in the pods the separation of sex and love from reproduction. Erika Nelson "Invasion of the Body Snatchers: Gender and Sexuality in Four Film Adaptations," *Extrapolation* 52, no. 1 (2011), 51–74, extends to the next three remakes this view of the pods as a threat to male dominance through the "male loss of reproductive control."

20. Mann, "'You're Next!'," 57, views "others" as those excluded from the dominant white, male culture. This would include not only women but also Mexican immigrants (reflected in the distribution of the pods by farm workers).
21. The studio also insisted that Siegel remove the comic dialogue, insisting that the film not mix comedy with horror. Kaminsky, "Don Siegel on the Pod Society (1976)," 134. See also Neil Badmington, "Pod Almighty!," 14.
22. The film's producer, Walter Wanger, had contemplated that Orson Welles, having famously voiced the *War of the Worlds* radio broadcast and movie, would voice the narrator. See Hoberman, J., "Paranoia and the Pods," 30.
23. Knöppler, *The Monster Always Returns*, 100, observes that Santa Mira's rational institutions fail in combating the alien pods and yet the psychiatrist and police in the studio-imposed ending are trustworthy.
24. Kaufman has claimed that his film is more a sequel than a remake of Siegel. Grant, *Invasion of the Body Snatchers*, 94; also Wald, *Contagious*, 204–212. For a reflection at the time, William Bates, "Body Snatching Pods Are Back, Courtesy of Philip Kaufman," *The New York Times*, January 7, 1979, https://www.nytimes.com/1979/01/07/archives/bodysnatching-pods-are-back-courtesy-of-philip-kaufman.html. The second film introduces the same characters with changes. The character Miles, a divorced, small-town doctor, becomes Matthew, a public health official. Becky, a divorcée, becomes Elizabeth, also a health department worker, who is living unhappily with a boyfriend. Jack Belicec, a successful mystery writer, becomes Jack Bellicec, a failed writer, and Nancy Belicec, a housewife, becomes Nancy Bellicec, the owner of a mud bath upon which husband and wife rely for their income. Dr. Kaufman, a small-town psychiatrist, becomes Dr. Kibner, a self-help guru.
25. Philip Kaufman directed several movies critical of Western culture, such as *The White Dawn* (1974), *The Wanderers* (1979) and *The Right Stuff* (1983). As for Kaufman's retrospective view of San Francisco, see David Weiner, "Why 'Invasion of the Body Snatchers' Still Haunts Its Director," *The Hollywood Reporter*, December 20, 2018, https://www.hollywoodreporter.com/movies/movie-news/invasion-body-snatchers-ending-still-haunts-director-1170220/.
26. Philip Kaufman and Stephen Farber, "Hollywood Maverick," *Film Comment* 15, no. 1 (1979): 28.
27. The film opens with pollution and environmental destruction. The alien species infects local plant life, and Matthew is initially shown visiting a restaurant to check on its food contamination. Watergate is evoked in Matthew's unsuccessful effort to alert the mayor to the alien invasion, and Jack and Elizabeth initially express the view that there's a "conspiracy" around them. Kaufman himself had a degree in history. See Michael Dempsey, "Invaders and Encampments: The Films of Philip Kaufman," *Film Quarterly* 32, no. 2 (1978): 17.
28. Ironically, Kaufman decided to cast Nimoy after reading his book *I Am Not Spock* in which he tried to break away from his character. Kaufman professed "to 'feel bad' about his decision." Bates, "Body-Snatching Pods Are Back, Courtesy of Philip Kaufman"; Kaufman and Farber, "Hollywood Maverick," 28.
29. Such bleak endings of New Hollywood movies were common between about 1967 and 1977. They begin with *Bonnie and Clyde* (1967), *The Graduate* (1967) and *Easy Rider* (1969), continued with *The Last Picture Show* (1971), *The Deer Hunter*

(1978) and *Taxi Driver* (1976). They are usually said to end with *Jaws* (1975) and *Star Wars* (1977). See Peter Biskind, *Easy Riders, Raging Bulls: How the Sex-Drugs-and-Rock 'N' Roll Generation Saved Hollywood* (New York: Simon & Schuster, 1998).
30. Kaufman and Farber, "Hollywood Maverick," 28.
31. Bates, "Body-Snatching Pods Are Back, Courtesy of Philip Kaufman."
32. Abel Ferrara directed the raw, violent films *Ms. 45* (1981) and *Bad Lieutenant* (1992) and would later direct such apocalyptic films as *The Addiction* (1995) and *4:44 Last Day* (2011).
33. Ferrara has claimed that the studio, Warner Brothers, which financed the large budget, came up with the setting of an army base. He also claims he would have preferred following Jack Finney's "brilliant" idea of focusing on a doctor in a small town. Ryan Lambie, "Abel Ferrara interview: Driller Killer, Bad Lieutenant, Body Snatchers," *Den of Geek*, November 23, 2016, https://www.denofgeek.com/movies/abel-ferrara-interview-driller-killer-bad-lieutenant-body-snatchers/.
34. Charles Moskos and John Sibley Butler, *All That We Can Be: Black Leadership and Racial Integration the Army Way* (New York: Basic Books, 1997).
35. For a psychoanalytic discussion of this Oedipal scene along with a similar analysis of the first three *The Body Snatchers* movies, see Kelly Hurley, "'Type H': Medicine, Psychiatry and Psychoanalysis in the Body Snatchers Films," *Horror Studies* 6, no. 2 (2015): 195–210.
36. For further discussion: Loock, "The Return of the Pod People."
37. Bennell's patient is played by Veronica Cartwright, the actor who had played the sole survivor, Nancy Bellicec, in Kaufman's 1978 movie version.
38. The spread of the virus and the disintegration of Bennell's family are often linked. For example, Dr. Tucker Kaufman's transformation into a pod person results in his son Oliver's awakening from a nightmare. One writer has interpreted the movie through the lens of a lengthy "custody battle" between Bennell and Kaufman, see Nelson, "Invasion of The Body Snatchers: Gender and Sexuality," 66.
39. Hausner has commented: "The story mainly revolves around the 'two children' she has. There's even a line in one of the dialogues: 'Which of your children will you choose?' Meaning her work or her son. I chose this similarity to make it obvious that the plant is her second child." She also noted, "The funny thing in 'Little Joe' is that you do have the possibility of a biological explanation for what is going on, but on the other hand there's also the option of a psychological one. It could also be that there's nothing 'real' happening at all, and it's all about ideas in the minds of the characters. To have the two options that play against each other was the joy of creating this story." Karin Schiefer, "Interview with Jessica Hausner," *Eurimages*, June 2018, https://rm.coe.int/interview-with-jessica-hausner/168091e731.
40. Marshall Shaffer, "'Little Joe' Director Jessica Hausner on Combining Genres and Maintaining a Personal Stamp [Interview]," *SlashFilm*, December 6, 2019, https://www.slashfilm.com/little-joe-director-interview/.
41. Chuck Bowen, "Interview: Jessica Hausner on *Little Joe* and the Ways of Being and Seeing," *Slant Magazine*, December 1, 2019, https://www.slantmagazine.com/film/interview-jessica-hausner-on-little-joe-and-the-ways-of-being-and-seeing/.
42. Karin Schiefer, "Interview with Jessica Hausner."

43. See Jessica Hausner, "Diesmal wollte ich es gemütlich!," *Der Standard*, May 23, 2014, https://www.derstandard.at/story/1397521284263/diesmal-wollte-ich-es-gemuetlich. After comparing the film to the Frankenstein story with its "monster" who yearns to be free, Hausner has said that she did not want to film a "remake" of Siegel's *Invasion of the Body Snatchers,* but rather offer a happy ending. If society is to function, everyone must lie and play a role. She describes the film's ending as a "twisted" happy ending about a mother who has felt guilty about her focus on work but is now able to let her son go and accept who she is. *Little Joe*, Magnolia Home Entertainment, released on March 10, 2020, "Q & A: Emily Beechum and Jessica Hausner (Film at Lincoln Center)," DVD.
44. Her film endorses the cultural logic of late capitalism whose characteristics include the disappearance of the individual subject, "a whole new culture of the image or the simulacrum," and a loss of historical context. Fredric Jameson, *Postmodernism, or, the Cultural Logic of Late Capitalism* (Durham: Duke University Press, 1991), 6 and 16.
45. Voltaire satirized in the ending of his novel *Candide* (1759) the optimism of the enlightenment philosopher Leibniz in which Pangloss, speaking for Leibniz, finds in the happy ending to the horrific series of events that Candide has endured throughout the novel as evidence that this is the "best of all possible worlds." Candide famously replied simply, "Let us cultivate our garden." Voltaire, *Candide* (New York: Boni & Liveright, 1918), 169.

CHAPTER 5

POPULARIZING THE PANDEMIC: THE *RESIDENT EVIL* FRANCHISE

Introduction

The changes and developments in disease movies over the last few decades did not just occur in individual movies or remakes. In the early 2000s, *Resident Evil*, a movie franchise, successfully capitalized on this expanded and evolving genre. It was based on two video games that were released in 1996 and 1999 and helped revive zombies in popular culture.[1] Capcom, the Japanese owner of the franchise, claimed as early as 1998 that *Resident Evil* had "contributed enormously" to the company's growth and helped make the new PlayStation console the leading system on the market.[2] The video games' success led over several decades to an expansion of the franchise into other media, including novels, plays and animated films. It also led Constantin Film, a German production company, to acquire the movie rights to the video game franchise.[3] The first film series would eventually include six movies released between 2002 and 2016.

Despite the commercial appeal of the franchise, the first movie's production process was torturous. After the success of the original *Resident Evil* video game, Capcom hired George Romero, the director of *Night of the Living Dead* and subsequent zombie movies, to direct an expensive $1.5 million TV commercial for the second video game, *Resident Evil 2*, and thereafter to draft a movie script.[4] Romero wrote a script in 1998 that followed the original game, but Capcom rejected the script and the five or six revisions Romero wrote over the next few years, eventually firing Romero.[5] In the meantime, Paul W. S. Anderson, who had earlier directed the commercially successful *Mortal Kombat* (1995), based on another video game, separately wrote a script for *Resident Evil*. Constantin Film thereafter brought him on board to direct the first film in what would become the *Resident Evil* franchise.[6] Anderson would write the scripts for all six films: *Resident Evil* (2002), *Resident Evil: Apocalypse* (2004), *Resident Evil: Extinction* (2007), *Resident Evil: Afterlife* (2010), *Resident Evil: Retribution* (2012) and *Resident Evil: The Final Chapter* (2016).[7] He would also direct four of the movies and produce all but the first. He remained "heavily involved" even in the films he did not direct, *Apocalypse* and *Extinction*, handpicking their directors.[8] Anderson claimed he was "not trying to [have the films] look like a video game" and attributed their success to their distinctive narrative, which he perceived as a balancing act in satisfying both video game fans and movie audiences.[9] Given his continuous, extensive involvement in all of the films, they represent his vision. These films also became a family affair when, while working on the franchise, Anderson married Milla Jovovich, who plays the main character in the series (Alice). Their daughter, Ever Anderson, would also play key roles (the Red Queen and the young Alicia Marcus) in the last movie, *The Final Chapter*.

Mainstream movie critics have consistently panned the six movies.[10] Roger Ebert placed the first two films upon their release on his "most hated" film list.[11] He described *Apocalypse* as "an utterly meaningless waste of time. There was no reason to produce it, except to make money, and there is no reason to see it, except to spend money. It is a dead zone, a film without interest, wit, imagination or even entertaining violence and special effects."[12] A critic for *The New Yorker* likewise wrote that "the films are best enjoyed out of sequence, with no prior knowledge of the plot" and that they "may resemble formulaic junk, concocted by committee in some corporate flavor-testing lab and served to those who have no taste."[13] The plots of the six movies are convoluted, inconsistent and, at times, incoherent. They are also openly derivative, as the individual movies take themes and narrative elements from other movies. While this derivativeness may, in part, be the cause for some of the negative reviews, the constant updating of themes and episodes from earlier movies to fit contemporary expectations also helps explain the franchise's enduring popularity. The films offered audiences known themes and expected scenes within a multi-media franchise, a formula that was successful in other franchises.[14] Even if an individual film or game in the franchise failed to deliver, consumers might complain but remained loyal.

All six *Resident Evil* movies, notwithstanding their critical drubbing, were hugely profitable, making this franchise at the time "easily the longest-running, highest-grossing film series ever based on a video game."[15] To date, Anderson's six films in the *Resident Evil* franchise have grossed over $1.2 billion. This popularity both in the United States and globally, despite the negative reviews, underscores the franchise's reflection and support of mainstream ideas and audience expectations about disease movies. It is evidence of Hollywood's focus on profit, but the franchise could not have made money if the underlying disease paradigm that the films depict had not changed over time. The *Resident Evil* franchise critiques individual, corporate villains who are responsible for the disease and its horrific effects. It also, however, largely fails to critique the structural reasons for that villainy and concludes with an imagined, hoped-for apocalyptic future where the world will simply be better, despite the consequences of a global pandemic that has killed most of humanity. It offers no alternative to multinational, corporate power other than the cartoonish triumph of good over such evil. The franchise condemns corporations, an easy target for its audience, even as the films themselves have financially benefited such corporations. Their supposed critique of corporate America coincides with the changes to disease films generally and corresponds to the transformation of American culture. If the early franchise films present disease as a containable biological weapon, the later films depict the biologically created disease as leading to an inevitable global pandemic and, in the concluding film, a posthuman transformation.

The franchise's most groundbreaking challenge to movie norms is its female lead. Diverging from its video game source, the franchise features Alice as the action hero of all six films and eventually humanity's savior.[16] She punishes those who threaten or violate her sexually and defeats those who try to control her, including a lover who betrays her. In contrast, the franchise links men, masculinity and patriarchy to greed and, in the franchise's last film, to a planned, global genocide.[17] Yet, while Alice is the lead character, the films largely conform to the standard narrative conventions of gender. Alice is a sexualized and fetishized object, evidenced by her attire or lack thereof.[18] In contrast to male action superheroes of the 2010s, such as Batman in *The Dark Knight Rises* (2012) and Captain America in *Avengers: Endgame* (2019), both of whom defeat their enemies and end happily with their romantic partners, Alice is denied personal happiness and remains consistently unattainable and apart, except for brief moments when she acts as a surrogate mother for children who quickly disappear.[19] Alice remains within gender norms which demand that women outperform men by triumphantly saving the world but at an emotional cost which requires that they remain alone.

Like her male superhero counterparts, however, Alice's success supports the contemporary capitalist paradigm in which only the select few triumph amidst the ruins of the social contract. Alice is last seen riding alone on her motorcycle in an apocalyptic landscape of her global employer's creation. The franchise advocates for the heroic individual who defeats the evil corporation, but like the many superhero movie franchises of the twenty-first century, assumes and advocates for capitalism as the natural order of the human species. The franchise also offers no cure for what ails the world and, in the end, supports the global capitalist ideals that it papers over with a female superhero.[20] The film assumes that disease will overwhelm humanity but prefers to overlook that outcome in favor of a clichéd triumph of good over evil.

This chapter focuses on the first and last episodes in the franchise – *Resident Evil* and *The Final Chapter* – and briefly discusses the four transitional films. The narrative arc of the franchise follows the trajectory of disease movies from the mid-1990s to the mid-2010s. The franchise begins with the release of a virus that creates slow-moving but containable zombies and develops into a global pandemic resulting in a post-apocalyptic landscape of zombies overrunning humanity and in which mutant creatures and artificial intelligence dominate the narrative. Yet, the franchise never explains how or why this change in the disease occurs, since it happens offscreen between the second and the third movies. The franchise is less interested in a nuanced exploration of causes and more focused on offering known themes to retain its audience. Its narrative accordingly changes from primarily a horror story to a stylized action film. The films also change in their perception of corporate capitalism. The first four movies – *Resident Evil, Apocalypse, Extinction* and *Afterlife* – place responsibility for the spread of the pandemic on a global corporation, the Umbrella Corporation. Corporate greed and rampant consumerism have turned the American population – literally – into mindless drones (or zombies), a recurring theme in zombie movies since the 1970s. However, *Retribution* and *The Final Chapter*, the last two episodes of the franchise, shift the focus and advocate for the technological transformation of humanity through cloning and artificial intelligence. The franchise becomes less a clichéd critique of global capitalism than an endorsement for an evolutionary change of the species to erase social and biological differences among humans, thereby furthering the goals of global capitalism by assimilating those differences within its narrative.

Nostalgia for an Imagined Containment: *Resident Evil* (2002)

Resident Evil, the first movie in the franchise, focuses on the outbreak of a disease known as the T-virus. The Umbrella Corporation is described as "the largest commercial entity in the United States . . . [whose] political and financial influence is felt everywhere . . . but whose massive profits are generated by military technology, genetic experimentation, and viral weaponry." It has genetically engineered the T-virus as a biological weapon in an underground research facility called the Hive which is located beneath Raccoon City. The Red Queen, Umbrella's computer system programmed to safeguard the Hive, has sealed it off with hundreds of workers inside. The Red Queen aims to contain the virus, which a corporate thief has deliberately released. Umbrella thereafter sends in a team of commandos to investigate. The team initially discovers Alice in an above ground mansion, the entry to the Hive, and succeeds in shutting down the Red Queen, though several commandoes are killed in the process. The zombies, who are the workers transformed by the T-virus, then kill the remaining members of the team with the Red Queen's assistance, and only Alice and one other survivor escape from the Hive. Umbrella scientists, however, capture both.

Anderson has said that the horror-science fiction movie *Alien* (1979) as well his favorite book, the Lewis Carroll children's fantasy *Alice in Wonderland* (1865), influenced the first film.[21] *Resident Evil* derives many of its ideas from the *Alien* franchise, including the franchise's early films' focus on a profit-driven, corrupt and powerful corporation as well as the evil artificial intelligence serving it. *Resident Evil*'s heroes naively believe that they can expose this corrupting influence on human society. *Resident Evil* is also a throwback to the older genre of zombie movies, such as Romero's *Night of the Living Dead*, though updated with more violence and gore. Like those older movies, *Resident Evil*'s slow-moving zombies attempt to overwhelm humans with their numbers. Moreover, although released in 2002, *Resident Evil* is similar to pre-millennium movies in its depiction of an infectious disease. Its plot focuses on local containment rather than a worldwide apocalypse and substitutes corporate wrongdoing for the military conspiracy of *Outbreak*. While other movies from the early 2000s, such as *28 Days Later*, would transform the zombie narrative, *Resident Evil* has little in common with them and belongs with the earlier paradigm of zombie movies.

Resident Evil's zombies consist of masses of undead, and the living, as in *Night of the Living Dead*, are slow to recognize how to kill them. In place of a TV news broadcaster in the 1968 film, the Red Queen must explain to the living that these undead are vulnerable to a head shot or the separation of the head from the body. Like the small group of humans in *Night of the Living Dead*, the members of the elite commando unit confuse the dead with the living, as when Matt (Eric Mabius), who is searching for his sister and will be the film's other survivor, confuses her for the zombie that she has become. The commando Rain (Michelle Rodriguez) is likewise later unable to shoot her squad member who has become a zombie, resulting in him biting her. There is no cure for the infection caused by these masses of undead. While Rain receives an antivirus that Umbrella has developed and it seems to cure her, moments later she becomes a zombie and attacks Alice and Matt.

Resident Evil's zombies, like Romero's zombies, serve as a metaphor for those who are already spiritually and emotionally dead because of their jobs and daily lives. The film equates the undead with their living counterparts through a humorous critique of corporate culture. Rain, for example, comments upon discovering Umbrella's workers, "All the people that were working here [in the Hive] are dead." Likewise, Kaplan, another team member, notes, "It's pretty goddamn obvious what they are. Lab coats, badges. Those people used to work here!" Working far below ground, separated from Raccoon City and with only a window's simulation of an urban landscape, these living inhabitants of the corporate culture in the Hive were already dead. The effects of the T-virus simply accelerated the process. "Even in death the human body still remains active," the Red Queen wryly observes. "The brain itself holds a small electrical charge that takes months to dissipate. The T-virus provides a massive jolt . . . Put quite simply, it reanimates the body." Like the undead consumers of the original *Dawn of the Dead* (1978), who instinctively wander in and around a suburban mall, these white-collar workers are brought back to life with, as the Red Queen elaborates, "the simplest of motor functions. Perhaps a little memory. Virtually no intelligence. They are driven by the basest of impulses . . . The need to feed." The virus has completed the transformation of these humans into drones, no different from the anonymous horde that had been laboring for Umbrella while still alive.

Resident Evil offers a clichéd critique of the capitalist Umbrella Corporation as the manifestation of what is wrong with American society that supports international corporations generating enormous profits at the expense of middle-class Americans. Its widespread "political and financial influence" is reflected in its creation of a secret testing facility for deadly diseases beneath the heavily urbanized Raccoon City. Alice, a corporate security officer, has sought to expose its wrongdoings, and Matt, with his history of exposing corporate corruption, claims that "corporations like Umbrella think they're above the law, but they're not." Yet, their combined efforts are quixotic and fail. Spence (James Purefoy), Alice's co-worker and one-time lover who stole the T-virus to sell for personal profit, is proven correct when he observes that "nothing ever changes," suggesting that such corporations will continue as before, regardless of their illegal practices. While Spence is killed twice (as a human and as a zombie) for his transgressions, Matt and Alice suffer the consequences of their idealism. Escaping from the Hive, Alice remarks to Matt that they "finally have the proof" of what Umbrella has done. Immediately thereafter Umbrella workers in hazmat suits appear and capture them both. When a short time later Alice awakens and escapes from a locked, hospital examination room, the film's cliffhanger ending reveals that the T-virus has broken out and infected Raccoon City. Corporate overlords, the movie argues, exploit any opportunity and punish all dissent in exercising their vast control over society.

Umbrella's AI, the Red Queen, represents the logical extension of the company's efforts at maximizing control over its employees, which the film underscores by repeatedly showing the commando team from the perspective of Umbrella's ubiquitous security cameras and hence from the Red Queen's point of view. Reflecting the notion of data-driven group-think, the Red Queen's underground research facility is known as the Hive. As an artificial intelligence, the Red Queen symbolizes how corporations rely on statistics, logic and surveillance to ensure its employees remain drones to protect its bottom line.

Figure 5.1 *Resident Evil* (2002): Alice encounters the Red Queen, the Umbrella Corporation's AI seeking to contain the T-virus within the underground Hive.

She causes the deaths of hundreds of Umbrella employees to contain the T-virus but maintains its secrecy as she attempts to prevent the virus from escaping. Just as in Lewis Carroll's story that Anderson based his script upon, Alice confronts and eventually escapes the Red Queen of this underground wonderland. When Alice brings the Red Queen back online so that she can identify an escape route from the Hive, the Red Queen immediately reverts to her cold, calculating approach, including plotting the moves needed to defeat Alice and the commando team to ensure containment. Refusing to open the locked door to the lab in which Alice, Matt and Rain are trapped even as the monstrous Licker mutant pounds on the glass, the Red Queen insists that Alice kill the infected Rain. In contrast to humans, the Red Queen "does not deal in chance" and disregards the antidote for Rain's infection sitting on the train not far away. Only the unexpected appearance of Kaplan, whom the others believed dead, enables all four to escape after he fries the Red Queen's circuitry. While this narrative emotionally favors Alice, the narratives of the later franchise movies will endorse the Red Queen's logic of containment and rehabilitate her as prescient.

Like most Hollywood movies, this first episode in the franchise offers a clear narrative arc. It begins in the mansion with Alice suffering from amnesia, follows her and the commando team to the heart of the Hive, and then depicts their desperate efforts to escape from the research facility and hordes of zombies. *Resident Evil* clearly identifies its heroes – Alice, Matt and Rain – and its villains – Spence and the Umbrella Corporation. Its structure is modeled after *Aliens* (the second movie of that franchise released in 1986), including its female hero and a military security team fighting unknown monsters. Alice reprises the role of Ripley in *Aliens* with the Umbrella's commando team modeled after its team of multiracial colonial marines.[22] Alice's development of skills as a warrior remains credible within the realm of a story in which the monsters are slow moving undead. Umbrella likewise represents a clear and obvious corporate bad actor, whose banality of evil causes disgust. And just like in *Aliens*, Alice's individualistic heroism will win the day (or nearly so).

Resident Evil straddles the disease movies of the mid-1990s through the mid-2000s with its clear identification of villains and heroes, unrelenting, suspenseful action and a nostalgia for an imagined containment. Like earlier films, such as *Outbreak*, *Resident Evil*'s outbreak is initially contained, though the cliffhanger ending reveals the unexplained spread of infection to the population of Raccoon City. Released in the same year as *28 Days Later*, it was less original in its depiction of a disease outbreak and the undead but made far more money at the box office, notwithstanding that critics panned *Resident Evil* with its clear heroes and villains. Unsurprisingly, the nefarious Umbrella triumphs, reflecting American audience expectations that corporations nearly always win – or at least in this first episode from which a sequel is already envisioned. In clearly identifying the source of the film's evil, however, the film also creates a binary morality, an "us versus them" paradigm, which serves both to disguise and reinforce a mythology in which the absence of a social contract informed by the common good weighs against America's ordinary citizens. Each person is alone and must individually – and heroically – confront such capitalist evil rather than as part of a body politic drawing together the differing social and biological interests. The film's focus on the Red Queen is highly unusual in a disease film even if reflective of contemporary movies, such as *The Matrix* (1999). This narrative choice – absent from the video games as well – anticipates the growing concerns about AI technology that would be developed in more detail in later science fiction movies, such as the *Alien* prequels, *Prometheus* (2012) and *Alien: Covenant* (2017). In hindsight this odd contrast lends it, perhaps paradoxically, greater importance as a movie somewhat behind its time about disease, but ahead of its time about technology, including artificial intelligence. While tempered by its cliff-hanging ending, it continues to promote the American capitalist mythology of the triumphant, heroic individual who tries to selflessly save the day and prevent a disease from killing everyone.

Transitions and New Paradigms: *Apocalypse* (2004), *Extinction* (2007), *Afterlife* (2010) and *Retribution* (2012)

The four middle episodes of the *Resident Evil* franchise, *Apocalypse*, *Extinction*, *Afterlife* and *Retribution*, are transitional films, continuing existing trends but sometimes breaking new ground. Viewed in hindsight after the release of all six films, they represent stepping-stones between the first movie, with its focus on an older disease film narrative, and the last movie, which reflects a new paradigm. The meandering plots of these movies makes plain that the development of the franchise was not the result of a detailed, long-term plan. With their inconsistent twists and turns, openings that supposedly summarize the prior episodes and cliffhanger endings, they recall the movie serials of the 1930s and 1940s, such as those about the adventures of Buck Rogers and Flash Gordon. In contrast to those early serials, the openings of these movies gloss over narrative inconsistencies as well as introduce new plot elements and character developments.[23]

The franchise's two overarching developments, however, are clear. First, a post-apocalyptic world replaced the imagined containment narrative of the first two movies. Second, while the focus on Umbrella remained, the company transformed from a problematic corporation to the catalyst for how and why humans must transform to survive. These transitional films offer little social critique and instead depict a pandemic as a cataclysmic event leading to social collapse and the rise of a benevolent, posthuman superhero. The world is "remade" into a "better" place, though the franchise never defines "better" and depicts the means for achieving "better" as simply a few (and in some cases technologically enhanced) individuals "doing good." This perpetuates the American myth that personal choice by a few heroic individuals can substantively improve the world.

Apocalypse, the second movie in the franchise and released in 2004, picks up where the cliffhanger ending of the first movie leaves off. It is set in Raccoon City and begins only a few weeks after Umbrella's reopening of the Hive. Umbrella has quarantined the entire city after the virus' spread throughout the city and at the same time wakes up Alice on whom it has experimented with the T-virus. The enhanced Alice eventually escapes from Raccoon City with a handful of survivors, and Umbrella detonates a nuclear weapon to stop the virus' spread beyond the city limits. In a coda, Umbrella scientist Dr. Alexander Isaacs (Iain Glen) oversees the revival and resurrection of Alice, who had died while escaping the blast. She soon escapes from Umbrella's lab with the help of her surviving friends.

This second film, like the first, replays the disease containment narrative common to earlier disease movies and does not yet reflect the ongoing change in disease movies. Umbrella contains the T-virus outbreak to Raccoon City and its environs, described in the film as "the Hot Zone," a call back to Preston's 1994 book. The film turns Umbrella into an even more militarized entity with significant surveillance capabilities, which reflects the then recent passage in response to 9/11 of the USA PATRIOT Act authorizing expansive government surveillance and the American government's increasing reliance on private, military contractors.[24] Umbrella's security forces even fire live ammunition at crowds of people trying to escape from Raccoon City while the city's hapless police force does nothing. At the end of the movie, Umbrella manages to hide its involvement in the nuclear blast that kills those whom Umbrella has prevented from escaping from Raccoon City.

Apocalypse continues to feature the traditional Hollywood story of good and evil. Alice's main opponent is the Umbrella Corporation, not the zombies. Umbrella corrupts everything good, including the T-virus. According to this film, Umbrella's employee Dr. Charles Ashford (Jared Harris), had invented the T-virus to cure his daughter of a genetic disease (a daughter whom Alice spends much of the film trying to rescue).[25] Umbrella, however, weaponized the T-virus in an effort to develop a mutant super-soldier. When Ashford disobeys Umbrella to save his daughter, an Umbrella administrator summarily executes him, while also acknowledging that "he was a valuable asset to the corporation." Umbrella's other employees are equally disposable. As one commando, Carlos Olivera (Oded Fehr), remarks after Umbrella abandons his squad to zombies, they were "expendable assets. And we've just been expended." Corporations, such as Umbrella, exploit and discard everyone. If Alice and the other survivors form a surrogate family to expose Umbrella's criminal actions, Umbrella triumphs by publicly branding them outlaws. Evil is readily identifiable, while heroes try to fight back.

The transition to a post-apocalyptic landscape as a result of the T-virus occurs anticlimactically in the opening voiceover of the third movie, *Extinction*, which takes place several years later. Alice summarily observes, "The Umbrella Corporation thought they'd contained the T-virus. Well, they were wrong . . . Within weeks, it had consumed the United States, within months the world." She then continues, "The virus didn't just wipe out human life. Lakes and rivers dried up, forests became deserts and whole continents were reduced to nothing more than barren wastelands. Slowly but surely, the Earth began to wither and die." *Extinction* and the remaining films in the franchise take place in this post-apocalyptic world. This global destruction is neither shown on screen nor explained until the final movie – and then inconsistently. The franchise shifts to meet changing genre expectations. *Extinction*, which was released in 2007, conforms to and reinforces how a disease film must now depict the complete collapse of society. It rapidly transforms without explanation the effects of a disease on the assumption that its audience will readily accept the change. Alice remains the heroic individual but is also a "Mad Max" road warrior who roams the wasteland until she rescues and joins a caravan of survivors led by Claire Redfield (Ali Larter), a video game character.

Extinction shifts many of the earlier thematic elements of the franchise. While corporate forces remain the villain, Umbrella now seeks to exploit zombies as "the basis for a docile workforce." The film also reverses its view of artificial intelligence. Focusing on Alice's efforts to stop Dr. Isaacs, who has become a powerful mutant by injecting himself with the T-virus, the movie tells how Alice succeeds in killing him with the support of the White Queen, another Umbrella AI. The White Queen, the Red Queen's "sister," openly praises the Red Queen as prescient in following "the most logical path for the preservation of human life" by sealing off the Hive in the first movie. In parallel, *Extinction* continues the transformation through technology of Alice into a posthuman hero, endowing her with additional, superhuman abilities, including telekinesis. And it introduces a yet another form of posthuman, namely clones developed in an Umbrella facility. These appear in an early scene in which Alice clones fill a genocidal grave and still later during the ending in which vast numbers of newly created Alice clones appear. All these – zombie workers, artificial intelligence, a superhero Alice and clones – represent future, technological alternatives to humans. This shift reflects the movie franchise's slow advancement toward the creation of a post-apocalyptic society which is best led by a new species.

The fourth film, *Afterlife,* takes place 18 months later and accentuates this post-apocalyptic, pandemic world. Alice and her clones attack Umbrella's Tokyo headquarters and kill most of its leadership during the opening scenes. Its CEO, Albert Wesker (Shawn Roberts), escapes, blows up all the clones, and injects Alice with an antivirus, taking away her powers. Alice soon reunites with Claire Redfield from the previous movie, helps a group of survivors in Los Angeles escape to a ship named *Arcadia*, which is unexpectedly revealed as another Umbrella research facility, and again defeats Wesker. The CEO escapes and in a cliffhanger ending orders an attack on the *Arcadia*.

Since Umbrella had failed in its creation of new worker zombies, it now relies upon the technology of scarab-like devices to compel its human servants. Wesker, who has replaced Dr. Isaacs as the main villain, has become a mutant who must consume fresh human DNA to stay alive. He resembles the traditional vampire sucking dry the blood of his victims, and his presence yet again shifts the critique of the franchise from the evil corporation to the elite owners and leaders of corporate America. This genetically modified elite represents the overriding threat in this new posthuman world. Alice, a "good" mutant (as a result of Umbrella's experiments) who is also a member of the new elite (as a result of her powers), stands in contrast to Wesker. That she voices her preference to remain human – "Thank you for making me human again," she tells Wesker – even at the price of losing her powers highlights the film's message that only altruistic, individual heroism offers salvation.[26]

Retribution, the fifth movie, begins with Umbrella's airstrike that kills most of the survivors on the *Arcadia*. Umbrella then retrieves Alice, placing her in an underground base in Siberia. In an unexplained plot twist, Wesker tells Alice that the Red Queen is directing the activities of Umbrella to destroy humanity. He offers to cooperate with Alice and subsequently sends a commando team to extract her from the Siberian base. Alice eventually escapes with a few others and travels to Wesker's headquarters in the White House where the remnants of the American military are preparing to fight a last stand battle against the zombie and mutant hordes.

Like the earlier films, *Retribution* adopts the uncontainable disease narrative and renews the franchise's focus on AI as evil with the Red Queen monitoring through security cameras Alice's efforts at escape. Evoking the scene from *The Matrix* in which Neo discovers vast rows of dormant humans in pods, Alice discovers a factory room in which massive numbers of clones hang from and come off conveyer belts, offering a horrific vision of the Red Queen's production of mindless automatons used to populate her endlessly repetitive simulations. The Red Queen imprints its clones "with basic memories. Just enough to ensure a correct emotional response," conjuring up the implanted memories of the replicants in *Blade Runner*. Where the audience has empathy for *Blade Runner*'s replicants, there is no such empathy for *Retribution*'s clones, who are blank slates with nothing to differentiate one from the other. As Ada Wong (Li Bingbing), a former Umbrella operative, explains to Alice, "In one life, [the same clone] could be a suburban housewife. The next, a businesswoman in New York. The next, a soldier working for Umbrella."[27] The Red Queen programs its clones to perform efficiently in a simulated environment, a horrific vision of the future in which Umbrella's attempts to find compliant workers has come to fruition.

Alice is initially attracted to this world, which seems to offer a happy if bland future, even if an Umbrella simulation. Evoking the attraction – and Cypher's choice – of the seeming perfection of the simulation in *The Matrix*, Alice momentarily visits her simulated home, gazes at photographs of her simulated family life, including her cloned husband and daughter, and yearns for this picture-perfect, if unreal suburb of Raccoon City.[28] Alice is also emotionally drawn to Becky, the daughter of an Alice clone, so that a member of the commando team must point out to Alice that Becky "is not your daughter. She is not even a real person" and that Becky's feelings for Alice and vice versa "are not real." When later encountering rows of Becky and Alice clones, revealing the truth behind this simulated world, Becky seeks assurances that Alice is her mother. Alice melodramatically replies, "I am now." While Alice serves as Becky's surrogate mother throughout this movie, Becky disappears without explanation in the next episode of the franchise.

The ending shows Wesker sitting at the presidential desk in the Oval Office and commanding the remains of the US military, symbolizing how corporations have absorbed America's body politic. Wesker then forcibly transforms Alice by injecting her with renewed superpowers. If humanity stands on the brink of extermination, then Alice represents America's messiah-like superhero. Like Neo in the cliffhanger ending of *The Matrix*, the posthuman Alice

Figure 5.2 *Resident Evil: Retribution* (2012): Alice and her clone daughter encounter the industrial production of massive numbers of their clones.

is humanity's best hope for defeating the army of undead, mutants and clones. She aptly observes, "I became different. Powerful. Unstoppable. As I got stronger, the human race became weaker. I tried my best to lead what survivors I could find to safety." Only Alice, a superhero, can defeat America's monsters in an unexpected alliance with the corporation that has created her. The irony is that Alice is herself a clone, as will be revealed in the last movie.

These four movies, *Apocalypse*, *Extinction*, *Afterlife* and *Retribution*, change the franchise from stories about containment of a viral disease to those in which a superhero created by movie special effects increasingly drive the narrative and in which the world infected by a technologically created pandemic seems increasingly chaotic and beyond human control, thereby necessitating that superhero.[29] Fear motivates the need for such a hero, and the violence increasingly accelerates. While *Extinction* opens with the standard action sequence in which Alice defeats a family of marauders, the opening scene of *Afterlife* consists of a prolonged commando attack in which Alice and her clones slaughter hundreds of Umbrella security guards. *The Matrix*, in particular, has become a key, derivative source for the action, exemplified by *Afterlife*'s final fight sequence in which Wesker dodges bullets in slow-motion like AI Agent Smith in *The Matrix* and even wears Smith's dark sunglasses. *Retribution* similarly features in its opening credits an innovative slow-motion depiction in reverse of the Umbrella's massive airstrike on the ship *Arcadia* and then self-consciously replays that sequence chronologically in normal time, underscoring the artifice of the depiction.

These changes in the franchise reflect parallel changes in disease movies generally and advance as well as capitalize on new disease movies. The slow-moving zombies in *Apocalypse* become in *Extinction* the fast-moving zombies introduced by *28 Days Later*. Moreover, the franchise begins as a story of rebellion against the forces of capitalism and becomes a story of social fragmentation and collapse and the need for a posthuman social order, even if the films never identify the lessons to be drawn from the old order or articulate the contours of the new one other than the necessity for a technologically-enhanced superhero.

The New Apotheosis: *The Final Chapter* (2016)

The Final Chapter opens with Alice waking up after the offscreen, last-stand battle. In yet another plot twist, the Red Queen returns to help Alice infiltrate back into the Hive to prevent Umbrella from wiping out the last surviving humans. After joining a few human survivors, including Claire Redfield, Alice learns that she is a clone of Alicia, the daughter of the developer of the T-virus and the original co-owner of Umbrella. Alicia has been hibernating with the Umbrella elite in the hopes of using the T-virus to wipe out humanity and create a new world order. With the help of both the Red Queen and Alicia, Alice eventually defeats Umbrella CEO Wesker, the cyborg Dr. Isaacs and a clone Dr. Isaacs, and then releases an airborne antivirus that over many weeks will kill all zombies and mutants. The movie ends with Alice leaving everyone behind and riding her motorcycle alone into Manhattan in the new, post-apocalyptic world.

The Final Chapter's plot extensively scrambles the earlier narratives, leaves unexplained the disappearance of several characters and introduces new story elements. It also revises the backstory. It contradicts the first movie, *Resident Evil*, in which the first "incident" occurred in the Hive, the second movie, *Apocalypse*, which featured a different scientist (Charles Ashford) who developed the T-virus for his daughter, and the explanation given in the immediately prior episode, *Retribution*, in which the T-virus was part of a bio-weapons arms race. Instead, *The Final Chapter* tells how the T-virus resulted from the efforts of the "crusading scientist Professor James Marcus" to find a cure for his daughter Alicia, that Umbrella learned that the T-virus had just a "small" adverse effect (turning people into zombies) and that Umbrella then used this effect for its own perverse goal of advancing a new world order. This explanation nullifies the plots of the previous five movies, including Alice's key role in Umbrella's nefarious efforts at world domination. *The Final Chapter* has also further accelerated the spread of infectious disease. If *Extinction* explained that the infection took weeks to spread within the United States and months to the rest of the world, *The Final Chapter* simply states that "the viral outbreak spread across the world within days."[30] As with other changes to the disease narrative during the course of the franchise, the last film inexplicably assumes this overwhelmingly rapid spread of the disease. *The Final Chapter* also changes without comment the role of the Red Queen from villain in *Retribution* to Alice's ally in defeating Umbrella in the person of its owner Dr. Isaacs.

Yet despite, or perhaps because of, these inconsistencies, *The Final Chapter* tells of Alice's success in her longstanding mission to destroy Umbrella with its vision of a new world order, though failing to depict what the improved future society might look like. Alice and the Red Queen reenact in *The Final Chapter* the roles of Ripley and Call from *Alien: Resurrection* (1997). In both, the pair defeats its human and non-human enemies, but where Ripley and Call end their journey on a paradisiacal Earth, Alice as a superhero ends her journey wandering alone across an apocalyptic wasteland. While initially Alice resists the Red Queen, the Red Queen convinces Alice to return to the Hive, and *The Final Chapter* eventually reveals that both characters are derivative, simultaneously created simulations of yet another character, Alicia. If the Red Queen resembles a perpetual motion machine, Alice, too, confesses, "Sometimes I feel like this has been my whole life. Running. Killing." And both experience revelatory moments. For the Red Queen, that moment consists of learning that Umbrella planned the end of the world through the spread of the T-virus, resulting in a logical conflict of her directives both to protect Umbrella employees and "value human life." Alice's transformative moment occurs when Isaacs tells her that she is not human but rather a clone of Alicia, but without her memories. That disclosure is enough to satisfy Alice, who replies, "I know who I am."[31]

If the human species is seemingly doomed to wander in a post-pandemic world, the film offers salvation through an evolution of the species. With its focus on posthuman characters, *The Final Chapter* recalls the myth of Frankenstein in which the "creature" outgrew its master, observing to Frankenstein, "You are my creator, but I am your master; obey!" Alice, too, is the creature who has outgrown her master.

> Isaacs: We've played a long game, you and I, but now it's over.
> Alice: Yes. Yes, it is.
> Isaacs: I made you.
> Alice: Yeah. Big mistake.

Alice's humor does not obscure the film's supposedly redemptive story begun earlier in the franchise. If Umbrella's development of the T-virus has threatened humans with extinction, that same technology has also resulted in an enhanced Alice as a model for the reinvention of the species or at least its newly enhanced and empowered elite. Alice proves her salvific role by passing a test in offering to sacrifice herself in order to wipe out the zombies, mutants and other creatures. As the Red Queen observes. "This is something no one at Umbrella would have done."

Corporate America personified through Umbrella remains the villain, but its villainy has shifted from exploiting humans for profit to killing billions in an attempt to remake the world in its own image for its shareholder elites.

Umbrella discovered a new means for conquering disease that had offered hope for the mid-twentieth century dream of a technological utopia. Yet, when the T-virus proved harmful by turning humans into zombies, "the corporation that had begun with such lofty ideals" was "seduced completely by greed and power," Alice observes. Even this observation understates Umbrella's depravity. Isaacs releases the T-virus not for money but in the belief that "we stand on the brink of Armageddon," whether through disease, fundamentalist states, global warming or uncontrollable population growth. He, therefore, proposes to the Umbrella board that "we end the world, but on our terms." An "orchestrated apocalypse" is preferable to an "unorchestrated" one. Umbrella will repopulate the Earth with its own people in charge. In *The Final Chapter*, Isaacs both clones and transforms himself into a cyborg. The T-virus serves as the corporate means at achieving the new world order for an evolved posthuman species.

The Final Chapter imbues its posthuman visions with religious overtones. In advocating for the need for an "orchestrated apocalypse," Isaacs assures the Umbrella board that there is Biblical precedent, since "it's been done once before with great success," referring to the story of Noah and the flood. He envisions how "when it's over, we will emerge onto a cleansed Earth," which "we can then reboot in our image." The cryogenically frozen, wealthy elite stored within the Hive are symbolic of the story of Noah's ark, and the aptly named Umbrella will serve to save these elites so as to achieve a new world order with yet more control, efficiency and profit.[32] Umbrella under Isaacs' leadership represents the teachings of the Old Testament, including its stories of violence and vengeance, that will guide the future.

In contrast, Alice represents Christ of the New Testament in her vision of a new humanity, although Alice as Christ offers no parables for the poor and the sick or even the suggestion of a Golden Rule. She simply redeems humanity through self-sacrifice in a belief that her path will lead to a better future. This idea had appeared briefly in earlier movies when Alice sacrificed herself to save others, was resurrected, and was recognized as the new messiah.[33] *The Final Chapter* makes her sacrifice more explicit, and Isaacs even identifies Alicia, Alice and the Red Queen as "the Trinity of Bitches," with Alice playing the role of Jesus, the innocent without memory, to Alicia's father and to the Red Queen's guiding spirit. That Milla Jovovich plays both Alice and Alicia and that her real-life daughter plays the Red Queen highlights the unity of this trinity. Alice again offers to sacrifice herself in the film's ending by releasing the antivirus, mistakenly believing that she, too, will die given that she, like the undead, is infected with the T-virus. When she unexpectedly survives, the Red Queen reflects, "You became something more than they [Umbrella] could ever have anticipated." Clone Ripley's observation about the altruistic AI Call in *Alien: Resurrection* – "I should have known. No human being is that humane." – applies to Alice, the posthuman superhero.

Figure 5.3 *Resident Evil: The Final Chapter* (2016): The Trinity of Bitches, Alice (center background), the Red Queen (background, facing Alice) and Alicia (right foreground), confront and defeat Umbrella's evil Dr. Isaacs (far left).

The Final Chapter completes the shift in the franchise's depiction of disease and hence the newly envisioned future of the human species. The T-virus has developed from a disease that might be contained to a pandemic that has resulted in a post-apocalyptic world in which survivors must fend for themselves. In the context of this global nightmare, Alice represents the means for transformation of the human species – or at least its newly elite members – to a posthuman form. While Isaacs argues in *The Final Chapter* that clones are "just a poor imitation or a worthless copy," Alice represents the imitation that surpasses the original. As Alicia acknowledges to Alice, "You are so much better than I ever could be." Recalling the corporate-created replicants of *Blade Runner*, whose creator observed were "more human than humans," the Red Queen similarly observes at the end of *The Final Chapter*, "The clone became more human than they [Umbrella's elite] ever could be." The *Resident Evil* franchise mirrors the values and global expansion of American capitalism with its simultaneously fragmented and connected world. The social contract depicted in *The Final Chapter* is completely broken, which is symbolized by the post-apocalyptic landscape infested with the undead remains of the human species. The posthuman clone Alice, the rogue creation of profit-driven Umbrella, has become the new face of humanity: the new apotheosis of American, global capitalism.

CONCLUSION

The *Resident Evil* movies have not drawn much scholarly attention, and a review of the single book on the *Resident Evil* franchise described the book as "undoubtedly problematic."[34] The movies themselves frequently beat the viewer into submission with their messages. And yet the incredible popularity of the franchise both in the United States and worldwide, notwithstanding the hostile reviews, underscores its cultural importance. These disease movies with their shifting narrative are neither impersonal, objective stories nor personal reflections, but an intertwined combination of both. The *Resident Evil* franchise serves as a useful lens in understanding the historical transformation of humanity's view of plagues, pandemics and zombies. The containment of the first two films became in the third film the story of a post-apocalyptic world as a result of corporate evil. The newly developed non-humans, such as clones and AI, seemingly overwhelm their corporate creators but also represent the desired solution through the evolutionary advancement of the human species. Technology, which created the viral disease in the first film, increasingly drives the narrative toward a posthuman world that advances an assimilating global capitalism. We gladly accept Alice as an alternative to America's corporate culture, represented by Umbrella's cryogenically frozen elite, and more importantly, as the model for our future selves. Such a model is, of course, as implausible as Umbrella's pure evil and simply offers a new world order that simultaneously offers it up as pure fantasy and yet also an endorsement of the truth of that fantasy. The franchise enables each of us to identify with the superhero Alice in a universal fantasy of our own making, even though in reality we are merely assimilated into and transformed by the needs of global capitalism, just like Alice.

Similar to Alice's repeated revivals and clonings, *The Final Chapter* was not the final chapter of the *Resident Evil* world. *Resident Evil* continues in a variety of iterations, including an anime TV series, *Resident Evil: Infinite Darkness* (2021), and a live-action TV series, *Resident Evil* (2022). In late 2021, Capcom, Sony and Constantin Film also rebooted the theatrical franchise with *Resident Evil: Welcome to Raccoon City*. Writing Alice out of the script and without Anderson's participation as screenwriter or director, the reboot attempted to return to the video game material, reflected by the inclusion of such fan-favorite characters as Chris and Claire Redfield and Jill Valentine. Its plot takes place in 1998, and Umbrella has sealed off Raccoon City in anticipation of containing a viral outbreak by obliterating the city. Like the previous six movies, *Welcome to Raccoon City* was largely panned by critics, but unlike Anderson's franchise it was far less successful commercially, making $42 million worldwide compared to *The Final Chapter*'s $314 million.

Anderson's *Resident Evil* franchise had remained consistent throughout its six episodes in its conformity to contemporary, cultural developments – from a belief in the possible containment of the undead to its faith in evolutionary development through a mix of scientific technology and the New Testament. The superhero Alice masquerades as an ordinary person who rises to the challenge of a fragmented world but, in fact, embodies the threat of a transformed species, a clone, in which differences, including uniqueness, disappear. She is an American hero for our times. That vision of a hero coincided with and advances the corporate goal of displacing through technology human infirmities with the efficiency of a utopian posthuman in which differences of identity disappear as the American hero is transformed into a fantasy superhero. If at times we seem to treat too seriously Anderson's convoluted stories comprising the *Resident Evil* franchise, its commercial success suggests that not doing so runs the risk of failing to understand the shifting mythologies of global capitalism. That its changing narrative arc parallels transformations in other stories over the same period, most obviously *The Body Snatchers* remakes in their varied artistic and commercial forms, reinforces that these ideas exist across critically acclaimed and panned movies and are not solely a means to generate profits for their corporate producers.

NOTES

1. The second game sold 3.6 million units in the first two months after its release. CAPCOM, "CAPCOM's Annual Report: FY 1998," 1999, 8, https://www.capcom.co.jp/ir/english/data/pdf/Annual1998.pdf.
2. CAPCOM, "CAPCOM's Annual Report: FY 1998," preface, 2 and 4.
3. "Constantin Buys 'Evil' Rights," *Variety*, January 15, 1997, https://web.archive.org/web/20191105095526/https://variety.com/1997/scene/vpage/constantin-buys-evil-rights-1117433527/. Alan McElroy was identified as the screenwriter for the movie.
4. The commercial was aired only in Japan. For the commercial, *CanadienDestroyer*, "Resident Evil 2 Commercial," July 1, 2006, https://www.youtube.com/watch?v=tnglxHaB6SY; for why it was released only in Japan, Rob McGregor, "George Romero's *Resident Evil*," 2021, http://www.new-blood.com/romeros.html.
5. David Crow, "The George Romero Resident Evil Movie You Never Saw," *Den of Geek*, March 12, 2018, https://www.denofgeek.com/games/the-george-romero-resident-evil-movie-you-never-saw/. Romero's original script is online: George Romero, "Resident Evil – by George A. Romero," https://imsdb.com/scripts/Resident-Evil.html. A Capcom producer later remarked that "Romero's script wasn't good, so Romero was fired." Matthew Chernov, "Why George Romero's 'Resident Evil' Film Failed to Launch," *Variety*, December 16, 2016, https://variety.com/2016/film/spotlight/resident-evil-george-romero-failed-1201942677/.
6. Matt Patches, "How the Mastermind Behind 'Resident Evil' Kept the Franchise Going for 15 Years," *Thrillist*, January 26, 2017, https://www.thrillist.com/entertainment/nation/resident-evil-movies-paul-ws-anderson-interview-resident-evil-the-final-chapter.
7. For clarity the subsequent discussion will refer to each film by their individual names (e.g., *Apocalypse*).
8. Patches, "Mastermind Behind 'Resident Evil.'"
9. Richard Trenholm, "Why Resident Evil Crushes Every Other Video Game Movie," *CNET*, January 25, 2019, https://www.cnet.com/news/resident-evil-the-most-successful-video-game-movie-series-milla-jovovich-paul-ws-anderson/. Anderson continued,

"What makes a successful video game doesn't necessarily make a successful movie. While you have to appeal to the core fanbase who love the game, you also have to make a film. You risk alienating the fans if you deviate too far, but if you don't deviate at all you kind of don't appeal to a movie audience. It's a fine line." Owen Williams, "Resident Evil Movies: The Complete Guide," *Empire*, June 25, 2021, https://www.empireonline.com/movies/features/resident-evil-movies-the-complete-guide/.

10. The movie ratings in the franchise range between 19–37 percent on Rotten Tomatoes. See their individual reviews in "Rotten Tomatoes," 2021, https://www.rottentomatoes.com/search?search=resident%20evil.
11. Roger Ebert, "Ebert's Most Hated," *RogerEbert.com*, August 11, 2005, https://www.rogerebert.com/roger-ebert/eberts-most-hated.
12. Roger Ebert, "Drab filmmaking the true evil in new 'Resident,'" *RogerEbert.com*, September 10, 2004, https://www.rogerebert.com/reviews/resident-evil-apocalypse-2004. Another reviewer claimed the films "are often considered, at best, 'videogame-inspired action schlock,'" Margo Collins, "'I Barely Feel Human Anymore': Project Alice and the Posthuman in the Films," in *Unraveling Resident Evil: Essays on the Complex Universe of the Games and Films*, ed. Nadine Farghaly (Jefferson: McFarland, 2014), 253.
13. Daniel Engber, "The Unusual Genius of the 'Resident Evil' Movies," *The New Yorker*, February 2, 2017, http://www.newyorker.com/culture/culture-desk/the-unusual-genius-of-the-resident-evil-movies. For a similar view on *Extinction*, in particular: Matt Zoller Seitz, "Las Vegas Under Siege by Zombies and a Mutant," *The New York Times*, September 24, 2007, https://www.nytimes.com/2007/09/24/movies/24evil.html. And for a similar view of the later *Retribution*: Jeannette Catsoulis, "Alice, Still Fighting to Save the World," *The New York Times*, September 14, 2012, https://www.nytimes.com/2012/09/15/movies/resident-evil-retribution-with-milla-jovovich.html.
14. These include *Star Wars* and the Marvel Cinematic Universe.
15. Trenholm, "Why Resident Evil Crushes."
16. Female action heroes date back to at least the 1960s with Mrs. Emma Peel played by Diana Rigg in the British television series *The Avengers* (1965–1968). Jovovich had played an action hero in Luc Besson's *The Fifth Element* (1997). While Anderson had initially relegated Jovovich to a secondary, passive role in the film, she insisted that he rework the movie's narrative. Milla Jovovich and Anderson's reflection on the franchise in the fall of 2022: Nicolas Rapold, "Paul W. S. Anderson and Milla Jovovich: A Marriage Built on Monsters," *The New York Times*, September 2, 2022, https://www.nytimes.com/2022/09/02/movies/paul-ws-anderson-milla-jovovich-resident-evil.html.
17. For a feminist take, Andrea Harris, "Woman as Evolution: The Feminist Promise of the *Resident Evil* Film Series," in *Race, Gender, and Sexuality in Post-Apocalyptic TV and Film*, ed. Barbara Gurr (New York: Palgrave Macmillan, 2015), 99–111.
18. For the classic discussion of the male gaze: Laura Mulvey, "Visual Pleasure and Narrative Cinema," in *Film Theory & Criticism*, 7th edition, eds. Leo Braudy and Marshall Cohen (New York: Oxford University Press, 2009), 711–722.
19. For the view that Alice is a hero, see Steven Gerrard, "'My Name Is Alice. And I Remember Everything.' Project Alice and Milla Jovovich in the Resident Evil

Films," in *Gender and Contemporary Horror in Film*, ed. Samantha Holland et al. (Bingley, UK: Emerald Publishing Limited, 2019), 205–18. But for the view of a trend of sexualizing female action heroes see Katy Gilpatric, "Violent Female Action Characters in Contemporary American Cinema," *Sex Roles* 62, no. 11 (2010): 734–46.
20. For a similar view on the first two movies, Stephen Harper, "'I could kiss you, you bitch.' Race, gender and sexuality in *Resident Evil* and *Resident Evil 2: Apocalypse*," *Jump Cut* 49 (2007), https://www.ejumpcut.org/archive/jc49.2007/HarperResEvil/. Harper also notes that Romero's zombies would be out of place with the themes of *Resident Evil*.
21. See Mark Salisbury, "Resident Evil: Girls, Guns and Ghouls," *Fangoria*, April 2002; Anderson's interest in science fiction is reflected in his other work, including his directing *Event Horizon* (1997) and *Alien vs. Predator* (2004).
22. Additional comparisons with *Aliens* include Rain (a professional Latina soldier) as Pvt. Vasquez and Matt (a kind-hearted survivor supportive of the lead protagonist) playing the role of Corporal Hicks. For a similar view, Harper, "'I could kiss you, you bitch.'"
23. The franchise is rife with these inconsistencies. Dr. Isaacs in *Apocalypse* and *Extinction* is an Umbrella employee who leads the project experimenting on Alice. After he goes rogue and becomes a mutant, Alice kills him at the end of *Extinction*. In *The Final Chapter*, however, two versions of Dr. Isaacs unexpectedly appear – the "real" Dr. Isaacs, the co-founder of Umbrella who has become a cyborg, and the clone Dr. Isaacs who kills his "real" counterpart. Supporting characters likewise appear and disappear throughout the franchise without explanation.
24. *Uniting and Strengthening America by Providing Appropriate Tools Required to Intercept and Obstruct Terrorism (USA PATRIOT) Act* of 2001, Public Law 107–56, *US Statutes at Large*: 115 (272). The USA PATRIOT Act, which included authorization for the secret collection of data on American citizens, passed in 2001 largely without debate or objection. The result of that expansion, including the cooperation between government and private enterprise, would only become apparent in 2013 when Edward Snowden went public. Laura Poitras and Glenn Greenwald, "NSA Whistleblower Edward Snowden: 'I Don't Want to Live in a Society That Does These Sort of Things' – Video," *The Guardian*, June 9, 2013, http://www.theguardian.com/world/video/2013/jun/09/nsa-whistleblower-edward-snowden-interview-video.
25. *Apocalypse* recalls John Carpenter's classic *Escape from New York* (1981) in which Snake Plissken tries to rescue the American President held by criminals in Manhattan, which the American government has converted into a maximum-security prison.
26. The film offers other examples of altruistic characters. For example, a former professional basketball player, another member of the 1 percent, goes out of his way to help the group of survivors in Los Angeles. On the other hand, a big-shot Hollywood producer looks out only for himself, aided by his former intern who continues to believe he can become a member of the elite through subservience.
27. The notion of constantly implanting new memories originated at least as early as *Dark City* (1998) in which aliens kidnap humans and replace each night their memories with new ones.

28. This returns to an opening scene in *Retribution*, which is a seven-minute dream by Alice who sees herself as one of her clones living a classic suburban life violently disturbed by a zombie outbreak.
29. The films mirror the rising popularity of the big budget, superhero movies of Marvel and DC Comics, which, in turn, coincided with the fears introduced by 9/11 and the war on terror.
30. In yet another example of inconsistency, the ending of *Apocalypse* takes place three weeks after the original incident in the Hive. There is no indication, however, in the Umbrella research facility or outside, when Alice's allies come to her rescue, that the outbreak has continued to spread. The opening credits of *Extinction* simply announce the global spread.
31. Alice's statement is reminiscent of several biblical statements about God's being (e.g., Exodus 3:14, John 14:6).
32. Isaacs' clone, too, is engaged in a religious mission. He is described as engaged in a "cleansing operation" to "cast out" the unbelievers and prominently wears a cross, while his vehicles are likewise conspicuously affixed with crosses.
33. Earlier movies hint at rather than insist upon the heavy-handed religious symbolism of *The Final Chapter*. For example, Alice sacrifices herself when she dies in *Apocalypse* to save the young Angela Ashford, or later in *Extinction* when she stays behind alone to confront Dr. Isaacs. Alice is resurrected in *Apocalypse* when she reawakens in a liquid tank (from which she is extracted by Isaacs the scientist clergy) and in *Retribution*, she falls dead from an explosion into water and then appears in a cross-like effect against the water's surface. Alice appears as the new messiah in *Apocalypse* when she unexpectedly crashes through on her motorcycle the church's stained-glass windows of the main sanctuary and she then defeats a mutant by bringing a giant cross down upon it.
34. Nadine Farghaly, ed. *Unraveling Resident Evil: Essays on the Complex Universe of the Games and Films* (Jefferson: McFarland, 2014); the review of the book is Lars Schmeink, "Review of *Unraveling Resident Evil: Essays on the Complex Universe of the Games and Films* ed. Nadine Farghaly, and *'We're all Infected'*: Essays on AMC's The Walking Dead and the Fate of the Human, ed. Dawn Keetley," in the *Journal of the Fantastic in the Arts* 27, no. 1 (2016): 162–66. For another article see Gwyneth Peaty, "The Afterlives of Alice: Reanimating the Gothic Heroine in the *Resident Evil* Franchise," in *Gothic Afterlives: Reincarnations of Horror in Film and Popular Media*, ed. Lorna Piatti-Farnell (Lanham: Rowman & Littlefield, 2019), 29–40.

CHAPTER 6

MOVIE MYTHS: THE COVID-19 PANDEMIC

INTRODUCTION

When COVID-19 transformed in early 2020 from an epidemic in China to a global pandemic, Americans sought to make sense of its unprecedented challenges. Public health practitioners, politicians and academics scrambled to respond. Uncertainty reigned. Even basic answers, such as the number of cases or the ways in which the disease spread, were unclear in early 2020 and continued to change. More immediate questions about effective measures to protect oneself from COVID – from wearing masks to wiping down packages with bleach – were hotly debated. In retrospect, this chaotic beginning is normal in the early days of a novel disease, echoing similar debates over the spread and prevention of HIV/AIDS. Scientific explanations changed as more evidence accumulated. Scientists arrived at answers to pressing questions about COVID – wearing masks, social distancing and vaccines – remarkably fast from an historical perspective. But the speed of science was matched, and overtaken, in the United States by miscommunication and misinformation. Social media and some loud public voices, including then US President Donald Trump, influenced people in directions inconsistent with the developing consensus of the scientific community. Although uncertainties and changes are part of the scientific process, the public seemed unaccustomed to these ups and downs that had monumental social, economic, political and personal consequences, leading to confusion and ultimately reducing trust in both science and scientists who personified – literally on TV in many cases – the answers. Although most people were trying to protect themselves and their loved ones, fear and anxiety often carried the day.

Historical comparisons to previous pandemics were one popular way to find answers or readymade lessons that some thought could save lives. In the American context, though, historical lessons were stated, but rarely made an impact.[1] Fictional stories about disease instead offered a widely diverse American population answers from disparate perspectives as to what the future might look like and how to act in the "new normal" of COVID. The most accessible, and remembered, were stories from the last few decades, which offered depictions of what people thought, or feared, was to come.[2] Films, in particular, helped structure responses through their fictional yet compelling stories, offering the illusion of certainty but, in fact, leading to further misunderstandings and inconsistent or even chaotic behavior.[3] Stories of recent films helped stoke fears that COVID would lead to a demographic collapse or economic breakdown. These disease movies shaped early responses to the pandemic, even if their worst-case scenarios never materialized. Interest in movies peaked quickly in early 2020 but after only a few months the experience of living with COVID took precedence. Disease movies faded from public consciousness by mid-spring 2020.

The first part of this chapter discusses how movie myths and reality blurred and how movies briefly but significantly influenced responses to COVID. Movies played several roles in discourse, especially between January and April 2020, in different countries. This chapter focuses on two case studies. In Britain, *28 Days Later* offered comparisons with daily COVID life and a language to describe 2020's unprecedented, shared experiences. In the United States, *Contagion* presented an uncannily similar narrative to COVID, and viewers seemed to watch it to interpret COVID's trajectory and plan for the future. Within a few months, movies lost much of their attraction. Life under COVID, it turned out, was far less dramatic than movies suggested, though the differences obviously varied depending on individual circumstances. The wealthy departed to suburban and rural areas, white collar workers worked remotely, and blue-collar workers were required to continue working on site and had to endure daily exposure to possible sickness and death. Whatever their situation, from the mid-spring of 2020 onward Americans had settled into a routine that continued at least until vaccinations became available in early 2021. Subsequently, the pandemic has slowly become "background noise" that has lacked the excitement of movies or even daily politics, with each new variant briefly gaining attention. The announcement in spring 2022 of 1 million COVID deaths in the United States quickly became yesterday's news.[4]

Once Americans seemed to realize within a few months that the recent pandemic movie myths of societal collapse would not happen, individuals and groups responded to COVID according to their pre-COVID beliefs and values. While early American solidarity led to some limited state lockdowns and the passage of several stimulus bills to provide economic aid to both struggling businesses and individuals, within a year most people had returned to their pre-existing social perspectives, reflected, for example, in the sharply divided debate over how to balance the need for public health with a desire for personal liberty. COVID revealed significant problems in America, such as the need for a national, and even a global, public health agenda, while Democrats weaponized the Trump administration's inept COVID response to elect Joe Biden president in the 2020 election. They too, however, failed to address the structural problems COVID had revealed. The death toll continued from one administration to the next, while new diseases – such as monkeypox – appeared, revealing that little had structurally changed. Like movies of recent decades suggested, Americans were unable to improve, let alone solve, the broader social problems that ailed the country.

The second part of the chapter then examines how COVID has underscored the differences between recent disease films and the effects of a real disease. Movie stories had assumed that rational or scientific, even if also self-serving and corrupt at times, responses to a pandemic would prevail. Reality proved this was not the case. Moreover, while twenty-first century disease movies featured ever more catastrophic outcomes, they had also erased social and biological differences. Almost everyone in movies has an equal chance of dying. In such a fictional world, all Americans are created equal and everyone ultimately falls within an undifferentiated but equal mass of people struggling to survive. The exception to this rule are the wealthy (or politically connected), who abuse their power, but even this exception is depicted as a social norm. In reality, disparate groups in America – divided by race, age, gender, class, residency or political opinion – had distinctly different experiences of the pandemic, and the consequences of the pandemic differed from group to group. This contrast between movies and real life highlighted, in particular, how the fragmentation of American culture drove the experiences of and the responses to the pandemic in ways in which movies had not prepared the public.

Consuming Movie Pandemics during COVID

Interest in pandemic movies exploded as COVID spread globally. Movies were not alone, of course, since interest in all types of online, pandemic-related content substantially increased during the first three months of 2020.[5] As a "realistic" respiratory virus movie, *Contagion*, released a decade earlier, was the most popularly watched disease film. In January alone, its pirated downloads increased by 5,609 percent.[6] It soon rose to the top of charts in both the United States and the United Kingdom, reaching the top 10 by the end of January on iTunes, when it became clear that the virus had reached the United States.[7] It remained in the top ten most-viewed films on iTunes and the top fifteen most downloaded movies according to Google Trends through early March.[8] It peaked at second on the most viewed films list on iTunes on

March 16.[9] The same day, *Outbreak*, a twenty-five-year-old film, became the third most-watched film in the United States on Netflix.[10] Periodic reports in the media on these films drew more public attention to them, which further increased their popularity.

Media commentators differed on how to explain this phenomenon. Some believed that pandemic films served as a coping mechanism, suggesting that these films offered viewers a way to control their fear.[11] Others believed audiences were watching to reach the happy endings and feel better, since those endings show how "we ultimately beat the virus."[12] A third set of commentators suggested that fictionalized pandemic accounts offered a useful set of lessons to think through the present. *Moonlight* director Barry Jenkins pointed out that he watched *Contagion* because he "was really curious to see how well it would line up to what is happening right now . . . It was shocking. It felt like I was watching a documentary that has all these movie stars playing real people."[13] There was no single reason why people watched these movies, of course, and they plainly appealed for a variety of reasons.

COVID also inspired new disease movies that sought to exploit this new interest as well. *Corona* (2020), which was released in March 2020 and made headlines as the first COVID movie, focused on a Chinese woman stuck in an elevator with six others, highlighting the fear and racism the disease provoked.[14] *Corona Zombies* (2020), released in April as a straight to video movie imagined a COVID-caused zombie outbreak.[15] Similarly, *Songbird* (2020), released in December, focused on a futuristic COVID-23, while *After the Pandemic* (2022) featured an alternative scenario in which the pandemic's mortality was 98 percent. Still other movies used COVID as a background to comedy or romance, such as *Locked Down* (2021), *The End of Us* (2021) and *Recovery* (2021).[16] None of these films was a commercial success, and none had an immediately discernible impact on how people thought about COVID. While the public might have wanted to understand COVID, contemporary movies attracted far smaller audiences than established, earlier films.

The Blurring of COVID and the Movie Pandemic Landscape

COVID's outbreak and global spread played out like a movie script, and that similarity helped shape the public's perception of the pandemic. COVID slowly expanded from China to Iran to Europe to the United States, gradually resulting in the implementation of lockdowns to mitigate the disease's impact. From early on, international, national and local media compared the developing COVID pandemic to movie diseases.[17] Fictional film narratives and reality blurred.[18] Stills from movies were juxtaposed with photos from real events, such as runs on food at supermarkets or overburdened hospitals. Movie comparisons focused on film scenes which reflected COVID experiences, such as self-isolation at home and deserted streets of a post-apocalyptic world.

Figure 6.1 *Contagion* offered real-life lessons for those experiencing the unknowns of COVID-19. Composite image published by *Daily Mail Online* on March 4, 2020.

Pandemic movies, particularly films from the mid-1990s onward, entered COVID-related discussions almost immediately. Film and real-life events reinforced one another.[19] As early as January 23, 2020, the *New York Post* cited *Contagion* as the model for the development and spread of COVID.[20] Likewise, *The New York Times* review of *Outbreak* appeared on the front page of its online version in March with the title "now we're living the sequel."[21] Perhaps less expected was the significant place of zombie movies in discussions. Commentators, for example, compared real Israel's closing of its borders with the walls fictional Israel raised around the country in *World War Z*.[22] The media also featured a few references to older movies. An American baby-boomer, who was infected on the *Diamond Princess* cruise ship, remarked that the doctors and nurses checking him on board while quarantined looked like something out of *The Andromeda Strain*.[23] *The Wall Street Journal* even used the seventy-year-old *Panic in the Streets* to describe the urban COVID experience.[24] Given that these movies were less well known to audiences, though, they were unsurprisingly featured less often.

Movies helped their audiences understand the early, harsh lockdowns in many countries. These strict lockdowns led to the emptying of public spaces

Figure 6.2 *World War Z* (2013): Waves of zombies swarm up the wall to invade Israel.

Figure 6.3 *12 Monkeys* (1995): In 2035, animals roam the streets of Philadelphia while the few surviving humans of a global pandemic live underground.

in urban centers, reminding observers of the End Times. Stores closed, mass transit travel was reduced and car driving ceased almost entirely.[25] Recalling scenes from earlier disease films, such as *12 Monkeys*, some stories described how cities, suburbs and towns appeared to turn into natural habitats with wild animals prowling the streets.[26] The two films that featured commonly in comparisons to the present were *Contagion* and *28 Days Later*. Each was used primarily in the country that produced it, the United States and the United Kingdom, respectively.

British discussions about COVID prominently featured in *28 Days Later*, notwithstanding its post-apocalyptic zombie plot, especially emphasizing the unexpected speed of the changes to daily life and the empty streets. The media writings on the topic emphasized the emotions aroused, such as horror and awe, with some references to the thriller aspects. *The Daily Star*, for example, interviewed a British train driver in Wuhan who asked readers to "imagine a scene out of *28 Days Later*. There is no one on the streets, in a city bigger than London, it is weird. We have enough food to last us a week and we have water. I don't know what we are going to do when we have run out. We don't want to go outside."[27] The phrase "*28 Days Later* vibe" was adopted as a shorthand way of describing current events.[28] Moreover, some accounts described *28 Days Later* as a "disaster film," not a zombie or horror film, reframing a key element of the film's narrative to make it sound more realistic.[29] These accounts no longer envisaged differences between the more realistic disease films and zombie horror films in the context of the COVID "apocalypse" but instead began describing all of them as simply disease films.[30]

As COVID continued to spread and the number of deaths rose, *28 Days Later*, also became a shorthand to describe how people unexpectedly found themselves in a new, strange reality. As one observer put it, "Everyone is worried. Everyone's got this idea of *I am Legend* or *28 Days Later*. It is like that but without the zombies – there is nothing in the streets!"[31] The *Sun*'s film critic Jamie East wrote about his experience of becoming sick with COVID. "I'm Cillian Murphy [Jim, the protagonist] in *28 Days Later*," he wrote, "waking up wondering what the hell happened to the world."[32] A *Guardian* writer compared a group who were rafting in the Grand Canyon and emerged after twenty-five days to a COVID lockdown landscape to Jim in *28 Days Later* who awoke in a hospital after twenty-eight days to find London deserted.[33] The Hollywood star Jared Leto, who was on a silent retreat for a few weeks at the beginning of the pandemic, was also compared to Jim and his awakening when he returned to the world.[34] Observers continued to mention the movie for months thereafter, in both analytic articles and personal commentaries.[35] Even people who had never watched *28 Days Later* described their own experiences through the fictional narrative of the film.[36]

References to *28 Days Later* became both more common and explicit. In reports and opinion pieces on COVID, the British media frequently juxtaposed images of empty streets and roads during COVID with images from *28 Days Later*. By late March 2020, articles commenting on the images of abandoned streets had become clichés. Writers then shifted to cite the movie approvingly as "the apocalyptic beauty of lockdown Britain" and called upon readers to "appreciate the terrible beauty of the day the earth stood still."[37] Echoing those who had cited movie images of animals roaming the urban streets, writers pointed to the drop in gas emissions as a result of the mandated lockdowns as an indication that the world had begun to heal.[38] In effect, they sought immediate, positive outcomes from COVID, notwithstanding all the sick and dying people. Of course, once the public became acclimated to the new COVID reality, streets were reoccupied and animals returned to the woods. As formerly strange situations became normalized, *28 Days Later* lost its relevance and disappeared from discussions.

While *28 Days Later* offered a few specific points of comparison with COVID, the "hyper-realistic" *Contagion* was by far the most popular and enduring fictional narrative during the pandemic in American discourse. Its story seemed eerily similar to what was happening as COVID spread around the world. The CDC's enthusiastic endorsement of *Contagion* during its original release a decade earlier accelerated its use as a benchmark.[39] In the first few months of COVID, articles re-endorsed its accuracy, observing that *Contagion* was "meticulously researched," describing it as "an extremely prescient film," praising its "almost true-to-life plot," and claiming "it really foretold what we are experiencing today."[40] It was a "must-see movie," "essential" and a "fully realised, accurate vision of a pandemic," which one could watch "to see just how bad things can get."[41]

These opinions were neither exceptional nor limited to film critics and media pundits. Medical and health professionals even encouraged watching *Contagion* to understand the pandemic. A professor of medicine at the University of California, San Diego, claimed he "was taken aback at how realistic it was" when he first watched the movie and used the film to teach epidemiology.[42] The Director of the Center for Global Health and Security at Georgetown University noted that the movie has "scenes where it doesn't feel like a movie anymore." Although she added a disclaimer to her endorsement by acknowledging that fictional movies "are not documentaries," this caution hardly tamped down her endorsement for the factual insights that the film supposedly offered.[43]

Contagion offered several points of obvious comparison with COVID. Many noted that *Contagion*'s fictional virus (MEV-1) and COVID-19 are both airborne viruses that feature flu-like symptoms.[44] This led some to see *Contagion* as offering a means to foresee how COVID might end. As a CNN report noted, "the origin of the 'Contagion' virus could mirror the potential origin of the current coronavirus" and that, in turn, might reveal clues about how to find a scientific solution to COVID.[45] After all, movies such as *Panic in the Streets*, *Outbreak* and *World War Z*, had all agreed that finding the origin of a disease was an early, necessary step in developing a cure. In the new reality of COVID-19, the search for its origin became a central ideological and political source of debate. Several countries, particularly China and the United States, accused each other of developing COVID-19 as a biological weapon with no evidence.[46]

Since the public and media perceived the movie *Contagion* as a realistic depiction of a pandemic, the people who worked on the film became de facto pandemic experts. Published interviews with the movie's crew and its scientific consultants helped reinforce this view.[47] The film, as articles were quick to remind readers, was made with the advice of medical experts, and "dozens of scientists and doctors were brought on to consult" on the film's production, thereby legitimizing its message.[48] The two primary medical advisors on the film, Prof. Ian Lipkin and Dr. Larry Brilliant, were even heralded as "hero scientists."[49] Lipkin humbly bragged how "he's sorry it's so accurate," and asserted that it was "one of the things in my career I'm most proud of."[50] Steven Soderbergh, the film's director, was cast as "a leading cinematic expert on pandemics."[51] Whether truthful in his claims or projecting COVID onto the past, Soderbergh further enhanced the film's reputation by claiming that "everybody we [he and Scott Burns, the screenwriter] talked to when we were preparing the film, every expert, when we asked them how will the next one [pandemic] start, to a person, they said, wet market, Asia, there's probably going to be a bat involved. Literally all of them. Ten years ago, eleven years ago. So it's not a surprise."[52] The Directors' Guild of America even appointed Soderbergh to chair a committee that would consult with "top epidemiologists in the field" to help the film industry get back to work safely.[53] Burns, the screenwriter, reiterated Soderberg's claims after having "conducted months of in-depth research into the science of pandemics."[54] Whatever Soderberg or Burns thought at the time of the film's release or during the first few months of COVID, others within the film industry believed their knowledge was exceptional and useful.

The actors in *Contagion* also became popular media figures in the context of COVID. Despite her character's early death, Gwyneth Paltrow's experience on the set was enough to make her an expert. "Gwyneth is well versed in dealing with outbreaks," said one article.[55] Her otherwise unremarkable trip to Paris Fashion Week in February 2020 attracted widespread media attention, including her stylish £53 ($99) mask. "I've already been in this movie," she remarked.[56] Matt Damon's daughter's contraction of the virus became international news, since, in contrast to the father he had portrayed in *Contagion*, the real Damon had not protected his daughter.[57] The cast's newfound expertise was not entirely without some public benefit. Kate Winslet, Matt Damon, Laurence Fishburne, Jennifer Ehle and Marion Cotillard collaborated with Columbia University's School of Public Health to release videos in which they offered public health tips about COVID while also promoting the voices of scientists and public health experts and speaking against misinformation and racism.[58] Their public association through their work on *Contagion* had made them messengers, even if the effectiveness of their messages was unclear.

Contagion's depiction of misinformation and fake news also eerily mirrored reality during COVID. Observers compared Krumwiede, the film's blogger/conspiracy-theorist, to Alex Jones, Glenn Beck and Donald Trump with their charismatic TV and online presences and the legions of enthusiastic fans who followed incorrect medical advice to their detriment.[59] Like Krumwiede, some attempted to profit from the pandemic with holistic remedies.[60] Krumwiede's promotion of forsythia reminded some of President Trump's promotion of chloroquine, which he kept hawking without any factual basis as effective.[61]

Like *28 Days Later*, however, *Contagion* faded from discussions within a few months. Once people had adjusted to the new reality of COVID, they no longer needed fictional narratives to facilitate their learning of this new pandemic. The consequences of one's actions and the probable future trajectory of COVID became more evident, making films, such as *Contagion*, less relevant. The few exceptions occurred when people had to face novel situations. In one such example, Britain's Health Secretary explicitly cited *Contagion* in an interview as the reason he bought 100 million vaccine doses instead of the recommended 30 million – a decision that also prevented other countries from acquiring the vaccine.[62]

Of course, not all comparisons to movies were realistic, and humor and clickbait titles played a role. When monkeys snatched COVID blood test samples from a lab in India in late May 2020, the media compared the episode to movies with headlines such as "*28 Days Later* just became real" and "Real-Life Monkey Attack Is Eerily Like *Planet of the Apes*." The articles even included movie imagery to document their headlines.[63] In another example, a photo of anti-lockdown protestors squeezed against the glass doors of the statehouse during an anti-social distancing protest in Ohio in mid-April 2020 was humorously linked to images of zombies pressed against glass doors.[64]

While looking to films as a script for understanding COVID, most lessons ranged from the obvious to unhelpful. *Contagion*, for example, taught the public to watch for fake news and attempt to recreate normalcy at home, such as the home prom Mitch organizes for his daughter.[65] Such banal lessons did not help people perceive how the American response to COVID reflected the values of American culture. Movies suggested that people's actions might be selfish and individualistic but failed to note that political and social norms would drive potentially problematic responses on a broader scale. Since disease films had avoided addressing these kinds of issues, various groups drew different lessons from the same films. The public no longer seemed to perceive *Contagion* as a story about holding a prom at home but instead debated whether it was more appropriate to hold a prom at home or send your daughter to an in-school prom. Both had become rational responses for different communities.

The Wrong Lessons of Movie Stories

The use of movie fiction to help shape real-life events received only limited push back in the early, chaotic months of COVID. One writer criticized all post-1995 movies by arguing that culture has been "drenched in catastrophe porn for decades" and that once the pandemic did arrive, it turned out to be "so different from what we imagined."[66] From that perspective *Contagion* was the ultimate fantasy in imaging how COVID would unfold: simply and with clarity. It depicted its pandemic, MEV-1, in plain, dramatic and moral terms. Yet, it clearly missed the effects of COVID, which spread far more slowly than MEV-1, yet continued to evolve and spread for years killing hundreds of Americans per day even after two years of the pandemic. MEV-1 killed tens of millions worldwide within months before its vaccine began commercial distribution 133 days after the pathogen's first outbreak, effectively leading to the beginning of the end of the pandemic (and the end of the movie). COVID's disparate mortality rates, its politicization of institutional responses and the non-compliance with health efforts were all missing from disease movies.[67] Movie makers failed to anticipate the rejection of scientific answers to reduce human deaths and the politically driven changes to the CDC's response.

While early hyperbolic rhetoric described the pandemic as a game-changer, the simple takeaway after the first few months of lockdown was that the stakes were less visceral for society in aggregate than movies had suggested and that the status quo would persist. Overwhelming fear and anxiety of what might occur soon dissipated. As one writer remarked, "epidemic epics [such as] *28 Days Later* and *Contagion* feature fights to the death over scant resources, not the revival of meals on wheels."[68] The husband of a supermarket worker, who criticized the anxious shoppers abusing his wife, pointed out in an interview that "too many people have been watching *28 Days Later* and thinking we're going to run out of food, it's just got a wee bit out of hand."[69] The early panic over shortages of some commodities, such as toilet paper or cleaning supplies, faded once demand dropped. Observers concluded that the zombie genre, in particular, was "far too pessimistic and cynical about the human race" and that the breakdown of society leading to a post-apocalyptic world was unrealistic.[70] COVID offered men few stereotypically masculine opportunities to express their individuality and independence, except to refuse (sometimes violently) to follow public health guidelines by not wearing a mask or refusing to quarantine. Altogether solidarity was, at least initially, more common than open conflict, temporarily stretched and disrupted supply chains were largely resilient, and public utilities functioned. Movies depicted societal chaos and collapse, followed by the breakdown of the social contract, but this was far from reality after the first few months of confusion.

COVID's impact revealed how movies had offered misguided and unrealistic ideas, perhaps even numbing audiences to real world viruses in the absence of immediate devastation and chaos. The pre-vaccine case fatality rate (around 1 percent) during COVID is far lower compared to viruses such as Motaba (*Outbreak*), which kills 100 percent of its victims in two or three days, or MEV-1 (*Contagion*), which kills about 20 percent and resulted in tens of millions of deaths worldwide in the movie over just a few weeks (compared to COVID's anywhere from 6 to 20 million in its first few years).[71] Perhaps these lower numbers then resulted in complacency among the American government and general population, stymying government and social action and increasing the pandemic's spread and mortality rate.[72]

COVID revealed that the real pandemic narrative in the United States consisted of the stark inequalities of a fragmented American society, the result of decades of deliberate disinvestment in federal, state and local institutions and their ability to respond. The United States has featured a series of structural failures both responding to the initial outbreak and convincing its population to respond to the further spread of an infectious disease. As the middle and upper middle classes hid in their homes, invisible but essential workers, such as cleaners and drivers, risked their lives to maintain the country's economy in return for superficial sympathy and only minimal reward. The heroic elite, Hollywood-looking doctors of movies, who tried to find the origin of a disease and develop its cure, were absent, replaced in the real world with the anonymous, exhausted doctors and nurses who lived next door and faced COVID in a daily Sisyphean struggle.[73] Only the first few months in New York City (and a few other locations), where the changing of hospital shifts each evening led to daily cheers, broke the otherwise calm silence.[74] Once the panicked early days had ended, COVID-related deaths outside one's circle of family and acquaintances became normalized. Experts in policy and public health who appeared on American screens similarly fell short of the films' heroic doctors as they failed to stop the disease.[75] The wholesale privatization of public health had been slow and silent, resulting in mass numbers of people left largely on their own to improvise in finding solutions to an unknown and invisible virus. Movies had come to gloss over these American public health problems in the past few decades in their eager promotion of social collapse or a new social order.

Another important difference was also generally unstated. The film's drama – with heroes, villains and cliffhanger outcomes – was not how political leadership reacted to COVID. *Contagion* imagined a world divided between selfish politicians out to save themselves and individuals who made heroic sacrifices. Political behavior throughout COVID was far more cynical and self-serving. If a member of Congress in *Contagion* commandeered a plane to save himself, resulting in the abandonment of CDC agent Erin Mears, that was at least "personal" corruption. COVID corruption was far more mundane and based on simple greed. During COVID members of Congress attended a closed door COVID briefing in January 2020 and received information not yet public as the Trump administration continued to assure the public that COVID would readily be contained. Within days, several Republican senators, some of whom suggested to their constituents that COVID was not a threat, sold off stock that soon plummeted in value.[76] In a culture in which events are perceived through the lens of maximizing individual, capital returns to increase your assets, it is hardly surprising that those high in government with advance knowledge sought to benefit financially from the anticipated market disruption which COVID caused. Investigations were quietly closed several years later without any punishment or explanation.[77] In that respect, life was worse than the movies, since movie makers had not anticipated political profiteering. To the contrary, movies had largely advocated for the role of the individual in the effort at conquering increasingly global diseases and had ignored that such a focus fostered the very social disintegration that resulted in the post-apocalyptic landscape.

As COVID continued, political views further divided responses to COVID, reinforcing the structural problems in American public health. President Donald Trump's refusal to acknowledge the virus' impact publicly and push to have people return to their pre-COVID lives built on the cynical efforts to profit off the pandemic to ensure national economic numbers would help his re-election. Democrats pounced on the opportunity with then presidential candidate Joe Biden, stating two weeks before elections that anyone "responsible for that many deaths [220,000 at the time] should not remain as president of the United States of America."[78] Once in office, President Biden promoted greater public health efforts during his first half year in office, such as organizing an expedited vaccine rollout, encouraging mask wearing and offering Americans free at home tests.[79] Nevertheless, none of this stemmed the daily death toll, and Biden abandoned his position on COVID as variants reappeared in greater rapidity from the summer of 2021 onward. By late spring 2022, almost all remaining measures were gone. Biden's administration reverted to the basic conceit of contemporary American society: blame bad actors, such as the unvaccinated (which included those who refused the vaccine as well as those who could not take it) for their own sickness and death and for causing that of others. The vulnerable – senior citizens and the immunocompromised, among others – were left on their own to navigate a world in which the majority decided the pandemic was over even as hundreds continued to die every day. Individual responsibility and choice as a value trumped a possible debate on how to best balance, for example, economic and public health risks during the continuing waves of COVID variants. Wearing a mask or getting vaccinated became symbolic of individual choice rather than being perceived through the lens of a common good that might benefit everyone, whether economically, medically or morally.

What also became apparent in the United States after the initial panic buying disrupted supply lines and the heartbreaking stories of poverty was the banality of life for all but the essential workers. Rather than *Contagion*'s fights in pharmacies over forsythia or *28 Days Later*'s bloody zombie violence, "life has instead slowed down to an increasingly interior balancing act of worry, vigilance, uncertainty and yes, boredom."[80] Disease films have offered few cinematic portrayals of the slow horror of the hundreds of thousands who continued to die in the United States, largely sequestered from the public consciousness by being sealed off in hospitals, nursing homes, prisons or at home, with their funerals broadcast on Zoom. Pandemic films contained no discussion on how during COVID the super-rich, such as Amazon's Jeff Bezos, would almost double their wealth, or that the favored course of action for many of the upper and middle classes would be the unheroic practice of waiting the pandemic out while staying at home. An optimistic op-ed considered the average person as heroic, arguing that "most people don't panic and riot. Most become Matt Damon."[81] While the author pointed out that Matt Damon's character in *Contagion*, Mitch Emhoff, helped and protected others, he did not dwell on the fact that Emhoff undoubtedly spent more time sitting in his living room off-screen than he did in trying to prevent his daughter from leaving the house, fleeing the outbreak or searching for a gun in the surrounding suburbs.

COVID offered far less drama than any film and certainly no apocalyptic conflict even as politicians and government officials continued to play their traditional roles. President Trump remained the villain in the liberal narrative and Dr. Fauci became the villain of the conservative narrative, but neither adequately reflected COVID's story and both stories, in fact, reinforced the focus on individuals as responsible or irresponsible actors. While the Biden administration's response to COVID has been more scientifically centered than Trump's, both have focused on individuals rather than attempting to address the systemic causes of America's public health crisis.[82]

The Stories Missing in Movies

Hollywood movies about disease, like other Hollywood movies, obviously reflect the unstated cultural values of America. By ignoring that which does not conform to those values, most disease films failed to accurately depict, let alone anticipate, the stories of the early twenty-first century COVID pandemic. Economics and individual choice, not empathy or basic public health, drove America's response to COVID. The most significant impact of the pandemic in the United States was on marginalized groups, including those from lower socioeconomic classes, communities of color and the elderly. George Floyd's murder and the subsequent social protests galvanizing calls for change underscored how COVID discussions had often avoided cultural differences in America and the resulting disparate impact of the pandemic. Since the late twentieth century, the drive to maximize profits from a global movie market has resulted in disease movies that have increasingly ignored divisions within American society, such as race and politics, notwithstanding that these differences have informed how America has responded to all health issues, including COVID.

Disease movies also ignored the role of the United States in global politics, including the global inequalities it has helped perpetuate. While sometimes still featuring a foreign originating disease or identifying foreign bad actors, Hollywood disease movies pay little attention to the need for global cooperation, which is necessary to bring a pandemic under control, let alone acknowledge the existence of non-American governments. Movies such as *Contagion* portrayed China as the source of disease, but the country itself was largely absent from the narrative other than in a subplot.

In contrast to the United States, China's initial response, trying to entirely stop the spread of COVID, was based on its own, strikingly different value system. That response, assuming available data and statistics are accurately reported, led to lower death rates than in the United States and anywhere else in the developed world.[83] For two and a half years, the Chinese central government implemented a policy of "zero tolerance for local transmission (zero COVID)" and mobilized workers and resources to infected areas to contain COVID.[84] These numbers were achieved through ubiquitous surveillance and the Chinese state's policy to isolate millions who have no vote or choice. The newly empowered surveillance state applied to COVID has already been expanded to other threats to the body politic.[85]

In December 2022, China reversed its policy to remove all mitigation efforts with almost no prior notice. This may have been in response to widespread public protests.[86] Whatever caused this change, COVID was allowed to infect the entire country immediately so that by mid-January 2023 the Chinese government claimed that about 80 percent of the population had already been infected. While the official death count was reported as only 72,000 by the end of January 2023, non-Chinese experts estimated up to 1 million deaths.[87] The death toll is likely to remain unknown and a matter of future estimates and modeling, since China "has effectively stopped counting COVID cases and deaths . . . adopting new criteria for counting deaths that will exclude most fatalities from being reported."[88]

The United States used a discourse of individual freedom to promote elite, private economic interests while China initially positioned itself at the other end of the spectrum – a rhetoric of public health that strengthened central government control. As the pandemic continued, these underlying values – economic interests and central control – remained the key factors. In both countries, COVID was eventually "solved" by moving the goal posts and publicly declaring the pandemic over. A debate over some middle ground between the values at these opposite ends of the spectrum, economic interests and centralized control, is wholly absent from American movie narratives. Instead, Hollywood movies assume an economic-centered value system, which they then propagate through the rhetoric of individual freedom but which coincides with American, global capitalism and its longstanding prejudices and colonial attitudes.

The developed world's approach to COVID has reflected American capitalism's emphasis on private sector competition and individual responsibility.

The result was de facto "vaccine apartheid."[89] Wealthy countries hoarded vaccines (and anti-viral medicine) so that millions of doses expired in storage and the populations of poorer countries received few, if any, vaccines (or other medicine).[90] Wealthy countries pursued vaccine diplomacy, such as trading vaccine surpluses to poorer countries in return for political concessions, and vaccine war, such as imposing sanctions on Iran so that it could not purchase vaccines, resulting in civilian deaths.[91] Western pharmaceutical companies, who are generally absent from American disease movies, made enormous profits from these vaccines, notwithstanding that they developed them with government funding (whether directly or through funding of academic research). Not only did their ownership of vaccine intellectual property rights ensure continued future profits, but it also ensured that they would continue to profit through booster shots, while developing other drugs and remedies and keeping the rights to this medicine.[92] In parallel, pharmaceutical companies amassed vast amounts of private health data, which some governments, such as Israel, handed over without their citizens' consent to gain faster access to vaccines for local political benefit.[93]

As some health experts predicted, this fragmented approach to COVID vaccines resulted in the worldwide spread of COVID variants, including the Delta and Omicron variants and their subvariants. These have sickened and killed Americans, too, particularly the unvaccinated or the immunocompromised, while also making it clear that further future variants, for which the current vaccines may be less effective, are likely. To avoid addressing these challenges, the Biden administration has shifted to offer a set of tools to fight COVID (vaccines, booster shots, updated vaccines and anti-virals) and declared COVID over, even as the daily death toll remained in the hundreds.[94] The failure to address adequately COVID seems obvious when viewed historically. Inequality and social injustice, after all, have resulted in disproportionate suffering worldwide due to disease for centuries.[95] Movies seldom tell this story. To the contrary, Hollywood movies insist on American exceptionalism and the exclusion of others even as the gap between the wealthy and all others continues to increase and the obligations of the state to individuals in the United States continue to shrink.

Three years after the onset of COVID, the United States has failed to address the problems COVID had revealed and continues to feature a dysfunctional and neglected public health structure. As such, COVID will likely continue to claim deaths for many years. A long-term solution to COVID requires a denial of American exceptionalism, a recognition that all people should be equitably treated and an acknowledgement of the need to work together both globally and within the United States. These three ideas seem obvious but at present impossible to achieve, because they challenge contemporary values and require substantial political will. American capitalism favors both private markets and short-term profits, both of which are contrary to the collective needs for a long-term health solution.

By ignoring this paradigmatic reality, disease movies have problematically shaped COVID expectations and responses. The news media, for example, adopted the movie narrative in which disease and death equally affected everyone. Like *Outbreak*, which depicts an almost entirely white, small town as its focus of the outbreak, *Contagion* depicted homogeneous, middle-class cities and suburbs as its focus and shows the risks and deaths from MEV-1 as the same across all social groups. While a few elite government officials receive favored treatment by receiving the vaccine earlier, the focus remains on how everyone else receives the vaccine through a lottery. This generally equitable solution assures viewers that everyone, regardless of cultural identity, is equal. The heroes of these movies, like the heroes depicted in the media, are those individuals who rebel against "the system" even as their rebellion affirms that the common good has disappeared, reflecting an American culture in which only American exceptionalism remains.

The myth of a post-cultural identity that movies such as *Contagion* espouse advances the agenda of global capitalism, rendering vast populations throughout the world the same and resulting in yet a greater ability to maximize corporate profits for the few in America's post-industrial, information society. The focus on economics and freedom of choice as the key cultural values drove many of the divisive American policy decisions, such as the duration of lockdowns, the barring of mask mandates and the adoption of the "let 'er rip" approach which tolerated higher infection and death numbers in an attempt to let the pandemic burn through the population. Sickness, hospitalization and death were plotted against profit in a COVID cost-benefit analysis. Ironically, only movies from the pre-1980s, which commentators mentioned far more infrequently during COVID, grappled with the disparate impact of disease.[96] *Panic in the Streets* at least depicted the unequal impact of its disease based on class and ethnicity even if it argued for the policing of foreign, non-white immigrants and for the prevention of their entry into the United States with their inevitable carrying of diseases.[97] This more nuanced depiction of society was not adopted in considering how to think about achieving social cohesion when addressing COVID.

Finally, the standard dramatic arc of Hollywood movies failed to highlight the lengthy process of the pandemic, since these movies focus on the acute phase of disease, removed from its broader social, cultural and even personal context. A Hollywood movie, which requires a beginning, middle and end in that order and in two hours, is deceptive in its closure so that its disease narrative likewise suggests a similarly simplistic arc that should be replicated in real life. A romance film that ends with marriage, for example, fails to account for the formative experiences that led to the romance, as well as the many years afterwards in which the couple ages, may become divorced, and eventually dies. Richard Linklater's *Before* trilogy, after all, required almost two decades and three movies to reach this conclusion, which most other movies do not even attempt. So, too, most Hollywood disease narratives failed to take account of how humans in the years and decades after a disease outbreak may continue to suffer.[98] While Jory Emhoff in *Contagion* enjoys her romantic ending of a prom, neither she nor her father have to deal with the long-term consequences of the deaths of her stepmother and brother. The newly developed vaccine will be administered to everyone, and life appears to return to normality. By summer 2022, most Americans returned to their pre-pandemic habits, since they are "over" the pandemic, which is neither exciting nor news. Perhaps reflecting this attitude, the CDC has continuously relaxed its COVID guidance.[99] The result, it seems, has been to avoid a serious public discussion of COVID and its lessons.

COVID has demonstrated that technological utopianism, which disease movies promote, led to the simplistic view that science will save us with a vaccine and life will thereafter return to normal. COVID, however, has demonstrated that vaccine development and distribution are merely the end of the beginning of a pandemic. In retrospect, triumphal jubilations in wealthy countries that "defeated COVID" were woefully premature as the disease reemerged in more infectious variants and returned to re-infect people. Additionally, COVID can also result in long-term harm even with vaccines with the duration and specific impact unknown. Long COVID with its serious medical effects is already shaping the lives of many thousands in the United States.[100] While polio was supposedly wiped out in many countries, its survivors similarly continue to suffer from its lasting effects. It is the same story that those suffering from HIV in the United States have already endured and will likely continue to endure for decades.[101] Notwithstanding the classic Hollywood myths of conquest and invincibility or even the contemporary story of post-apocalyptic extinction, life under COVID is both more boring and unending.

Conclusion

This chapter has offered a snapshot in time as of the winter of 2022–2023 of the role of movies during the COVID pandemic in the United States. If early drafts of this chapter were written when COVID was still perceived as a threatening presence, vaccines a distant fiction and medical treatments non-existent, the reality of COVID has since changed a few times, with the spread of variants revealing that COVID did not offer a simple Hollywood ending with the development of the COVID vaccine. It is clear that in the first few months of COVID, Americans used movies to orient themselves. Yet, COVID has also illuminated how the stories told in movies create our cultural myths and shape our thinking in the present. In today's culture, reality and movies are intimately connected and have together resulted in stories that have guided our discourse, even when they have incorrectly focused and motivated our responses and ideas.

This intertwined relationship between reality and movies and the cultural myths they create and perpetuate can be helpful. These stories allow people to grasp ideas, concepts and possibilities that might otherwise have been difficult to understand. Before COVID, few people had much experience with a fast-spreading pandemic. It was difficult for many to understand the concept of an exponential increase in the spread of a disease or an R0 factor. Movies became one way to make sense of what was happening and helped establish a common discourse. Moreover, while their narratives were frequently problematic, biased and wrong, that does not mean they were useless. During the uncertain beginnings of COVID, when scientists, public health officials and politicians seemed to know few specifics about the new pandemic, movies functioned as more-or-less coherent narratives that offered ways to make sense of the unprecedented events unfolding in the real world.

Yet, movies' discourse also seized hold so powerfully even before COVID that the ideas underlying them could not be dislodged when different, more favorable outcomes for society might have been possible. The unexamined myths embedded in these movies drove discussions and resulted in behavior that frequently ran contrary to the interests of many. Given that our current system favors economics, it is not surprising, for example, that our movie myths elide over such differences as class, race, age or residency, and that America's conflicted response to COVID reflects the often-unstated omission of these differences from movie narratives. The result is a continuation of a fragmented America in which these differing needs remain unacknowledged and repressed. People may have understood what COVID was doing but too often acted in service to a narrative indifferent to the lives of themselves and those around them.

Will contemporary movie stories focusing on the End Times and the post-apocalyptic world continue to hold sway or will movies begin to question their own mythology by taking into account other values, including the unequal impact of pandemics in the twenty-first century? One writer has already predicted that future movies would continue to be "as grim and nihilistic as they ever were."[102] Zack Snyder's *Army of the Dead* (2021), which was released during COVID, bears out this pessimistic view. Snyder's film is made in the same style and with the same theme as his 2004 *Dawn of the Dead* remake.[103] The zombie outbreak results from a villainous army bioweapon, and the ending depicts a zombie possessing self-awareness and increased intelligence, thereby pointing to the possible apocalyptic triumph of zombies. The issue remains, however, whether we, as a society, will adopt new cultural myths, including those told through movies, that acknowledge the complexity of our differences and similarities and the need to reconcile the seeming conflict between individual and communal perspectives. The stories we tell in disease movies will only change when the creators of those stories, both the makers of the movies and their audiences, begin readjusting their views of American cultural values. COVID has demonstrated again that we are the makers of our own stories and that those stories inform whether and how we respond to the newly infectious diseases of an evolving world. Only collective, imaginative stories, however, will enable us to evolve by seeing our world through a new perspective in which a collective reality results in a more expansive social contract.

Notes

1. Kelsey Piper, "Here's How COVID-19 Ranks among the Worst Plagues in History," *Vox*, January 11, 2021, https://www.vox.com/future-perfect/21539483/covid-19-black-death-plagues-in-history; Oliver Milman, "Covid-19 Has Now Killed as Many Americans as the 1918–19 Flu Pandemic," *The Guardian*, September 21, 2021, https://www.theguardian.com/world/2021/sep/20/covid-19-death-toll-1918-flu-pandemic. And in summary, Merle Eisenberg, "Uses of History During the First Nine Months of COVID," *Perspectives in Biology and Medicine* 64, no. 3 (2021): 421–35.
2. See, for example, Evie Kendal, "Public Health Crises in Popular Media: How Viral Outbreak Films Affect the Public's Health Literacy," *Medical Humanities* 47, no. 1 (2021): 11–19.
3. For pandemics as stories: Charles E. Rosenberg, "What Is an Epidemic? AIDS in Historical Perspective"; and also Wald, *Contagious*.
4. The murder of George Floyd by police during his arrest for suspicion of using a counterfeit $20 bill and the ensuing nationwide, Black Lives Matter protests mirrored the disparate effects of COVID on persons of color. Even the January 6, 2021 insurrection at the US Capitol reflected the political divisions over how to address COVID.
5. Chris Lindahl, "Beyond 'Contagion': Interest in Outbreak Movies, Podcasts, and More Surges Across the Internet," *IndieWire*, March 17, 2020, https://www.indiewire.com/2020/03/contagion-pandemic-outbreak-movies-coronavirus-1202218477/.
6. Press Trust of India, "Pandemic and Disaster Stories on Screen: To See or to Not See, That Is the Question," *Business Standard India*, April 17, 2020, https://www.business-standard.com/article/pti-stories/pandemic-and-disaster-stories-on-screen-to-see-or-to-not-see-that-is-the-question-120041700771_1.html.
7. UK: Robbie Collin, "Trying Not to Panic about Coronavirus? Then Don't Rewatch Contagion," *Telegraph*, March 27, 2020, https://www.telegraph.co.uk/films/0/trying-not-panic-coronavirus-dont-rewatch-contagion/; US: David Mack, "Everyone Is Watching 'Contagion,' A 9-Year-Old Movie About A Flu Outbreak," *BuzzFeed News*, March 3, 2020, https://www.buzzfeednews.com/article/davidmack/contagion-movie-coronavirus; for more detailed data, Julia Alexander, "Contagion Shows the Lengths People Go to Watch a Movie They Can't Stream," *The Verge*, March 7, 2020, https://www.theverge.com/2020/3/7/21164769/contagion-streaming-netflix-hulu-cinemax-itunes-download-torrent-coronavirus; Ernesto Van der Sar, "Coronavirus Outbreak Triggers Surge in Pirated Downloads of the Film 'Contagion,'"

TorrentFreak, March 7, 2020, https://torrentfreak.com/coronavirus-outbreak-triggers-surge-in-pirated-downloads-of-the-film-contagion/.
8. *CE Noticias Financieras English*, "Coronavirus, from Reality to Fiction to Prediction," March 8, 2020, https://advance.lexis.com/api/document?collection=news&id=urn:contentItem:5YCS-JG21-JBJN-M14R-00000-00&context=1516831.
9. "Top iTunes Movie Rentals Charts and Movie Trailer on iTunes Store USA 2020," *iTopChart*, March 17, 2020, https://web.archive.org/web/20200317160316/https://itopchart.com/us/en/movies/.
10. Charles Bramesco, "Exposure Therapy: Why We're Obsessed with Watching Virus Movies," *The Guardian*, March 16, 2020, https://www.theguardian.com/film/2020/mar/16/coronavirus-movies-why-are-we-obsessed-contagion-films.
11. See Heather Kelly, "People Have Found a Way to Cope with Pandemic Fears: Watching 'Contagion,'" *The Washington Post*, March 6, 2020, https://www.washingtonpost.com/technology/2020/03/06/contagion-streaming/.
12. Other observers noted that these films end well: Benjamin Bullard, "Self-Quarantined? Here Are 5 Pandemic Movies Where We Ultimately Beat the Virus," *SYFY WIRE*, March 13, 2020, https://www.syfy.com/syfywire/5-movies-people-win-for-your-coronavirus-quarantine; Torsten Landsberg, "In Times of Coronavirus, Looking at How Hollywood Films Portray Virus Outbreaks," *DW.COM*, June 3, 2020, https://www.dw.com/en/in-times-of-coronavirus-looking-at-how-hollywood-films-portray-virus-outbreaks/a-52665150.
13. Nicole Sperling, "'Contagion,' Steven Soderbergh's 2011 Thriller, Is Climbing Up the Charts," *The New York Times* March 4, 2020, https://www.nytimes.com/2020/03/04/business/media/coronavirus-contagion-movie.html.
14. Mostafa Keshvari, *Corona* (GrandMuse Pictures, 2020).
15. Given the need for the cast and crew to self-isolate, the movie features only one actor, and much of it consists of redubbed earlier zombie movies as well as videos of Donald Trump and COVID events: Stuart Heritage, "Corona Zombies: The Terrible Movie We Might Just Need Right Now," *The Guardian*, April 13, 2020, https://www.theguardian.com/film/2020/apr/13/corona-zombies-film-full-moon-features.
16. Dan Solomon, "A New Genre of Film Is Already Here: COVID Movies," *Texas Monthly*, March 24, 2021, https://www.texasmonthly.com/arts-entertainment/pandemic-movies-just-getting-started/.
17. For a relevant pre-COVID framing, see Lynteris, *Human Extinction*; for a few examples: New Zealand: Brittany Keogh, "Coronavirus: What Does Declaring a Pandemic for COVID-19 Mean?," *Stuff*, March 12, 2020, https://www.stuff.co.nz/national/health/coronavirus/119997644/outbreak-or-pandemic-translating-coronavirus-jargon-into-human-speak; Italy: Angela Giuffrida, "'This Is Not a Film': Italian Mayors Rage at Virus Lockdown Dodgers," *The Guardian*, March 23, 2020, https://www.theguardian.com/world/2020/mar/23/this-is-not-a-film-italian-mayors-rage-coronavirus-lockdown-dodgers; Bangladesh: Niaz Alam, "World Leaders Pretend," *Dhaka Tribune*, March 21, 2020, https://www.dhakatribune.com/opinion/2020/03/21/world-leaders-pretend; Ireland: Michael McNiffe, "Mick McNiffe comment: Ireland's War with Coronavirus Is Like a Sci-Fi Movie – Hopefully It Has a Happy Ending," *Irish Mirror*, March 25, 2020, https://www.irishmirror.ie/news/news-opinion/mick-mcniffe-comment-irelands-war-21754374; Australia: Hans van

Leeuwen, "Life in London's Lockdown: How the Real Becomes Surreal," *The Australian Financial Review*, March 25, 2020, https://www.afr.com/world/europe/life-in-london-s-lockdown-how-the-real-becomes-surreal-20200326-p54e0i.

18. "Fiction offers us a framework to think about reality" (orig. French "la fiction nous offre des grilles pour penser la réalité") in Christian Chelebourg, "Virus, quarantaine et paranoïa: quand la réalité rejoint la fiction," *The Conversation*, February 18, 2020, http://theconversation.com/virus-quarantaine-et-parano-a-quand-la-realite-rejoint-la-fiction-132027.

19. Geoffrey Macnab, "Infected Hollywood: Why Filmmakers Love Disease," *Independent*, February 20, 2020, https://www.independent.co.uk/independent-premium/culture/coronavirus-panic-in-the-streets-bfi-contagion-outbreak-zombie-films-a9341801.html.

20. Lia Eustachewich, "People Are Freaking out That Coronavirus Outbreak Is like 'Contagion,'" January 23, 2020, *New York Post*, https://nypost.com/2020/01/23/people-are-freaking-out-that-coronavirus-outbreak-is-like-contagion/.

21. Wesley Morris, "'Outbreak' Was a Hit in 1995. Now We're Living the Sequel," *The New York Times* March 30, 2020, https://www.nytimes.com/2020/03/30/movies/outbreak-movie-coronavirus.html.

22. Hannah Brown, "Did World War Z Predict Israel's Response to Coronavirus?," *The Jerusalem Post*, March 10, 2020, https://www.jpost.com/israel-news/world-war-c-did-world-war-z-predict-israels-response-to-covid-19-620342.

23. Carl Goldman, "I Have the Coronavirus. So Far, It Hasn't Been That Bad for Me," *The Washington Post*, February 28, 2020, https://www.washingtonpost.com/outlook/2020/02/28/i-have-coronavirus-so-far-it-isnt-that-bad/.

24. Terry Teachout, "The Time Has Come Again for 'Panic in the Streets,'" *The Wall Street Journal*, March 4, 2020, https://www.wsj.com/articles/the-time-has-come-again-for-panic-in-the-streets-11583352180.

25. Jennifer Valentino-DeVries, Ella Koeze, and Sapna Maheshwari, "Virus Alters Where People Open Their Wallets, Hinting at a Halting Recovery," *The New York Times*, August 18, 2020, https://www.nytimes.com/interactive/2020/08/18/business/economy/coronavirus-economic-recovery-states.html.

26. Radhika Chalasani, "Photos: Wildlife Roams during the Coronavirus Pandemic," *ABC News*, April 22, 2020, https://abcnews.go.com/International/photos-wildlife-roams-planets-human-population-isolates/story?id=70213431.

27. Siba Jackson, "Brit Stranded in Coronavirus 'ground Zero' with City Deserted like '28 Days Later,'" *Dailystar.co.uk*, January 26, 2020, https://www.dailystar.co.uk/news/latest-news/brit-stranded-coronavirus-ground-zero-21364581.

28. See, for example, Brigid Delaney, "Travelling through Asia during the Coronavirus: It's Like I Have the Whole Place to Myself," *The Guardian*, March 5, 2020, https://www.theguardian.com/commentisfree/2020/mar/06/travelling-through-asia-during-the-coronavirus-its-like-i-have-the-whole-place-to-myself; David Ellis, "No reservation? No Problem: London's Top Restaurants, Pubs and Bars Accepting Walk-Ins," *Evening Standard*, April 28, 2021, https://www.standard.co.uk/reveller/restaurants/london-top-restaurants-pubs-bars-accepting-walk-ins-no-reservations-b929450.html. See also *The Economist*, "Foot Traffic Has Fallen Sharply in Cities with Big Coronavirus Outbreaks," *The Economist*, March 14,

2020, https://www.economist.com/graphic-detail/2020/03/14/foot-traffic-has-fallen-sharply-in-cities-with-big-coronavirus-outbreaks.
29. Stephen Matthews and Sam Blanchard, "Fourteen UK Patients Are Tested for Coronavirus: Suspected Victims Are Taken into Isolation after Returning from Wuhan with Flu-like Symptoms as Health Secretary Is Urged to Order Checks on Passengers on ALL Flights from China," *Daily Mail Online*, January 23, 2020, https://www.dailymail.co.uk/health/article-7920907/Coronavirus-fears-Scotland-two-Chinese-patients-rushed-hospital.html.
30. Slugan, "Pandemic (Movies)."
31. Kristy Dawson, "Dad Stuck in Italy Coronavirus Zone with No Health Care for Baby," *TeessideLive*, March 13, 2020, https://www.gazettelive.co.uk/news/teesside-news/dad-stuck-italy-coronavirus-zone-17918238.
32. Jamie East, "Coronavirus Has Left Me Feeling like I'm in 28 Days Later and Been Hit by a Train – It's the Worst I've Felt in My Life," *The Sun*, March 19, 2020, https://www.thesun.co.uk/news/11213289/coronavirus-suffering-28-days-later/.
33. Naaman Zhou, Christopher Knaus, and Amy Remeikis, "Australian Shares Plunge 6.4% and AFL Season to Start as Planned amid Covid-19 Outbreak – as It Happened," *The Guardian*, March 18, 2020, https://www.theguardian.com/world/live/2020/mar/18/australia-coronavirus-live-updates-test-kits-covid19-nsw-victoria-qld-schools-latest-news-update.
34. Bethany Minelle, "Coronavirus: What Can We Learn from a Hollywood Pandemic? The Positives from Four Outbreak Films," *Sky News*, April 29, 2020, https://news.sky.com/story/coronavirus-can-pandemic-disaster-films-help-us-navigate-the-outbreak-11979655.
35. A bus driver in Dublin: Patrick Freyne, "Rush Hour on a Dublin Bus: 'They're All Ghost Buses Now,'" *The Irish Times*, April 18, 2020, https://www.irishtimes.com/life-and-style/people/rush-hour-on-a-dublin-bus-they-re-all-ghost-buses-now-1.4230714; a local newspaper in York: Chloe Laversuch, "28 Days Later: York in Coronavirus Lockdown," *The Press*, April 19, 2020, https://www.yorkpress.co.uk/news/18388214.28-days-later-york-coronavirus-lockdown/; a metro driver in Newcastle: Tom Parmenter, "Coronavirus in Newcastle: Novelty of Lockdown Gives Way to Fear of Economic Recession," *Sky News*, May 15, 2020, https://news.sky.com/story/coronavirus-in-newcastle-novelty-of-lockdown-gives-way-to-fear-of-economic-recession-11988544; Calum Marsh, "As Outdated Ads Linger a Hundred Days Later, a City Feels like an Apocalyptic St. Patrick's Day," *National Post*, June 27, 2020, https://nationalpost.com/entertainment/as-outdated-ads-linger-a-hundred-days-later-a-city-feels-like-an-apocalyptic-st-patricks-day; in Australia as well: Ted Clarke, "Locked Down Under in New Zealand," *Prince George Citizen*, June 28, 2020, https://www.princegeorgecitizen.com/local-news/locked-down-under-in-new-zealand-3740764.
36. Clarissa Place, "Trader Woke up from Operation to Discover Country Was in Lockdown," *Norwich Evening News*, June 17, 2020, https://www.eveningnews24.co.uk/news/shop-owner-norwich-wakes-up-nnuh-lockdown-1771246.
37. The comment refers to the science fiction movie *The Day the Earth Stood Still* (1951). Of course, that display was hardly experienced as "beautiful." Jonathan Jones, "Apocalyptic Vision: The Unsettling Beauty of Lockdown Is Pure Sci-Fi,"

The Guardian, April 29, 2020, https://www.theguardian.com/artanddesign/2020/apr/29/apocalyptic-vision-the-unsettling-beauty-of-lockdown-britain-is-pure-sci-fi-coronavirus.
38. Chris Mooney, Brady Dennis and John Muyskens, "Global Emissions Plunged an Unprecedented 17 Percent during the Coronavirus Pandemic," *The Washington Post*, May 19, 2020, https://www.washingtonpost.com/climate-environment/2020/05/19/greenhouse-emissions-coronavirus/.
39. Thomas R. Frieden, "CDC Director on 'Contagion': Deadly Viruses Could Spread Fast," *The Atlantic*, September 10, 2011, https://www.theatlantic.com/health/archive/2011/09/cdc-director-on-contagion-deadly-viruses-could-spread-fast/244849/.
40. Quotes are from, respectively: Zak Hepburn, "A Film Critic and Scientist Review Pandemic Films in the Era of Coronavirus," *ABC News*, June 7, 2020, https://www.abc.net.au/news/2020-06-08/film-critic-scientist-review-pandemic-films-in-era-of-covid-19/12149784; James Oliver, "Apocalypse Now: How to Find Coronavirus Comfort in Catastrophe Movies," *New European*, April 6, 2020, https://web.archive.org/web/20200406125020/https://www.theneweuropean.co.uk/top-stories/apocalypse-now-how-to-find-coronavirus-comfort-in-catastrophe-movies-1-6591127; Matthew Fisher, "Pandemics like the Coronavirus Crisis Inspire Outbreaks of Art," *Global News*, April 21, 2020, https://globalnews.ca/news/6839544/coronavirus-art-movies-books/; TVEyes – *BBC 1 Northern Ireland 4*, "A Question of Sport – 01:35 AM GMT," April 6, 2020, https://advance.lexis.com/api/document?collection=news&id=urn:contentItem:5YKP-K5P1-DY08-32YP-00000-00&context=1516831.
41. Jason Guerrasio, "How 'Contagion' Became a Must-See Movie during the Coronavirus Pandemic," *Insider*, April 3, 2020, https://www.insider.com/how-contagion-became-a-must-see-movie-during-the-coronavirus-2020-4; Devansh Sharma, "In Times of Coronavirus Outbreak, Why Steven Soderbergh's 2011 Medical Thriller Contagion Makes for Essential Viewing," *Firstpost*, March 11, 2020, https://www.firstpost.com/entertainment/in-times-of-coronavirus-outbreak-why-steven-soderberghs-2011-medical-thriller-contagion-makes-for-essential-viewing-8138601.html; Wesley Morris, "For Me, Rewatching 'Contagion' Was Fun, Until It Wasn't," *The New York Times*, March 10, 2020, https://www.nytimes.com/2020/03/10/movies/contagion-movie-coronavirus.html.
42. Beth Accomando, "UC San Diego Professor Uses 'Contagion' Film To Teach Epidemiology," *KPBS Public Media*, March 23, 2020, https://www.kpbs.org/news/midday-edition/2020/03/23/uc-san-diego-professor-uses-contagion-film-teach-e.
43. Travis M. Andrews, "Sure, Binge 'Contagion' and Other Pandemic Movies Right Now. But Their Creators Urge You to Watch with Caution," *The Washington Post*, March 19, 2020, https://www.washingtonpost.com/arts-entertainment/2020/03/19/contagion-outbreak-stand-pandemic-movie-caution/.
44. Commentators struggled to find dissimilarities. The *Los Angeles Times*, for example, noted, that in *Contagion* the pandemic began in Macau and Gwyneth Paltrow's character died of a swelling of the brain, while COVID's first epicenter was Wuhan and encephalitis is not a symptom of COVID. Soumya Karlamangla, "I've Seen 'Contagion' Four Times. No, the Coronavirus Outbreak Isn't the Same," *Los Angeles*

Times, March 11, 2020, https://www.latimes.com/california/story/2020-03-11/coronavirus-contagion-outbreak-movie-comparison.

45. Kristen Rogers, "'Contagion' vs. Coronavirus: The Film's Connections to a Real Life Pandemic," *CNN*, April 2, 2020, https://www.cnn.com/2020/04/02/movies/contagion-movie-versus-coronavirus-scn-wellness/index.html.

46. Despite an early scientific study published in *Nature Medicine* and an initial near consensus among scientists that COVID developed naturally and not in lab, the theory continues to circulate. See Bob Hunt, Justin Gmoser, and Victoria Barranco, "How We Know the COVID-19 Coronavirus Wasn't Made in a Lab," *Business Insider*, December 6, 2020, https://www.businessinsider.com/coronavirus-lab-man-made-myth-debunked-2020-6; Jon Cohen, "Call of the Wild: Why Many Scientists Say It's Unlikely That SARS-CoV-2 Originated from a 'Lab Leak,'" September 2, 2021, https://www.science.org/content/article/why-many-scientists-say-unlikely-sars-cov-2-originated-lab-leak. Over time the belief by the public that COVID originated in a lab has grown dramatically, see Alice Miranda Ollstein, "POLITICO-Harvard Poll: Most Americans Believe Covid Leaked from Lab," *Politico*, July 9, 2021, https://www.politico.com/news/2021/07/09/poll-covid-wuhan-lab-leak-498847. While the evidence for such a theory is purely circumstantial – the location of a virology lab working on coronaviruses in Wuhan – the American public, regardless of political affiliation, has increasingly come to believe that the Chinese government either created the virus or that Chinese containment measures were slipshod. This is mirrored by the seriousness with which it is promoted by high-ranking officials – including President Trump, who personally articulated it, and President Biden, who ordered an intelligence commission to study it. For the study in *Nature Medicine*, Kristian G. Andersen et al., "The Proximal Origin of SARS-CoV-2," *Nature Medicine* 26, no. 4 (2020): 450–52. For Donald Trump, BBC News, "Coronavirus: Trump Stands by China Lab Origin Theory for Virus," *BBC News*, May 1, 2020, https://www.bbc.com/news/world-us-canada-52496098, for both countries: Sarah Peterson and Wendy Mesley, "Covid-19 Blame Game Intensifies with Online Ad Campaigns Paid for by China and the US," *CBC*, May 10, 2020, https://www.cbc.ca/news/world/coronavirus-covid-china-united-states-political-campaign-1.5555245. For China blaming Trump, Io Dodds, "China Floods Facebook with Undeclared Coronavirus Propaganda Ads Blaming Trump," *The Telegraph*, April 5, 2020, https://www.telegraph.co.uk/technology/2020/04/05/china-floods-facebook-instagram-undeclared-coronavirus-propaganda/.

47. Ruben V. Nepales, "Why 'Contagion,' out in 2011, Accurately Foretold Coronavirus Pandemic," *Jakarta Post*, April 26, 2020, https://www.thejakartapost.com/life/2020/04/26/why-contagion-out-in-2011-accurately-foretold-coronavirus-pandemic.html.

48. Christina Farr, "The Medical Advisors for the Movie 'Contagion' Saw a Pandemic Coming, but Got One Big Thing Wrong," *CNBC*, April 14, 2020, https://www.cnbc.com/2020/04/14/contagion-movie-advisors-anticipated-pandemic.html.

49. Isaac Feldberg, "'Contagion' Writer, Scientific Adviser Reflect on Film's Newfound Relevance amid Coronavirus Crisis," *Fortune*, February 12, 2020, https://fortune.com/2020/02/12/contagion-scott-z-burns-larry-brilliant-interview-coronavirus-fears/.

50. Cal Revely-Calder, "How Contagion Got Coronavirus Right – by the Film's Science Advisor," *The Telegraph*, May 4, 2020, https://www.telegraph.co.uk/films/0/contagion-coronavirus-science/.
51. Mark Olsen, "'Contagion' Director Steven Soderbergh on Hollywood Reopening: 'We're Going to Get Back to Work,'" *Los Angeles Times*, May 21, 2020, https://www.latimes.com/entertainment-arts/movies/story/2020-05-21/steven-soderbergh-hollywood-reopening-coronavirus-contagion; Anousha Sakoui and Ryan Faughnder, "Reopening California: Hollywood Is Figuring out How to Start Rolling Again," *Los Angeles Times*, April 28, 2020, https://www.latimes.com/entertainment-arts/business/story/2020-04-28/coronavirus-reopening-california-hollywood-production-restart.
52. Olsen, "'Contagion' Director Steven Soderbergh on Hollywood Reopening."
53. Erik Hayden, "'Contagion' Helmer Steven Soderbergh to Lead Directors Guild's COVID-19 Committee," *The Hollywood Reporter*, April 16, 2020, https://www.hollywoodreporter.com/news/general-news/steven-soderbergh-lead-directors-guild-committee-covid-19-impact-1290639/.
54. Soumya Karlamangla, "How the makers of 'Contagion' saw an outbreak like coronavirus coming," March 11, 2020, https://www.latimes.com/california/story/2020-03-11/coronavirus-contagion-outbreak-accuracy-movie.
55. Rebecca Lawrence, "'I'm paranoid and panicked': Gwyneth Jets to Paris with a Face Mask amid Coronavirus Outbreak," *Mail Online*, February 26, 2020, https://www.dailymail.co.uk/tvshowbiz/article-8046557/Gwyneth-jets-Paris-face-mask-amid-coronavirus-outbreak.html.
56. Christie D'Zurilla, "Wearing a Mask, Gwyneth Paltrow Cracks a Coronavirus Joke: 'I've Already Been in This Movie,'" *Los Angeles Times*, February 26, 2020, https://www.latimes.com/entertainment-arts/story/2020-02-26/gwyneth-paltrow-kate-hudson-face-mask-coronavirus.
57. Hannah Yasharoff, "Matt Damon Talks Coronavirus and 'Contagion,' Reveals His Daughter Had Virus 'Early on,'" *USA Today*, May 13, 2020, https://www.usatoday.com/story/entertainment/celebrities/2020/05/13/coronavirus-matt-damon-contagion-daughter-contracting-virus/5181774002/; "'Contagion' Star Matt Damon Reveals His Eldest Daughter Had Coronavirus in New York," *The Week*, May 14, 2020, https://www.theweek.in/news/entertainment/2020/05/14/contagion-star-matt-damon-reveals-eldest-daughter-had-coronavirus-new-york.html.
58. "Coronavirus: Contagion Cast Share Covid-19 Advice," *BBC News*, March 31, 2020, https://www.bbc.com/news/technology-52105472. Each video was watched by tens to hundreds of thousands of people and they are the most popular videos uploaded to YouTube by Columbia's School of Public Health. Columbia Public Health, "Control the Contagion," 2021, https://www.youtube.com/playlist?list=PL1UKNqoJNj9-ZhoAKuGlbNBcW4T9lCUOt.
59. Alissa Wilkinson, "The 2011 Film Contagion Is Even More Relevant in 2020, and Not Just Because of Coronavirus," *Vox*, February 4, 2020, https://www.vox.com/2020/2/4/21120178/contagion-movie-coronavirus-itunes-fake-news; Jason Bailey, "The Ending of Steven Soderbergh's Contagion, Revisited," *Vulture*, January 30, 2020, https://www.vulture.com/2020/01/contagion-movie-ending-coronavirus-and-pandemic-panic.html; Ali Walker, "Coronavirus: The Movie," *Politico*, April 1, 2020, https://www.politico.eu/article/coronavirus-the-movie-pandemic/.

60. Sperling, "'Contagion' Is Climbing Up the Charts."; see the FDA's response in warning letters to companies promoting elderberry from March 6, 2020 FDA – Center for Food Safety and Applied Nutrition, "Herbal Amy Inc – 604813 – 03/06/2020," *Center for Food Safety and Applied Nutrition*, March 6, 2020, https://www.fda.gov/inspections-compliance-enforcement-and-criminal-investigations/warning-letters/herbal-amy-inc-604813-03062020. For chloroquine see Rogers, "'Contagion' vs. Coronavirus." Interestingly, when Prof. Ian Lipkin, one of the science advisors on the film, contracted COVID, he treated himself with hydroxychloroquine, see Katrina Manson, "Virologist behind 'Contagion' Film Criticises Leaders' Slow Responses," *Financial Times*, April 18, 2020, https://www.ft.com/content/6e9b4fe7-b26e-45b9-acbd-2b24d182e914.
61. Walker, "Coronavirus: The Movie"; *National Institutes of Health*, "Chloroquine or Hydroxychloroquine, and/or Azithromycin," Covid-19 Treatment Guidelines, September 29, 2021, https://www.covid19treatmentguidelines.nih.gov/therapies/antiviral-therapy/chloroquine-or-hydroxychloroquine-and-or-azithromycin/; for another example, Matt Novak, "Instagram Muscleman Arrested For Allegedly Peddling Fake Covid-19 Cure," *Gizmodo*, March 26, 2020, https://gizmodo.com/instagram-muscleman-arrested-for-allegedly-peddling-fak-1842507108.
62. James Felton, "The UK's Vaccine Plan Was Inspired By The Matt Damon Movie Contagion," *IFLScience*, February 3, 2021, https://www.iflscience.com/the-uks-vaccine-plan-was-inspired-by-the-matt-damon-movie-contagion-58615.
63. Titles from Seren Morris, "'28 Days Later' Just Became Real After Monkeys Escape From Lab With COVID-19 Blood Test Samples," *Newsweek*, May 29, 2020, https://www.newsweek.com/28-days-later-planet-apes-movie-monkeys-escape-covid-19-samples-1507402; Jun Chung, "Real-Life Monkey Attack Is Eerily Like Planet of the Apes," *ScreenRant*, May 29, 2020, https://screenrant.com/planet-apes-twitter-trending-monkeys-coronavirus-samples/. For another example, Emma Parker, "Monkeys 'Escape with Coronavirus Test Samples after Attacking Lab Assistant,'" *Dailystar.co.uk*, May 29, 2020, https://www.dailystar.co.uk/news/world-news/monkeys-escape-coronavirus-test-samples-22108572.
64. Poppy Noor, "Fury and Despair: Behind the Viral Image of Americans Protesting against Lockdown," *The Guardian*, April 18, 2020, https://www.theguardian.com/artanddesign/2020/apr/18/ohio-protest-repoen-viral-image-photojournalist-joshua-bickel; Frank Carnevale, "Photo of Protesters at Ohio Statehouse Compared to Zombie Movie," *TribLIVE.com*, April 19, 2020, https://triblive.com/news/world/photo-of-protester-at-ohio-statehouse-compared-to-zombie-movie/. Notably the photographer spoke out strongly against comparing people with zombies and preferred instead to express sympathy towards the protestors, since he understood "that everybody's experience [of this pandemic] is different."
65. Minelle, "Coronavirus: What Can We Learn?"
66. Laurie Penny, "This Is Not the Apocalypse You Were Looking For," *Wired*, March 30, 2020, https://www.wired.com/story/coronavirus-apocalypse-myths/.
67. See for example, Farr, "The Medical Advisors for the Movie 'Contagion.'"
68. Janice Turner, "In Times of Fear We Put Our Faith in Hoarding," March 7, 2020, *The Times*, https://www.thetimes.co.uk/article/in-times-of-fear-we-put-our-faith-in-hoarding-s2zsf599t.

69. Helen Le Caplain and Kelly-Ann Mills, "Coronavirus: Man Slams 'Apocalypse-Fearing' Panic Buyers for Tesco Worker Wife's Tears," *Mirror*, March 17, 2020, https://www.mirror.co.uk/news/uk-news/coronavirus-man-slams-apocalypse-fearing-21708289.
70. Daniel W. Drezner, "What I Learned About the Coronavirus World From Watching Zombie Flicks," *Foreign Policy*, April 11, 2020, https://foreignpolicy.com/2020/04/11/what-i-learned-about-coronavirus-world-from-zombie-movies/.
71. As of early May 2022, however, that estimate had tripled to 15 million. See Katie Shepherd and Niha Masih, "Nearly 15 Million Deaths related to Covid-19, WHO Estimates," *The Washington Post*, May 5, 2022, https://www.washingtonpost.com/health/2022/05/05/covid-excess-global-deaths-nearly-15-million/. This might even be too low, see Richard Van Noorden, "Covid Death Tolls: Scientists Acknowledge Errors in WHO Estimates," *Nature* 606, no. 7913 (2022): 242–44.
72. Adam Wren, "What I Learned About Coronavirus From Binge-Watching 10 Hours of Virus Movies," *Politico*, March 21, 2020, https://www.politico.com/news/magazine/2020/03/21/pandemic-movies-coronavirus-140043.
73. Qijun Han and Daniel R. Curtis, "Epidemics, Public Health Workers, and 'Heroism' in Cinematic Perspective," *Visual Studies* 36, no. 4–5 (2021), 450–462; Penny, "This Is Not the Apocalypse You Were Looking For."
74. Lauren M. Johnson, "New York City Spent Two Minutes Clapping for Coronavirus First Responders," *CNN*, March 27, 2020, https://www.cnn.com/2020/03/27/us/new-york-claps-for-first-responders-trnd/index.html.
75. Early, uncertain statements from national health expert Dr. Anthony Fauci led to conservatives' rejection of him as an authority, which extended to the vaccines he had come to personify. Natasha Korecki and Sarah Owermohle, "Attacks on Fauci Grow More Intense, Personal and Conspiratorial," *Politico*, June 4, 2021, https://www.politico.com/news/2021/06/04/fauci-attacks-personal-conspiratorial-491896; CNN, "DeSantis PAC Selling 'Don't Fauci My Florida' Merch. Hear Dr. Fauci's Reaction," *CNN Video*, July 17, 2021, https://www.cnn.com/videos/politics/2021/07/17/florida-desantis-pac-merch-dr-anthony-fauci-reaction-intv-sot-acosta-nr-vpx.cnn.
76. Eric Lipton and Nicholas Fandos, "Senator Richard Burr Sold a Fortune in Stocks as G.O.P. Played Down Coronavirus Threat," *The New York Times*, March 19, 2020, https://www.nytimes.com/2020/03/19/us/politics/richard-burr-stocks-sold-coronavirus.html; Shane Goldmacher, "Kelly Loeffler and Richard Burr Were Briefed on Coronavirus. Then They Sold Stocks. What Now?" *The New York Times*, March 20, 2020, https://www.nytimes.com/2020/03/20/us/politics/kelly-loeffler-richard-burr-insider-trading.html. This was the tip of the proverbial iceberg, as suspected insider trading appears widespread among United States lawmakers. See Kate Kelly, Adam Playford and Alicia Parlapiano, and Ege Uz, "Stock Trades Reported by Nearly a Fifth of Congress Show Possible Conflicts," *The New York Times*, September 13, 2022, https://www.nytimes.com/interactive/2022/09/13/us/politics/congress-stock-trading-investigation.html.
77. Kate Kelly, "S.E.C. Inquiry Into Former Senator's Stock Sales Is Closed Without Charges." *The New York Times*, January 6, 2023, https://www.nytimes.com/2023/01/06/us/politics/burr-sec-inquiry-closed.html.

78. CNN, "Biden: 'Anyone Who's Responsible for That Many Deaths Should Not Remain as President,'" *CNN*, October 22, 2020, https://edition.cnn.com/politics/live-news/presidential-debate-coverage-fact-check-10-22-20/h_1f0bf1c810464cc902c6a3687467ed32.
79. For plans, Jon Cohen and Meredith Wadman, "Biden Proposes a Science-Led New Deal to End Pandemic Suffering," *Science*, January 15, 2021, https://www.science.org/content/article/biden-proposed-science-led-new-deal-end-pandemic-suffering; but for real plans implemented as of Summer 2022: "National COVID-19 Preparedness Plan," *The White House*, accessed September 9, 2022, https://www.whitehouse.gov/covidplan/.
80. Mary McNamara, "Column: Flesh-Eating Apocalyptic Films and Shows Didn't Prepare Us for This Pandemic's Horror," *Los Angeles Times*, April 2, 2020, https://www.latimes.com/entertainment-arts/story/2020-04-02/coronavirus-pandemic-tips-movies.
81. Dan Gardner, "We're Not 'Contagion' – Disasters like the Coronavirus Bring out the Best in People," *The Boston Globe*, April 3, 2020, https://www.bostonglobe.com/2020/04/03/opinion/were-not-contagion-disasters-like-coronavirus-bring-out-best-people/.
82. For Biden's administration attempts to follow the science, see Jeff Tollefson, et al., "Has Biden Followed the Science? What Researchers Say," *Nature* 601, no. 7894 (January 20, 2022): 491–93, https://www.nature.com/articles/d41586-022-00108-4.
83. Observers have doubted the veracity of Chinese official numbers. For official numbers: World Health Organization, "China: WHO Coronavirus Disease (Covid-19) Dashboard With Vaccination Data," *World Health Organization*, October 8, 2022, https://covid19.who.int/region/wpro/country/cn.
84. For a list of measures adopted by China and its strategy see Qiulan Chen et al., "Rapid and Sustained Containment of Covid-19 Is Achievable and Worthwhile: Implications for Pandemic Response," *BMJ* 375 (2021). https://www.bmj.com/content/375/BMJ-2021-066169.
85. For an investigative report on electronic surveillance in China, see Paul Mozur, Muyi Xiao, and John Liu, "'An Invisible Cage': How China Is Policing the Future," *The New York Times*, June 25, 2022, https://www.nytimes.com/2022/06/25/technology/china-surveillance-police.html; and Isabelle Qian, Muyi Xiao, Paul Mozur and Alexander Cardia, "Four Takeaways From a Times Investigation Into China's Expanding Surveillance State," *The New York Times*, updated July 26, 2022, https://www.nytimes.com/2022/06/21/world/asia/china-surveillance-investigation.html.
86. Kathy Huang and Mengyu Han, "Did China's Street Protests End Harsh COVID Policies?" *Council on Foreign Relations*, December 14, 2022, https://www.cfr.org/blog/did-chinas-street-protests-end-harsh-covid-policies.
87. Helen Davidson, "Eight in 10 People in China Caught Covid Since Early December, Say Officials," *The Guardian*, January 23, 2023, https://www.theguardian.com/world/2023/jan/23/80-of-people-in-china-caught-Covid-since-early-december-say-officials.
88. Owen Dyer, "Covid-19: China Stops Counting Cases as Models Predict A Million Or More Deaths" *BMJ* 380 (2023): 2. For a perspective from rural China, see Selina Wang, "After 3 years of Covid, CNN Went into Rural China for Lunar New Year. Here's What We Found and How Officials Tried Stopping Us", *CNN*,

January 27, 2023, https://edition.cnn.com/2023/01/27/china/rural-china-lunar-new-year-covid-intl-hnk-dst/index.html.

89. Reuters, "World Has Entered Stage of 'Vaccine Apartheid' – WHO Head," *Reuters*, May 17, 2021, https://www.reuters.com/business/healthcare-pharmaceuticals/world-has-entered-stage-vaccine-apartheid-who-head-2021-05-17/.

90. Economist Intelligence, "Rich Countries Will Get Access to Coronavirus Vaccines Earlier than Others," *Economist Intelligence Unit*, December 18, 2020, https://www.eiu.com/n/rich-countries-will-get-access-to-coronavirus-vaccines-earlier-than-others/; and Sheryl Gay Stolberg, "As Poor Nations Seek Covid Pills, Officials Fear Repeat of AIDS Crisis," *The New York Times*, May 8, 2022, https://www.nytimes.com/2022/05/08/us/politics/covid-pills-global-aids-hiv.html.

91. Reuters, "Iran Urges Biden to Lift Sanctions Affecting Medicines as It Fights COVID-19," *Reuters*, January 26, 2021, https://www.reuters.com/article/health-coronavirus-iran-int-idUSKBN29V1G2.

92. Lucy Hooker and Daniele Palumbo, "Covid Vaccines: Will Drug Companies Make Bumper Profits?," *BBC News*, December 18, 2020, https://www.bbc.com/news/business-55170756; Michael Safi, "Oxford/AstraZeneca Covid Vaccine Research 'Was 97% Publicly Funded,'" *The Guardian*, April 15, 2021, https://www.theguardian.com/science/2021/apr/15/oxfordastrazeneca-covid-vaccine-research-was-97-publicly-funded. See Michael Erman and Manas Mishra, "Pfizer Sees Robust COVID-19 Vaccine Demand for Years, $26 Bln in 2021 Sales," *Reuters*, May 4, 2021, https://www.reuters.com/business/healthcare-pharmaceuticals/pfizer-lifts-annual-sales-forecast-covid-19-vaccine-2021-05-04/.

93. Ilan Ben Zion, "Israel's Data-for-Vaccines Deal with Pfizer Raises Privacy Concerns," *Times of Israel*, January 18, 2021, https://www.timesofisrael.com/israels-data-for-vaccines-deal-with-pfizer-raises-privacy-concerns/.

94. Sheryl Gay Stolberg, "Biden Says the Pandemic Is Over. But at Least 400 People Are Dying Daily," *The New York Times*, September 19, 2022, https://www.nytimes.com/2022/09/19/us/politics/biden-covid-pandemic-over.html.

95. As just one example, death rates in 1900 among poor Indians under colonial British rule in Bombay (modern Mumbai) were over 20 times as high as the death rates among colonial European populations. Ira Klein, "Plague, Policy and Popular Unrest in British India," *Modern Asian Studies* 22, no. 4 (1988): 729.

96. Although a few movies, such as *Children of Men*, discuss social groups from the perspective of race and class, these movies and the issues that they raised were not discussed in the context of COVID.

97. Rebecca Kaplan, "A Silent, Savage Menace."

98. There are a few exceptions to this, such as *Longtime Companion* (1989).

99. Lena H. Sun and Joel Achenbach, "CDC Loosens Coronavirus Guidance, Signaling Strategic Shift," *The Washington Post*, August 11, 2022, https://www.washingtonpost.com/health/2022/08/11/cdc-coronavirus-recommendations.

100. Zeynep Tufekci, "If You're Suffering After Being Sick With Covid, It's Not Just in Your Head," *The New York Times*, August 25 2022, https://www.nytimes.com/2022/08/25/opinion/long-covid-pandemic.html.

101. For these ideas and polio, Dóra Vargha, *Polio Across the Iron Curtain: Hungary's Cold War with an Epidemic* (Cambridge: Cambridge University Press, 2018); and

on the need to change stories, Dóra Vargha, "Reconsidering the Dramaturgy," *Bulletin of the History of Medicine* 94, no. 4 (2020): 690–98.
102. Donald Clarke, "What Kinds of Films Will We Watch in the Post Covid-19 Era?" *The Irish Times*, April 25, 2020, https://www.irishtimes.com/culture/what-kinds-of-films-will-we-watch-in-the-post-covid-19-era-1.4235926.
103. A prequel film and an anime series were scheduled for release on Netflix, with another untitled sequel in development. See Borys Kit, "Zack Snyder's 'Army of the Dead': Prequel and Anime Series in the Works," *The Hollywood Reporter*, September 3, 2020, https://www.hollywoodreporter.com/movies/movie-news/zack-snyders-army-of-the-dead-prequel-and-anime-series-in-the-works-4054508/.

CONCLUSION

The Historical Arc of Disease Movies

Literary and artistic works help people understand the social norms of behavior and define for them humanity's place within the universe. While religion offers the eternal truths of the gods, secular stories and works of fiction have offered cultural myths that reflect and influence their historical moments. They are no less paradigmatic. Humans create, tell and revise their stories as a way of expressing faith and identifying truth in a world which appears to be constantly changing or otherwise uncertain. If Homer's pre-Christian *Iliad* depicts the tragic heroism of Achilles, the aristocratic, god-like male warrior, then 2,500 years later during the Renaissance Shakespeare's *King Lear* (1606) softens that image into the tragedy of a mortal, self-aggrandizing old man. If George Eliot in *Middlemarch* (1871) at the height of the British Empire rejects the journey of the aspiring Dorothea Brooke and favors instead the mundane life Mary Garth and Fred Vincy anonymously lived, then Edith Wharton's *The Age of Innocence* (1920), a post-World War I novel that looks back upon the Gilded Age, darkens that story. Literary and artistic works – whether popular or intellectual – seek to make sense of their cultural moment, which seems entirely natural to those residing within and, at times, arbitrary in retrospect.

The invention of movies at the end of the nineteenth century coincided with the rise of industrial capitalism. Hollywood soon developed a method of production in its studio system that was reflective of that industrial model, and its movie language furthered those values through a seamless style of storytelling,

Figure C.1 The warrior Achilles of the *Iliad* is immortalized on a Greek jar (ca. 530–520 BC).

even as Hollywood's producers denied that its entertainment provided anything other than a means for diversion and relaxation for its audience. That audience was initially American but soon became global as a result of Hollywood's expansive production and distribution, the imitation of Hollywood's model for entertainment by non-American studios and the long reach of the American empire. Ironically, industrial capitalism with its continuous attempts to maximize private gain through ever-increasing efficiency created the very need for escape through such passive entertainment. Movies were less about the art of understanding and more about the enjoyment of a momentary freedom from work as well as the reinforcement of American cultural values.[1]

The most commercially successful directors of Hollywood over the past century have reinforced and reified through their storytelling American values, such as the myths of Victorian innocence (D. W. Griffith), the comforts and discomforts of middle-class suburbia (Steven Spielberg) or the limitless powers of elitist superheroes (the Russo brothers). Some Hollywood directors, such as John Ford in his depiction of the American West and Kathryn Bigelow in her embrace and critique of Hollywood genres, have occasionally sought to combine the personal and the commercial and explore the origins and contours of cultural myths. At the same time, more nuanced, political voices, such as Robert Altman, Spike Lee and Kelly Reichardt, have remained largely invisible to mainstream audiences even if they might be critically celebrated.

Disease movies follow the same production pattern and conform to the American cultural values of their time. The earliest of these movies depict a local disease and identify the non-white, non-American and non-Christian outsider as responsible for its spread – the voodoo master in *White Zombie*, the lower-class Asian stowaway in *Pacific Liner* and the illegal immigrant in *Panic in the Streets*. The standard solution was containment. Representatives of the public good, typified by Dr. Ehrlich in *Dr. Ehrlich's Magic Bullet* or Dr. Wood in *The Killer that Stalked New York*, applied reason and used science to find a solution. As Chapter 1 discusses, mid-twentieth century disease movies reflected the increasingly globalized world of their times. Yet, the same movies also highlighted concerns about diseases spreading more easily to the American mainland. The heroic, public servant Dr. Reed in *Panic in the Streets* is keenly aware of this new situation and is willing to give up some of his personal aspirations to ensure the functioning of society. As he stops the plague from spreading beyond New Orleans, he asserts how "we're all in a community, the same one!" referring to the entire United States and even beyond as opposed to thinking only about his neighborhood or family. As the Cold War continued, disease films also offered the opportunity for critiques of society and its norms. In the socially turbulent late 1960s, *Night of the Living Dead* depicts a disease that threatens the entire American East Coast. It serves as metaphor for the racism, sexism and constraints of the "traditional" family that infect America. Efforts at containing the outbreak and ensuring a cohesive society result, however, in wanton violence by roving white militias that shoot and kill infected and non-infected alike. *Shivers* a decade later focuses on a bioengineered parasite that a local doctor releases in an upper-middle class apartment complex. Disease serves as a metaphor for the excesses of the counterculture, and the film's ending features all the infected residents driving out to infect the rest of the country.

By the 1990s, globalization and the appearance of new terrifying diseases, such as Ebola, made American concerns about outbreaks and epidemics at home more acute. Not only was the public more aware of these diseases, but increasingly connected global trade and communications accelerated this changing perspective. The idea that these diseases could reach anywhere in the world within a day became popular.[2] As Chapter 2 points out, *Outbreak* represented an early reflection of this shift, depicting the horrors of a fictional yet supposedly realistic disease. Its Motaba virus originated in the jungles of Zaire but quickly crosses the ocean, passes through US Customs, and spreads through tiny droplets in a movie theater to the small, California town of Cedar Creek. From a twenty-first century perspective, these movies retained a sense of triumph. A maverick hero or two working outside institutional constraints could still contain the disease and protect society, ensuring a happy ending. Post-Cold War American triumphalism and exceptionalism, the economically roaring 1990s and America's newfound position as the single global superpower offered a sufficient veneer to paper over the growing structural cracks in this nostalgic model.

This geopolitical and cultural configuration was not sustainable. Movies steadily began to feature diseases that triumphed over human efforts at containment and resulted in a global pandemic, as Chapter 3 reveals. The catalyzing political event was 9/11.[3] *Resident Evil* and *28 Days Later* the following year were representatives of both the revival of zombies in popular culture and a new disease cinema. Despite their dark plots and themes, both movies end with the apparent containment and eradication of the disease (even if leaving open the possibility of a sequel).[4] The overarching shift continued. Movies such as *Contagion*, *World War Z* and *Black Death* around the end of the first decade of the twenty-first century reveal the inherent faults in the containment paradigm, which was severely flawed and temporary at best. Despite the hopeful note on which movies such as *Children of Men* or *The Invasion* ended, they highlighted the many persistent weaknesses of humanity and the problematic values holding society together. The apocalypse and near-demise of humanity became ever more common and even inevitable as seen in *Resident Evil: Extinction*. The remake of *Dawn of the Dead* likewise underscored the shift, since it removes much of the original's social critique, revels in the visual pleasures of its violence, and ends with credits depicting the likely death of its few survivors.

The 2008 recession and its aftermath further spurred this post-apocalyptic thinking. American institutions, such as the state, its elite and multinational corporations, openly ignored the plight of the majority of the country's population, let alone the populations of other countries. Films during the 2010s, unsurprisingly, portrayed these institutions as failing in their duties. Increasingly they depicted the unraveling of American society across all levels, from the social contract between the state and its citizens, all the way down to personal relations in local communities. Some films had zombie apocalypse narratives, with the new threat of undifferentiated masses of fast zombies, which was created in *28 Days Later*, expanded in *Dawn of the Dead* and perfected in *World War Z*, overrunning any semblance of stability the few human survivors attempted to maintain. Other films argued that humans must evolve. *Little Joe* focused on technological utopianism, contending that bioengineered contentment could lead to a zombie population that was, in fact, a better version of humanity. *Resident Evil: Retribution* and *The Final Chapter* likewise suggested a technological solution by artificially developing new humans through cloning, artificial intelligence or other forms of unregulated, scientific experimentation. Even zombie comedies, such as *Zombieland* or

The Dead Don't Die, featured a new, post-apocalyptic society with new rules and new adventures. What all movies agreed on is that the apocalyptic transition will arrive sooner rather than later and that it will be extremely fast, fitting the increased speed in which the world moved. Viruses would spread and kill almost as rapidly as other end-of-world scenarios, which in the mid-twentieth century would have focused on other threats, such as nuclear war in movies. This dark vision resonated with increasing frequency and urgency in the face of real-world challenges, such as global warming and emerging infectious diseases, as became apparent with the global spread of COVID-19.

Depicting an End of Times Landscape

Contemporary disease films continue the trend of the previous decades, featuring apocalyptic or post-apocalyptic landscapes in which society ceases to exist. While such films may be fictional, hypothetical or unrealistic, they nevertheless suggest that rapid, massive mortality and chaos are the expected outcome of a disease outbreak. These films emphasize that society is hopelessly fragmented, preferring to depict a new world order while eschewing constructive criticism of the current system. They highlight how society has failed the material and aspirational needs of its citizens, increasingly alienating them from democratic norms and encouraging authoritarianism. The mythology of current movies reflects contemporary culture in which elite power is maintained through technologies that have replaced community and democracy with simulated networks and digital surveillance. If earlier movies, such as *Pacific Liner*, depicted the containment of a local outbreak through a commonly accepted view of the majority's social norms, post-apocalyptic movies, such as *Train to Busan*, cater to audiences who no longer perceive themselves as part of such norms. The powerless and disenfranchised audiences of the early twenty-first century frequently imagine the destruction of the state and its elite as the only seemingly logical, "critical" response. Movies, in turn, visualize this destruction in an accessible and attractive form. They no longer so much seek to allay anxiety as seek to persuade that this new world offers the pleasures of conformity with its abundance of material comforts.[5]

Contemporary disease films also reflect how twenty-first century capitalism with a focus on technological utopianism has simultaneously dehumanized American citizens. Surveillance – whether for supposed national security or economic reasons – has become ubiquitous.[6] Here as well the trend is clear. If there was previously some pushback against increased surveillance in the early 2000s, such as critiques of the USA PATRIOT Act, the 2010s have largely led to an abandonment of the effort to control such surveillance. The common assumption is that states and corporations possess and use personal data and its use is acceptable. The *Resident Evil* franchise reflects and reifies this transformation of surveillance technology. If the first movie features cameras within the Hive research facility, by the last movie Umbrella's surveillance is global and perfect, apparent in its knowledge of the exact location of all 4,472 surviving humans.

While some of the recent disease films have become more diverse in their casting to reflect American society, these films rarely afford space to discuss how new ideas and different values from marginalized groups might be centered or how including their beliefs might facilitate a more inclusive society. Capitalism's incessant demand for conformity to ensure greater efficiency leads then to the near-absence of any discussion in recent disease movies of these differences, such as gender, race, class, ethnicity and age. Instead, films subsume these groups into a monolithic mass, depicting individuals as seeking the same outcome: to enter the globalized, capitalist elite who, once they have achieved materialistic success, will inevitably treat those who have not (regardless of their identity) as mere cast offs while protecting their own gated community of family and friends. If the global problems of the twenty-first century – such as climate change and new infectious diseases – require global solutions, movies opt to portray competition over cooperation, further unraveling the cohesion of American society.

While this erasure of cultural and biological human differences exists in many Hollywood films, it features conspicuously in so-called realistic disease films, such as *Contagion*. In its ostensibly happy ending the government implements a random lottery based on birth dates – rather than considering cultural or biological factors that might affect the individual need for the vaccine in a real-life pandemic. *Contagion*'s exception to this lottery is the class of elites, who receive the vaccine first and exploit the system to take care of those in their "lifeboat," to paraphrase the film's CDC Director Cheever. Laurence Fishburne, a black actor who plays Cheever, is simply a member of the elite who wants to protect his loved ones first, rather than change the status quo. Films might identify the obvious villains, but they ignore the cultural paradigm that frames and drives behavior in Western countries and furthers the interests of American, global capitalism. Cheever's behavior coincides with capitalism's advocacy of an individualism which celebrates those securing the largest boat.

The bleakness of recent disease films, including the increasingly numerous post-apocalyptic movies, results from their depiction of an inability to escape this paradigm or envision a new paradigm offering some form of personal and collective salvation. The same loss of faith or hope appears in other movie genres in recent decades. For example, the science fiction movie *The Matrix* (1999), which influenced the *Resident Evil* film series, depicts humans as asleep in vast fields of pods, alluding to the pods from *Invasion of the Body Snatchers* and revealing that humanity has lost its battle with the artificial intelligence it had developed. While the human hero Neo defeats the program known as Agent Smith and frees humanity, the real world into which humans will awaken is grey and barren. Unsurprisingly, some humans prefer the enjoyment of a virtual, fake steak dinner in the Matrix simulation rather than eat the gruel of reality, a "choice" which *Little Joe* affirms.

This pessimism informs the dark endings to nearly all recent apocalyptic movies, such as *It Comes at Night* (2017), in which an infectious disease wipes out an isolated, seemingly self-sufficient family, or *Army of the Dead*, in which a surviving protagonist escapes the intelligent zombies who have overwhelmed Las Vegas only to become infected himself. If contemporary movies seek to find a realistic alternative to capitalism, they consistently fail in that effort. In *The Matrix*'s supposedly optimistic ending Neo defeats Agent Smith by entering his body and destroying him from within. Yet, that ending confirms Smith's view of humans as a virus which consumes its surrounding environment rather than develop "a natural equilibrium" within it. "Human beings are a disease, a cancer of this planet. You're a plague and we [AI] are the cure," Mr. Smith tells Morpheus – only to succumb to that human disease. In the supposed comedy *The Dead Don't Die*, the sole heroic survivor, a katana-wielding female mortician, is revealed to be an alien who can escape the zombie outbreak on a UFO. The only surviving human is Hermit Bob, a recluse who watches through his binoculars as zombies defeat the other human survivors one by one and laments, "What a fucked-up world."

The COVID Story

The increase in disease movies over the last few decades reflects the widespread assumption that new pandemics are imminent. This had become a common point of discussion over the past quarter century. Experts had repeatedly warned of such a scenario, and films increasingly visualized how this might unfold.[7] Governments, especially the United States, invested billions in infectious disease surveillance, biological defense and other preparations for an anticipated outbreak.[8] These investments contained or at least mitigated earlier outbreaks, such as SARS, MERS and Zika. The political will and available resources were insufficient to meet the challenge of COVID.

Most countries responded slowly to the threat of COVID in early 2020. Consistent with recent movies, nearly all government and other institutions failed to contain the disease. Before COVID, many commentators had viewed the United States as the country best prepared to deal with a pandemic.[9] It even had an advance, early warning, since information from China and European countries demonstrated COVID's devastating effects.[10] Nevertheless, COVID quickly revealed how cultural values and politics drove the United States' response, sidelining scientists and public health experts and leading to disproportionately high American fatalities. Not only did the country's federalized system of government fragment its approach but the American administration exacerbated that fragmentation by further emphasizing individual responsibility instead of collective action. Inconsistent border closings, scattered contact tracing, poor testing and mask wearing refusal resulted in the continuing spread and increasing mortality of COVID. This especially affected marginalized groups, such as the infirm, the impoverished, the non-white and the aged. Moreover, the federal government abandoned mitigation efforts to states and local governments, resulting in conflicting and contradictory policies, and the lack of a common health care system left many sick on their own. The United States quickly experienced product shortages – ventilators, masks, toilet paper and hand sanitizers – since its distribution system was built to maximize profit through hyper-efficiency, allowing for little elasticity in the face of sudden increased demand. Scenes of empty shelves in supermarkets evoked scenes from movies, and alarmist media reports featured long lines at food banks or farmers who had to plow under crops that could no longer reach the market.[11]

Contrary to movies, COVID did not result in the End Times. Society did not collapse. American institutions, both private and public sectors, continued to function. States often "rationally" decided to allow the disease to infect, sicken and kill people, focusing less on saving lives by mitigating the spread of COVID than on reopening businesses to protect "the economy" as if it was a binary choice between maintaining a cultural belief or preventing the deaths of humans. While early commentators suggested that the pandemic would level social differences and reduce inequality, that view quickly proved naïve, if not completely wrong.[12] After a brief plunge, American stock markets rallied within a few months of COVID's widescale spread in the United States to all-time highs in approval of government policy, enriching the wealthy. COVID both revealed the structural problems in the United States and reinforced the elite, capitalist paradigm through which too many people framed their thoughts and behavior. The United States was hardly alone in such framing and was instead mirrored by many other developed countries, such as the United Kingdom.

COVID likewise revealed the chasm between science as an ongoing practice in the real world and its depiction in movies. Movies told two-hour stories about readymade, easy solutions to disease outbreaks, even if audiences might recognize them as dramatic stories and unrealistic. Dr. Reed in *Panic in the Streets* immediately identifies pneumonic plague as the threat to New Orleans and vaccinates officials possibly infected. Within days, Dr. Daniels in *Outbreak* finds the monkey that is the Motaba virus carrier and then develops and distributes a cure. Dr. Hextall in *Contagion* within a few months develops a vaccine to MEV-1, which the American government quickly produces for worldwide distribution. In contrast, COVID revealed to the broader public that science is a long process full of fits and starts. As infections spread and deaths mounted, clear answers from experts were few, infrequent and repeatedly revised. That public discourse questioned the efficacy of science should have surprised no one. The distrust of science has a long tradition. Eighteenth century popular culture, for example, had caricatured early smallpox vaccines as turning people into cows.[13] Contemporary social media, including President Trump's tweets, delivered consistently misleading, false information, resulting in the further distrust of science. All this contributed to a paradox. While science developed effective COVID vaccines extraordinarily fast in historical terms, a substantial portion of the American population declined these vaccines for political reasons. This reaction was inconceivable on the movie screen.

The importance of global cooperation or of American global leadership was similarly absent from movies, which preferred to focus on the American narrative while excluding other governments. By the end of the second full year of the pandemic, the disease had become an accepted part of life in America and western Europe, with few regulations in place as their populations returned to a pre-COVID environment of supposed normality, notwithstanding the adverse impact on those still susceptible to COVID. Monkeypox, while acknowledged as a "health emergency" both within the United States and globally, initially at least was largely ignored, as if nothing was learned from the COVID experience.[14]

If during the early days of COVID movies offered stories to help make some sense of this pandemic, COVID within a few months made clear the differences between reality and these movie stories. Ironically, however, the myths of these stories often seemed to resonate more than the developing science.[15] This is hardly surprising and is perhaps most aptly summed up by the famous line from John Ford's *The Man Who Shot Liberty Valance* (1962) that acknowledged the resonance of cultural myths, in this case that of the American western – "This is the West, sir. When the legend becomes fact, print the legend."

Movie Myths and Stories for the Future

In 2010, *Black Death* replayed much of the same narrative and revisited many of the same themes as *The Seventh Seal* half a century earlier, exploring, in particular, personal behavior against the background of a fraying social order during an incomprehensible, horrific pandemic, the fourteenth century Black Death. The films' differing approaches reflect the change in humanity's self-perception and in the relationship between individuals and their social environment, which is discussed in this book. While *Black Death* is the more realistic film in its depiction of the plague and the banal, daily reality of medieval life, it also depicts a disillusioned humanity in which each person faces a material world alone with no expectation of any improvement, let alone hope of a spiritual redemption. The young monk, Osmund, is manipulated by persuasive individuals and powerful institutions in which he has placed his faith, so that he eventually kills his own lover. While he ultimately survives his ordeal, blind vengeance consumes him, and he devotes the remainder of his life to torturing and burning innocent women whom he perceives as witches. "I like to think that he found peace, that he continued seeing beauty in the world," the

CONCLUSION

Figure C.2 *Black Death* (2010): The knight, Ulric, revels in his infection of villagers with the Black Death even as they quarter him.

soldier Wolfstan's voiceover dryly observes at the end of the film. But peace through torture and death is surely no peace at all. Osmund, who is corrupted by institutionalized religion, uses the guise of that same religion to descend into savagery and inflict inhumane punishment. Life has no purpose other than the metes and bounds of what the savage surveys.

The unrealistic but poetically composed *The Seventh Seal* also portrays institutionalized religion as corrupt. The theologian who had a decade earlier encouraged the knight Antonius Block to go on crusade has become a thief who tries to rape a mute servant girl and bullies the artist Jof. Yet, in contrast to *Black Death*, *The Seventh Seal* rejects the materialistic view of Jöns, the knight's squire, who claims that "love is the blackest of all plagues." The film endorses the disillusioned Block's revelation and his sense of achieving personal redemption. This knight, who had sought knowledge of God but found only emptiness, rejects institutionalized religion and finds serenity and faith in a momentary, secular communion with Jof and his family. He acknowledges to Jof's wife Mia, "I shall remember this hour of peace . . . the strawberries, the bowl of milk . . . your faces in the dusk. Michael asleep, Jof with his lute."[16] Distracting Death so that Jof and his family might escape, he expresses satisfaction to Death in having performed one meaningful deed on behalf of others before his own death. *The Seventh Seal* offers a vision of humanity in which each person is not the measure of all things so each is not alone. In contrast to the tormented life of Osmund, who inflicts only suffering and fear in *Black Death*, Block in the *The Seventh Seal* finds meaning and renewed faith.

Human myths reflect, define and inform the human species. Movie stories about disease likewise shape our experience not only in their factual accuracy (or inaccuracy) but also in how we perceive ourselves in the context of community

Figure C.3 *The Seventh Seal* (1957): The knight, Antonius Block, finds personal salvation in the midst of the Black Death from a momentary, secular communion with Jof and his family.

and within the universe, struggling with both the science and the cultural values that characterize us through these stories. Disease movies serve that purpose and, as this book has shown, they depict increasingly dark images of humanity, a trend that began during the industrial era more than a century ago. The poet William Butler Yeats had famously, prophetically signaled the darkness after witnessing the horrors of World War I, asking in "The Second Coming" (1919), "And what rough beast, its hour come round at last, / Slouches towards Bethlehem to be born?" Humanity has created the means for its own destruction, even if the specific threats have shifted for now from war and nuclear weapons to ecocide and disease. COVID suggests ways in which disease movies might (or might not) help us in the future. Certainly, the misunderstandings about science even in the United States, the supposedly most "advanced" country, and the differing impact of COVID throughout the world should inform how movies might more closely mirror as well as progressively reform reality.

Myths about disease need not be dark. That they are today says much about us. During the mid-twentieth century polio pandemic, Dr. Jonas Salk invented a vaccine but did not patent it. He mythically believed that his vaccine was a shared good that humanity on both sides of the Cold War should enjoy. As he rhetorically asked, "Could you patent the sun?"[17] Salk's vision of vaccines is in stark contrast to COVID vaccines today that have led to massive profit for a few pharmaceutical companies and, not surprisingly, a backlash against them. Salk's mythic story of a common social good is clearly at odds with the values of contemporary capitalism, and similar types of narratives only infrequently appear today in movies – and then are framed as a childhood fantasy, not the reality of adulthood. This anecdotal story about Salk, which is largely absent from disease and vaccine culture, highlights the need for a new, alternative mythology for contemporary disease films. While film stories cannot immediately change reality, they can alter the direction of our future by changing our perspective of the world which we share.

The alternative is to continue down the current path of disease movies in which plagues, pandemics and zombies result in the destruction of society through the extinction of the species, whether by death through ecocide or war or by technological transformation. The historical myths of humankind and the recent experience of COVID suggest that we do ill to ourselves and future generations in dismissing such visions of diseased cinema as mere stories. Movie stories, like all stories we tell, are formed from the shards and chaos of events in life. In telling those stories, we define who we are, who we want to be, and how we might get there. Seeing our contemporary world through the enactment of our myths reveals the social cracks and fault lines as well as highlights those uncomfortable truths we prefer to ignore. In this sense, disease movies serve as a form of cultural truth telling, and we deny that truth at our own peril.

Notes

1. John Belton, *American Cinema/American Culture*, 5th edition (New York: McGraw-Hill Education, 2017).
2. This idea appeared already in *Panic in the Streets* as Reed exclaims that "[a]nybody that leaves here [New Orleans] can be in any city in the country within ten hours. I could leave here today and I can be in Africa tomorrow. And whatever disease I had would go right with me!" It did not, however, gain further traction at the time.
3. Dahlia Schweitzer, "When Terrorism Met the Plague: How 9/11 Affected the Outbreak Narrative," *Cinema Journal* 56, no. 1 (2016): 118–23.
4. Lars Schmeink, *Biopunk Dystopias: Genetic Engineering, Society, and Science Fiction* (Liverpool: Liverpool University Press, 2016), 205; and Schweitzer, *Going Viral*, 154–58.
5. See Susan Sontag, "The Imagination of Disaster," *Commentary*, October 1, 1965, https://www.commentary.org/articles/susan-sontag/the-imagination-of-disaster/ in which she wrote about 1950s science fiction movies: "These [science fiction] films reflect world-wide anxieties, and they serve to allay them . . . [T]he science fiction film . . . is concerned with the aesthetics of destruction, with the peculiar beauties to

be found in wreaking havoc, making a mess. And it is in the imagery of destruction that the core of a good science fiction film lies."
6. For earlier responses: Becki A. Graham, "Post-9/11 Anxieties: Unpredictability and Complacency in the Age of New Terrorism in Dawn of the Dead," in *Race, Oppression and the Zombie: Essays on Cross-Cultural Appropriations of the Caribbean Tradition*, eds. Christopher M. Moreman and Cory Rushton (Jefferson: McFarland, 2011), 124–38.
7. Starting in the mid-1990s in Laurie Garrett, *The Coming Plague: Newly Emerging Diseases in a World out of Balance*; and as another example in 2018, Ed Yong, "What Bill Gates Fears Most," *The Atlantic*, April 27, 2018, https://www.theatlantic.com/science/archive/2018/04/what-bill-gates-fears-most/559007/.
8. For positive implementation of these techniques in Australia and New Zealand, Geoffrey W. Rice, "How Reminders of the 1918–19 Pandemic Helped Australia and New Zealand Respond to COVID-19," *Journal of Global History* 15, no. 3 (2020): 421–33.
9. David Elliott, "These Are the Countries Best Prepared for Health Emergencies," *World Economic Forum*, February 12, 2020, https://www.weforum.org/agenda/2020/02/these-are-the-countries-best-prepared-for-health-emergencies/; Niall McCarthy, "The Countries Best And Worst Prepared For An Epidemic [Infographic]," *Forbes*, January 27, 2020, https://www.forbes.com/sites/niallmccarthy/2020/01/27/the-countries-best-and-worst-prepared-for-an-epidemic-infographic/.
10. One video from a hospital in Northern Italy showed a continuous shot of doctors, nurses, and patients in an overcrowded hospital room over which the narrator observes, "They're fighting a war here and they're losing." Such videos were duplicated elsewhere, including New York City. For the story, Stuart Ramsay, "Coronavirus: Italy's Hardest-Hit City Wants You to See How COVID-19 Is Affecting Its Hospitals," *Sky News*, March 20, 2020, https://web.archive.org/web/20200320114010/https://news.sky.com/story/coronavirus-they-call-it-the-apocalypse-inside-italys-hardest-hit-hospital-11960597.
11. Nicholas Kulish, "'Never Seen Anything Like It': Cars Line Up for Miles at Food Banks," *The New York Times*, April 8, 2020, https://www.nytimes.com/2020/04/08/business/economy/coronavirus-food-banks.html; David Yaffe-Bellany and Michael Corkery, "Dumped Milk, Smashed Eggs, Plowed Vegetables: Food Waste of the Pandemic," *The New York Times*, April 11, 2020, https://www.nytimes.com/2020/04/11/business/coronavirus-destroying-food.html.
12. See, for example, Kyrill Hartog, "Black Death Historian: 'A Coronavirus Depression Could Be the Great Leveller,'" *The Guardian*, April 30, 2020, https://www.theguardian.com/world/commentisfree/2020/apr/30/walter-scheidel-a-shock-to-the-established-order-can-deliver-change; and Sean Illing, "Can a Pandemic Remake Society? A Historian Explains," *Vox*, April 9, 2020, https://www.vox.com/policy-and-politics/2020/4/9/21174760/coronavirus-covid-19-inequality-walter-scheidel.
13. For the caricature, Sandra Carpenter, "The Cow-Pock,-or-The Wonderful Effects of the New Inoculation!" *The Morgan Library & Museum*, February 25, 2021, https://www.themorgan.org/blog/cow-pock-or-wonderful-effects-new-inoculation.
14. Sheryl Gay Stolberg and Apoorva Mandavilli, "As Monkeypox Spreads, US Declares a Health Emergency," *The New York Times*, August 4, 2022, https://www.nytimes.

com/2022/08/04/health/monkeypox-emergency-us.html. Mark Johnson, "World Ignored Monkeypox Threats, Including Signs of Sexual Transmission," *The Washington Post*, August 12, 2022, https://www.washingtonpost.com/health/2022/08/12/monkeypox-virus-origins-nigeria-sexual-transmission/. The threat, at least in the United States, has declined as of early 2023. Apoorva Mandavilli, "Monkeypox Appears to Recede, but Risks and Uncertainties Linger," *The New York Times*, September 26, 2022, https://www.nytimes.com/2022/09/26/health/monkeypox-vaccine.html.

15. For a discussion of its significance, Robert Alpert, "Kathryn Bigelow's Zero Dark Thirty: A Case Study on Mythmaking and Making History," *Jump Cut* 57 (2016), https://www.ejumpcut.org/archive/jc57.2016/-Alpert-0Dark30/index.html.

16. Translation from *The Seventh Seal*, directed by Ingmar Bergman (1957: New York, The Criterion Collection, 1998), DVD.

17. Jane S. Smith, *Patenting the Sun: Polio and the Salk Vaccine*, 1st edition (New York: William Morrow & Co, 1990); but also Brian Palmer, "Jonas Salk: Good at Virology, Bad at Economics," *Slate*, April 14, 2014, https://slate.com/technology/2014/04/the-real-reasons-jonas-salk-didnt-patent-the-polio-vaccine.html. COVID was the context of a rare polio outbreak in the US in 2022: Apoorva Mandavilli, "Polio Was Almost Eradicated. This Year It Staged a Comeback," *The New York Times*, August 18, 2022, https://www.nytimes.com/2022/08/18/health/polio-new-york-malawi.html.

BIBLIOGRAPHY

"1986 State of the Union Address," C-SPAN.org, February 4, 1986, https://www.c-span.org/video/?125975-1/1986-state-union-address.

"28 Days Later." *Box Office Mojo.* https://www.boxofficemojo.com/title/tt0289043/.

"28 Weeks Later." *Box Office Mojo.* https://www.boxofficemojo.com/title/tt0463854/.

Aaltola, Mika. "Contagious Insecurity: War, SARS and Global Air Mobility." *Contemporary Politics* 18, no. 1 (2012): 53–70.

Accomando, Beth. "UC San Diego Professor Uses 'Contagion' Film To Teach Epidemiology." *KPBS Public Media*, March 23, 2020. https://www.kpbs.org/news/midday-edition/2020/03/23/uc-san-diego-professor-uses-contagion-film-teach-e.

Adkins, Lisa, Martijn Konings, and Melinda Cooper. *The Asset Economy: Property Ownership and the New Logic of Inequality.* Medford: Polity Press, 2020.

Alam, Niaz. "World Leaders Pretend." *Dhaka Tribune*, March 21, 2020. https://www.dhakatribune.com/opinion/2020/03/21/world-leaders-pretend.

Alexander, Julia. "Contagion Shows the Lengths People Go to Watch a Movie They Can't Stream." *The Verge*, March 7, 2020. https://www.theverge.com/2020/3/7/21164769/contagion-streaming-netflix-hulu-cinemax-itunes-download-torrent-coronavirus.

Alpert, Robert. "AI at the Movies and the Second Coming." *Senses of Cinema*, no. 88 (2018). https://www.sensesofcinema.com/2018/feature-articles/ai-at-the-movies-and-the-second-coming/.
———. "George Romero's Night of the Living Dead and Diary of the Dead: Recording History." *CineAction*, 95 (2015): 16.
———. "George Romero's Zombie Movies: The Fragmentation of America." *Senses of Cinema*, no. 98 (2021). https://www.sensesofcinema.com/2021/feature-articles/george-romeros-zombie-movies-the-fragmentation-of-america/.
———. "Kathryn Bigelow's Zero Dark Thirty: A Case Study on Mythmaking and Making History." *Jump Cut 57* (2016). https://www.ejumpcut.org/archive/jc57.2016/-Alpert-0Dark30/index.html.
Andersen, Kristian G., Andrew Rambaut, W. Ian Lipkin, Edward C. Holmes, and Robert F. Garry. "The Proximal Origin of SARS-CoV-2." *Nature Medicine* 26, no. 4 (2020): 450–52.
Andrews, Travis M. "Sure, Binge 'Contagion' and Other Pandemic Movies Right Now. But Their Creators Urge You to Watch with Caution." *The Washington Post*, March 19, 2020. https://www.washingtonpost.com/arts-entertainment/2020/03/19/contagion-outbreak-stand-pandemic-movie-caution/.
Appadurai, Arjun. "Disjuncture and Difference in the Global Cultural Economy." *Theory, Culture & Society* 7, no. 2–3 (1990): 295–310.
Badmington, Neil. "Pod Almighty!; Or, Humanism, Posthumanism, and the Strange Case of Invasion of the Body Snatchers." *Textual Practice* 15, no. 1 (2001): 5–22.
Bailey, Jason. "The Ending of Steven Soderbergh's Contagion, Revisited." *Vulture*, January 30, 2020. https://www.vulture.com/2020/01/contagion-movie-ending-coronavirus-and-pandemic-panic.html.
Bates, William. "Body-Snatching Pods Are Back, Courtesy of Philip Kaufman." *The New York Times*, January 7, 1979. https://www.nytimes.com/1979/01/07/archives/bodysnatching-pods-are-back-courtesy-of-philip-kaufman.html.
BBC News. "Coronavirus: Contagion Cast Share Covid-19 Advice." *BBC News*, March 31, 2020. https://www.bbc.com/news/technology-52105472.
———. "Coronavirus: Trump Stands by China Lab Origin Theory for Virus." *BBC News*, May 1, 2020. https://www.bbc.com/news/world-us-canada-52496098.
Beard, William. *The Artist as Monster: The Cinema of David Cronenberg*. Buffalo: University of Toronto Press, 2001.
Beck, Richard. "Talking Point: Inanimate Fact and Iraq War Experience." *Film Quarterly* 62, no. 1 (2008): 8–9.
Beiner, Guy, ed. *Pandemic Re-Awakenings: The Forgotten and Unforgotten "Spanish" Flu of 1918–1919*. Oxford: Oxford University Press, 2021.

Beisecker, Dave. "Afterword: Bye-Gone Days: Reflections on Romero, Kirkman and What We Become," in *"We're All Infected": Essays on AMC's The Walking Dead and the Fate of the Human*, edited by Dawn Keetley, 201–14. Jefferson: McFarland, 2014.

Belton, John. *American Cinema/American Culture*. 5th edition. New York: McGraw-Hill Education, 2017.

Ben Zion, Ilan. "Israel's Data-for-Vaccines Deal with Pfizer Raises Privacy Concerns." *Times of Israel*, January 18, 2021. https://www.timesofisrael.com/israels-data-for-vaccines-deal-with-pfizer-raises-privacy-concerns/.

Benedictow, Ole Jørgen. *The Black Death, 1346–1353: The Complete History*. Rochester: Boydell Press, 2004.

Benton, Adia. "Border Promiscuity, Illicit Intimacies, and Origin Stories: Or What Contagion's Bookends Tell Us About New Infectious Diseases and a Racialized Geography of Blame." *Somatosphere*, March 6, 2020. http://somatosphere.net/forumpost/border-promiscuity-racialized-blame/.

Bergman, Ingmar, dir. *The Seventh Seal*. New York, The Criterion Collection, 1998, DVD.

Biodrowski, Steve. "Interview: George Romero Documents the Dead." *Cinefantastique*, February 15, 2008. https://web.archive.org/web/20160404150058/http://cinefantastiqueonline.com/2008/02/interview-george-romero-documents-the-dead-part-1/.

———. "Retro Review: 15th Anniversary Screening of 28 Days Later w/ John Murphy." *Hollywood Gothique*, December 2, 2017. http://new.hollywoodgothique.com/retro-review-15th-anniversary-screening-28-days-later-w-john-murphy/.

Bishop, Kyle W. *How Zombies Conquered Popular Culture: The Multifarious Walking Dead in the 21st Century*. Jefferson: McFarland, 2015.

———. "The Sub-Subaltern Monster: Imperialist Hegemony and the Cinematic Voodoo Zombie." *The Journal of American Culture* 31, no. 2 (2008): 141–52.

Biskind, Peter. *Easy Riders, Raging Bulls: How the Sex-Drugs-And Rock 'N' Roll Generation Saved Hollywood*. New York: Simon & Schuster, 1998.

Black, Winston. *The Middle Ages: Facts and Fictions*. Santa Barbara: ABC-CLIO, 2019.

Boluk, Stephanie, and Wylie Lenz. "Infection, Media, and Capitalism: From Early Modern Plagues to Postmodern Zombies." *Journal for Early Modern Cultural Studies* 10, no. 2 (2010): 126–47.

———. "Introduction: Generation Z, the Age of Apocalypse," in *Generation Zombie : Essays on the Living Dead in Modern Culture*, edited by Stephanie Boluk and Wylie Lenz, 1–17. Jefferson: McFarland, 2011.

Bowen, Chuck. "Interview: Jessica Hausner on *Little Joe* and the Ways of Being and Seeing." *Slant Magazine*, December 1, 2019. https://www.

slantmagazine.com/film/interview-jessica-hausner-on-little-joe-and-the-ways-of-being-and-seeing/.
Braidotti, Rosi. *The Posthuman*. Cambridge: Polity Press, 2013.
Bramesco, Charles. "Exposure Therapy: Why We're Obsessed with Watching Virus Movies." *The Guardian*, March 16, 2020. https://www.theguardian.com/film/2020/mar/16/coronavirus-movies-why-are-we-obsessed-contagion-films.
Brandt, Allan M. "How AIDS Invented Global Health." *New England Journal of Medicine* 368, no. 23 (2013): 2149–52.
Brennan, Judy. "Just What the Doctor Ordered." *Los Angeles Times*, January 15, 1995. https://www.latimes.com/archives/la-xpm-1995-01-15-ca-20291-story.html.
Brooks, Max. *World War Z: An Oral History of the Zombie War*. New York: Three Rivers Press, 2006.
Brown, Hannah. "Did World War Z Predict Israel's Response to Coronavirus?," *The Jerusalem Post*, March 10, 2020. https://www.jpost.com/israel-news/world-war-c-did-world-war-z-predict-israels-response-to-covid-19-620342.
Brown, Wendy. *Undoing the Demos: Neoliberalism's Stealth Revolution*. New York: Zone Books, 2017.
Bruin-Molé, Megen de. "Killable Hordes, Chronic Others and 'Mindful' Consumers: Rehabilitating the Zombie in Twenty-First-Century Popular Culture," in *Embodying Contagion: The Viropolitics of Horror and Desire in Contemporary Discourse*, edited by Sandra Becker, Megen de Bruin-Molé, and Sara Polak, 159–78. Cardiff: University of Wales Press, 2021.
Bullard, Benjamin. "Self-Quarantined? Here Are 5 Pandemic Movies Where We Ultimately Beat the Virus." *SYFY WIRE*, March 13, 2020. https://www.syfy.com/syfywire/5-movies-people-win-for-your-coronavirus-quarantine.
Byrge, Duane. "'Outbreak': THR's 1995 Review." *The Hollywood Reporter*, March 10, 2020, originally published March 8, 1995. https://www.hollywoodreporter.com/news/general-news/outbreak-review-movie-1995-1281560/.
Caduff, Carlo. *The Pandemic Perhaps: Dramatic Events in a Public Culture of Danger*. Oakland: University of California Press, 2015.
Cady, Kathryn A., and Thomas Oates. "Family Splatters: Rescuing Heteronormativity from the Zombie Apocalypse." *Women's Studies in Communication* 39, no. 3 (2016): 308–25.
Caldwell, Thomas. "Shivers." *Senses of Cinema* 19 (2002). http://sensesofcinema.com/2002/cteq/shivers/.
CAPCOM. "CAPCOM's Annual Report: FY 1998," 1999. https://www.capcom.co.jp/ir/english/data/pdf/Annual1998.pdf.
Caplain, Helen Le, and Kelly-Ann Mills. "Coronavirus: Man Slams 'Apocalypse-Fearing' Panic Buyers for Tesco Worker Wife's Tears." *Mirror*,

March 17, 2020. https://www.mirror.co.uk/news/uk-news/coronavirus-man-slams-apocalypse-fearing-21708289.

CanadienDestroyer, "Resident Evil 2 Commercial," July 1, 2006. https://www.youtube.com/watch?v=tnglxHaB6SY.

Carnevale, Frank. "Photo of Protesters at Ohio Statehouse Compared to Zombie Movie." *TribLIVE.com*, April 19, 2020. https://triblive.com/news/world/photo-of-protester-at-ohio-statehouse-compared-to-zombie-movie/.

Carpenter, Sandra. "The Cow-Pock,-or-The Wonderful Effects of the New Inoculation!" *The Morgan Library & Museum*, February 25, 2021. https://www.themorgan.org/blog/cow-pock-or-wonderful-effects-new-inoculation.

Carson, Rachel. *Silent Spring*. New York: Fawcett Crest, 1962.

Cashill, Robert. "'There'll Be No More Tears': The Shifting Identities of Invasion of the Body Snatchers." *Cineaste Magazine* 44, no. 2 (2019): 3–7.

Catsoulis, Jeannette. "Alice, Still Fighting to Save the World." *The New York Times*, September 14, 2012. https://www.nytimes.com/2012/09/15/movies/resident-evil-retribution-with-milla-jovovich.html.

CBC News, "Killer virus Ebola breaks out in 1995," October 3, 2014. https://www.youtube.com/watch?v=v2e7TeCR--w.

CDC. "Symptoms | Plague | CDC," Centers for Disease Control and Prevention. https://www.cdc.gov/plague/symptoms/index.html.

CE Noticias Financieras English. "Coronavirus, from Reality to Fiction to Prediction," March 8, 2020. https://advance.lexis.com/api/document?collection=news&id=urn:contentItem:5YCS-JG21-JBJN-M14R-00000-00&context=1516831.

Chaganti, Seeta. *Strange Footing: Poetic Form and Dance in the Late Middle Ages*. Chicago: University of Chicago Press, 2018.

Chalasani, Radhika. "Photos: Wildlife Roams during the Coronavirus Pandemic." *ABC News*, April 22, 2020. https://abcnews.go.com/International/photos-wildlife-roams-planets-human-population-isolates/story?id=70213431.

Chelebourg, Christian. "Virus, quarantaine et paranoïa: quand la réalité rejoint la fiction," *The Conversation*, February 18, 2020. http://theconversation.com/virus-quarantaine-et-parano-a-quand-la-realite-rejoint-la-fiction-132027.

Chen, Qiulan, Lance Rodewald, Shengjie Lai, and George F. Gao. "Rapid and Sustained Containment of Covid-19 Is Achievable and Worthwhile: Implications for Pandemic Response." *BMJ* 375 (2021). https://www.bmj.com/content/375/BMJ-2021-066169.

Chernov, Matthew. "Why George Romero's 'Resident Evil' Film Failed to Launch." *Variety*, December 16, 2016. https://variety.com/2016/film/spotlight/resident-evil-george-romero-failed-1201942677/.

Christie, Deborah, and Sarah Juliet Lauro, eds. *Better off Dead: The Evolution of the Zombie as Post-Human*. New York: Fordham University Press, 2011.

Chung, Jun. "Real-Life Monkey Attack Is Eerily Like Planet of the Apes." *ScreenRant*, May 29, 2020. https://screenrant.com/planet-apes-twitter-trending-monkeys-coronavirus-samples/.

Clarke, Donald. "What Kinds of Films Will We Watch in the Post Covid-19 Era?" *The Irish Times*, April 25, 2020. https://www.irishtimes.com/culture/what-kinds-of-films-will-we-watch-in-the-post-covid-19-era-1.4235926.

Clarke, Ted. "Locked Down Under in New Zealand." *Prince George Citizen*, June 28, 2020. https://www.princegeorgecitizen.com/local-news/locked-down-under-in-new-zealand-3740764.

CNN, "Biden: 'Anyone Who's Responsible for That Many Deaths Should Not Remain as President.'" *CNN*, October 22, 2020. https://edition.cnn.com/politics/live-news/presidential-debate-coverage-fact-check-10-22-20/h_1f0bf1c810464cc902c6a3687467ed32.

CNN, "DeSantis PAC Selling 'Don't Fauci My Florida' Merch. Hear Dr. Fauci's Reaction." *CNN Video*, July 17, 2021. https://www.cnn.com/videos/politics/2021/07/17/florida-desantis-pac-merch-dr-anthony-fauci-reaction-intv-sot-acosta-nr-vpx.cnn.

Cohen, Jon. "Call of the Wild: Why Many Scientists Say It's Unlikely That SARS-CoV-2 Originated from a 'Lab Leak,'" September 2, 2021. https://www.science.org/content/article/why-many-scientists-say-unlikely-sars-cov-2-originated-lab-leak.

Cohen, Jon, and Meredith Wadman. "Biden Proposes a Science-Led New Deal to End Pandemic Suffering." *Science*, January 15, 2021. https://www.science.org/content/article/biden-proposed-science-led-new-deal-end-pandemic-suffering.

Cohn, Samuel K. "The Black Death: End of a Paradigm." *American Historical Review* 107, no. 3 (2002): 703–38.

Collin, Robbie. "Trying Not to Panic about Coronavirus? Then Don't Rewatch Contagion." *The Telegraph*, March 27, 2020. https://www.telegraph.co.uk/films/0/trying-not-panic-coronavirus-dont-rewatch-contagion/.

Collins, Margo. "'I Barely Feel Human Anymore': Project Alice and the Posthuman in the Films," in *Unraveling Resident Evil: Essays on the Complex Universe of the Games and Films*, edited by Nadine Farghaly, 201–15. Jefferson: McFarland, 2014.

Columbia Public Health, *Control the Contagion*, 2021. https://www.youtube.com/playlist?list=PL1UKNqoJNj9-ZhoAKuGlbNBcW4T9lCUOt.

Commentary by Danny Boyle and Alex Garland, "Alternative Theatrical Ending." *28 Days Later*. Directed by Danny Boyle. London: 20th Century Fox Home Entertainment, 2003, DVD.

Commentary by Jeanine Basinger. *Jezebel*, directed by William Wyler. Burbank, Warner Home Video, 2000, DVD.

Conis, Elena. *How to Sell a Poison: The Rise, Fall, and Toxic Return of DDT*. New York: Bold Type Books, 2022.

Cook, Alethia H. "Securitization of Disease in the United States: Globalization, Public Policy, and Pandemics." *Risk, Hazards & Crisis in Public Policy* 1, no. 1 (2010): 11–31.

Cooke, Jennifer. *Legacies of Plague in Literature, Theory and Film*. New York: Palgrave Macmillan, 2009.

Cooper, Melinda. *Family Values: Between Neoliberalism and the New Social Conservatism*. New York: Zone Books, 2017.

Cornelius, Michael G., and Sherry Ginn, eds. *Apocalypse TV: Essays on Society and Self at the End of the World*. Jefferson: McFarland, Publishers, 2020.

Cowie, Peter. *Ingmar Bergman: A Critical Biography*. New York: Limelight Editions, 1992.

Crawfurd, Raymond. *Plague and Pestilence in Literature and Art*. Oxford: Clarendon Press, 1914.

Crockett, Zachary, and Javier Zarracina. "How the Zombie Represents America's Deepest Fears." *Vox*, October 31, 2016. https://www.vox.com/policy-and-politics/2016/10/31/13440402/zombie-political-history.

Crosby, Alfred W. *America's Forgotten Pandemic: The Influenza of 1918*. 2nd edition New York: Cambridge University Press, 2003.

———. *Epidemic and Peace, 1918*. Westport: Greenwood Press, 1976.

Crow, David. "The George Romero Resident Evil Movie You Never Saw." *Den of Geek*, March 12, 2018. https://www.denofgeek.com/games/the-george-romero-resident-evil-movie-you-never-saw/.

Danks, Adrian. "Panic in the Streets." *Senses of Cinema* 2, January 2000. http://sensesofcinema.com/2000/feature-articles/panic/.

Dargis, Manohla. "Looking Apocalypse in the Eye." *The New York Times*, August 4, 2011. https://www.nytimes.com/2011/08/05/movies/rise-of-the-planet-of-the-apes-stars-james-franco-review.html.

Davidson, Helen. "Eight in 10 People in China Caught Covid Since Early December, Say Officials." *The Guardian*, January 23, 2023. https://www.theguardian.com/world/2023/jan/23/80-of-people-in-china-caught-covid-since-early-december-say-officials.

"Dawn of the Dead (Comparison: Theatrical Version and Director's Cut)." *Movie-Censorship.com*. https://www.movie-censorship.com/report.php?ID=1988.

Dawson, Kristy. "Dad Stuck in Italy Coronavirus Zone with No Health Care for Baby." *TeessideLive*, March 13, 2020. https://www.gazettelive.co.uk/news/teesside-news/dad-stuck-italy-coronavirus-zone-17918238.

Decker, Lindsey. "Transatlantic Genre Hybridity in Danny Boyle's *28 Days Later*." *Horror Studies* 7, no. 1 (2016): 95–110.

Dehority, Walter. "Infectious Disease Outbreaks, Pandemics, and Hollywood – Hope and Fear Across a Century of Cinema." *JAMA* 323, no. 19 (2020): 1878–80.

Delaney, Brigid. "Travelling through Asia during the Coronavirus: It's Like I Have the Whole Place to Myself." *The Guardian*, March 5, 2020. https://www.theguardian.com/commentisfree/2020/mar/06/travelling-through-asia-during-the-coronavirus-its-like-i-have-the-whole-place-to-myself.

Dempsey, Michael. "Invaders and Encampments: The Films of Philip Kaufman." *Film Quarterly* 32, no. 2 (1978): 17–27.

Dendle, Peter. *The Zombie Movie Encyclopedia*. Jefferson: McFarland, 2010.

———. *The Zombie Movie Encyclopedia, Volume 2: 2000–2010*. Jefferson: McFarland, 2012.

———. "Zombie Movies and the 'Millenial Generation,'" in *Better off Dead: The Evolution of the Zombie as Post-Human*, edited by Deborah Christie and Sarah Juliet Lauro, 175–86. New York: Fordham University Press, 2011.

Dillard, R. H. W. "Night of the Living Dead: It's Not Just Like a Wind That's Passing Through," in *American Horrors: Essays on the Modern American Horror Film*, edited by Gregory Albert Waller, 14–29. Urbana: University of Illinois Press, 1987.

Dodds, Io. "China Floods Facebook with Undeclared Coronavirus Propaganda Ads Blaming Trump." *The Telegraph*, April 5, 2020. https://www.telegraph.co.uk/technology/2020/04/05/china-floods-facebook-instagram-undeclared-coronavirus-propaganda/.

Drezner, Daniel W. "What I Learned About the Coronavirus World From Watching Zombie Flicks." *Foreign Policy*, April 11, 2020. https://foreignpolicy.com/2020/04/11/what-i-learned-about-coronavirus-world-from-zombie-movies/.

Dyer, Owen. "Covid-19: China Stops Counting Cases as Models Predict A Million Or More Deaths." *BMJ* 380 (2023): 2. https://www.bmj.com/content/380/bmj.p2.

D'Zurilla, Christie. "Wearing a Mask, Gwyneth Paltrow Cracks a Coronavirus Joke: 'I've Already Been in This Movie.'" *Los Angeles Times*, February 26, 2020. https://www.latimes.com/entertainment-arts/story/2020-02-26/gwyneth-paltrow-kate-hudson-face-mask-coronavirus.

E! News, "'Outbreak' Sounds Like Coronavirus 25 Years Later: Rewind | E! News," https://www.youtube.com/watch?v=ga1yTAsXksk.

East, Jamie. "Coronavirus Has Left Me Feeling like I'm in 28 Days Later and Been Hit by a Train – It's the Worst I've Felt in My Life." *The Sun*,

March 19, 2020. https://www.thesun.co.uk/news/11213289/coronavirus-suffering-28-days-later/.

Ebert, Roger. "Drab filmmaking the true evil in new 'Resident'." *RogerEbert.com*, September 10, 2004. https://www.rogerebert.com/reviews/resident-evil-apocalypse-2004.

———. "Ebert's Most Hated." *RogerEbert.com*, August 11, 2005. https://www.rogerebert.com/roger-ebert/eberts-most-hated.

———. "Pity they can't always remain babies." *RogerEbert.com*, August 3, 2011. https://www.rogerebert.com/reviews/rise-of-the-planet-of-the-apes-2011.

The Economist. "Foot Traffic Has Fallen Sharply in Cities with Big Coronavirus Outbreaks." *The Economist*, March 14, 2020. https://www.economist.com/graphic-detail/2020/03/14/foot-traffic-has-fallen-sharply-in-cities-with-big-coronavirus-outbreaks.

Economist Intelligence Unit. "Rich Countries Will Get Access to Coronavirus Vaccines Earlier than Others." *Economist Intelligence Unit*, December 18, 2020. https://www.eiu.com/n/rich-countries-will-get-access-to-coronavirus-vaccines-earlier-than-others/.

Eisenberg, Merle. "Uses of History During the First Nine Months of COVID." *Perspectives in Biology and Medicine* 64, no. 3 (2021): 421–35.

Eisenberg, Merle, and Lee Mordechai. "The Justinianic Plague and Global Pandemics: The Making of the Plague Concept." *The American Historical Review* 125, no. 5 (2020): 1632–67.

Elliott, David. "These Are the Countries Best Prepared for Health Emergencies." *World Economic Forum*, February 12, 2020. https://www.weforum.org/agenda/2020/02/these-are-the-countries-best-prepared-for-health-emergencies/.

Ellis, David. "No Reservation? No Problem: London's Top Restaurants, Pubs and Bars Accepting Walk-Ins." *Evening Standard*, April 28, 2021. https://www.standard.co.uk/reveller/restaurants/london-top-restaurants-pubs-bars-accepting-walk-ins-no-reservations-b929450.html.

Engber, Daniel. "The Unusual Genius of the 'Resident Evil' Movies." *The New Yorker*, February 2, 2017. http://www.newyorker.com/culture/culture-desk/the-unusual-genius-of-the-resident-evil-movies.

Erman, Michael, and Manas Mishra. "Pfizer Sees Robust COVID-19 Vaccine Demand for Years, $26 Bln in 2021 Sales." *Reuters*, May 4, 2021. https://www.reuters.com/business/healthcare-pharmaceuticals/pfizer-lifts-annual-sales-forecast-covid-19-vaccine-2021-05-04/.

Eustachewich, Lia. "People Are Freaking out That Coronavirus Outbreak Is Like 'Contagion,'" *New York Post*, January 23, 2020. https://nypost.com/2020/01/23/people-are-freaking-out-that-coronavirus-outbreak-is-like-contagion/.

EW Staff. "Inside 'Outbreak' Fever." *Entertainment Weekly*, April 21, 1995. https://ew.com/article/1995/04/21/inside-outbreak-fever/.
Farghaly, Nadine. *Unraveling Resident Evil: Essays on the Complex Universe of the Games and Films*. Jefferson: McFarland, 2014.
Farr, Christina. "The Medical Advisors for the Movie 'Contagion' Saw a Pandemic Coming, but Got One Big Thing Wrong." *CNBC*, April 14, 2020. https://www.cnbc.com/2020/04/14/contagion-movie-advisors-anticipated-pandemic.html.
FDA – Center for Food Safety and Applied Nutrition. "Herbal Amy Inc – 604813 – 03/06/2020." *Center for Food Safety and Applied Nutrition*. March 6, 2020. https://www.fda.gov/inspections-compliance-enforcement-and-criminal-investigations/warning-letters/herbal-amy-inc-604813-03062020.
Fee, Elizabeth, and Daniel M. Fox, eds. *AIDS: The Making of a Chronic Disease*. Berkeley: University of California Press, 1992.
Feldberg, Isaac. "'Contagion' Writer, Scientific Adviser Reflect on Film's Newfound Relevance amid Coronavirus Crisis," *Fortune*, February 12, 2020. https://fortune.com/2020/02/12/contagion-scott-z-burns-larry-brilliant-interview-coronavirus-fears/.
Felton, James. "The UK's Vaccine Plan Was Inspired By The Matt Damon Movie Contagion." *IFLScience*, February 3, 2021. https://iflscience.com/the-uks-vaccine-plan-was-inspired-by-the-matt-damon-movie-contagion-58615.
Fisher, Matthew. "Pandemics like the Coronavirus Crisis Inspire Outbreaks of Art." *Global News*, April 21, 2020. https://globalnews.ca/news/6839544/coronavirus-art-movies-books/.
Fissell, Mary E., Jeremy A. Greene, Randall M. Packard, and James A. Schafer Jr. "Introduction: Reimagining Epidemics." *Bulletin of the History of Medicine* 94, no. 4 (2020): 543–61.
Fraser, Nancy. "Contradictions of Capital and Care." *New Left Review*, no. 100 (2016): 99–117.
Fraser, Steve, and Gary Gerstle, eds. *The Rise and Fall of the New Deal Order, 1930–1980*. Princeton: Princeton University Press, 1989.
Freyne, Patrick. "Rush Hour on a Dublin Bus: 'They're All Ghost Buses Now.'" *The Irish Times*, April 18, 2020. https://www.irishtimes.com/life-and-style/people/rush-hour-on-a-dublin-bus-they-re-all-ghost-buses-now-1.4230714.
Frieden, Thomas R. "CDC Director on 'Contagion': Deadly Viruses Could Spread Fast." *The Atlantic*, September 10, 2011. https://www.theatlantic.com/health/archive/2011/09/cdc-director-on-contagion-deadly-viruses-could-spread-fast/244849/.
Froula, Anna. "Prolepsis and the 'War on Terror': Zombie Pathology and the Culture of Fear in 28 Days Later . . ." in *Reframing 9/11: Film, Popular Culture and the "War on Terror*," edited by Jeff Berkenstein, Anna Froula, and Karen Randell, 195–208. New York: Continuum, 2010.

Gagne, Paul R. *The Zombies That Ate Pittsburgh: The Films of George A. Romero*. New York: Dodd, Mead, 1987.

Galbraith IV, Stuart. *The Toho Studios Story: A History and Complete Filmography*. Lanham: Scarecrow Press, 2008.

Gardner, Dan. "We're Not 'Contagion' – Disasters like the Coronavirus Bring out the Best in People." *The Boston Globe*, April 3, 2020. https://www.bostonglobe.com/2020/04/03/opinion/were-not-contagion-disasters-like-coronavirus-bring-out-best-people/.

Garrett, Laurie. *The Coming Plague: Newly Emerging Diseases in a World out of Balance*. New York: Farrar, Straus and Giroux, 1994.

———. "Plague Warriors." *Vanity Fair*, August 1, 1995. https://www.vanityfair.com/news/1995/08/ebola-africa-outbreak.

Gerlach, Neil A. "From Outbreak to Pandemic Narrative: Reading Newspaper Coverage of the 2014 Ebola Epidemic." *Canadian Journal of Communication* 41, no. 4 (2016): 611–630.

———. "Visualizing Ebola: Hazmat Suite Imagery, the Press, and the Production of Biosecurity." *Canadian Journal of Communication* 44, no. 2 (2019): 191–210.

Gerlach, Neil A., and Sheryl N. Hamilton. "Trafficking in the Zombie: The CDC Zombie Apocalypse Campaign, Diseaseability and Pandemic Culture." *Refractory: A Journal of Entertainment Media* 23 (2014). https://refractory-journal.com/cdc-zombie-apocalypse-gerlach-hamilton/.

Gerrard, Steven. "'My Name Is Alice. And I Remember Everything.' Project Alice and Milla Jovovich in the Resident Evil Films," in *Gender and Contemporary Horror in Film*, edited by Samantha Holland, Robert Shail, and Steven Gerrard, 205–18. Bingley: Emerald Publishing Limited, 2019.

Ghabra, Haneen Shafeeq, and Marouf A. Hasian. "World War Z, The Zombie Apocalypse, and the Israeli State's Monstering of Palestinian 'Others.'" *Communication and Critical/Cultural Studies* 17, no. 2 (2020): 183–98.

Giddens, Anthony. *The Consequences of Modernity*. Stanford: Stanford University Press, 1990.

Gilman, Ernest B. *Plague Writing in Early Modern England*. Chicago: University of Chicago Press, 2009.

Gilpatric, Katy. "Violent Female Action Characters in Contemporary American Cinema." *Sex Roles* 62, no. 11 (2010): 734–46.

Girard, René. "The Plague in Literature and Myth." *Texas Studies in Literature and Language* 15, no. 5 (1974): 833–50.

Giuffrida, Angela. "'This Is Not a Film': Italian Mayors Rage at Virus Lockdown Dodgers." *The Guardian*, March 23, 2020. https://www.theguardian.com/world/2020/mar/23/this-is-not-a-film-italian-mayors-rage-coronavirus-lockdown-dodgers.

Gladwell, Malcolm. "The Plague Year." *New Republic*, July 17, 1995. https://newrepublic.com/article/62521/the-plague-year.

Goldmacher, Shane. "Kelly Loeffler and Richard Burr Were Briefed on Coronavirus. Then They Sold Stocks. What Now?" *The New York Times*, March 20, 2020. https://www.nytimes.com/2020/03/20/us/politics/kelly-loeffler-richard-burr-insider-trading.html.

Goldman, Carl. "I Have the Coronavirus. So Far, It Hasn't Been That Bad for Me." *The Washington Post*, February 28, 2020. https://www.washingtonpost.com/outlook/2020/02/28/i-have-coronavirus-so-far-it-isnt-that-bad/.

Gomel, Elana. "The Plague of Utopias: Pestilence and the Apocalyptic Body." *Twentieth Century Literature* 46, no. 4 (2000): 405–33.

Goss, Brian Michael. "Unmasking the Monster(s) in 28 Weeks Later." *Film International* 15, no. 2 (2017): 99–113.

Graham, Becki A. "Post-9/11 Anxieties: Unpredictability and Complacency in the Age of New Terrorism in Dawn of the Dead," in *Race, Oppression and the Zombie: Essays on Cross-Cultural Appropriations of the Caribbean Tradition*, edited by Christopher M. Moreman and Cory Rushton, 124–38. Jefferson: McFarland, 2011.

Grant, Barry Keith. *Invasion of the Body Snatchers*. London: Bloomsbury, 2010.

———. "Sensuous Elaboration: Reason and the Visible in the Science-Fiction Film," in *Alien Zone II: The Spaces of Science-Fiction Cinema*, edited by Annette Kuhn, 16–30. New York: Verso, 1999.

———. "Taking Back the Night of the Living Dead: George Romero, Feminism, and the Horror Film," in *The Dread of Difference: Gender and the Horror Film*, edited by Barry Keith Grant, 2nd edition, 228–40. Texas Film Studies Series. Austin: University of Texas Press, 2015.

Guerrasio, Jason. "How 'Contagion' Became a Must-See Movie during the Coronavirus Pandemic." *Insider*, April 3, 2020. https://www.insider.com/how-contagion-became-a-must-see-movie-during-the-coronavirus-2020-4.

Gunn, James, and Michael Tolkin. "Dawn of the Dead (Screenplay)," April 24, 2003. http://www.horrorlair.com/movies/scripts/dawnofthedead_2004.pdf.

Gunn, James, Michael Tolkin, and Scott Frank. "Dawn of the Dead (Screenplay)," August 19, 2003. https://www.scriptslug.com/assets/scripts/dawn-of-the-dead-2004.pdf.

Hadouchi, Olivier. *Kinji Fukasaku: un ineaste critique dans le chaos du Xxème siècle*. Paris: Harmattan, 2009.

Haeseler, Rob. "Hollywood Invades Humboldt County / Ferndale Profits from 'Outbreak' Cash Infusion." *SFGATE*, April 17, 1995. https://www.sfgate.com/entertainment/article/Hollywood-Invades-Humboldt-County-Ferndale-3036529.php.

Hamilton, Sheryl N. "Mediating Disease Cultures." *Canadian Journal of Communication* 44, no. 2 (2019): 151–56.

Han, Qijun, and Daniel R. Curtis. "Epidemics, Public Health Workers, and 'Heroism' in Cinematic Perspective." *Visual Studies* 36, no. 4–5 (2021): 450–462.

——. *Infectious Inequalities: Epidemics, Trust, and Social Vulnerabilities in Cinema*. New York: Routledge, 2022.

——. "Suspicious Minds: Cinematic Depiction of Distrust during Epidemic Disease Outbreaks." *Medical Humanities* 47, no. 2 (2020): 248–256.

Handling, Piers, ed. *The Shape of Rage: The Films of David Cronenberg*. Toronto: New York Zoetrope, 1983.

Haraway, Donna. "A Manifesto for Cyborgs: Science, Technology, and Socialist Feminism in the 1980s." *Socialist Review* 80 (1985): 65–108.

Harper, Stephen. "'I could kiss you, you bitch.' Race, gender and sexuality in *Resident Evil* and *Resident Evil 2: Apocalypse*." *Jump Cut* 49 (2007). https://www.ejumpcut.org/archive/jc49.2007/HarperResEvil/.

Harris, Andrea. "Woman as Evolution: The Feminist Promise of the Resident Evil Film Series," in *Race, Gender, and Sexuality in Post-Apocalyptic TV and Film*, edited by Barbara Gurr, 99–111. New York: Palgrave Macmillan, 2015.

Hartog, Kyrill. "Black Death Historian: 'A Coronavirus Depression Could Be the Great Leveller.'" *The Guardian*, April 30, 2020. https://www.theguardian.com/world/commentisfree/2020/apr/30/walter-scheidel-a-shock-to-the-established-order-can-deliver-change.

Harvey, David. *A Brief History of Neoliberalism*. New York: Oxford University Press, 2005.

Haskell, Molly. *From Reverence to Rape: The Treatment of Women in the Movies*. 3rd edition Chicago: University of Chicago Press, 2016.

Hauskeller, Michael, Thomas D. Philbeck, and Curtis D. Carbonell. "Posthumanism in Film and Television," in *The Palgrave Handbook of Posthumanism in Film and Television*, edited by Michael Hauskeller, Thomas D. Philbeck, and Curtis D. Carbonell, 1–7. New York: Palgrave Macmillan, 2015.

Hausner, Jessica. "Diesmal wollte ich es gemütlich!" *Der Standard*, May 23, 2014. https://www.derstandard.at/story/1397521284263/diesmal-wollte-ich-es-gemuetlich.

Havert, Nik. *The Golden Age of Disaster Cinema: A Guide to the Films, 1950–1979*. Jefferson: McFarland, 2019.

Hayden, Erik. "'Contagion' Helmer Steven Soderbergh to Lead Directors Guild's COVID-19 Committee." *The Hollywood Reporter*, April 16, 2020. https://www.hollywoodreporter.com/news/general-news/steven-soderbergh-lead-directors-guild-committee-covid-19-impact-1290639/.

Hayles, N. Katherine. *How We Became Posthuman: Virtual Bodies in Cybernetics, Literature, and Informatics*. Chicago: University of Chicago Press, 1999.

Hays, J. N. *The Burdens of Disease: Epidemics and Human Response in Western History*. Revised edition. New Brunswick: Rutgers University Press, 2009.
Heinlein, Robert A. *Starship Troopers*. New York: G. P. Putnam's Sons, 1959.
Heinze, Rüdiger, and Jochen Petzold. "No More Room in Hell: Utopian Moments in the Dystopia of 28 Days Later." *Zeitschrift für Anglistik und Amerikanistik* 55, no. 1 (2007): 53–68.
Hepburn, Zak. "A Film Critic and Scientist Review Pandemic Films in the Era of Coronavirus." *ABC News*, June 7, 2020. https://www.abc.net.au/news/2020-06-08/film-critic-scientist-review-pandemic-films-in-era-of-covid-19/12149784.
Heritage, Stuart. "Corona Zombies: The Terrible Movie We Might Just Need Right Now." *The Guardian*, April 13, 2020. https://www.theguardian.com/film/2020/apr/13/corona-zombies-film-full-moon-features.
Hirst, L. Fabian. *The Conquest of Plague*. Oxford: Clarendon Press, 1953.
Hobbes, Thomas. *Three-Text Edition of Thomas Hobbes's Political Theory: The Elements of Law, De Cive, and Leviathan*. Edited by Deborah Baumgold. Cambridge: Cambridge University Press, 2017.
Hoberman, J. "Paranoia and the Pods." *Sight and Sound* 4, no. 5 (1994): 28–31.
Hooker, Lucy, and Daniele Palumbo. "Covid Vaccines: Will Drug Companies Make Bumper Profits?" *BBC News*, December 18, 2020. https://www.bbc.com/news/business-55170756.
Huang, Kathy and Mengyu Han. "Did China's Street Protests End Harsh COVID Policies?" *Council on Foreign Relations*, December 14, 2022. https://www.cfr.org/blog/did-chinas-street-protests-end-harsh-covid-policies.
Hunt, Bob, Justin Gmoser, and Victoria Barranco. "How We Know the COVID-19 Coronavirus Wasn't Made in a Lab." Business Insider, December 6, 2020. https://www.businessinsider.com/coronavirus-lab-manmade-myth-debunked-2020-6.
Hurley, Kelly. "'Type H': Medicine, Psychiatry and Psychoanalysis in the Body Snatchers Films." *Horror Studies* 6, no. 2 (2015): 195–210.
Illing, Sean. "Can a Pandemic Remake Society? A Historian Explains." *Vox*, April 9, 2020. https://www.vox.com/policy-and-politics/2020/4/9/21174760/coronavirus-covid-19-inequality-walter-scheidel.
"Introduction by Ingmar Bergman." *Cries and Whispers*. Stockholm, Sweden, The Criterion Collection, 2015, DVD.
iTopChart. "Top iTunes Movie Rentals Charts and Movie Trailer on iTunes Store USA 2020," *iTopChart*, March 17, 2020. https://web.archive.org/web/20200317160316/https://itopchart.com/us/en/movies/.
Jackson, Kevin. *Nosferatu: Eine Symphonie des Grauens*. London: Palgrave Macmillan, 2013.
Jackson, Siba. "Brit Stranded in Coronavirus 'Ground Zero' with City Deserted 'like 28 Days Later.'" *Dailystar.co.uk*, January 26, 2020. https://

www.dailystar.co.uk/news/latest-news/brit-stranded-coronavirus-ground-zero-21364581.

Jameson, Fredric. *Postmodernism, or, The Cultural Logic of Late Capitalism*. Durham: Duke University Press, 1991.

Johnson, Lauren M. "New York City Spent Two Minutes Clapping for Coronavirus First Responders." *CNN*, March 27, 2020. https://www.cnn.com/2020/03/27/us/new-york-claps-for-first-responders-trnd/index.html.

Johnson, Mark. "World Ignored Monkeypox Threats, Including Signs of Sexual Transmission." *The Washington Post*, August 12, 2022. https://www.washingtonpost.com/health/2022/08/12/monkeypox-virus-origins-nigeria-sexual-transmission/.

Jones, Jonathan. "Apocalyptic Vision: The Unsettling Beauty of Lockdown Is Pure Sci-Fi." *The Guardian*, April 29, 2020. https://www.theguardian.com/artanddesign/2020/apr/29/apocalyptic-vision-the-unsettling-beauty-of-lockdown-britain-is-pure-sci-fi-coronavirus.

Kaminsky, Stuart M. "Don Siegel on the Pod Society (1976)," in *The Science Fiction Film Reader*, edited by Gregg Rickman. Milwaukee: Limelight Editions, 2009.

Kaplan, Rebecca. "A Silent, Savage Menace: Reassessing 'Panic in the Streets.'" *Science History Institute – Distillations: Using Stories from Science's Past to Understand Our World*, June 30, 2020. https://www.sciencehistory.org/distillations/a-silent-savage-menace-reassessing-panic-in-the-streets.

Karlamangla, Soumya. "How the makers of 'Contagion' saw an outbreak like coronavirus coming." *Los Angeles Times*, March 11, 2020. https://www.latimes.com/california/story/2020-03-11/coronavirus-contagion-outbreak-accuracy-movie.

———. "I've Seen 'Contagion' Four Times. No, the Coronavirus Outbreak Isn't the Same." *Los Angeles Times*, March 11, 2020. https://www.latimes.com/california/story/2020-03-11/coronavirus-contagion-outbreak-movie-comparison.

Kaufman, Philip and Stephen Farber. "Hollywood Maverick." *Film Comment* 15, no. 1 (1979): 26–31.

Kazan, Elia. *Elia Kazan: A Life*. New York: Knopf, 1988.

Keane, Stephen. *Disaster Movies: The Cinema of Catastrophe*. 2nd edition. New York, Wallflower Press, 2006.

Keetley, Dawn, ed. *"We're All Infected": Essays on AMC's The Walking Dead and the Fate of the Human*. Jefferson: McFarland, 2014.

Kellner, Douglas. *Cinema Wars: Hollywood Film and Politics in the Bush-Cheney Era*. Malden: Wiley-Blackwell, 2010.

———. "Social Apocalypse in Contemporary Hollywood Film," in *The Routledge Companion to Cinema and Politics*, edited by Yannis Tzioumakis and Claire Molloy, 13–28. London: Routledge, 2016.

Kelly, Heather. "People Have Found a Way to Cope with Pandemic Fears: Watching 'Contagion.'" *The Washington Post*, March 6, 2020. https://www.washingtonpost.com/technology/2020/03/06/contagion-streaming/.

Kelly, Kate. "S.E.C. Inquiry Into Former Senator's Stock Sales Is Closed Without Charges." *The New York Times*, January 6, 2023. https://www.nytimes.com/2023/01/06/us/politics/burr-sec-inquiry-closed.html.

Kelly, Kate, Adam Playford, Alicia Parlapiano, and Ege Uz. "Stock Trades Reported by Nearly a Fifth of Congress Show Possible Conflicts." *The New York Times*, September 13, 2022. https://www.nytimes.com/interactive/2022/09/13/us/politics/congress-stock-trading-investigation.html.

Kendal, Evie. "Public Health Crises in Popular Media: How Viral Outbreak Films Affect the Public's Health Literacy." *Medical Humanities* 47, no. 1 (2021): 11–19.

Keogh, Brittany. "Coronavirus: What Does Declaring a Pandemic for Covid-19 Mean?" *Stuff*, March 12, 2020. https://www.stuff.co.nz/national/health/coronavirus/119997644/outbreak-or-pandemic-translating-coronavirus-jargon-into-human-speak.

Keshvari, Mostafa, writer/director. *Corona*. GrandMuse Pictures, 2020.

Kilday, Gregg. "Peter Bogdanovich on Barbra Streisand: 'Funny, Cute and Kind of a Wiseass.'" *The Hollywood Reporter*, April 19, 2013. https://www.hollywoodreporter.com/movies/movie-news/peter-bogdanovich-barbra-streisand-funny-434860/.

Kit, Borys. "Zack Snyder's 'Army of the Dead': Prequel and Anime Series in the Works." *The Hollywood Reporter*, September 3, 2020. https://www.hollywoodreporter.com/movies/movie-news/zack-snyders-army-of-the-dead-prequel-and-anime-series-in-the-works-4054508/.

Klein, Ira. "Plague, Policy and Popular Unrest in British India." *Modern Asian Studies* 22, no. 4 (1988): 723–55.

Knöppler, Christian. *The Monster Always Returns: American Horror Films and Their Remakes*. New York: Columbia University Press, 2017.

Korecki, Natasha, and Sarah Owermohle. "Attacks on Fauci Grow More Intense, Personal and Conspiratorial." *Politico*, June 4, 2021. https://www.politico.com/news/2021/06/04/fauci-attacks-personal-conspiratorial-491896.

Korte, Barbara. "Envisioning a Black Tomorrow? Black Mother Figures and the Issue of Representation in *28 Days Later* (2003) and *Children of Men* (2006)," in *Multi-Ethnic Britain 2000+*, edited by Lars Eckstein, Barbara Korte, Eva Ulrike Pirker, and Christoph Reinfandt, 315–25. Leiden: Brill, 2008.

Kuklenski, Valerie. "Germ Warfare." *People*, March 20, 1995. https://www.upi.com/Archives/1995/03/20/People/8649795675600/.

Kulish, Nicholas. "'Never Seen Anything Like It': Cars Line Up for Miles at Food Banks." *The New York Times*, April 8, 2020. https://www.nytimes.com/2020/04/08/business/economy/coronavirus-food-banks.html.

Kuttner, Robert. "Free Markets, Besieged Citizens." *New York Review of Books*, July 21, 2022. https://www.nybooks.com/articles/2022/07/21/free-markets-besieged-citizens-gerstle-kuttner/.

Lambie, Ryan. "Abel Ferrara Interview: Driller Killer, Bad Lieutenant, Body Snatchers." *Den of Geek*, November 23, 2016. https://www.denofgeek.com/movies/abel-ferrara-interview-driller-killer-bad-lieutenant-body-snatchers/.

Landsberg, Torsten. "In Times of Coronavirus, Looking at How Hollywood Films Portray Virus Outbreaks." *DW.COM*, June 3, 2020. https://www.dw.com/en/in-times-of-coronavirus-looking-at-how-hollywood-films-portray-virus-outbreaks/a-52665150.

Lang, Brent. "'Outbreak' Writers on How the Movie's Deadly Illness Compares to the Coronavirus Pandemic." *Variety*, April 15, 2020. https://variety.com/2020/film/news/outbreak-writers-25-year-anniversary-coronavirus-covid-19-1234580608/.

Lauro, Sarah Juliet. *The Transatlantic Zombie: Slavery, Rebellion, and Living Death*. New Brunswick: Rutgers University Press, 2015.

———, ed. *Zombie Theory: A Reader*. Minneapolis: University of Minnesota Press, 2017.

Laversuch, Chloe. "28 Days Later: York in Coronavirus Lockdown." *York Press*, April 19, 2020. https://www.yorkpress.co.uk/news/18388214.28-days-later-york-coronavirus-lockdown/.

Lawrence, Rebecca. "'I'm paranoid and panicked': Gwyneth Jets to Paris with a Face Mask amid Coronavirus Outbreak." *Daily Mail Online*, February 26, 2020. https://www.dailymail.co.uk/tvshowbiz/article-8046557/Gwyneth-jets-Paris-face-mask-amid-coronavirus-outbreak.html.

Lederberg, Joshua. "Infectious History." *Science* 288, no. 5464 (April 14, 2000): 287–93.

Leeder, Murray. "Invasion of the Body Snatchers." *Oxford Bibliographies*, July 24, 2018. https://www.oxfordbibliographies.com/view/document/obo-9780199791286/obo-9780199791286-0297.xml.

Leeuwen, Hans van. "Life in London's Lockdown: How the Real Becomes Surreal." *The Australian Financial Review*, March 25, 2020. https://www.afr.com/world/europe/life-in-london-s-lockdown-how-the-real-becomes-surreal-20200326-p54e0i.

LeGacy, Arthur. "'The Invasion of the Body Snatchers': A Metaphor for the Fifties." *Literature/Film Quarterly* 6, no. 3 (1978): 285–92.

Leistle, Bernhard, ed. *Anthropology and Alterity: Responding to the Other*. New York: Routledge, 2017.

Lindahl, Chris. "Beyond 'Contagion': Interest in Outbreak Movies, Podcasts, and More Surges Across the Internet." *IndieWire*, March 17, 2020. https://www.indiewire.com/2020/03/contagion-pandemic-outbreak-movies-coronavirus-1202218477/.

Link, Vernon B. *A History of Plague in the United States of America*. Washington: US Government Printing Office, 1955.
Lipton, Eric, and Nicholas Fandos. "Senator Richard Burr Sold a Fortune in Stocks as GOP Played Down Coronavirus Threat." *The New York Times*, March 19, 2020. https://www.nytimes.com/2020/03/19/us/politics/richard-burr-stocks-sold-coronavirus.html.
Loock, Kathleen. "The Return of the Pod People: Remaking Cultural Anxieties in Invasion of the Body Snatchers," in *Film Remakes, Adaptations and Fan Productions: Remake | Remodel*, edited by Kathleen Loock and Constantine Verevis, 122–44. London: Palgrave Macmillan, 2012.
Lovell, Alan. *Don Siegel: American Cinema*. London: British Film Institute, 1975.
Luckhurst, Roger. *Zombies: A Cultural History*. London: Reaktion Books, 2015.
Luhning, Holly. "Cronenberg's: Contagion and Community." in *Body Horror and Shapeshifting*, edited by Jessica Folio and Holly Luhning, 33–40. Leiden: Brill, 2014.
Lynteris, Christos. "The Epidemiologist as Culture Hero: Visualizing Humanity in the Age of 'the Next Pandemic.'" *Visual Anthropology* 29, no. 1 (2016): 36–53.
———. *Human Extinction and the Pandemic Imaginary*. New York: Routledge, 2020.
———. "The Imperative Origins of COVID-19." *L'Homme* no. 234–235 (2020): 21–32.
———. *Visual Plague: The Emergence of Epidemic Photography*. Cambridge: MIT Press, 2022.
MacInnis, Allan. "Sex, Science, and the 'Female Monstrous': Wood Contra Cronenberg, Revisited." *CineAction*, no. 88 (June 22, 2012): 34–43.
Mack, David. "Everyone Is Watching 'Contagion,' A 9-Year-Old Movie About A Flu Outbreak." *BuzzFeed News*, March 3, 2020. https://www.buzzfeednews.com/article/davidmack/contagion-movie-coronavirus.
Macnab, Geoffrey. "Infected Hollywood: Why Filmmakers Love Disease." *Independent*, February 20, 2020. https://www.independent.co.uk/independentpremium/culture/coronavirus-panic-in-the-streets-bfi-contagion-outbreak-zombie-films-a9341801.html.
Malone, Tyler. "The Zombies of Karl Marx: Horror in Capitalism's Wake." *Literary Hub*, October 31, 2018. https://lithub.com/the-zombies-of-karl-marx-horror-in-capitalisms-wake/.
Mandavilli, Apoorva. "Monkeypox Appears to Recede, but Risks and Uncertainties Linger." *The New York Times*, September 26, 2022. https://www.nytimes.com/2022/09/26/health/monkeypox-vaccine.html.
———. "Polio Was Almost Eradicated. This Year It Staged a Comeback." *The New York Times*, August 18, 2022. https://www.nytimes.com/2022/08/18/health/polio-new-york-malawi.html.

Mann, Katrina. "'You're Next!': Postwar Hegemony Besieged in 'Invasion of the Body Snatchers.'" *Cinema Journal* 44, no. 1 (2004): 49–68.
Manson, Katrina. "Virologist behind 'Contagion' Film Criticises Leaders' Slow Responses." *Financial Times*, April 18, 2020. https://www.ft.com/content/6e9b4fe7-b26e-45b9-acbd-2b24d182e914.
Marsh, Calum. "As Outdated Ads Linger a Hundred Days Later, a City Feels like an Apocalyptic St. Patrick's Day." *National Post*, June 27, 2020. https://nationalpost.com/entertainment/as-outdated-ads-linger-a-hundred-days-later-a-city-feels-like-an-apocalyptic-st-patricks-day.
Martin, Karl. "The Failure of a Pseudo-Christian Community in a Nation-State in Crisis: 28 Days Later." *Journal of Religion & Film* 18, no. 2 (2014), Article 6.
Maslin, Janet. "The Hero Is Hoffman, The Villain a Virus." *The New York Times*, March 10, 1995. https://www.nytimes.com/1995/03/10/movies/film-review-the-hero-is-hoffman-the-villain-a-virus.html.
Matthews, Stephen, and Sam Blanchard. "Fourteen UK Patients Are Tested for Coronavirus: Suspected Victims Are Taken into Isolation after Returning from Wuhan with Flu-like Symptoms as Health Secretary Is Urged to Order Checks on Passengers on ALL Flights from China." *Daily Mail Online*, January 23, 2020. https://www.dailymail.co.uk/health/article-7920907/Coronavirus-fears-Scotland-two-Chinese-patients-rushed-hospital.html.
McCarthy, Niall. "The Countries Best and Worst Prepared For An Epidemic [Infographic]." *Forbes*, January 27, 2020. https://www.forbes.com/sites/niallmccarthy/2020/01/27/the-countries-best-and-worst-prepared-for-an-epidemic-infographic/.
McCarty, E. Berryhill, and Lance Wahlert. "Lessons on Surviving a Pandemic From 35 Years of AIDS Cinema." *AMA Journal of Ethics* 23, no. 5 (2021): 423–27.
McGregor, Rob. "George A. Romero's *Resident Evil*," 2021. http://www.new-blood.com/romeros.html.
McKay, Richard A. *Patient Zero and the Making of the AIDS Epidemic*. Chicago: University of Chicago, Press, 2017.
McLarty, Lianne. "'Beyond the Veil of Flesh': Cronenberg and the Disembodiment of Horror," in *The Dread of Difference: Gender and the Horror Film*, edited by Barry Keith Grant, 259–80. Austin: University of Texas Press, 1996.
McNamara, Mary. "Column: Flesh-Eating Apocalyptic Films and Shows Didn't Prepare Us for This Pandemic's Horror." *Los Angeles Times*, April 2, 2020. https://www.latimes.com/entertainment-arts/story/2020-04-02/coronavirus-pandemic-tips-movies.
McNeill, William. *Plagues and Peoples*. Garden City: Anchor Books, 1976.
McNiffe, Michael. "Mick McNiffe comment: Ireland's War with Coronavirus Has Become a Sci-Fi Movie – Hopefully It Has a Happy Ending." *Irish*

Mirror, March 25, 2020. https://www.irishmirror.ie/news/news-opinion/mick-mcniffe-comment-irelands-war-21754374.

Menadue, Christopher B. "Pandemics, Epidemics, Viruses, Plagues, and Disease: Comparative Frequency Analysis of a Cultural Pathology Reflected in Science Fiction Magazines from 1926 to 2015." *Social Sciences & Humanities Open* 2, no. 1 (2020): 100048.

Mills, C. Wright. *White Collar: the American Middle Classes*. New York: Oxford University Press, 1951.

Milman, Oliver. "Covid-19 Has Now Killed as Many Americans as the 1918–19 Flu Pandemic." *The Guardian*, September 21, 2021. https://www.theguardian.com/world/2021/sep/20/covid-19-death-toll-1918-flu-pandemic.

Minelle, Bethany. "Coronavirus: What Can We Learn from a Hollywood Pandemic? The Positives from Four Outbreak Films." *Sky News*, April 29, 2020. https://news.sky.com/story/coronavirus-can-pandemic-disaster-films-help-us-navigate-the-outbreak-11979655.

Mitchell, Scott, and Sheryl N. Hamilton. "Playing at Apocalypse: Reading Plague Inc. in Pandemic Culture." *Convergence* 24, no. 6 (2018): 587–606.

Moeller, Susan D. *Compassion Fatigue: How the Media Sell Disease, Famine, War and Death*. London: Routledge, 1999.

Mooney, Chris, Brady Dennis and John Muyskens. "Global Emissions Plunged an Unprecedented 17 Percent during the Coronavirus Pandemic." *The Washington Post*, May 19, 2020. https://www.washingtonpost.com/climate-environment/2020/05/19/greenhouse-emissions-coronavirus/.

Morris, Seren. "'28 Days Later' Just Became Real After Monkeys Escape From Lab With COVID-19 Blood Test Samples." *Newsweek*, May 29, 2020. https://www.newsweek.com/28-days-later-planet-apes-movie-monkeys-escape-covid-19-samples-1507402.

Morris, Wesley. "For Me, Rewatching 'Contagion' Was Fun, Until It Wasn't." *The New York Times*, March 10, 2020. https://www.nytimes.com/2020/03/10/movies/contagion-movie-coronavirus.html.

———. "'Outbreak' Was a Hit in 1995. Now We're Living the Sequel." *The New York Times*, March 30, 2020. https://www.nytimes.com/2020/03/30/movies/outbreak-movie-coronavirus.html.

Morse, Stephen S. "Factors in the Emergence of Infectious Diseases." *Emerging Infectious Diseases* 1, no. 1 (1995): 7–15.

Moskos, Charles, and John Sibley Butler. *All That We Can Be: Black Leadership and Racial Integration The Army Way*. New York: Basic Books, 1997.

Mozur, Paul, Muyi Xiao, and John Liu. "'An Invisible Cage': How China Is Policing the Future." *The New York Times*, June 25, 2022. https://www.nytimes.com/2022/06/25/technology/china-surveillance-police.html.

Mulvey, Laura "Visual Pleasure and Narrative Cinema," in *Film Theory & Criticism*, 7th edition, eds. Leo Braudy and Marshall Cohen, 711–22. New York: Oxford University Press, 2009,

Muntean, Nick, and Matthew Thomas Payne. "Attack of the Livid Dead: Recalibrating Terror in the Post-9/11 Zombie Film," in *The War on Terror and American Popular Culture: September 11 and Beyond*, eds. Andrew Schopp and Matthew B. Hill, 239–58. Madison: Fairleigh Dickinson University Press, 2009.

Nasiruddin, Melissa, Monique Halabi, Alexander Dao, Kyle Chen, and Brandon Brown. "Zombies – A Pop Culture Resource for Public Health Awareness." *Emerging Infectious Diseases* 19, no. 5 (2013), 809–13.

"National COVID-19 Preparedness Plan." *The White House*, accessed September 9, 2022. https://www.whitehouse.gov/covidplan/.

National Institutes of Health. "Chloroquine or Hydroxychloroquine, and/or Azithromycin." COVID-19 Treatment Guidelines, September 29, 2021. https://www.covid19treatmentguidelines.nih.gov/therapies/antiviral-therapy/chloroquine-or-hydroxychloroquine-and-or-azithromycin/.

Nelson, Erika. "Invasion of The Body Snatchers: Gender and Sexuality in Four Film Adaptations." *Extrapolation* 52, no. 1 (2011): 51–75.

Nepales, Ruben V. "Why 'Contagion,' out in 2011, Accurately Foretold Coronavirus Pandemic." *Jakarta Post*, April 26, 2020. https://www.thejakartapost.com/life/2020/04/26/why-contagion-out-in-2011-accurately-foretold-coronavirus-pandemic.html.

Nerlich, Brigitte, and Christopher Halliday. "Avian Flu: The Creation of Expectations in the Interplay between Science and the Media." *Sociology of Health & Illness* 29, no. 1 (2007): 46–65.

Neve, Brian. *Elia Kazan: The Cinema of an American Outsider*. London: Bloomsbury Academic, 2009.

———. "Elia Kazan's First Testimony to the House Committee on Un-American Activities, Executive Session, 14 January 1952." *Historical Journal of Film, Radio and Television* 25, no. 2 (2005): 251–72.

Newbury, Michael. "Fast Zombie/Slow Zombie: Food Writing, Horror Movies, and Agribusiness Apocalypse." *American Literary History* 24, no. 1 (2012): 87–114.

Newby, Richard. "How '28 Days Later' Changed the Horror Genre." *The Hollywood Reporter*, June 29, 2018. https://www.hollywoodreporter.com/heat-vision/have-get-a-quiet-place-killed-zombie-genre-1121491.

Newman, Kim. "The Diseased World." *Filmmaker Magazine*, Summer 2003. https://www.filmmakermagazine.com/archives/issues/summer2003/features/diseased_world.html.

Nietzsche, Friedrich. *The Portable Nietzsche*. ed. Walter Kaufman. New York: Viking Press, 1968.

Niles, Steve. *28 Days Later: The Aftermath*. New York: Dey Street Books, 2007.
Noor, Poppy. "Fury and Despair: Behind the Viral Image of Americans Protesting against Lockdown." *The Guardian*, April 18, 2020. https://www.theguardian.com/artanddesign/2020/apr/18/ohio-protest-repoen-viral-image-photojournalist-joshua-bickel.
Novak, Matt. "Instagram Muscleman Arrested For Allegedly Peddling Fake Covid-19 Cure." *Gizmodo*, March 26, 2020. https://gizmodo.com/instagram-muscleman-arrested-for-allegedly-peddling-fak-1842507108.
Oliver, James. "Apocalypse Now: How to Find Coronavirus Comfort in Catastrophe Movies." *New European,* April 6, 2020. https://web.archive.org/web/20200406125020/https://www.theneweuropean.co.uk/top-stories/apocalypse-now-how-to-find-coronavirus-comfort-in-catastrophe-movies-1-6591127.
Ollstein, Alice Miranda. "POLITICO-Harvard Poll: Most Americans Believe Covid Leaked from Lab." *Politico*, July 9, 2021. https://www.politico.com/news/2021/07/09/poll-covid-wuhan-lab-leak-498847.
Olsen, Mark. "'Contagion' Director Steven Soderbergh on Hollywood Reopening: 'We're Going to Get Back to Work.'" *Los Angeles Times*, May 21, 2020. https://www.latimes.com/entertainment-arts/movies/story/2020-05-21/steven-soderbergh-hollywood-reopening-coronavirus-contagion.
Orwell, George. *Animal Farm*. New York: Harcourt, Brace, and Company, 1946.
Osterhammel, Jürgen. *Globalization: A Short History*. Princeton: Princeton University Press, 2005.
Ostherr, Kirsten. *Cinematic Prophylaxis: Globalization and Contagion in the Discourse of World Health*. Durham: Duke University Press, 2005.
Otto, Jeff. "An Interview with Writer James Gunn." *IGN*, March 26, 2004 (updated May 21, 2012). https://www.ign.com/articles/2004/03/26/an-interview-with-writer-james-gunn?page=1.
"Outbreak." *Rotten Tomatoes*. https://www.rottentomatoes.com/m/outbreak.
"Outbreak (1995)." *Box Office Mojo*. https://www.boxofficemojo.com/title/tt0114069/.
"Outbreak (1995) – Financial Information." *The Numbers*. https://www.the-numbers.com/movie/Outbreak.
Paffenroth, Kim. *Gospel of the Living Dead: George Romero's Visions of Hell on Earth*. Waco: Baylor University Press, 2006.
Palmer, Brian. "Jonas Salk: Good at Virology, Bad at Economics." *Slate*, April 14, 2014. https://slate.com/technology/2014/04/the-real-reasons-jonas-salk-didnt-patent-the-polio-vaccine.html.
"Panic in the Streets." *AFI Catalog of Feature Films: The First 100 years 1893–1993.* https://catalog.afi.com/Film/26448-PANIC-IN-THE-STREETS.

Pappas, Georgios, Savvas Seitaridis, Nikolaos Akritidis, and Epaminondas Tsianos. "Infectious Diseases in Cinema: Virus Hunters and Killer Microbes." *Clinical Infectious Diseases* 37, no. 7 (2003): 939–42.

Parker, Emma. "Monkeys 'Escape with Coronavirus Test Samples after Attacking Lab Assistant.'" *Dailystar.co.uk*, May 29, 2020. https://www.dailystar.co.uk/news/world-news/monkeys-escape-coronavirus-test-samples-22108572.

Parmenter, Tom. "Coronavirus in Newcastle: Novelty of Lockdown Gives Way to Fear of Economic Recession." *Sky News*, May 15, 2020. https://news.sky.com/story/coronavirus-in-newcastle-novelty-of-lockdown-gives-way-to-fear-of-economic-recession-11988544.

Patches, Matt. "How the Mastermind Behind 'Resident Evil' Kept the Franchise Going for 15 Years." *Thrillist*, January 26, 2017. https://www.thrillist.com/entertainment/nation/resident-evil-movies-paul-ws-anderson-interview-resident-evil-the-final-chapter.

Pearl, Monica. "AIDS and New Queer Cinema," in *New Queer Cinema: A Critical Reader*, edited by Michele Aaron, 23–36. New Brunswick: Rutgers University Press, 2004.

Peaty, Gwyneth. "The Afterlives of Alice: Reanimating the Gothic Heroine in the *Resident Evil* Franchise," in *Gothic Afterlives: Reincarnations of Horror in Film and Popular Media*, edited by Lorna Piatti-Farnell, 29–40. Lanham: Rowman & Littlefield, 2019.

Penny, Laurie. "This Is Not the Apocalypse You Were Looking For." *Wired*, March 30, 2020. https://www.wired.com/story/coronavirus-apocalypse-myths/.

Peterson, Sarah, and Wendy Mesley. "COVID-19 Blame Game Intensifies with Online Ad Campaigns Paid for by China and the US | CBC News." *CBC*, May 10, 2020. https://www.cbc.ca/news/world/coronavirus-covid-china-united-states-political-campaign-1.5555245.

Piper, Kelsey. "Here's How Covid-19 Ranks among the Worst Plagues in History." *Vox*, January 11, 2021. https://www.vox.com/future-perfect/21539483/covid-19-black-death-plagues-in-history.

Place, Clarissa. "Trader Woke up from Operation to Discover Country Was in Lockdown." *Norwich Evening News*, June 17, 2020. https://www.eveningnews24.co.uk/news/shop-owner-norwich-wakes-up-nnuh-lockdown-1771246.

Platts, Todd K. "A Comparative Analysis of the Factors Driving Film Cycles: Italian and American Zombie Film Production, 1978–82." *Journal of Italian Cinema & Media Studies* 5, no. 2 (2017): 191–210.

———. "From White Zombies to Night Zombies and Beyond: The Evolution of the Zombie in Western Popular Culture," in *The Supernatural Revamped: From Timeworn Legends to Twenty-First-Century Chic*, edited by Barbara Brodman and James E. Doan, 219–35. Madison: Fairleigh Dickinson University Press, 2016.

———. "The Unmade Undead: A Post-Mortem of the Post-9/11 Zombie Cycle," in *Shadow Cinema: The Historical and Production Contexts of Unmade Films*, edited by James Fenwick, Kieran Foster, and David Eldridge, 251–66. New York: Bloomsbury Publishing, 2020.

Poitras, Laura, and Glenn Greenwald. "NSA Whistleblower Edward Snowden: 'I Don't Want to Live in a Society That Does These Sort of Things' – Video." *The Guardian*, June 9, 2013. http://www.theguardian.com/world/video/2013/jun/09/nsa-whistleblower-edward-snowden-interview-video.

Polak, Sara. "Preparedness 101: 'Zombie Pandemic' and the Ebola Scare – How the CDC's Use of Zombie Pop Culture Helped Fan a Nationalist Outbreak Narrative," in *Embodying Contagion : The Viropolitics of Horror and Desire in Contemporary Discourse*, edited by Sandra Becker, Megen de Bruin-Molé, and Sara Polak, 41–59. Cardiff: University of Wales Press, 2021.

Pollitzer, R. *Plague*. Geneva: World Health Organization, 1954.

Press Trust of India. "Pandemic and Disaster Stories on Screen: To See or to Not See, That Is the Question." *Business Standard India*, April 17, 2020. https://www.business-standard.com/article/pti-stories/pandemic-and-disaster-stories-on-screen-to-see-or-to-not-see-that-is-the-question-120041700771_1.html.

Preston, Richard. "Crisis in the Hot Zone: Lessons from an Outbreak of Ebola." *The New Yorker*, October 18, 1992. https://www.newyorker.com/magazine/1992/10/26/crisis-in-the-hot-zone.

———. *The Hot Zone*. New York: Random House, 1994.

———. "The Vaccine Debacle." *The New York Times*, October 2, 1994. https://www.nytimes.com/1994/10/02/opinion/the-vaccine-debacle.html.

"Q & A: Emily Beechum and Jessica Hausner (Film at Lincoln Center)." *Little Joe*. Magnolia Home Entertainment, 2020, DVD.

Qian, Isabelle, Muyi Xiao, Paul Mozur, and Alexander Cardia. "Four Takeaways From a Times Investigation Into China's Expanding Surveillance State." *The New York Times*, June 21, 2022. https://www.nytimes.com/2022/06/21/world/asia/china-surveillance-investigation.html.

Quammen, David. *Spillover : Animal Infections and the next Human Pandemic*. New York: W.W. Norton & Co., 2012.

Ramsay, Stuart. "Coronavirus: Italy's Hardest-Hit City Wants You to See How COVID-19 Is Affecting Its Hospitals." *Sky News*, March 20, 2020. https://web.archive.org/web/20200320114010/https://news.sky.com/story/coronavirus-they-call-it-the-apocalypse-inside-italys-hardest-hit-hospital-11960597.

Rapold, Nicolas. "Paul W. S. Anderson and Milla Jovovich: A Marriage Built on Monsters." *The New York Times*, September 2, 2022. https://www.

nytimes.com/2022/09/02/movies/paul-ws-anderson-milla-jovovich-resident-evil.html.

Raza Kolb, Anjuli Fatima. *Epidemic Empire: Colonialism, Contagion, and Terror, 1817–2020*. Chicago: University of Chicago Press, 2021.

Redding, David W., Peter M. Atkinson, Andrew A. Cunningham, Gianni Lo Iacono, Lina M. Moses, James L. N. Wood, and Kate E. Jones. "Impacts of Environmental and Socio-Economic Factors on Emergence and Epidemic Potential of Ebola in Africa." *Nature Communications* 10, no. 4531 (2019).

Reuters. "World Has Entered Stage of 'Vaccine Apartheid' – WHO Head." *Reuters*, May 17, 2021. https://www.reuters.com/business/healthcare-pharmaceuticals/world-has-entered-stage-vaccine-apartheid-who-head-2021-05-17/.

Reuters. "Iran Urges Biden to Lift Sanctions Affecting Medicines as It Fights COVID-19." *Reuters*, January 26, 2021. https://www.reuters.com/article/health-coronavirus-iran-int-idUSKBN29V1G2.

Revely-Calder, Cal. "How Contagion Got Coronavirus Right – by the Film's Science Advisor." *The Telegraph*, March 27, 2020. https://www.telegraph.co.uk/films/0/contagion-coronavirus-science/.

Rice, Geoffrey W. "How Reminders of the 1918–19 Pandemic Helped Australia and New Zealand Respond to COVID-19." *Journal of Global History* 15, no. 3 (2020): 421–33.

Riesman, David. *The Lonely Crowd; a Study of the Changing American Character*. New Haven: Yale University Press, 1950.

Robey, Tim. "George A. Romero: Why I Don't like The Walking Dead." *The Telegraph*, November 8, 2013. https://www.telegraph.co.uk//culture/film/10436738/George-A-Romero-Why-I-dont-like-The-Walking-Dead.html.

Rodgers, Daniel T. *Age of Fracture*. Cambridge: Belknap Press, 2012.

Rogers, Kristen. "'Contagion' vs. Coronavirus: The Film's Connections to a Real Life Pandemic." *CNN*, April 2, 2020. https://www.cnn.com/2020/04/02/movies/contagion-movie-versus-coronavirus-scn-wellness/index.html.

Romero, George. "Resident Evil – by George A. Romero." Script. https://imsdb.com/scripts/Resident-Evil.html.

Rosen, George. *A History of Public Health*. Expanded edition. Baltimore: Johns Hopkins University Press, 1993.

Rosenberg, Charles E. "What Is an Epidemic? AIDS in Historical Perspective." *Daedalus* 118, no. 2 (1989): 1–17.

——. "What Is and Was an Epidemic." *Bulletin of the History of Medicine* 94, no. 4 (2020): 755–56.

"Rotten Tomatoes." 2021. https://www.rottentomatoes.com/search?search=resident%20evil.

Safi, Michael. "Oxford/AstraZeneca Covid Vaccine Research 'Was 97% Publicly Funded.'" *The Guardian*, April 15, 2021. https://www.theguardian.com/science/2021/apr/15/oxfordastrazeneca-covid-vaccine-research-was-97-publicly-funded.

Sakoui, Anousha, and Ryan Faughnder. "Reopening California: Hollywood Is Figuring out How to Start Rolling Again." *Los Angeles Times*, April 28, 2020. https://www.latimes.com/entertainment-arts/business/story/2020-04-28/coronavirus-reopening-california-hollywood-production-restart.

Salisbury, Mark. "Resident Evil: Girls, Guns and Ghouls." *Fangoria*, April 2002.

Sanjek, David. "Dr. Hobbes's Parasites: Victims, Victimization, and Gender in David Cronenberg's 'Shivers.'" *Cinema Journal* 36, no. 1 (1996): 55–74.

Sarasohn, Lisa T. *Getting under Our Skin: The Cultural and Social History of Vermin*. Baltimore: Johns Hopkins University Press, 2021.

Schaller, Michael. "Japan and the Cold War, 1960–1991," in *The Cambridge History of the Cold War: Volume 3: Endings*, edited by Melvyn P. Leffler and Odd Arne Westad, 3:156–80. Cambridge: Cambridge University Press, 2010.

Schiefer, Karin. "Interview with Jessica Hausner." *Eurimages*, June 2018. https://rm.coe.int/interview-with-jessica-hausner/168091e731.

Schmeink, Lars. *Biopunk Dystopias: Genetic Engineering, Society, and Science Fiction*. Liverpool: Liverpool University Press, 2016.

——. "Review of *Unraveling Resident Evil: Essays on the Complex Universe of the Games and Films; 'We're all Infected': Essays on AMC's The Walking Dead and the Fate of the Human*, by Nadine Farghaly and Dawn Keetley. *Journal of the Fantastic in the Arts* 27, no. 1 (95) (2016): 162–66.

Schopp, Andrew, and Matthew B. Hill. "Attack of the Livid Dead: Recalibrating Terror in the Post-9/11 Zombie Film," in *The War on Terror and American Popular Culture: September 11 and Beyond*, edited by Andrew Schopp and Matthew B. Hill, 239–58. Madison: Fairleigh Dickinson University Press, 2009.

Schrader, Paul. "Notes on Film Noir." *Film Comment* 8, no. 1 (1972): 8–13.

Schweitzer, Dahlia. *Going Viral: Zombies, Viruses, and the End of the World*. New Brunswick: Rutgers University Press, 2018.

——. "Pushing Contagion: How Government Agencies Shape Portrayals of Disease." *Journal of Popular Culture* 50, no. 3 (2017): 445–65.

——. "When Terrorism Met the Plague: How 9/11 Affected the Outbreak Narrative." *Cinema Journal* 56, no. 1 (2016): 118–23.

Seitz, Matt Zoller. "Las Vegas Under Siege by Zombies and a Mutant." *The New York Times*, September 24, 2007. https://www.nytimes.com/2007/09/24/movies/24evil.html.

Shaffer, Marshall. "'Little Joe' Director Jessica Hausner on Combining Genres and Maintaining a Personal Stamp (Interview)." *SlashFilm*, December 6, 2019. https://www.slashfilm.com/little-joe-director-interview/.

Sharma, Devansh. "In Times of Coronavirus Outbreak, Why Steven Soderbergh's 2011 Medical Thriller Contagion Makes for Essential Viewing." *Firstpost*, March 11, 2020. https://www.firstpost.com/entertainment/in-times-of-coronavirus-outbreak-why-steven-soderberghs-2011-medical-thriller-contagion-makes-for-essential-viewing-8138601.html.

Shepherd, Katie, and Niha Masih. "Nearly 15 Million Deaths Related to Covid-19, WHO Estimates." *The Washington Post*, May 5, 2022. https://www.washingtonpost.com/health/2022/05/05/covid-excess-global-deaths-nearly-15-million/.

Shilts, Randy. *And the Band Played On: Politics, People, and the AIDS Epidemic*. New York: St. Martin's Press, 1987.

Slugan, Mario. "Pandemic (Movies): A Pragmatic Analysis of a Nascent Genre." *Quarterly Review of Film and Video* 39, no. 4 (2021): 890–918.

Smith, Jane S. *Patenting the Sun: Polio and the Salk Vaccine*. New York: William Morrow & Co, 1990.

Soles, Carter. "'And No Birds Sing': Discourses of Environmental Apocalypse in *The Birds* and *Night of the Living Dead*." *ISLE: Interdisciplinary Studies in Literature and Environment* 21, no. 3 (2014): 526–37.

Solomon, Dan. "A New Genre of Film Is Already Here: COVID Movies." *Texas Monthly*, March 24, 2021. https://www.texasmonthly.com/arts-entertainment/pandemic-movies-just-getting-started/.

Sontag, Susan. *Illness as Metaphor*. New York: Farrar, Straus and Giroux, 1978.

———. "The Imagination of Disaster." *Commentary*, October 1965. https://www.commentary.org/articles/susan-sontag/the-imagination-of-disaster/.

Sperling, Nicole. "'Contagion,' Steven Soderbergh's 2011 Thriller, Is Climbing Up the Charts." *The New York Times*, March 4, 2020. https://www.nytimes.com/2020/03/04/business/media/coronavirus-contagion-movie.html.

Squakenet, "The Typing of the Dead Gameplay (PC Game, 2000)," February 12, 2015. https://www.youtube.com/watch?v=Zs3M6oDcPlU.

Steel, David. "Plague Writing: From Boccaccio to Camus." *Journal of European Studies* 11, no. 2 (1981): 88–110.

Steffen-Fluhr, Nancy. "Women and the Inner Game of Don Siegel's 'Invasion of the Body Snatchers.'" *Science Fiction Studies* 11, no. 2 (1984): 139–53.

Stern, Alexandra Minna, and Howard Markel. "The Public Health Service and Film Noir: A Look Back at Elia Kazan's *Panic in the Streets* (1950)." *Public Health Reports* 118, no. 3 (2003): 178–83.

Stolberg, Sheryl Gay. "As Poor Nations Seek Covid Pills, Officials Fear Repeat of AIDS Crisis." *The New York Times*, May 8, 2022. https://www.nytimes.com/2022/05/08/us/politics/covid-pills-global-aids-hiv.html.

———. "Biden Says the Pandemic Is Over. But at Least 400 People Are Dying Daily." *The New York Times*, September 19, 2022. https://www.nytimes.com/2022/09/19/us/politics/biden-covid-pandemic-over.html.

Stolberg, Sheryl Gay and Apoorva Mandavilli. "As Monkeypox Spreads, US Declares a Health Emergency," *The New York Times*, August 4, 2022. https://www.nytimes.com/2022/08/04/health/monkeypox-emergency-us.html.

Sturtevant, Paul B. *The Middle Ages in Popular Imagination: Memory, Film and Medievalism*. London: I. B. Tauris, 2018.

Sun, Lena H., and Joel Achenbach. "CDC Loosens Coronavirus Guidance, Signaling Strategic Shift." *The Washington Post*, August 11, 2022. https://www.washingtonpost.com/health/2022/08/11/cdc-coronavirus-recommendations/.

Teachout, Terry. "The Time Has Come Again for 'Panic in the Streets.'" *The Wall Street Journal*, March 4, 2020. https://www.wsj.com/articles/the-time-has-come-again-for-panic-in-the-streets-11583352180.

Tenner, Edward. *The Efficiency Paradox: What Big Data Can't Do*. New York: Knopf Doubleday, 2018.

Tollefson, Jeff, Max Kozlov, Amy Maxmen, and Alexandra Witze. "Has Biden Followed the Science? What Researchers Say." *Nature* 601, no. 7894 (January 2022): 491–93.

Tomes, Nancy. *The Gospel of Germs : Men, Women, and the Microbe in American Life*. Cambridge: Harvard University Press, 1998.

Tomes, Nancy J., and John Harley Warner. "Introduction to Special Issue on Rethinking the Reception of the Germ Theory of Disease: Comparative Perspectives." *Journal of the History of Medicine and Allied Sciences* 52, no. 1 (1997): 7–16.

Toronto International Film Festival, "George A. Romero Interview." November 2, 2012. https://www.youtube.com/watch?v=uCpJKakWVRc.

Trenholm, Richard. "Why Resident Evil Crushes Every Other Video Game Movie." *CNET*, January 25, 2019. https://www.cnet.com/news/resident-evil-the-most-successful-video-game-movie-series-milla-jovovich-paul-ws-anderson/.

Trimble, Sarah. "(White) Rage: Affect, Neoliberalism, and the Family in *28 Days Later* and *28 Weeks Later*." *Review of Education, Pedagogy, and Cultural Studies* 32, no. 3 (2010): 295–322.

Truffaut, Francois. *Hitchcock*. New York: Simon & Schuster, 1967.

Tufekci, Zeynep. "If You're Suffering After Being Sick With Covid, It's Not Just in Your Head." *The New York Times*, August 25, 2022. https://www.nytimes.com/2022/08/25/opinion/long-covid-pandemic.html.

Turkle, Sherry. *Alone Together: Why We Expect More from Technology and Less from Each Other*. New York: Basic Books, 2011.

Turner, Janice. "In Times of Fear We Put Our Faith in Hoarding." *The Times*, March 7, 2020. https://www.thetimes.co.uk/article/in-times-of-fear-we-put-our-faith-in-hoarding-s2zsf599t.

TVEyes – BBC News 24. "A Question of Sport – 01:35 AM GMT." June 4, 2020. https://advance.lexis.com/api/document?collection=news&id=urn:contentItem:5YKP-K5P1-DY08-32YP-00000-00&context=1516831.

United States Constitution, Amendment V.

Ungar, Sheldon. "Global Bird Flu Communication: Hot Crisis and Media Reassurance." *Science Communication* 29, no. 4 (2008): 472–97.

———. "Hot Crises and Media Reassurance: A Comparison of Emerging Diseases and Ebola Zaire." *British Journal of Sociology* 49, no. 1 (1998): 36–56.

Uniting and Strengthening America by Providing Appropriate Tools Required to Intercept and Obstruct Terrorism (USA PATRIOT) Act of 2001, Public Law 107–56, US Statutes at Large: 115 (272).

Valentino-DeVries, Jennifer, Ella Koeze, and Sapna Maheshwari. "Virus Alters Where People Open Their Wallets, Hinting at a Halting Recovery." *The New York Times*, August 19, 2020. https://www.nytimes.com/interactive/2020/08/18/business/economy/coronavirus-economic-recovery-states.html.

Van der Sar, Ernesto. "Coronavirus Outbreak Triggers Surge in Pirated Downloads of the Film 'Contagion.'" *TorrentFreak*, March 7, 2020. https://torrentfreak.com/coronavirus-outbreak-triggers-surge-in-pirated-downloads-of-the-film-contagion/.

Van Noorden, Richard. "COVID Death Tolls: Scientists Acknowledge Errors in WHO Estimates." *Nature* 606, no. 7913 (2022): 242–44.

Vann, Michael G. *The Great Hanoi Rat Hunt: Empire, Disease, and Modernity in French Colonial Vietnam*. New York: Oxford University Press, 2019.

Vargha, Dóra. *Polio Across the Iron Curtain: Hungary's Cold War with an Epidemic*. Cambridge: Cambridge University Press, 2018.

———. "Reconsidering the Dramaturgy." *Bulletin of the History of Medicine* 94, no. 4 (2020): 690–98.

Variety. "Constantin Buys 'Evil' Rights." January 15, 1997. https://web.archive.org/web/20191105095526/https://variety.com/1997/scene/vpage/constantin-buys-evil-rights-1117433527/.

Voltaire, *Candide*. New York: Boni & Liveright, 1918.

Wald, Priscilla. *Contagious: Cultures, Carriers, and the Outbreak Narrative*. Durham, NC: Duke University Press, 2008.

Walker, Ali. "Coronavirus: The Movie." *Politico*, April 1, 2020. https://www.politico.eu/article/coronavirus-the-movie-pandemic/.

Walter, Ben. "Simon Pegg Interviews George A Romero." *The Tomb, Time Out Movie Blog*, September 8, 2005. https://web.archive.org/web/20070217113705/http:/www.timeout.com:80/film/news/631.html.

Wang, Selina. "After 3 years of Covid, CNN went into rural China for Lunar New Year. Here's what we found and how officials tried stopping us." *CNN*, January 27, 2023. https://edition.cnn.com/2023/01/27/china/rural-china-lunar-new-year-COVID-intl-hnk-dst/index.html.

Washer, Peter. *Emerging Infectious Diseases and Society*. New York: Palgrave Macmillan, 2010.

———. "Representations of SARS in the British Newspapers." *Social Science & Medicine* 59, no. 12 (2004): 2561–71.

The Week. "'Contagion' Star Matt Damon Reveals His Eldest Daughter Had Coronavirus in New York." *The Week*, May 14, 2020. https://www.theweek.in/news/entertainment/2020/05/14/contagion-star-matt-damon-reveals-eldest-daughter-had-coronavirus-new-york.html.

Weiner, David. "Why 'Invasion of the Body Snatchers' Still Haunts Its Director." *The Hollywood Reporter*, December 20, 2018. https://www.hollywoodreporter.com/movies/movie-news/invasion-body-snatchers-ending-still-haunts-director-1170220/.

Weinraub, Bernard. "Two Films, One Subject. Uh-Oh. In Hollywood, the Race Is On." *The New York Times*, June 23, 1994. https://www.nytimes.com/1994/06/23/movies/two-films-one-subject-uh-oh-in-hollywood-the-race-is-on.html.

———. "Wrestling a Virus to the Screen." *The New York Times*, March 19, 1995. https://www.nytimes.com/1995/03/19/movies/film-wrestling-a-virus-to-the-screen.html.

Wetmore, Jr., Kevin J. *Back from the Dead: Remakes of the Romero Zombie Films as Markers of Their Times*. Jefferson: McFarland, 2011.

Wheeling, Kate, and Max Ufberg. "'The Ocean Is Boiling': The Complete Oral History of the 1969 Santa Barbara Oil Spill." *Pacific Standard*, April 18, 2017. https://psmag.com/news/the-ocean-is-boiling-the-complete-oral-history-of-the-1969-santa-barbara-oil-spill.

Wilkinson, Alissa. "The 2011 Film Contagion Is Even More Relevant in 2020, and Not Just Because of Coronavirus." *Vox*, February 4, 2020. https://www.vox.com/2020/2/4/21120178/contagion-movie-coronavirus-itunes-fake-news.

Williams, G. Christopher. "Birthing an Undead Family: Reification of the Mother's Role in the Gothic Landscape of 28 Days Later." *Gothic Studies* 9, no. 2 (2007): 33–44.

Williams, Owen. "Resident Evil Movies: The Complete Guide." *Empire*, June 25, 2021. https://www.empireonline.com/movies/features/resident-evil-movies-the-complete-guide/.

Williams, Tony. *The Cinema of George A. Romero: Knight of the Living Dead*. 2nd edition. London: Wallflower Press, 2015.

———. "Doomsday, Past, Present and Future: Kinji Fukasaku's Virus." *Asian Cinema* 19 (2008): 215–31.

———. *George A. Romero: Interviews*. Jackson: University Press of Mississippi, 2011.

Wood, Robin. "Cronenberg: A Dissenting View," in *The Shape of Rage: The Films of David Cronenberg*, edited by Piers Handling, 115–35. Toronto: New York Zoetrope, 1983.

———. "The Dark Mirror: Murnau's Nosferatu," in *Robin Wood on the Horror Film : Collected Essays and Reviews*, edited by Barry Keith Grant, 119–32. Detroit: Wayne State University Press, 2018.

———. *Hollywood from Vietnam to Reagan . . . and Beyond*. Expanded and revised edition. New York: Columbia University Press, 2003.

———. "An Introduction to the American Horror Film," in *American Nightmare: Essays on the Horror Film*, edited by Andrew Britton, 7–28. Toronto: Festival of Festivals, 1979.

———. *Robin Wood on the Horror Film: Collected Essays and Reviews*. Edited by Barry Keith Grant. Detroit: Wayne State University Press, 2018.

World Health Organization. "China: WHO Coronavirus Disease (COVID-19) Dashboard With Vaccination Data." October 8, 2022. https://covid19.who.int.

Wren, Adam. "What I Learned About Coronavirus From Binge-Watching 10 Hours of Virus Movies." *Politico*, March 21, 2020. https://www.politico.com/news/magazine/2020/03/21/pandemic-movies-coronavirus-140043.

Yaffe-Bellany, David, and Michael Corkery. "Dumped Milk, Smashed Eggs, Plowed Vegetables: Food Waste of the Pandemic." *The New York Times*, April 11, 2020. https://www.nytimes.com/2020/04/11/business/coronavirus-destroying-food.html.

Yasharoff, Hannah. "Matt Damon Talks Coronavirus and 'Contagion,' Reveals His Daughter Had Virus 'Early on.'" *USA Today*, May 13, 2020. https://www.usatoday.com/story/entertainment/celebrities/2020/05/13/coronavirus-matt-damon-contagion-daughter-contracting-virus/5181774002/.

Yong, Ed. "What Bill Gates Fears Most." *The Atlantic*, April 27, 2018. https://www.theatlantic.com/science/archive/2018/04/what-bill-gates-fears-most/559007/.

Zhou, Naaman, Christopher Knaus, and Amy Remeikis. "Australian Shares Plunge 6.4% and AFL Season to Start as Planned amid Covid-19 Outbreak – as It Happened." *The Guardian*, March 18, 2020. http://www.theguardian.com/world/live/2020/mar/18/australia-coronavirus-live-updates-test-kits-covid19-nsw-victoria-qld-schools-latest-news-update.

Zimmer, Thomas. *Welt ohne Krankheit Geschichte der internationalen Gesundheitspolitik 1940–1970*. Göttingen: Wallstein Verlag, 2017.

Zinsser, Hans. *Rats, Lice and History*. Boston: Little, Brown, and Company, 1935.

Zuboff, Shoshana. *The Age of Surveillance Capitalism: The Fight for a Human Future at the New Frontier of Power*. New York: PublicAffairs, 2019.

INDEX

Note: Page numbers in *italics* indicate illustrations. 'n' indicates notes.

Adams, Brooke, 117
The Addiction (1995), 137n
After the Pandemic (2022), 164
The Age of Innocence (Wharton; novel), 192
AIDS/HIV, 10, 53, 54, 77n, 125, 161
Airport (1970), 51n
Alice in Wonderland (Carroll; book), 143
Alien franchise
   Alien (1979), 46, 143
   Alien 3 (1985), 46
   Alien: Covenant (2017), 146
   Alien: Resurrection (1997), 153, 154
   Alien vs. Predator (2004), 149n
   Aliens (1986), 46, 146, 159n
   Prometheus (2012), 146
   Resident Evil, influenced by, 46, 143, 146, 153, 154
Altman, Robert, 194
American Westerns, 61, 110, 133n, 200
Amour Fou (2014), 128
And the Band Played On (1993), 77n
Anderson, Paul W. S., 139–40, 143, 156, 157–8n, 158n

The Andromeda Strain (1971), 42, 107n, 165
Animal Farm (Orwell; novel), 103
Antiviral (2012), 105
Anwar, Gabrielle, 120
"The Apocalypse Bug" (CNN special), 2
Apocalypse Now (1979), 104
apocalyptic disease movies *see* post-apocalyptic and posthuman narratives
Army of the Dead (2021), 179, 191n, 198
Ashford, Charles, 152
Austrian movies, 128, 134n
The Avengers (TV series, 1965–1968), 158n
Avengers: Endgame (2019), 141
The Avengers movies, 17

Back to the Future (1985), 46, 108n
Bad Lieutenant (1992), 137n
Basinger, Jeanine, 47n
The Batman (2022), 109n
Beck, Glenn, 169
Beecham, Emily, *128*
Bel Geddes, Barbara, 33, 34
Bergman, Ingmar, 25, 36, 37, 48n, 49n

237

Besson, Luc, 158n
Bezos, Jeff, 174
biblical references, 6–7, 43, 85, 91, 104, 154, 156, 160n
Biden, Joe, 163, 173, 174
Bigelow, Kathryn, 193
Bio Zombie (1998), 80n
biological weapons and bioterrorism, 42, 44, 53, 56, 64, 120, 141, 142, 168
Black Death (fourteenth-century plague outbreak), 13, 25, 36, 86, 88, 200
The Black Death (2010), 86, 88–90, 195, 200–1, *201*
Black Lives Matter movement, 180n
Blade Runner (1982), 46, 109n, 150
bleakness, trend toward, 119, 132, 136–7n, 197–8
Blindness (2008), 105
Blood Quantum (2019), 84
Bloodsuckers from Outer Space (1984), 45
B-movies, 7, 10, 20n, 27, 45
The Body Snatcher (stolen cadaver movie, 1945), 134n
Body Snatchers (1993), 111, 119–23
The Body Snatchers movies (on pod people), 14, 16, 110–33
  adaptations and take-offs, 134n
  Body Snatchers (1993), 111, 119–23
  capitalism in, 111, 117, 132, 133, 138n
  environmental concerns in, 117, 120, 136n
  family and marriage in, 115–16, 118, 121, 126, 127
  Finney novel inspiring, 110, 111, 112, 113, 117, 127, 132, 133–4n, 137n
  gender/race issues in, 111, 112, 113, 115–16, 118, 122, 123, 125–7, 132, 133, 135–6n, 135n
  government and military, critiques of, 122–3, 127, 136n
  human nature as problem, in *The Invasion*, 125–7
  The Invasion (2007), 84, 111, 123–7, *124*, 130, 132, 195
  Invasion of the Body Snatchers (1956), 9, 43, 107n, 111, 113–16, *114*, 117, 119, 120, 126, 132, 138n
  Invasion of the Body Snatchers (1978), 9, 111, 116–19, 120, 129, 132, 136n

Little Joe (2019), 111, 127–32, *128*, 133, 137n, 138n, 198
  The Matrix influenced by, 197
  posthumanism of *Little Joe*, 127–32, 133
  remakes, changes across eras revealed by, 110–12, 133n
  Resident Evil franchise compared, 157
  social conformity in, 111, 113–16, 119, 120–2, 132–3, 135n
  They Live (1988) compared, 46
Bogdanovich, Peter, 79n
Bonnie and Clyde (1967), 136n
Das Boot (1981), 56
Boyle, Danny, 77–8n, 80n, 81n
Brilliant, Larry, 169
Bringing Up Baby (1938), 79n
British movies, 55, 56, 63, 65–7, 74–5, 80n, 84, 88–90, 107n, 128, 167
The Brood (1979), 50n
Burns, Scott, 169
Burrell, Ty, 70

Cabin Fever (2002), 73–4
Canadian movies, 25–6, 42–3, 44, 50n, 84
Candide (Voltaire; novel), 138n
Cannes Film Festival, 120
Capcom, 139, 156
capitalism
  in *Body Snatchers* movies, 111, 117, 132, 133, 138n
  consumer capitalism critiqued, 68–73, 79n
  COVID-19 pandemic and, 175–6, 177
  disease linked directly to, 83n, 102
  as driver of change in American society and disease movies, 4–5
  in early disease movies, 9, 25, 27, 28, 33, 46
  global capitalism, 4–6, 14, 18n, 63–4, 85, 90, 96, 156, 175–6, 177
  informational capitalism, 100
  post-apocalyptic/posthuman narratives and, 14, 16, 84, 85–6, 87, 90, 96, 100, 102, 103, 106, 196–7
  in *Resident Evil* franchise, 141–2, 144, 152, 156
  surveillance capitalism, 18–19n
Carpenter, John, 46, 159n

Carriers (2009), 105
Carroll, Lewis, 143
Carson, Rachel, 10
Cartwright, Veronica, 117, 137n
Center for Global Health and Security, Georgetown University, 168
Centers for Disease Control and Prevention (CDC), 13, 61, 92, 93, 123, 132, 168, 172
Chelebourg, Christian, 182n
Children of Men (2006), 86–8, *88*, 89, 90, 101, 190n, 195
China
  in *Contagion*, 91, 94
  COVID-19 in, 161, 164, 168, 175, 185n, 189n, 198
  in *I Am Legend* (novel), 41
  in *The Invasion*, 125
  28 Days Later based on incident in, 80n
  Virus, absence from, 51n
chloroquine/hydroxychloroquine, in COVID outbreak, 170, 187n
cholera, 25, 27
Civil Rights movement, 25, 40, 41
classical mythology, references to, 6–7, 66, 101, 108n, 192, *193*
Cloverfield (2008), 109n
CNN, 168
Cohen, Larry, 46
Cold War, 9, 10, 26, 30, 38, 44–5, 49n, 56–7, 63, 112, 113, 119–20, 134–5n, 194–5
Collins, Margo, 158n
colonialism
  globalization of diseases and, 7, 10–11
  "the other"/foreign sources, in early disease movies, 7–8, 9, 24–8, 30–2, 34, 194
Columbia University School of Public Health, 169
comedies
  COVID-19 pandemic and, 164
  parodic post-apocalyptic/posthuman movies, 13, 84, 96–7, 105, 107n, 195–6
  removal of comic dialogue from 1957 *Invasion of the Body Snatchers*, 136n
  screwball comedies, 62, 79n
  see also romantic comedies

The Coming Plague (Garrett; book), 2
Communism, 31, 48n, 113, 134n
conformity, social, 111, 113–16, 119, 120–2, 132–3, 135n
Connor, Kit, 128
Connors, Chuck, 51n
Constantin Film, 139, 140, 156
Contagion (2011)
  COVID-19 pandemic and, 162, 163–4, *165*, 166, 168–74, 177, 178, 184–5n, 186n, 199
  false cure (forsythia) in, 94, 170, 173
  marginalized people/communities, failure to consider, 191
  as post-apocalyptic film, 13, 78n, 85–6, 90–6, *95*, 97, 101, 108n, 195
  scientific realism, claims of, 91, 94, 168–9
containment narratives
  early disease movies, successful containment in, 3, 8, 24–8, 30–3, 35–6, 38, 42
  nostalgia for imagined containment in *Resident Evil* (2002), 142–6, 156
  post-apocalyptic and posthuman narratives, failure of containment in, 3, 12–13, 14, 84–5, 150
  rise of viral disease movies and threats to containment, 3, 10, 12, 14, 55, 56–63, 195
Corona (2020), 164
Corona Zombies (2020), 164, 181n
Cotillard, Marion, 93, 169
counterculture, in *Invasion of the Body Snatchers* (1978), 116–19
COVID-19 pandemic, 6, 12, 16, 161–80, 198–200
  Andromeda Strain and, 165
  capitalism and, 175–6, 177
  CDC, critiques of, 132
  consumption of disease movies during, 162, 163–4, 179
  Contagion and, 162, 163–4, *165*, 166, 168–74, 177, 178, 184–5n, 186n, 199
  disconnect between disease movies and real pandemic experience, 163, 170–8, 200
  disease movies influenced by, 164, 179, 202

COVID-19 pandemic (*cont.*)
  disease movies shaping real-world responses to, 162, 164–70, *165*, *166*, 179
  dramatic arc of Hollywood stories versus, 177–8
  global politics of, 174–6
  heroic action, expectations regarding, 172, 188n
  hospital videos during, 204n
  I Am Legend and, 167
  lethality of movie viruses versus, 171–2
  origins of disease, search for, 107n, 168, 185n
  Outbreak and, 54, 164, 165, 168, 171, 177, 199
  Panic in the Streets and, 165, 168, 177, 199
  Planet of the Apes and, 85, 170
  political behavior during, 161, 163, 169–70, 172–3
  post-apocalyptic/posthuman movie trend and, 196
  science and technology, attitudes toward, 106, 161–2, 178, 188n, 199–200
  societal collapse, fears of, 162, 171, 199
  structural change not resulting from, 162–3
  structural effects of gender, race, age and socioeconomics, 16, 163, 173–8
  12 Monkeys and, *166*
  28 Days Later and, 162, 166–8, 170, 171, 173
  vaccines for, 161, 170–1, 173, 176–8, 188n, 199–200, 202–3
  World War Z and, 165, *166*, 168
Craig, Daniel, 123
Crawfurd, Raymond, 7
The Crazies (1973), 42, 107n
Cries and Whispers (1972), 49n
"Crisis in the Hot Zone" (Preston; *New Yorker* article), 1, 54
Crockett, Davy, 73
Cronenberg, David, 42, 50n, 51n
cures
  disease cures leading to pandemics, in movies, 83n, 84, 85, 100, 154
  forsythia in *Contagion*, 94, 170, 173
hydroxychloroquine/chloroquine, in COVID outbreak, 170, 187n; *see also* vaccines
Curtis, Daniel, 16

The Daily Star (newspaper), 167
Damon, Matt, 91, *165*, 169, 174
Dark City (1998), 159n
The Dark Knight Rises (2012), 141
Davis, Bette, 47n
Dawn of the Dead (1978), 56, 67–8, 144
Dawn of the Dead (2004), 56, 67–73, *69*, 76, 77, 82–3n, 120, 179
Dawn of the Planet of the Apes (2014), 85, 100, 103–4, 109
Day of the Dead (1985), 45–6
The Day the Earth Stood Still (1951), 183n
The Dead Don't Die (2019), 84, 105–6, 195, 198
The Deer Hunter (1978), 136–7n
Defoe, Daniel, 7, 15
Dempsey, Patrick, 58
Diary of the Dead (2007), 15
Dieterle, Daniel, 29
Directors' Guild of America, 169
disaster movies, 10, 17, 42–4, 51n
disease movies, 1–17, 192–203
  American culture, as means of understanding, 3–6
  bleakness, trend toward, 119, 132, 136–7n, 197–8
  capitalism as driver of change in, 4–5
  COVID-19 pandemic and, 6, 12, 16, 161–80, 198–200; *see also* COVID-19 pandemic
  early disease movies (to early 1990s), 6–10, 24–47, 194; *see also* early disease movies
  function of, 200–3
  historical arc/periodization of, 3, 15–16, 192–6
  infectious disease epidemics, mid-1990s concerns about, 1–3
  post-apocalyptic and posthuman narratives (2006–present), 12–17, 84–106, 195–8; *see also* post-apocalyptic and posthuman narratives

remakes, changes across eras revealed by, 110–12
rise of viral disease movies (mid-1990s to 2007), 10–12, 53–77, 194–5; see also rise of viral disease movies
video, online and board games compared, 16–17, 69, 80n
Douglas, Paul, 32, *33*
Dr. Ehrlich's Magic Bullet (1940), 29, 29–30, 194
Dr. Strangelove (1964), 45
Dracula (1931), 26
Dracula (Stoker; novel), 7
Dworet, Lawrence, 57–8, 78n

early disease movies (to early 1990s), 6–10, 24–47, 194
  B-movies versus mainstream movies, 7–8, 10, 20n
  capitalism in, 9, 25, 27, 28, 33, 46
  containment narratives of, 3, 8, 24–8, 30–3, 35–6, 38, 42
  existing social values, confirmation of, 24–8, 30–1, 35–6, 41, 43
  family and marriage in, 25, 33–4, 37, 38–9
  gender/race issues in, 15, 25, 26–7, 28, 30, 34, 35, 38, 39–41, 50n
  government and military, critiques of, 41, 42, 44–5
  heroic public servants in, 9, 28–30, 32–6, 42, 194
  individual choice/individualism in, 3, 29, 32, 35, 36–7, 45–7
  literary origins of, 6–7
  optimism of, 24–5, 42, 46–7
  "the other"/foreign sources, focus on, 7–8, 9, 24–8, 30–2, 34, 194
  personal redemption, disease as means of, 35–7
  pre-World War II movies, 25, 26–30
  Reagan years, shift in cultural ideology, and hiatus in, 45–6
  scientific and technological advancement, reflecting, 7, 8–9, 24, 28–9, 42
  societal ills, disease as means of exploring, 9–10, 20n, 25–6, 33–4, 36–7, 38–46
  zombies, 7–8, 26–7, 38–41, 46

Earth Day, 10
Earthquake (1974), 51n
East, Jamie, 167
East of Eden (1955), 47n
Eastman, Marilyn, 39
Easy Rider (1969), 136n
Ebert, Roger, 109n, 140
Ebola, 1–3, 12, 54, 56, 58, 78n, 81n, 106, 194
Ehle, Jennifer, 93, 169
Eisenberg, Jesse, 108n
Eliot, George, 192
Elise, Christine, 121
emerging infectious diseases, 10, 13, 53–4
The End of Us (2021), 164
environmental concerns
  in *Body Snatchers* movies, 117, 120, 136n
  in *Night of the Living Dead*, 49n
  in post-apocalyptic and posthuman narratives, 95, 106
  in viral disease movies from mid-1990s, 10, 11, 54, 65–6, 78n, 79n
Erin Brockovich (2000), 90
Ermey, R. Lee, 122
Escape from New York (1981), 159n
The Escapist (2008), 109n
eXistenZ (1999), 50n

A Face in the Crowd (1957), 47n
The Faculty (1998), 134n
false cures
  forsythia in *Contagion*, 94, 170, 173
  hydroxychloroquine/chloroquine, in COVID outbreak, 170, 187n
family and marriage
  in *Body Snatchers* movies, 115–16, 118, 121, 126, 127
  in *Contagion*, 91–3
  in *Dawn of the Dead* remake, 72–3
  in *Living Dead* movies, 15, 25, 38–9, 194
  in *Outbreak*, 59–62
  in *Panic in the Streets*, 33–4
  patriarchal hero, nostalgia for, in *Zombieland* and *World War Z*, 86, 96–9
  in *Rise of the Planet of the Apes*, 102
  in *Seventh Seal*, 37
  in *28 Days Later*, 66–7

Fanny and Alexander (1983), 48n
fascism, 27
Fauci, Anthony, 174, 188n
Fehr, Oded, 148
feminism *see* gender/race issues
Ferndale, CA, filming of *Outbreak* in, 79n
Ferrara, Albert, 120, 137n
The Fifth Element (1997), 158n
Fight Club (1999), 108n
film noir, 31, 33, 36, 48n, 135n
Final Cut (2022), 84
Finney, Jack, 110, 112, 132, 137n
Fishburne, Lawrence, 92, 169, 197
Flight of the Living Dead (2007), 107n
Floyd, George, 174, 180n
Flu (2013), 105
The Fly (1986), 50n
Ford, Glenn, 51n
Ford, John, 193, 200
Foree, Ken, 67–8, 70–1
foreign sources, movie diseases originating with, 7–8, 9, 24–8, 30–2, 34, 194
Four Weddings and a Funeral (1994), 79n
4:44 Last Day (2011), 137n
Franco, James, 101
Frankenstein (Shelley; novel), 101, 109n, 109n, 138n, 153
Freeman, Morgan, 1, 56
French movies, 84
Fukasaku, Kinji, 44, 51n
Full Metal Jacket (1987), 122

Garland, Alex, 77–8n, 81n
Gates, Larry, 114
gender/race issues
  in *Body Snatchers* movies, 111, 112, 113, 115–16, 118, 122, 123, 125–7, 132, 133, 135–6n, 135n
  COVID-19 pandemic and structural effects of, 16, 163, 173–8
  in early disease movies, 15, 25, 26–7, 28, 30, 34, 35, 38, 39–41, 50n
  global capitalism and, 5, 6
  origins of female action heroes, 158n
  "the other"/foreigners as disease vectors, 7–8, 9, 24–8, 30–2, 34
  in post-apocalyptic and posthuman narratives, 13, 84, 88, 98, 100, 104

Resident Evil franchise, female lead in, 141–2
  rise of viral disease movies and, 58–9, 64, 67, 70, 72, 82n
  sexualization of female action heroes, 159n
Gentlemen's Agreement (1947), 47n
Gerlach, Neil, 14
germ theory, 7, 24
German movies, 88–90, 128, 139
Gilliam, Terry, 63
Girard, René, 9, 47n
The Girlfriend Experience (2009), 90
Gladwell, Malcolm, 12
Glen, Iain, 147
global capitalism, 4–6, 14, 18n, 63–4, 85, 90, 96, 156, 175–6, 177
global politics and COVID-19, 174–6
global recession (2008), 195
globalization, 7, 10–12, 14, 18n, 53–5, 57, 59, 63–4, 76, 125
Goldblum, Jeff, 118
Gone with the Wind (1939), 47n
government and military
  in *Body Snatchers* movies, 122–3, 127, 136n
  COVID-19 pandemic, political behavior during, 161, 163, 169–70, 172–3
  in early disease movies, 41, 42, 44–5
  in *Outbreak* (1995), 59–61, 79n
  in post-apocalyptic/posthuman narratives, 92, 98–9, 104
  in *Resident Evil* franchise, 147–8, 150
The Graduate (1967), 136n
Green Light (1937), 28–9
Griffith, D. W., 193
Groundhog Day (1994), 79n
The Guardian (newspaper), 167
Guardians of the Galaxy (2014, 2017), 68
Gulf War, 120
Gunn, James, 68, 72, 82–3n

Halloween III: Season of the Witch (1983), 134n
Hamilton, Sheryl, 14
Han, Chin, 93
Han, Qijun, 16
Hardman, Karl, 39

INDEX

Harper, Stephen, 159n
Harrelson, Woody, 104
Harris, Jared, 148
#Alive (2020), 105
Hausner, Jessica, 128, 129, 132, 137n, 138n
Hebrew Bible, mass destruction narratives in, 6–7
Heinlein, Robert, 108n, 134n
heroic action
  in *Body Snatchers* movies, 118
  in COVID-19 pandemic, 172, 188n
  in early disease movies, 9, 28–30, 32–6, 194
  patriarchal hero, nostalgia for, 86, 96–9
  post-apocalyptic/posthuman narratives, individual heroism in, 85, 88, 90–6
  in *Resident Evil* movies, 146
  rise of viral disease movies from mid-1990s and, 12, 55, 57, 60–1, 76–7
Heston, Charlton, 100, 101, 104
Hirschbiegel, Oliver, 123
historical arc/periodization of disease movies, 3, 15–16, 192–6
Hitchcock, Alfred, 38, 49n
HIV/AIDS, 10, 53, 54, 77n, 125, 161
Hobbes, Thomas, 42, 43, 50n, 125
Hoffman, Dustin, 1, 2, 56, 62, 78n
Homer, 118, 192
horror and science fiction genres, combination of, 15, 46, 106
The Hot Zone (Preston; book), 1–2, 54, 78n, 80n, 147
House Committee on Un-American Activities (HUAC), 48n
House of the Dead (1996), 65
human nature as problem, in *The Invasion* (2007), 125–7
Hussein, Sadam, 80n
Hussey, Olivia, 51n
hydroxychloroquine/chloroquine, in COVID outbreak, 170, 187n

I Am Legend (2007 movie), 74, 83n, 84, 167
I Am Legend (Matheson; novel), 38, 41–2, 74
I Married A Monster from Space (1958), 134n
I Walked with a Zombie (1943), 27

I Was a Teenage Zombie (1987), 10
Iliad (Homer; epic), 192, *193*
imperialism, 11, 59, 83n, 101, 109n
In the Line of Fire (1993), 56
India in 1900, socioeconomic status and death rates in, 190n
Indian Ocean tsunami (2004), 76
individual choice/individualism
  Body Snatchers movies and, 14, 117–18, 121–2
  in early disease movies, 3, 29, 32, 35, 36–7, 45–7
  global capitalism and, 4–5, 17
  human nature as problem, in *The Invasion* (2007), 125–7
  in post-apocalyptic/posthuman narratives, 90–6
  in *Resident Evil* movies and, 146
  rise of disease movies and, 55–7, 59, 61, 63, 64, 67, 71–3
infertility pandemic, in *Children of Men* (2006), 86–8
Influenza Pandemic (1918–1920), 8, 13
informational capitalism, 100
Invaders from Mars (1953), 134n
The Invasion (2007), 84, 111, 123–7, *124*, 130, 132, 195
Invasion of the Body Snatchers (1956), 9, 43, 107n, 111, 113–16, *114*, 117, 119, 120, 126, 132, 138n
Invasion of the Body Snatchers (1978), 9, 111, 116–19, 120, 129, 132, 136n, 136n
Invasion of the Pod People (2007), 134n
Invisible Adversaries (1977), 134n
Iraq War (2003–2011), 75, 76, 125
It Came from Outer Space (1953), 134n
It's A Wonderful Life (1946), 45

Jameson, Fredric, 52n, 138n
Japanese movies, 26, 43–5, 51n, 65, 84, 139, 157n
Jaws (1975), 58, 137n
Jenkins, Barry, 164
La Jetée (1962), 63
Jews and Judaism, 7, 26, 30, 47n
Jezebel (1938), 9, 28, 46, 47n
Jones, Alex, 169

243

Jones, Duane, 40, 50n
A Journal of the Plague Year (Defoe; book), 7, 15
Jovovich, Milla, 140, *145*, 154, 158n
Junk (2000), 80n
Justice League (2017), 68

Kaufman, Philip, 116–17, 119, 126, 132, 136n
Kazan, Elia, 30, 31, 47–8n
Kennedy, George, 51n
Kennedy, Robert, 41
Kidman, Nicole, 123, *124*
Kikwit, Zaire, Ebola outbreak in, 1–2, 11, 54
The Killer that Stalked New York (1950), 36, 46, 194
King, Martin Luther, Jr., 41, 50n
King Lear (Shakespeare; play), 192
King of the Zombies (1941), 27
Knöppler, Christian, 134n, 136n
Kopelson, Arnold, 78n
Korean movies, 13, 84, 105
Korobkina, Inna, 68

Land of the Dead (2005), 74
Larter, Ali, 148
The Last Man (Shelley; novel), 7
The Last Man on Earth (1964), 37–8, 41–2
The Last Picture Show (1971), 136n
Law, Jude, 92
Lederberg, Joshua, 54, 64
Lee, Spike, 194
Leibniz, Gottfried, 138n
Leno, Jay, 69
Let Me In (2010), 109n
Leto, Jared, 167
Lewton, Val, 134n
LGBTQ+ community, 10, 53, 71, 72
Life Force (1985), 80n
Lipkin, Ian, 169, 187n
Lithgow, John, 101
Little Joe (2019), 111, 127–32, *128*, 133, 137n, 138n, 198
Locked Down (2021), 164
The Lonely Crowd (Reisman; book), 135n
Longtime Companion (1989), 10, 77n
Los Angeles Times, 184–5n

Lourdes (2009), 128
Lugosi, Bela, 26, 27
Lynteris, Christos, 13

Mabius, Eric, 143
McCarthy, Joe, 134n
McCarthy, Kevin, 113, 119
McElroy, Alan, 157n
MacGuffin, 38, 49n
Maggie (2015), 105
mainstream vs. B-movies, 8, 20n
Mainwaring, Daniel, 135n
malaria, 3
mall, *Dawn of the Dead* movies set in, 67–73
Man of Steel (2013), 68
The Man Who Shot Liberty Valence (1962), 200
Mann, Katrina, 135n
marginalized people/communities
    COVID-19 pandemic, structural effects of, 16, 163, 173–8
    disease control based on quarantining of, 24–5, 26
    in film versus actual disease outbreaks, 6
    movies' failure to fully treat, 197
    "the other"/foreigners, in early disease movies, 7–8, 9, 24–8, 30–2, 34, 194
    see also gender/race issues
Marley, Bob, 74
marriage *see* family and marriage
Marshall Plan, 32
Marxism, 27
Matheson, Richard, 37–8, 41
The Matrix (1999), 146, 150, 151, 197–8
Mayhem (2017), 105
Mears, Erin, 172
MERS, 13, 106, 198
Meteor (1979), 51n
Middlemarch (Eliot; novel), 192
military *see* government and military
Mills, C. Wright, 135n
monkeypox, 163, 200, 204–5n
Monty Python, 63, 107n
Mortal Kombat (1995), 140
Mostel, Zero, 33
Ms. 45 (1981), 137n
Murphy, Cillian, *65*, 167

Murphy, Reilly, 120
Murray, Bill, 97

Napoleon III (emperor), 9
Nature Medicine (journal), 185n
Nelson, Erika, 135n
neoliberalism, 4, 46, 52n
New Deal order, 4
New York Post (newspaper), 165
New York Times (newspaper), 1, 165
New Yorker (magazine), 1, 54, 140
Nietzsche, Friedrich, 109n
Night of the Creeps (1986), 45
Night of the Living Dead (1968), 9–10, 15, 25–6, 38–41, 46, 194
  Body Snatchers movies and, 117
  Dawn of the Dead compared, 67, 73
  origins of disease in, 49n, 107n
  Resident Evil franchise and, 139, 143
  Shivers and *Virus* compared, 42, 43
  still from, 39
  28 Weeks Later compared, 74
Nimoy, Leonard, 117, 136n
9/11, 11, 53, 64, 65, 70, 76, 147, 160n, 195
99 River Street (1953), 48n
Nixon presidency, 117
noir films, 31, 33, 36, 48n, 135n
Northam, Jeremy, 123
Nosferatu: A Symphony of Horror (1922), 7, 8, 26
nuclear weapons, 45, 100, 113, 125

Ocean movies (2001, 2004, 2007), 90
O'Dea, Judith, 39
O'Donnell, Rosie, 69
Olmos, Edward James, 51n
The Omega Man (1971), 41–2
On the Waterfront (1954), 47n
One Cut of the Dead (2017), 84
O'Neal, Ryan, 62
Orwell, George, 103
"the other," in early disease movies, 7–8, 9, 24–8, 30–2, 34, 194
Outbreak (1995), 1–2, 11–12, 54, 55, 56–63, 76, 194–5
  Body Snatchers (1993) compared, 120, 122
  Contagion (2011) compared, 95
  COVID-19 pandemic and, 54, 164, 165, 168, 171, 177, 199
  Dawn of the Dead (2004) compared, 76, 77
  Ferndale, CA, filming in, 79n
  government and military critiqued in, 59–61, 79n
  as initial "pandemic genre" movie, 17n
  Panic in the Streets, *Outbreak* as working title of, 78n13
  Panic in the Streets compared, 55, 56–7, 58, 59, 61, 63
  production issues with, 78n
  Resident Evil (2002) compared, 143, 146
  as romantic comedy, 62
  scientific realism, claims of, 57–8, 78n
  stills from, 2, 60
  12 Monkeys compared, 63–4
outbreak narrative, development of, 12, 58–62
outer space, disease originating from, 9, 38, 42
Oyelowo, David, 102

Pacific Liner (1939), 27–8, 194, 196
The Painted Veil (1934), 27
Palance, Jack, 31
Paltrow, Gwyneth, 91, 95, 169, 184n
Pandemic (2016), 105
Pandemic (board game), 16
pandemic narratives and the pandemic imaginary, 12–13
Panic in the Streets (1950), 9, 30–6, 46
  Body Snatchers novel compared, 112, 113
  Contagion compared, 92, 93
  COVID-19 pandemic and, 165, 168, 177, 199
  heroic public servants in, 9, 30, 32–6, 194
  Night of the Living Dead compared, 38, 41
  "the other," in early disease movies, and, 25–6, 30–2, 34, 48n, 194
  Outbreak as working title of, 78n
  Outbreak compared, 55, 56–7, 58, 59, 61, 63
  pneumonic plague in, 31, 48n, 199
  potential global spread of disease in, 203n

245

Panic in the Streets (1950) (*cont.*)
   Seventh Seal compared, 36, 37
   Shivers compared, 43
   still from, *33*
   World War Z compared, 98
Parasite (1982), 10
Pasteur, Louis, 9, 29
Pax Americana, 53, 76
periodization of disease movies, 3, 15–16
Persona (1966), 48n
personal redemption, disease as means of, 35–7
Petersen, Wolfgang, 56
Phifer, Mekhi, 68
Philadelphia (1993), 10, 77n
Pitt, Brad, 79n, 108n
plague
   AIDS as Black Death of twentieth century, 10
   Black Death (fourteenth-century plague outbreak), 13, 25, 36, 86, 88, 200
   The Black Death (2010 movie), 86, 88–90, 195, 200–1, *201*
   pneumonic plague, in *Panic In the Streets,* 31, 48n, 199
   The Seventh Seal (1957), 6, 25, 36–7, 46–7, 86, 89, 90, 200, 201, *202*
Plague (2014), 105
Plague Inc. (online game), 16
Planet of the Apes, original franchise (1968–1973), 100, 101, 103, 104–5
Planet of the Apes, twenty-first century trilogy (2011–2017), 14, 85–6, 100–5, 107n, 170
pneumonic plague, 31, 48n, 199
pod people movies *see Body Snatchers* movies
Polidori, John, 7
polio, 202–3
politics *see* government and military
Polley, Sarah, 68
Pontypool (2008), 84
Pool, Robert Roy, 78n
The Poseidon Adventure (1972), 10, 51n
Postal (2007), 107n
post-apocalyptic and posthuman narratives (2006–present), 12–17, 84–106, 195–8
   capitalism in, 14, 16, 84, 85–6, 87, 90, 96, 100, 102, 103, 106, 196–7
   concept of posthumanism, 5, 18–19n
   containment, failure of, 3, 12–13, 14, 84–5, 150
   COVID-19 pandemic and, 196
   development of, in *Body Snatcher* franchise (*Little Joe,* 2019), 127–32, 133
   development of, in *Resident Evil* franchise, 141, 142, 147–57
   environmental issues in, 95, 106
   failure of modern social contract explored in, 14
   family and marriage in, 86, 91–3, 96–9, 102
   gender/race issues in, 13, 84, 88, 98, 100, 104
   in genres other than disease movies, 17
   government and military, critiques of, 92, 98–9, 104
   happy endings, mid-1990s/2000s disease movies moving away from, 55–6, 63–7, 70–5
   hope and pessimism for posthuman societies, 100–5
   horror and science fiction genres combined in, 15, 106
   individual heroic action in, 85, 88, 90–6
   Japanese precursor to (*Virus,* 1980), 43–5, 90
   pandemic narratives and the pandemic imaginary, 12–13, 14
   parodic and comedic movies, 13, 84, 96–7, 105, 107n
   patriarchal hero, nostalgia for, 86, 96–9
   science and technology, failures of, 87, 100, 106
   social collapse and disintegration in, 84–5, 86, 90–6, 152, 196
   spiritual faith in, 86–90
   surveillance in, 196–7
   unrealistic assumptions about disease effects, 12, 16
   zombie movies, 13–14, 64–5, 84
Preston, Richard, 1–2, 12, 54, 80n, 147
Pretty Woman (1990), 79n
Project Nim (2011), 107n
Prometheus (2012), 146

Psycho (1960), 38–9
The Puppet Masters (Heinlein; novel), 134n

Rabid (1977), 9, 10, 50n, 51n, 107n
race/racism *see* gender/race issues
Reagan, Ronald, and Reaganism, 45, 46, 133n
Recovery (2021), 164
Reeves, Matt, 103, 109n
Reichardt, Kelly, 194
religion *see* spiritual faith
remakes, changes across eras revealed by, 110–12, 133n
Resident Evil franchise, 14, 16, 139–57, 195
  Alien franchise, influence of, 46, 143, 146, 153, 154; *see also Alien* franchise
  capitalism in, 141–2, 144, 152, 156
  corporate America, critique of, 141, 142, 144–6, 148, 150, 153–4, 156
  critical and popular reception of, 140–1, 155–6, 158n
  female lead in, 141–2
  government and military, critiques of, 147–8, 150
  historical trajectory of disease movies followed by, 142, 146–7, 151–2, 156
  inconsistencies within, 140, 147, 148, 152–3, 159n, 160n
  individualistic heroism in, 146
  The Matrix, influence of, 146, 150, 151, 197
  post-apocalyptism and posthumanism in, 141, 142, 147–57
Resident Evil (2002), 139–40, 142–6, *145*, 152
Resident Evil (TV series, 2022), 156
Resident Evil: Afterlife (2010), 140, 142, 146–7, 149, 151
Resident Evil: Apocalypse (2004), 79n24, 140, 142, 146–8, 151, 152, 159n, 160n
Resident Evil: Extinction (2007), 84, 140, 142, 146–7, 148–9, 151, 152, 159n, 160n, 195
Resident Evil: The Final Chapter (2016), 85, 140, 142, 152–5, *155*, 156, 159n, 160n, 195

Resident Evil: Infinite Darkness (anime TV series, 2021), 156
Resident Evil: Retribution (2012), 140, 142, 146–7, 149–51, *151*, 152, 160n
Resident Evil: Welcome to Racoon City (2021), 156
  Romero and, 139, 157n, 159n
  spiritual faith in, 154, 160n
  surveillance in, 196–7
  video game, 16, 65, 139, 157n
Reston, VA, monkey virus outbreak in, 54
Return of the Living Dead (1985), 80n
Revenge of the Zombies (1943), 27
Reynolds, Burt, 69
Rhames, Ving, 68
Ridley, Judith, 39
Riesman, David, 135n
Rigg, Diana, 158n
The Right Stuff (1983), 136n
The Rise of the Planet of the Apes (2011), 85, 100–5, *103*, 107n, 109n
rise of viral disease movies (mid-1990s to 2007), 10–12, 53–77, 194–5
  containment, threats to, 3, 10, 12, 14, 55, 56–63, 195
  emergence of new infectious diseases influencing, 10, 53–4
  environmental concerns and, 10, 11, 54, 65–6, 78n, 79n
  family and marriage in, 59–62, 66–7, 72–3
  fast zombies, development of, 55, 65, 69, 80n
  gender/race issues, 58–9, 64, 67, 70, 72, 82n
  globalization of economy/ communications/diseases and, 10–11, 53–5, 57, 59, 63–4, 76
  happy endings, move away from, 55–6, 63–7, 70–5
  heroic action in, 12, 55, 57, 60–3, 76–7
  individual choice/individualism in, 55–7, 59, 61, 63, 64, 67, 71–3
  insecurity and uncertainty, American sense of, 2–3, 11–12, 54–5, 59–60, 62, 64–5, 69–70, 76–7
  outbreak narrative, development of, 12, 58–62
  scientific realism and, 57–8

247

A River Runs Through It (1992), 108n
Roberts, Shawn, 149
Robocop (1987 and 2014), 109n, 133n
Rocky Mountain spotted fever, 28–9
Rodriguez, Michelle, 143
romantic comedies
  COVID-19 pandemic and, 164
  mid-1990s resurgence of, 62, 79n
  Outbreak (1995) as, 62
  zombie movies as, 13–14, 105
Romero, George
  American culture, critiquing, 20n
  Dawn of the Dead (1978) and, 56, 67–8
  Dawn of the Dead (2004) and, 83n
  Night of the Living Dead (1968) and, 9, 15, 38, 41, 42, 46, 49n, 67, 73, 74, 143
  on race in *Night of the Living Dead*, 50n
  Resident Evil franchise and, 139, 157n, 159n
  28 Days Later rejecting format of, 65
Rosenberg, Charles, 12
Ross, Gaylen, 68
Russia *see* Cold War; Communism; Soviet Union/Russia
Russo, Rene, 1, 56, 58, 62
Russo brothers, 193
Rwandan genocide, 80n

Salk, Jonas, 202–3
SARS, 13, 106, 124, 198
Sawdust and Tinsel (1953), 48n
Scanners (1981), 50n
Scenes from a Marriage (1973), 48n
Schwarzenegger, Arnold, 105
Schweitzer, Dahlia, 14
science fiction
  combinations of horror and science fiction genres, 15, 46, 106
  filling gap of disease movies in 1980s and early 1990s, 46
  in post-apocalyptic/posthuman narratives, 85
  Susan Sontag on, 203–4n
scientific and technological advancement
  AIDS epidemic overturning earlier assumptions about, 10
  in *Body Snatchers* films, 124
  Contagion's claims of scientific realism, 91, 94, 168–9
  COVID-19 pandemic and attitudes toward, 106, 161–2, 178, 188n, 199–200
  cures for diseases leading to pandemics, 83n, 84, 85, 100, 154
  early disease movies reflecting, 7, 8–9, 24, 28–9, 42
  modern lack of faith in, 15, 42
  Outbreak's claims of scientific realism, 57–8, 78n
  popularity of science fiction movies and, 46
  post-apocalyptic/posthuman narratives showing failure of, 87, 100, 106
  utopianism, technological, 8–9, 133, 157, 178, 195, 196
screwball comedies, 62, 79n
"The Second Coming" (Yeats; poem), 202
Serkis, Andy, 101
The Seventh Seal (1957), 6, 25, 36–7, 46–7, 86, 89, 90, 200, 201, 202
Sex, Lies, and Videotape (1989), 90
sexual revolution, 25–6, 42–3
Shakespeare, William, 192
Shaun of the Dead (2004), 107n
Shelley, Mary, 7, 15, 109n
Shivers (1976), 9, 25–6, 42–3, 46, 50n, 194
Side Street (1950), 48n
Siegel, Don, 113–14, 116, 119, 132, 134–5n, 134n, 135n, 136n, 138n
Silent Spring (Carson; book), 10
slaves and slavery, 28
Sleepless in Seattle (1993), 79n
Slugan, Mario, 16
smallpox, 36, 200
small-town America
  in *Body Snatchers* movies, 111, 112, 115, 116–17, 132, 135n
  globalization and disintegration of, 76
  in *Outbreak*, 1, 57, 59–60, 62, 64
Smiles of a Summer Night (1955), 48n
Snowden, Edward, 159n
Snyder, Zack, 68, 179
The Social Network (2010), 108n
society/societal values

confirmations of, in early disease movies, 24–8, 30–1, 35–6, 41, 43
conformity, 111, 113–16, 119, 120–2, 132–3, 135n,
counterculture, in *Invasion of the Body Snatchers* (1978), 116–19
COVID-19 pandemic, fears of collapse and disintegration in, 162, 171, 199
COVID-19 pandemic, structural change not resulting from, 162–3
disease as means of exploring problems in, 9–10, 20n, 25–6, 33–4, 36–7, 38–45
existing social values, movie confirmation of, 24–5, 26
new social contract, in *Rise of the Planet of the Apes*, 102–3, 105
"the other"/foreigners as threats to, 9–10, 20n, 25–6, 33–4, 36–7, 38–46
post-apocalyptic/posthuman narratives, collapse and disintegration in, 84–5, 86, 90–6, 152, 196
Reagan years, shift in cultural ideology, and silo-ing of, 45–6
see also capitalism; family and marriage; small-town America
socioeconomic status and structural effects of COVID, 173–8
Soderbergh, Steven, 90, 169
Solo, Robert, 120
Songbird (2020), 164
Sontag, Susan, 9, 49n, 203–4n
Sony Pictures, 156
Soviet Union/Russia, 38, 41, 44, 45, 51n, 57, 68, 125
see also Cold War; Communism
Spielberg, Steven, 193
spiritual faith
biblical references, 6–7, 43, 85, 91, 104, 154, 156, 160n
in *Black Death,* 201
in post-apocalyptic/posthuman narratives, 86–90
in *Resident Evil* franchise, 154, 160n
in *Seventh Seal,* 25, 36–7, 46–7, 201
Star Trek franchise, 46, 52n
Star Wars franchise, 46, 52n, 137n
Starship Troopers (Heinlein novel, and movie, 1997), 108n

Steffen-Fluhr, Nancy, 135n
Stevenson, Robert Louis, 7
Stoker, Bram, 7
The Story of Louis Pasteur (1936), 9, 29
The Strange Case of Dr. Jekyll and Mr. Hyde (Stevenson; novel), 7
Strange Invaders (1983), 134n
A Streetcar Named Desire (1951), 47n
Streisand, Barbara, 62
The Stuff (1985), 9, 46
The Suicide Squad (2021), 68
The Sun (newspaper), 167
Sundance Film Festival, 80n
Superman franchise, 46, 52n
surveillance capitalism, 18–19n
surveillance in post-apocalyptic/posthuman narratives, 196–7
Sutherland, Donald, 56, *60,* 117
The Swarm (1978), 51n
syphilis, 25, 26, 30

Taxi Driver (1976), 137n
technological utopianism, 8–9, 133, 157, 178, 195, 196
technology see scientific and technological advancement
The Ten Commandments (1956), 101
Terminator (1984), 46
Terminator 2: Judgment Day (1991), 17, 23n
They Live (1988), 46
The Thing (1982), 134n
3:10 to Yuma (1957 and 2007), 133n
300 (2007), 68
Tora! Tora! Tora! (1970), 51n
Total Recall (1990), 46
Towering Inferno (1974), 10, 51n
Train to Busan (2016), 13, 84, 105, 196
Troy (2004), 108n
Trump, Donald, 161, 163, 169–70, 173, 174, 185n, 200
tsunami, Indian Ocean (2004), 76
12 Monkeys (1995), 55, 63–4, 79n, 86, 108n, 166
20th Century Fox, 54
28 Days Later (2002), 6, 55, 63, 65–7, 195
Body Snatchers (1993) compared, 120
COVID-19 pandemic and, 162, 166–8, 170, 171, 173

28 Days Later (2002) (*cont.*)
　Dawn of the Dead compared, 73
　digital video and 35 mm film used in, 81–2n
　as first movie in projected trilogy, 74
　genre classification of, 80n, 81n
　graphic novel bridging to *28 Weeks Later*, 81n
　international success of, 83n
　representation of disease in, 81n
　Resident Evil franchise compared, 143, 146, 152
　Shaun of the Dead as parody of, 107n
　still from, *65*
　at Sundance Film Festival, 80n
　theatrically released ending to, 67, 73, 77–8n
　28 Weeks Later compared, 75
　Zombieland compared, 97
28 Weeks Later (2007), 56, 73–5, 83n, 84
The Typing of the Dead (video game, 1999), 80n

UK *see* British movies
Ungar, Sheldon, 12
United Nations, 97, 99
USA PATRIOT Act (2001), 147, 159n, 196
utopianism, technological, 8–9, 133, 157, 178, 195, 196

vaccines
　in COVID-19 pandemic, 161, 170–1, 173, 176–8, 188n, 199–200, 202–3
　in early disease movies, 8–9, 24, 28, 30, 38, 42, 45
　in later disease movies, 13, 85, 90–4, 96, 98, 99, 108n, 124–7, 197, 199
　polio, 202–3
　smallpox, 200
vampires and vampire movies
　Dracula (1931), 26
　The Last Man on Earth (1964) and Matheson's *I Am Legend*, 37–8
　Nosferatu: A Symphony of Horror (1922), 7, *8*, 26
　Polidori's *The Vampyre*, 7
　Stoker's *Dracula*, 7

Vaughn, Robert, 51n
Versus (2000), 80n
video, online and board games, 16–17, 69, 80n
Videodrome (1983), 50n
Vietnam War, 25, 40, 41, 44
Viral (2016), 105
Virus/Day of Resurrection (1980), 26, 43–5, 51n, 90
Viva Zapata! (1952), 47n
Voltaire, 138n

Wald, Priscilla, 12, 14
The Walking Dead franchise (TV; 2010–2022), 16, 108n
Wall Street (1987), 57
Wall Street Journal, 165
The Wanderers (1979), 136n
Wanger, Walter, 136n
War for the Planet of the Apes (2017), 85, 100, 103, 104–5
War of the Worlds (radio broadcast and movie), 136n
Warm Bodies (2013), 13, 105
Warner Brothers, 54, 79n, 137n
Washer, Peter, 21n
Watergate, 117
Wayne, Keith, 39
Weber, Jake, 68
Weird Science (1985), 108n
Welles, Orson, 136n
westerns, 61, 110, 133n, 200
Wharton, Edith, 192
What's Up Doc? (1972), 62, 79n
When Harry Met Sally (1989), 79n
Whitaker, Forest, 121–2
White Collar: the American Middle Classes (Mills; book), 135n
White Dawn (1974), 136n
White Zombie (1932), 8, 26–7, 131, 194
Whitshaw, Ben, *128*
Widmark, Richard, 31, *33*, 34
Wild Zero (1999), 80n
Winslet, Kate, 92, 95, 169
Wirth, Billy, 120
women *see* gender/race issues
World Health Organization (WHO), 93, 98

World War Z (2013), 13, 86, 96, 97–9, 100, 108–9n, 165, *166*, 168, 195
Wright, Jeffrey, 126
Wyatt, Rupert, 103, 109n
Wynter, Dana, 113

Yeats, William Butler, 202
yellow fever, 9, 25, 28

Zika virus, 198
Zombieland (2009), 13, 84, 86, 96–7, 100, 108n, 195
Zombieland: Double Tap (2019), 84
zombies and zombie movies

Body Snatchers movies, pod people as zombies in, 111
decline of, in 1980s and early 1990s, 80n
early disease movies, 7–8, 26–7, 38–41, 46
fast zombies, development of, 55, 65, 69, 80n, 120, 151–2
parodic and comedic versions, 13, 84, 96–7, 105
post-apocalyptic and posthuman narratives, 13–14, 64–5, 84
pre-film zombies, 20n
see also disease movies
Zuboff, Shoshana, 18–19n

EU representative:
Easy Access System Europe
Mustamäe tee 50, 10621 Tallinn, Estonia
Gpsr.requests@easproject.com